HELP YOURSELF TOWARDS MENTAL HEALTH

HELP YOURSELF TOWARDS MENTAL HEALTH

Courtenay Young

KARNAC

First published in 2010 by
Karnac Books Ltd
118 Finchley Road, London NW3 5HT

Copyright © 2010 Courtenay Young.

The right of Courtenay Young to be identified as the author of this work has been asserted in accordance with §§ 77 and 78 of the Copyright Design and Patents Act 1988.

All rights reserved. No part of this publication may be reproduced, stored in a retrieval system, or transmitted, in any form or by any means, electronic, mechanical, photocopying, recording, or otherwise, without the prior written permission of the publisher.

British Library Cataloguing in Publication Data

A C.I.P. for this book is available from the British Library

ISBN 978 1 85575 474 4

Edited, designed and produced by The Studio Publishing Services Ltd,
www.studiopublishingservicesuk.co.uk
e-mail: studio@publishingservicesuk.co.uk

Printed in Great Britain

www.karnacbooks.com

CONTENTS

ABOUT THE AUTHOR ix

INTRODUCTION xi

A definition of mental health 1
Stepped care and self-help 13

STRESS 29

Basic information 31
Self-help for stress 41
Stress and modern life 47
Fitting exercise into your life 51
Different types of exercise 55
Relaxation 59
Meditation and mindfulness 67
Symptoms of stress 73
Other anti-stress exercises 77
Stress and life events 81

DEPRESSION — 85

Self-help for depression — 87
Working with depression — 97
Foods for depression — 101
Somatic aspects of depression — 107
Different views of depression — 111
Emotional expression in depression — 117
Basic working principles for depression — 123
A bit about anti-depressant drugs — 129
Negative emotions — 133
Thoughts and moods in depression — 145
Thinking distortions in depression — 149
Common irrational belief systems — 153
How to change your negative thinking — 157

THE PROCESS — 163

Your inner process — 165
Points to remember — 177

ANXIETY — 181

About anxiety — 183
Relaxation — 195
Social anxiety — 201
Panic attacks — 205
Working with panic attacks — 209
Phobias — 215
General anxiety disorder — 219

SELF-ESTEEM ISSUES — 223

Introducing issues of self-esteem — 225
Improving self-esteem — 237
Becoming more assertive — 247

WHAT WORKS? — 253

An overview of what works — 255
Self-awareness — 265

Legitimate needs	271
Asserting yourself	279
Responding to criticism	285

FAMILY ISSUES — 293

Bereavement and grieving	295
Having to care for others	307
Information for carers and families	313
Parents at home, parents at work	319
Relationship issues	323
Relationship difficulties	331
Divorce and separation	339

OTHER ISSUES — 347

Anger management	349
Sleep issues	365
Problems at work	373
Weight, body image, and eating issues	379
Chronic fatigue syndrome	385
Twelve-step programmes	395
Trauma and post traumatic stress disorder	399
Self-harm	401
Money worries	409
Ageing issues	413
Travel	419

WELL-BEING — 423

Natural health	425
The path to mental health	439
The road to change	449
Wider and different perspectives	453

SOURCES OF INFORMATION — 457
REFERENCES — 471

ABOUT THE AUTHOR

Courtenay Young is a registered psychotherapist, who has been accredited in various methods of humanistic, transpersonal, and body-orientated psychotherapies, and who has worked in a wide variety of different ways and in different situations throughout the mental health field over the past twenty years.

He was resident psychotherapist at the Findhorn Foundation, an international spiritual community located in north-east Scotland, for over seventeen years, and then started working in the NHS in various departments of clinical psychology and GP surgeries as a psychotherapist and counsellor. He currently lives near Edinburgh.

He has had several chapters and articles published, and is currently also writing a book on the subject of psycho-physiology, and a book on spiritual emergencies. He helps to edit a couple of psychotherapy journals and produces the EABP Bibliography of Body-Psychotherapy.

He can be contacted by e-mail: courtenay@courtenay-young.com, and his website is www.courtenary-young.com.

Recovery is happening when people can live well in the presence or absence of mental health problems. Believe in your own power to make a positive difference.

Introduction

This book is designed as a self-help aid for people with depression, anxiety, or with issues of low self-esteem. Unfortunately, these problems seem to be very common and are often associated with unnatural levels of stress. About 97% of people with any form of mental health "issues" are just ordinary people with anxiety and/or depression. These "issues" are nothing to do with mental illness. They are mostly natural reactions to life situations that are overwhelming, or have been very difficult. People perhaps just need to understand this, and work at reducing their stress levels. In this way, very effective work can be done with such self-help techniques. These are mostly relatively straightforward suggestions, but they are not at all easy to put into practice. Many of these problems have been "medicalized" and the "treatment" given is via a doctor and is often pharmaceutical. This is unfortunate: even more unfortunate is that only about 24% of people with these problems get any form of treatment, and this is mostly medication. Only about 9% get therapy or counseling (NICE Office of Statistics, 2000). However, most of these problems can probably be solved with better life skills. Many of them could be avoided by better emotional education, probably in primary school. In this way, much of what I am doing as a therapist is not psychological, not arcane, and not scientific; it is mostly commonsense, friendly support, and advice.

When I began to work with patients in the NHS in Scotland, many of them had been referred by their GP to a counselling service or a department of clinical psychology for some therapy, usually cognitive behavioural therapy (CBT). This method is used in the NHS mainly because it is, supposedly, evidence-based. However, many other forms of therapy are just as effective or useful, and are also supported by research studies. Apparently the best therapy comes from a caring, empathetic, and skilled professional: the therapeutic relationship is actually the most efficacious component in any psychotherapy, and this is evidenced from many world-wide meta-studies. Personally, I have veered away from the standard form of CBT, as I find that the clients and patients consider it rather boring, so I have adopted a more eclectic style that seems to work with many people. I have also been frequently told that being with a (person-centred) counsellor who just nods and essentially repeats back to you what you have said is quite ineffective. Therefore, I find myself working quite proactively. One method or modality does not suit everybody. If a particular therapy is to work for you, then it must be suited to you: it does not require you to "fit" the therapy. So you will need to find your own pathway.

I put these notes together when I found myself saying the same sort of thing over and over again to many of my patients, especially as, in the past four years, I have been referred over 500 new clients. This book is, therefore, a compilation of such notes from a variety of methods and perspectives. It is also, I hope, written in a language and style that is friendly and of use to the client. The notes and suggestions I present are just that: notes and suggestions. They try to be pragmatic. They might help to indicate a possible new direction or focus. They might provoke different perspectives, thoughts, and ideas, or they might suggest exercises and new routines to follow. They might even support a process of healing. However, every person is an individual, and, as such, must develop—perhaps from these pages—their own methods of coping and their own path to recovery. I hope that the emphasis on self-discovery and self-empowerment forms a consistent theme throughout the book.

Since I work largely within a medical setting, people come with the expectation of being helped; some do not like being told that they have to do the work themselves. Others come feeling that they really need some help and some simple, pragmatic solutions that they can carry out themselves. Unfortunately, there are no magic wands. It is my hope that the notes in this book have been helpful. I seem to get off to quite a good start with many of the people I see and they seem to get better quite quickly. So, maybe this particular style actually works.

Self-help is reasonably effective, especially for anxiety and depression. Various self-help resources have been utilized for this book, both from within clinical psychology and psychotherapy, and from other books and pamphlets. I do not claim to be anything like unique, or even exceptionally proficient in offering such self-help techniques. The mental health organization MIND produces a good basic series, as do many other organizations. I would like to thank the authors of all of these sources for the effort and clarity that have been put into their thinking and for the way they have influenced me. In trying to emulate their material, I hope I have given all these people appropriate credit for their hard work and inspiration.

Thanks are given especially to the members of the department of Clinical Psychology, Hartwoodhill Hospital, NHS Lanarkshire; the Cramond Medical Practice; the Ratho Medical Centre; the NE Edinburgh Psychology Dept., NHS Lothian; the "MoodJuice" team, and the staff of the Adult Clinical Psychology department, NHS Forth Valley; clients referred through various Employee Assistance Programmes (EAPs); the support staff of all these; and the staff and clients of the Moray Association for Mental Health (MAMH). I also would like to thank many other colleagues and clinicians, friends, and family for their feedback.

However, most sincere thanks are also given to all of you, those clients and patients who have given me a unique access into some of the most intimate aspects of your lives. Your difficulties and struggles have inspired these writings. Your feedback, suggestions, responses, ideas, and conversations have also been worked into these notes-I hope effectively. Without you, I am just a single person in a small room.

Courtenay Young
Edinburgh, 2010

A definition of "mental health"

This phrase "mental health" is used in a number of different ways. First, it can be a goal, something to be attained and retained. We all want to be physically and mentally healthy. We define physical health in terms of our abilities: the ability to move freely, eat well, enjoy our bodies, work, play, and rest, etc., or in terms of absence—the absence of any illness, medical condition, discomfort, etc. We could also similarly define mental health as the ability to contribute to relationships with other people; to function reasonably productively (given any limitations of age, or physical health or abilities); to enjoy the usual opportunities for pleasure in life; to care about others; to conform (mostly) to normal social and legal requirements; and to have a reasonable set of social and problem-solving skills, etc.

Given these definitions, I believe that one of the fundamental requirements for both physical and mental health is self-awareness. Without this, we are unaware of how we are, who we are, and what is happening to us: essentially we become lost. Stress and distress is often a key factor in "losing" ourselves, or losing touch with others and consensual reality. That is when things start to go wrong.

In Powell's *The Mental Health Handbook* (2006), there are "Seven keys to mental health". These are: (1) take responsibility (do not blame); (2) be flexible in your thinking; (3) confront rather than avoid difficulties and frustration; (4) look after your own needs; (5) express yourself; (6) strive for balance; and (7) develop and maintain relationships. Valuable as these are, this useful list does not define mental health: instead, it tries to give us a road map of "how to get there"—but "there" is not really determined. I expand on another list later in this book (see the section: "The path to mental health").

However, this is also more of a preventive definition (how to stop *not* being "there") by a linking of mental health with basic physical health and a degree of social and personal happiness. In addition, it is quite self-defined, as you determine where "there" is for you, often according to your previous experience. Sometimes the experience has been one of being depressed for a time, or having anxiety states, so that you do not want to go "there" again. But it may be wrong to see "there" as being the opposite of mental health, mental illness. These conditions have nothing to do with mental illness, despite the increasing medicalization of mental health issues and professionals. Mental health is much more than the absence of mental illness.

The actual definition of mental health thus becomes slightly opaque. A more humanistic paradigm defines mental health as having the capacity for "self-actualization", which is quite an active concept, or having a high degree of "authenticity" that is more internal and self-reflective. However, this also feels somewhat self-defined, as it becomes clearer that self-actualization is *you* determining what *you* need, and authenticity is again focused on a "true" self. You have to be in the paradigm to understand it. If you are anxious or depressed, then you are not your usual self, and therefore it is difficult to self-actualize.

There is a wider tendency to see mental health and happiness as almost the same thing, or at least, in retrospect,

unhappiness = mental un-health = distress.

I am deliberately avoiding the dreaded phrase "mental illness" for the reasons explained, and because mental health and mental illness are not opposite ends of a spectrum, but two totally different concepts.

So, let us try for a definition: mental health is the ability to ward off unpleasant mood states, to adjust to changing situations, and to cope with stress and distress. This ability prevents us from lapsing into a depression, anxiety state, or other form of distress: this is an ongoing task or process. Happiness (sometimes confused with pleasure) is when we feel good about ourselves, our lives, and what is happening around us. This is a more temporary situation, or as a result of ongoing mental health. We have to maintain this definition: it is an active principle. We do not achieve mental health and then expect to stay there for the rest of our lives. Another couple of mainstream definitions are as follows:

> Mental health can be conceptualized as a state of well-being in which the individual realizes his or her own abilities, can cope with the normal stresses of life, can work productively and fruitfully, and is able to make a contribution to his or her community.
>
> In this positive sense, mental health is the foundation for well-being and effective functioning for an individual and for a community. This core concept of mental health is consistent with its wide and varied interpretation across cultures.
>
> Mental health and mental health disorders are determined by multiple and interacting social, psychological, and biological factors, as are health and illness in general. [World Health Organization, 2007]

Mental health has, therefore, nothing to do with intelligence; and neither is lack of mental health a form of mental illness; there is no easy flip-flop diagnosis—sane or insane. So, what is mental health in this context? One key component of mental health is the ability to withstand negative events, or very difficult situations. This can be considered as a form of resilience or psychological hardiness. And we must continue to resist the more rigid medical paradigms: doctors are (very well) trained—but only in pathology. However, they rarely see "well" people and they sometimes only know health as a lack of illness. Quite frankly, they are not properly trained in health. They might prevent you from getting sick(er), but they do not—or have not up to now—done very much to keep you well, to promote health, and to avoid sickness.

Life is difficult. Things happen to us. One of the major sources of (reactive) depression is becoming overwhelmed by stressful life events around you. There is nothing "wrong" with you, but you have become depressed because of "wrong" things happening to you. Those who are mentally healthy can resist this onslaught for a little longer: those who have less resilience get overwhelmed sooner, or for longer. There is a gradient of aptitude. This is not a condemnation of those who become depressed; it can give hope that such ability can be improved relatively easily. It is hoped that this book can help to strengthen these facilities.

Happiness has two parts to it: a pleasure component of how good you feel about yourself at any one moment: and a satisfaction component, when (after reflection) we are reasonably content with our lives—for the moment, anyway. There is evidence that people who have a higher degree of satisfaction have a stronger resilience to coping with difficulties. Many people who seek happiness, sometimes quite desperately, are less satisfied with their lives and are symptomatic of (possibly) a lower level of mental health. Again we have a gradient, a fulfilment spectrum. The search for contentment has also fascinated philosophers through history.

Thus, one measure to improve mental health could be to re-examine one's goals and basic life expectations; how do you operate on a day-to-day basis; do you expect life to be reasonably difficult; does what you do make you more satisfied? Or, are you upset or distressed whenever there is a difficulty; do you expect that life should be easy or that nothing should go wrong; are you are constantly chasing after something you thought was important, but when or if you get it, will you still be unhappy? These are important questions. However, happiness is a skill that can also be learnt. But it does not happen, or come, from outside of yourself.

In this sort of context, one cornerstone of mental health can be seen as being able to manage one's mood, temper, or attitude, and, thus, one's responsiveness to both the external environment (a spouse or boss) and to the internal environment (feelings and thoughts). If being in control and being responsive are important, then methods of "treatment" that require one to seek external advice, get professional help, take this drug, or follow that particular method could possibly be counter-productive. This book is designed to try to enhance your feelings of awareness, control and flexibility.

Mental health problems can affect us all. Occasionally they can become serious and develop serious complications (mental illness) but this is very rare. For most people, their "ordinary" problems include stress, anxiety, unhappiness, distress, loneliness, lack of self-esteem, difficulty with relationships, and the lack of the ability to cope with adverse circumstances. Mental health therefore encompasses a sense of well-being and the ability to cope in adversity: it contains various factors such as resilience, confidence, a sense of being able to cope (mastery), coherence, optimism (or hope), the ability to initiate, a degree of emotional intelligence, and the ability to sustain and develop relationships.

However, mental health is still too often used as a euphemism for the absence of mental illness: particularly poignant for people who have been classified (rightly or wrongly) as actually having been mentally ill, or having had a "mental health episode" or breakdown. MIND, SANE, the Scottish Association for Mental Health (SAMH) and other organizations doing excellent work with such a population utilize this form of definition. Some of those people have been genuinely "ill". So, let us now examine the concept of mental illness a little bit further.

The common major mental illnesses are: severe and enduring depression (very much nastier and deeper than anyone normally experiences); bipolar depression (which used to be called manic-depression); schizophrenia (also very poorly defined); dementia (Alzheimer's and various other forms of mental ageing); and a variety of quite severe personality disorders. Many of these are categorized in classifications like *DSM-IV* (the 1994 American Psychiatric Association's *Diagnostic and Statistical Manual of Mental Disorders*). The other main classification of mental illness is in the *International Statistical Classification of Diseases and Related Health Problems* (ICD). Unfortunately, these diagnostics also classify things that are not mental illnesses: there is an increasing medicalization of "normal" life reactions. The medical model of mental illness does not really work, and in practice it might even be iatrogenic (self-generating by doctors).

There are also a few people suffering from physical brain damage (from biological reasons or injuries) and those who are severely psychologically damaged (often by trauma) and who (as yet) have been ineffectually treated. There is debate as to whether they are mentally ill, though sometimes they are certainly treated as such.

Psychology and psychiatry has—for a long time—focused on diagnosis, assessment, and types of treatment, rather than on prevention. This is probably a huge mistake. There is a wealth of knowledge that is not being tapped. Over the past 150 years or so, we have started to learn what does *not* work. Prevention is therefore usually always more efficient than treatment. But we do not intervene. Mental problems, emotional difficulties, and psychological disturbances really can be prevented, or the incidence of them can be diminished considerably: first, by improving people's emotional coping strategies and their problem solving abilities, and second, by re-examining their expectations and components of what makes them satisfied: their general well-being. Some of this, much of this, is down to education and increasing the incidence of emotional intelligence. This is a form of discovery—through experience—that makes us realize that if we do this, and that, others may well do that and this in return.

Definitely, we all want to try to end the insidious forms of discrimination that still persist around mental illness. At various times I emphasize that this—whatever it is that you are experiencing and suffering from—is *not* mental illness. With depression, for example, about 25–30% of the population get depressed at one point or another, but only a very small percentage of all the people who get depressed have depression as an illness. And (perhaps) only a very tiny proportion of the total population are those who may have developed a mental illness.

"Illness" is often a metaphor, in many situations, for distress; and it is usually social, family, work and environmental circumstances that engender most distress. Unfortunately, we have become totally obsessed with the medical model. Thus, we need to step outside of this and consider the true nature of happiness, and the causes of such distress.

The conditions dealt with in this book are things that can, and mostly do, happen to anyone. We can all get overstressed, anxious, or depressed. If this state persists, we may feel we need some help. But we do not necessarily *have* to see a doctor, counsellor, psychotherapist, psychologist, or psychiatrist. These are specialists for people who are ill. You are not ill; neither are you mentally ill. You can help yourself—given the right attitude and conditions.

This book could be a first step. Wanting to read it does not mean that you are crazy or insane: you may be a bit depressed, anxious, or feeling rotten about yourself. Wanting to read this book, or one like it, means that you are starting to increase your awareness, take more control over your life, and over your mental and physical health, and be both responsive to that which is around you, and more responsible for your thoughts, feelings, and actions towards other people and your environment. That's healthy! It is a great first step. Thus, more and more people are looking at self-help techniques to readjust their mental health in a positive and empowered way.

New approaches to mental health are now being offered by a range of institutions and people, from the National Institute for Health and Clinical Excellence (NICE), the body that informs the NHS what treatments it can safely and economically offer, to new types of thinking from very respected doctors and from the alternative or complementary health arena. Recommended, first and foremost, is a "stepped-care" approach to anxiety and depression, with guided self-help being an important (essential) part of the first step.

David Servan-Schrieber (2005) recommends a wide battery of techniques, all of them tried out for efficacy in university hospitals in the USA, and many promoted by other well-known doctors. Similar techniques include:

- a better understanding of how the brain and the body interact;
- living with greater "heart coherence" (because we experience feelings in our bodies, rather than our heads);
- using eye movement desensitization and reprocessing (EMDR) after emotional traumas;
- Using light therapy and dawn simulation—especially for seasonally affected disorders (SAD);
- trying Yoga, Tai Chi, Chi Gong or acupuncture;
- some diet therapy: focusing on Omega-3 fatty acids, drinking more water, taking vitamin B complex, eating "five-a-day" and avoiding too much sugar, salt, etc.;
- lots of aerobic exercise, followed by structured relaxation, thus helping rebalance the autonomic nervous system (ANS);

- increased touch: encouragement and help towards finding intimacy and better relationships (love); more rich, friendly social contacts;
- enhancing (honest) emotional communication;
- moving beyond self-psychology towards finding a wider and more meaningful connection with society, the wider world, and a meaningful life.

This sort of "broadband" approach, a smörgasboard of whatever is available and appropriate for you, also offers a form of self-empowerment drawn essentially from the resources that surround you. These are often largely untapped—by you—until now. They can help you to heal, but (unfortunately) *you* are going to have to do the work and make the effort to heal.

The really hard work is starting from the position of being inflicted, afflicted, or suffering, or a victim of the anxiety or depression, or feeling that there is something wrong with you, or however you see yourself. This view is usually totally incorrect. This is the medical model's perspective again.

Anxiety, depression, stress and low self-esteem are really nothing to do with any form of illness. They are more a part of the human condition. Philosophers have been asking, and trying to answer, questions about these aspects of life for thousands of years. The main religions (Hinduism, Buddhism, Christianity, Judaism, Islam) are also, in part, attempts to provide answers to these problems.

Instead, consider the position of something "bad" having happened to you. Do not—for a single moment—think that this something is in any way justified; that you have done something wrong, and are now (justly) suffering. This is not a punishment. Become a little more resilient instead: fight back to regain your rightful position of health and sense of rightness. Something happened to you. That's a pity. You tripped and fell. All right. Fortunately, nothing's broken. But do you lie there waiting for someone to come along and help you to your feet, or do you get up and continue on your journey? Certainly, take a few minutes to get over the shock of the fall, wipe your knee, adjust your clothing, dust yourself off, or whatever, and then you naturally continue on your journey. The first few paces will be tentative, limping a little, perhaps. Then you continue onwards.

The essence of all this is extremely simple, but it is not necessarily going to be easy. You are going to have to work at this—harder perhaps than anything you have done before. Miracles rarely happen, but hard work (patience, persistence, and perseverance) can move you across mountains. However, the main part of the journey, and the hardest part, will be when you start to "go inside" and look at yourself. It is also the most fascinating part: therein lies the secret of true happiness.

Our state of mind is only partially influenced by what has happened, or by physical factors. Much depends on how we think about things, our expectations, hopes, dreams, and desires, and these affect what we then put into practice, our behaviours, our habits and patterns of reaction. These can be changed quite easily. This is the basis of cognitive–behavioural therapy (CBT)—that a new understanding leads to different patterns of behaviour. However, I hope that the sections in this book go a little further than CBT; they are not just a simplistic, step-by-step, mental health manual. I will think I have failed if they have not also started you on a journey of self-exploration.

It is not always possible to avoid negative thoughts and feeling in a depressed mood, but one of the secrets of happiness, or mental balance, is to be able to notice when you are choosing the depressed, or the anxious, path, and when you are looking after your self. This is basic awareness; it is essential. The other key element that we shall return to again and again is what new direction, or new behaviour, is needed. The answer is simple, but not easy to find: it is the one that works for you. You are probably stressed, anxious, depressed, or have low self-esteem, mainly because you have been living your life according to what other people have been telling you (parents, church, school, society, bosses, and managers, etc.). This is now not working so well for you. So, you need to make a change towards something that works better for you. In order to find out what does work better for you, you may have to rediscover a little bit about who you really are. We shall come back to this point again and again.

Your life-style can also affect your mood. The most obvious way is in the life–work balance. This is not to say there is no "life" when you are at work, but that the balance is between work and leisure, what you *have* to do and what you *want* to do, being productive and relaxing, being focused and being reflective. Both sides are needed for a healthy lifestyle. If you are feeling a lot of stress at work, this will affect your home life. If life at home has just gone pear-shaped, this affects your abilities at work. But also, success at work can make you feel better about yourself at home, and a new baby or relationship has (often) positive impacts at work. We need to look, not just for a good balance in terms of time spent, but also in terms of satisfaction gained. Unfortunately, for men, priorities and self-esteem are often more wrapped up in their life and what they are doing at work, and for women, the balance tends to revolve more around how everyone is feeling at home. This may be traditional, but not all traditions are good ones, or give total satisfaction. If women feel that they are not "just" a housewife and mother, but also have a recognized, valued, and respected role out in society, then they will probably be happier. When men discover that there are real benefits—and a great deal of pleasure—to be had from spending more time at home and really being a part of the family with their children, they start to redefine their work–life priorities.

The important "feel-good" factors (we assume that these will promote feelings of "happiness" and/or "mental health") are not a new Porsche, or wide-screen plasma television, or a washing line of clean clothes. These can give quite temporary gratifications. Then a new model comes out, or it rains in some way on these aspirations, and the "must-have" cycle starts all over again. Instead, what can work better is:

- the ability to express yourself, your feelings and your needs;
- some success in aiming for and attaining achievable goals;
- having time to enjoy little, simple things (both at work, at home, and elsewhere);
- a healthy mix of exercise, relaxation, good diet, and reasonable sleep;
- doing something different occasionally: treats, outings, holidays, celebrations;
- quality time spent, both with friends and family (colleagues even), and by oneself;
- reasonably enjoyable work and—most importantly—appreciative feedback;
- a little more self-awareness and self-understanding.

The usual factors that diminish one's quality of life are:

- too much stress, for too long, and especially with several conflicts and changes;
- doing something you have come to dislike, or being in a situation that you now dislike;
- too high expectations of yourself;
- expectations coming towards you that you feel you cannot fulfil;
- negative thoughts and feelings (including those about yourself);
- very strong internal feelings (anger, guilt, rage, frustration, envy, jealousy, etc.).

So, self-esteem is very important in mental health, and in general well-being. A reasonable level of self-esteem means that we can appreciate ourselves, and our worth; we are clearer about what we want or what works for us, and then we can take our proper place in the world. A moderately increased level of self-esteem aids us towards having a more positive attitude towards our self, and to others, and about life in general. Self-esteem is usually, naturally, much higher in small children and then it is slowly diminished by social conditioning, rejections, disappointments, failures, negativity, and abuse. However, to get over these setbacks successfully and restore our self-esteem in adult life, we need to rebuild or reclaim our self-esteem. This is dealt with more specifically later in the book.

Hence, we come full-circle back to the concept of resilience. We need to, and we can, bounce back and reclaim our selves and our lives, despite the earlier setbacks or areas of our childhood where we could have, or should have, received more of what we needed. This is a way to start to give it to your self. Hopefully, in the process, you will also begin to explore your self, and think and discover more about what you really want out of life, the universe, and everything. This book does not provide "The Answer", but it might help you explore some of the proper questions.

Stepped care and self-help

A "stepped care" approach to mental health is now becoming the norm within the National Health Service. What this means is that there are various steps to be taken in assisting people with their mental health issues.

The first step is usually a combination of "watchful waiting" by the GP and, more importantly, encouraging the use of self-help techniques. In the NICE *Guidelines for Anxiety* (No. 22) and *Depression* (No. 23), "Bibliotherapy" (reading about your issues, or problems), and "Social Prescribing" are also considered important. All these come before psychological assistance or any medical treatment (medication).

Before considering any form of treatment for stress, depression, anxiety, low self-esteem, problems with bereavement or loss, or any other conditions of distress, a self-help approach should really be considered first. There is probably nothing actually wrong with you, just that much has happened to you. There may well have been a number of things that you, the "patient", have done, or have tried to do, already, but they have not fully helped you yet. This does not mean that they are wrong, just that other things might also be helpful. There might also be information "out there" that you have not been able to access yet. There might be other resources—voluntary organizations, specialist support groups—that you are not aware of. These should probably be explored first, before you are referred to, or ask for, counselling, and especially before you get any medication. These latter options are now identified as being the second and/or third steps.

Thus, initial explorations of self-help will ideally happen before you are referred to a counsellor, or while you are waiting for your first appointment (there is often a waiting list; one hopes for not too long). Once you get to see a counsellor, s/he will probably check what you have done already with regard to this first step, and, if nothing, then may recommend it. These weeks of waiting can thus be put to very good use. Within this self-help first step, there are five main areas of really important activity:

Exercise The best form of self-help for anxiety, stress, or depression is aerobic exercise: this is where you get somewhat out of breath, and possibly a little hot and sweaty. This does *not* have to be in a gym: a power-walk along the canal, in the park, up a hill, or round a golf course is just as good; so is a game of tennis or badminton, a long bike ride, a kick-about with the kids, or 20–30 lengths in the pool. You should try to do this type of exercise for a *minimum* of three to four times a week, for a *minimum* of 30–45 minutes each time. Make it enjoyable if you can: take the Walkman or MP3 player with your favourite music. Make it varied: when it is raining hard, dig out the exercise bike and set it up in the garage or on the landing; or double-dig the vegetable garden; or cycle to work; or something like that. Try to work this sort of aerobic exercise much more into your daily and weekly routine. It really does help.

Relaxation You should also find ways to relax as much as possible, for a *minimum* of twenty minutes, ideally twice daily. How often do you *not* sit down and have a proper tea break, or take a walk in the park at lunchtime? Proper relaxation, at regular intervals, is a very useful stress-buster. Yoga (before or after work), Tai Chi (in the early morning), any form of meditation, or using a relaxation method like Progressive Relaxation or the Autogenic Technique are all very effective ways of relaxing. So is lying on the sofa listening to Mozart or Chopin on a pair of headphones, or having a long, languid Radox bath. It is really important to try to build something like this into your daily routine on a regular basis. Other suggestions include: try using a music tape or audio book, rather than listening to the news or radio when driving to work, or to the shops; try out the concept of a half-hour (or more) siesta when at home during the day; or try to reinstate whatever you used to do for relaxation, now long dropped because "you didn't feel like it" or "hadn't enough time". Relaxation works best, either first thing in the morning, or sometime after you have done your exercise.

Information This is sometimes called Bibliotherapy. There are lots of self-help information booklets available nowadays. NHS Trusts often produce them; there is an excellent series from the mental health charity Mind (www.mind.org.uk: go to "Information", "Booklets" then the "Understanding" series) or many other Internet sites can be accessed (search for "self help mental health"; or go to MoodJuice: www.moodjuice.scot.nhs.uk; or some of the other similar sites listed in the "Sources of information" section towards the end of this book.

Social prescribing This is a phrase to encourage you to widen your range of contacts and "social community". When we are stressed, anxious, or depressed, or have low self-esteem, we tend to close in on ourselves. We lose touch with some friends or family. We don't think, "There must be others out there who can help". There are lots of voluntary organizations, specialist support groups, and like-minded people who can, and would, like to help, and often involving people who have gone through something similar. Use these "experts"!

General Look after your general health; drink lots of water daily; eat regularly; do NOT abuse alcohol, cigarettes, or processed food; try to get regular sleep; and try to talk to family and friends. Just because you feel that currently you are not (the normal) "you" does not mean you are ill and/or you need help. What do you need to do to become "you" again?

Stepped care: counselling and/or medication

This book emphasizes self-help techniques, but it is worthwhile to mention some of the alternatives. Step 2 in a stepped care approach to mental health is counselling (psychological intervention) and/or Step 3: counselling with an appropriate medication. The NICE Guidelines are very clear about this in relation to anxiety and depression: however, the same can also be said for stress, bereavement, relationship difficulties, work stress, financial problems, etc., which are not normally seen as medical issues. The NHS usually recommends cognitive–behavioural therapy (CBT) or "evidence-based" therapy, although there is no real evidence that any one method of psychological intervention is fundamentally better than any other.

Ideally, medication should only be taken if counselling is not available, or when counselling—by itself—has been proven not to be effective enough. According to the NICE Guidelines, if the patient's distress is sufficient to warrant appropriate medication, then counselling should be provided as well. So, it is very important to discuss these points with your doctor: ask for a twenty-minute appointment. He or she should be able to refer you to an appropriate counsellor, and discuss other options, if nothing is available locally. S/he can also discuss whether medication might be appropriate for you.

Counselling is a non-invasive technique. One can consider it more as a gentle reminder, or an educational top-up, when things are going badly. The counsellor (depending on the style that they were trained in) can offer reflections on whatever you tell them, or make suggestions as to ways forward. Counsellors, psychotherapists, community psychiatric nurses (CPNs), someone from a department of clinical psychology, and psychological therapists all do forms of counselling. Many studies have been done about the efficacy of counselling and other psychological approaches, and generally it has been shown to be efficacious; the benefits tend to last and there are very few side effects. However much depends on the therapeutic contact, or relationship, between you and the counsellor. The counselling should be professional and ethical, as well as caring and supportive. Incidentally, counselling and medication can work together very well, if necessary, possibly better than either one or the other by themselves.

Unfortunately, the availability of counselling in the NHS is somewhat patchy: it can mean waiting for a while (often 2–3 months minimum, sometimes 7–9 months), sessions are often limited, and not all areas have access to counselling services. Counselling—when it happens—is reasonably effective, though it is quite costly, both in time and money. So this is why self-help has been targeted as the first step: it is cheaper (for everybody), much more accessible, and easily the most effective, as well as being self-empowering. These pages are not a substitute for counselling, but can work as a supplement.

Medication

Medication for mental health issues can have some drawbacks. The first is that a medical treatment is often being used for a non-medical problem or life issue. Furthermore, not everyone likes taking such medications; and they do not solve your basic problems, though they can often help to relieve some of the symptoms. It is a bit like wearing a buoyancy aid when in the water. They keep your head above the water, but they do not teach you how to swim. Some medications replace or increase the effect of natural neurotransmitters (like serotonin) in the brain, some can take a while (2–3 weeks) to start working, some can sometimes have an unpleasant side-effect, some (anti-anxiety) can be quite addictive, and care needs to be taken when coming off some of these medications. Having said all that, there are a great number of people who use such medications regularly, over long periods, and to good effect, without any real problems. Generally, we are much better off from having these medications available. Sometimes they can be overused, or over-prescribed. In most cases, medication should initially be prescribed with some counselling.

Later steps

Later steps in a stepped care approach to mental health might involve longer-term counselling, or in-depth psychotherapy, possibly with a psychotherapist or clinical psychologist. This would usually be only for people with severe and enduring (chronic) problems. Waiting lists for such specialist therapeutic appointments can be quite long (even up to eighteen months). So keep practising what you read in this book in the meantime.

Another possibility might be a quick referral to a medical specialist, a psychiatrist, usually just to ensure that there is nothing organically wrong (for example, a brain tumour or epilepsy), or if the prescribed medication does not seem to be working properly, or if you are having too many side-effects. These later steps apply only to a very small percentage of referrals. None of these steps means that you are "mad" or "going crazy", even if you think that this might be happening to you. Insanity is, thankfully, very rare. The chances really are that you will have nothing seriously psychologically or organically wrong with you. But that does not mean to say that there is nothing wrong, or that you should do nothing. What is wrong, almost certainly, is that life has gone a little pear-shaped; that the balance between nice things and nasty things has become disturbed; that you have become over-stressed; or that something "bad" has happened to knock you back a bit.

Try to find the level of intervention that is right for you. Get more information, widen your social horizons, do some exercise, relax, discuss these issues with your GP, step back and look at yourself and your life a little, and things should improve.

A typical GP counselling service

This section should give you some information about a typical GP counselling service, and should answer some of the questions that you might have about the sort of counselling service typically available through most GP practices. Most people, at some time in their life, feel the need to talk about or get support for problems that they may be having. Sometimes it is just not possible to talk to family, friends, or your partner: perhaps they may be too close, or they might even be part of the problem. Counselling can therefore give you an opportunity to talk about things that may be troubling you with an objective, understanding, and professional outsider

What is counselling?

- Counselling is essentially a one-to-one talking therapy.
- Counselling offers a private, confidential, reliable, and judgement-free place to talk about your worries and concerns.

- Counselling can help clarify important decisions you may need to make now.
- When emotional difficulties have their roots in the past, talking them over with a counsellor can help you understand them better, and this can help you see past situations in a new light.
- Counselling can help you to rediscover or develop new resources within your self, enabling you to approach life in a more effective and personally satisfying way.
- Counselling can be most helpful when the time is right for you, when you feel ready, and are able to think and talk about what is happening with you and around you.

What does counselling involve?

An NHS counselling service is free and access is through the GP surgery. It usually involves fifty-minute sessions weekly or fortnightly with a trained and accredited psychotherapist or counsellor, experienced in working with people with a variety of emotional problems. All such counselling takes place at the surgery (or clinic) within usual office hours. After an initial session, the counsellor will agree to see you for a number of sessions, according to your need, with occasional reference to the GP who referred you.

The counselling will inevitably be time-limited (i.e., the number of sessions is limited—sometimes to about six). The counsellor may take or make some notes; however, these will not appear on your medical record. The counsellor will keep what you discuss with them within the strict bounds of professional confidentiality: they can only break this confidentiality under certain extreme circumstances; for example, if by not doing so, the person might harm him or herself or others, or if a court orders them to.

Counselling can help with:

- Relationship problems.
- Stress, depression, anxiety and low self esteem.
- Bereavement and other loss; for example, miscarriage and abortion.
- Coming to terms with traumatic events; for example, accidents, life changes, etc.
- Sexual difficulties and addictive behavioural patterns.

- Coping with violence and abuse.
- Work difficulties: bullying, redundancy, problems with colleagues.
- Self-harm.

Counselling is not suitable for:

- People with a mental illness or something that affects their ability to make relationships, to concentrate, and to attend regularly. Examples include: severe depression, psychotic illness, etc.
- People with severe post traumatic stress disorder (PTSD).
- People who are currently engaged in extreme forms of self-destructive behaviour, prolonged substance abuse, alcohol abuse, or eating disorders.
- People with a history of violent behaviour.

There are specialist treatment services available for all of these problems. Ask your GP.

Referral process

If you think you would benefit from counselling, then you should ask for a counselling referral from your GP. Ask for a twenty-minute appointment with the GP to discuss this initially.

Appointments

If you have to cancel or change an arranged appointment, please ring the surgery as soon as possible. Please bear in mind that because of the nature and rhythm of counselling sessions, changing your appointment at less than a week's notice will probably mean that your particular session cannot be given to another client. This wastes an hour of the counsellor's limited time.

Registration

The counsellor should be registered with a professional body, such as BACP, UKCP, COSCA, or similar: this will have been checked out by the surgery.

Alternatives

There are usually local alternatives to an NHS counselling service. Sometimes counselling is done through a church, a specialist service (for drug addicts, alcoholics, rape victims, etc.), or through a voluntary organization like Relate, or Cruse (for bereavement).

Initial interview format

At the start of a counselling relationship, it is fairly important for the counsellor to have sufficient information to help establish an overview of the client's situation. These are some of the headings that might be useful to that process. The counsellor may, or may not, ask you questions about some, or all, of these headings.

Case history and information checklist

Presenting problem(s)

> Referral reason
> Client's view/description
> Any recent changes or developments
> Why is help being sought? Now?
> Significant history of complaint. Onset, Duration.
> Difficulties in functioning: precipitating factors, moderating factors, severity.
> Any other significant history.
> Coping strategies: alcohol, tranquillizers, avoidance, etc.
> Effect on others: reinforcement, what motivated referral, etc.

Demographic history

> Occupation: length of time, other significant jobs/interests.
> Marital/partnership status, partner's occupation.
> Children: number, names, ages, at home or left, occupations, health.
> Social status, work status, extended family, significant relations(hips).
> Stressful life events.

Developmental history

Original family: position in family, siblings, parents.
Overview of early family life.
Significant events in childhood and adolescence.
Educational history: success, failure, trauma, changes, primary, secondary, tertiary.
Occupational history: work, work relationships, ups/downs.
Social history: childhood friends, adolescence experiences, long-term friends.
Psychosexual history.

Medical/psychological history and attitudes

Previous psychiatric, psychological, counselling, help.
Other relevant medical history.
Current medication: side effects.
Preventing moods and thoughts.
Any significant attitudes/beliefs/religion.
Any abnormal sensory experiences.
Any oddities? Posture, movement, interjections, memory, dissonance.
Assessment of intellectual/cognitive functioning.
Any need for more specialist assessment/tests.

Lifestyle questions

Smoking, drinking, drugs (including caffeine, chocolate, sugar, etc.).
Diet: water, fruit/vegetables, vitamins.
Exercise: how, what, how often?
Relaxation: physical/mental/meditation; pleasure/leisure.
Self-image.
Presentation: observations.

Formulations

Goals, aims, understanding.
Motivation, expectations, outcomes.

What differences could help/result?
Therapeutic relationship: quality, contact, frequency, contract.
Formulation: process/intervention proposals, prognosis.

Psychotherapy, psychology, psychiatry

The variety of mental health services and the difference between counselling, psychotherapy, psychology, and psychiatry seem to be very confusing to many people, and there are also community psychiatric nurses (CPNs), psychological therapists, and community mental health teams (CMHTs) to be found, as well as local associations for mental health and much within the voluntary sector. Any attempt to outline who does what, in these complex overlapping fields, will probably provide a totally inadequate description and thus might annoy many colleagues in these mental health professions: apologies are extended now. The government is also having some difficulty determining some of these overlaps and responsibilities. Soon, some of these professions will probably be regulated within the Health Professions Council and much more access to psychological therapists will be created. The field is also changing rapidly.

Counsellors, as mentioned previously, tend to be members of the British Association of Counselling and Psychotherapy (BACP), the UK Register of Counsellors (UKRC), the Psychotherapeutic Counselling (PC) section of the UK Council for Psychotherapy (UKCP), or similar accrediting bodies (AHPP, COSCA, etc.). They have typically had 2–3 years of experiential training in one or another of the many forms of counselling: cognitive–behavioural, humanistic, psychodynamic, person-centred, etc. The main goal of counselling, largely a vocational occupation, is providing personal support with certain specific issues or with emotional and relational difficulties.

Psychotherapy is an activity that is done by a mental health professional. It differs from counselling in that, typically, it might last for longer, it might work with problems that seem more well-established or that originated earlier, and it might help you to go deeper into your understanding of who you are and why you are having difficulties. Typically, a psychotherapist has had at least four years of theoretical and experiential training at a post-graduate level of entry, often has had considerable experience of psychotherapy himself or herself, and is probably a registered member of the UKCP, the main UK professional accrediting body for psychotherapists, or a member of similar professional associations in psychotherapy.

The goal of psychotherapy should be that the professional is working with you towards the reduction of any symptoms of anxiety, depression, stress, distress, or low-self esteem, and towards a position of increased self-empowerment. There are many different methods, modalities, streams, or approaches within psychotherapy: psychoanalysis, psychodynamic psychotherapy, systemic psychotherapy, family therapy, group analysis or therapy, cognitive–behavioural therapy, humanistic psychotherapy, integrative psychotherapy, body-orientated psychotherapy, hypno-psychotherapy, and psychotherapy for specialist groups such as children and adolescents. Labels like Gestalt, Transactional Analysis, Existential, Psychosynthesis, Process Orientated, etc. are also used. Fuller descriptions are found on the UKCP web site (www.psychotherapy.org.uk).

Psychology and the training of psychologists—and there are also many different types of psychologist (educational, occupational, clinical, etc.)—is somewhat more academic. Typically, they have both a first degree and a Masters degree in psychology, often a doctorate (PhD) as well, and will almost certainly be a chartered member of the British Psychological Society (BPS) and/or registered with the Health Professions Council (HPC). Most chartered clinical psychologists work in the National Health Service and practise a form of psychotherapy, often CBT-based. Educational psychologists mostly work with school children having difficulties; occupational psychologists are more focused towards helping people in employment. Many psychologists undertake active research.

A psychiatrist is a medical doctor, who has then specialized further in mental health problems and in psychopathology (mental illness). This involves a minimum of 8–9 years of professional training. Psychiatrists are usually members of the Royal College of Psychiatry. Their main focus, in a medical setting, is to determine whether the problems that people are having are related to any symptoms of an underlying organic problem and to help doctors

(GPs) and other health professionals determine the best form of medication, especially if the patient is continuing to have difficulties or side-effects. Many psychiatrists work in hospitals, or are attached to community mental health teams (CMHTs): some practise psychotherapy as well.

Community psychiatric nurses (CPNs) are qualified nurses who have specialized in, and have some training in, mental health. They largely work in the community, see people needing regular medical treatments and injections, providing support, counselling and sometimes psychotherapy, and frequently visit patients and families in their homes. Occupational Therapists and Social Workers also work in CMHTs and frequently provide much of the basic therapeutic contact with people having long-term difficulties.

"Psychological therapist" is a fairly new title that we may be seeing a lot more of. The Improved Access to Psychological Therapies (IAPT) initiative by the Department of Health wants to create 5,000–10,000 more psychological therapists. Typically, they will have about 6–12 weeks' training. They might be excellent in helping people with self-help and social prescribing at Step 1 (see above), possibly providing twenty-four-hour telephone support. Most of the rest of the psychological professions, though supportive of this extra level, have some serious reservations about these people giving counselling or psychotherapy to members of the public.

All these people form the teams of mental health professionals: some work in hospitals, some specialize in working with children and adolescents, some work with people in prison, others with psycho-geriatrics, or specialist client groups. Some prescribe and give medication, others do not. They all work together—remarkably well and efficiently.

Associations for Mental Health support people, usually with chronic mental (long term) health issues, or if someone has just come out of an extended hospital admission and does not have a good local support system. These people are not mad or crazy: they may have been damaged or scarred by profound trauma, emotional deprivation, or by life stresses that overwhelmed them totally for a while, and sometimes even by bad experiences in hospital or with (various types of) medication. They really do need some extra help and support initially, usually non-medical, and may need some background help and support to put things "right" again, or if things get a bit bumpy occasionally. Don't we all!

These associations often employ local staff and are usually funded out of a variety of resources: Mental Health grants, Social Services support, National Lottery grants, local fund-raising, etc. If there is not one in your area, please consider starting one up. They are really great grass-roots organizations, run locally, for a specific group of people whose needs are usually not very well met. They can even be quite democratically run, in that the clients are often members of the association and have a say in the running of the organization and the various activities. This is another form of self-help.

Typical projects run by such associations might be:

- A "stay-at-home" project to assist people with long-term mental health issues to stay at home, rather than going back into hospital again. People with such issues are often very isolated and lonely and need a little back-up and support in the community to stay at home. Initially, this might be quite a lot when such people first emerge from a hospital admission and have to rebuild their lives, but things can settle down relatively quickly and they should then need only regular background support and the availability of a support worker or extra resources only occasionally.
- Another type of project can be a "back-to-work" scheme, in which local employers and voluntary associations are contacted with a view to their assisting someone to get back in to the regularity of work after a long hospital admission for mental health issues. There is still a lot of prejudice around, and local employers often need the reassurance of a case-worker in the background before they will consider a placement. As the person re-establishes their confidence and gains new skills, he or she becomes more independent and is often taken on permanently, or can get a subsequent job independently.
- Befriending schemes are where someone who may be socially isolated is allocated a "friend" or volunteer—often someone with previous mental health issues—to meet with them on a regular basis. This helps to build confidence and reintroduces the person to social activities.

- Help-lines and local (rural) support schemes are quite common, especially if a significant proportion of the population are geographically or socially remote.
- Day Centres and other types of projects can provide a comprehensive local support system that addresses both the needs of the people concerned, and also those of the wider community.

Such a local mental health association can work successfully in a number of ways to reduce prejudice, widen networks, and normalize the experience of people with such issues. This improvement of life-quality, especially for those who have suffered mental illness (and the often accompanying discrimination) is badly needed.

Voluntary sector organizations

These, and there are many, are increasingly providing much mental health care at a grass roots level. National organizations such as MIND, National Schizophrenia Foundation (NSF), Depression Alliance, SANE, Breathing Space, Carers UK, Mental Health Foundation, Samaritans, Threshold, etc., provide good basic mental health information and several types of more specialist mental health services. There are many local mental health voluntary organizations as well: too many to list. Thank heavens for the development of the Internet and efficient search engines such as Google or Ask Jeeves. Anyone with access to a home computer, an Internet café, or the local library can now easily find out what is available locally. If you feel you are "computer-challenged" or a "technophobe", then there are lots of people who will willingly help you.

STRESS

Basic information

Stress is one the major problems facing all of us today. We were simply just not designed—we did not evolve—to live in cities, to work in offices and factories, and especially to live at the pace that we seem to live at now, and it is getting worse! Essentially, our bodies are not able to cope very well with the number, variety, and constancy of the stressors found in modern everyday life. They are able to do an amazing amount, but we work longer, commute further, shop more, stay awake longer, and sleep 20% less than we did 100 years ago. This eventually causes stress overload—physically, emotionally and mentally. In the UK, it is estimated that at least 40 million working days are lost each year because of stress. Psycho-physiological disorders (those concerning the body–mind) are nearly always caused by stress, or are considerably worsened by stress. Stress also damages our immune systems, and this then has further implications on our health.

Causes of stress

The causes of stress are numerous and include: major life changes and life events; noise; crowds; poor sleep, bad diet, unhealthy lifestyle; alcohol or drug misuse (also symptoms of stress); aggravation and abuse; pressure to perform (work, school, sports, etc.); traffic; chemicals; trauma; poverty; discrimination; frustration; pregnancy; work pressures; negative emotions; loneliness; family conflicts; money worries; alienation; uncertainty; illness; unemployment; sexual problems; identity problems; relationship difficulties; going to school or college; Christmas; loss of any kind, including theft, relationship break-up, divorce, redundancy, abandonment, death (of someone close to you)—anything can cause stress!

Symptoms

The physical symptoms of stress are very varied. You may experience:

- feeling tired all the time;
- your body feeling heavy and listless;
- worsening sleep patterns;
- either a poor appetite, or cravings for certain foods: chocolate, junk food, coffee, alcohol;
- constipation or diarrhoea;
- constantly breaking down into tears;
- low sex drive;
- nervous habits like nail biting, hair pulling, skin picking, etc.
- breathless feelings;
- anger;
- general malaise and lack of energy;
- spots, blemishes, or skin rash;
- hard to relax;
- muscle tension;
- trembling or shaking;
- shortness of breath;
- feeling sick, or nausea;
- pounding heart or racing pulse;
- fast breathing;
- dry mouth;
- hot flushes or chills;

- feeling sick;
- "butterflies" in the stomach;
- headaches and/or migraines;
- restlessness.

The emotional symptoms of stress are also varied. You may experience:

- feeling so low or sad that you want to cry all the time;
- feelings of anger or irritation;
- depression;
- feelings of low self-esteem and of nothing good around you (pessimism);
- feeling inadequate or helpless;
- loss of interest in friends, activities, social life, etc.;
- finding it very hard to make decisions;
- low motivation;
- loss of all desires;
- unable to make contact with friends;
- finding emotional expression very hard;
- general anxiety;
- procrastination (putting off things);
- confusion.

Health implications

Stress has been ascribed as a major factor in cardiovascular disorders (hypertension and coronary heart disease); diabetes; asthma and other respiratory disorders; colds and fevers; ulcers and gastritis; several skin disorders; backaches; headaches; the speed in growth of several cancers; chronic infections; infertility and sexual disorders. Stress also negatively affects our intake of cigarettes, alcohol, sugar and carbohydrates, legal and illegal drugs; family, social and work relationships; our capacity for pleasure, our levels of tolerance, and our general sense of self-esteem. It also increases our aggression. In short, stress is a killer. Yet, ironically, it is based on an early animalistic survival system: the "fight-or-flight" mechanism.

Understanding stress

Any perception of threat—it does not have to be real—triggers this basic survival mechanism. A number of hormones, mainly adrenalin and cortisol, automatically flood through your body and prime it for intense physical activity—to fight or run—in order to survive.

If, at this point in time, you actually undertake the strenuous physical activity that your body is now primed for, your body will relax naturally afterwards. However, most of the "threats" are perceived ones and not real, and thus we do not often react physically, at that moment. The hormones therefore do not get burnt off by the resultant physical activity, so the physical symptoms persist and the body stays alert.

We may not have been able to relax properly before the next time the adrenal system is triggered, so the new tensions will sit on top of the old ones. Thus, we build up layer upon layer of stress. Then we start to worry about being stressed, or making mistakes, or being snappy or rude with people, and the resulting anxiety adds further to our levels of stress.

We need to find ways out of this cycle of stress, anxiety (and possibly even resultant depression). Some level of anxiety is good, helpful, and healthy. It keeps us safe, it helps us stay alert; without it we might get hit crossing the road, or we could not pass exams, or be able to deal with a crisis. Too much stress and our levels of anxiety debilitate us. Chronic (long-term) stress and anxiety can make us very ill indeed.

In an ongoing study at the Harvard Medical School of people who live to a hundred and beyond, one of the findings is that longevity was not a result of having avoided stress, but of having responded to it efficiently and effectively. There are several things that you can do to help to reduce considerably your levels of psychological or physiological stress. These work best in conjunction with each other, and most practitioners would agree that a combination of these is the only, repeat only, way to reverse long-standing (chronic) stress conditions. They share one common feature: they all help the body to restore its natural functioning. Your body–mind is beautifully designed to heal itself, and it will do so, given half a chance. However, if your anxiety states get too high, or are not really relevant, or remain at high levels long after the stimulus has passed, then you are probably seriously over-stressed, and possibly also restressing yourself. Alternatively, if you are depressed and cannot respond to a worsening situation, your stress will increase, which will compound the depression. All this requires you to take active steps to address stress and rebalance your basic bodily systems.

The very best thing that you can possibly do to combat your stress is almost certainly to do some aerobic exercise on a regular basis. This intense physical activity really helps you to burn off any built-up stress hormones and helps to rebalance your basic level of functioning (your Autonomic Nervous System). Regular aerobic exercise is thus a great first step. It also makes you feel better—you produce endorphins, the nice hormones that make you happy.

Once you start to do any physical exercise regularly, the very next thing to do is to learn how to relax physically. What happens in a state of relaxation is that your body begins to switch to a place where:

- your mind is not so alert and is more tranquil;
- you are not producing so many stress hormones (adrenalin, cortisol);
- your breathing rate is slower and your breathing is probably deeper;
- your heart rate is slower and your blood pressure is lower;
- you may start to feel tired and sleepy;
- your muscles begin to relax;
- your digestion starts up again.

It is quite simple to *learn* how to relax; however, it is not at all easy to *do*. Doing it properly might be the hardest thing you ever did in your whole life.

If these basic self-healing methods are *not* being utilized, then nothing much else written about in this book can make a great deal of difference. Your body will still be under stress; it will prevent you from feeling better. So you may need to learn how to do this sort of exercise and relaxation rhythm properly. The ideal—though you may not be able to achieve this immediately—is to get to the point where you are doing about forty-five minutes of aerobic exercise 3–4 times, or even five times, per week. This aerobic exercise should be combined with some relaxation, either first thing in the morning or later in the day, ideally lasting about twenty minutes, and you should try to do this 8–9 times per week. Get some coloured stickers from the stationer; use a wall calendar, and give yourself a red sticker every time you do more than about 30–45 minutes of aerobic exercise; and give yourself a green sticker for each period of at least twenty minutes of relaxation. This pattern is easy to monitor and the new rhythm really does work as it helps to rebalance your basic bodily system in a relatively short space of time.

Even people in a wheelchair, or with physical difficulties can find a way to do some aerobic exercise. You do not have to jog or be fit in order to get out of breath and a little hot and sweaty. Any aerobic exercise is basically good for you. If you have any serious physical difficulties, ask your doctor for a referral to a physiotherapist.

It is clear that different people have different thresholds of stress. Some of these are obviously due to how much other stress they are carrying. "Hardy" people—those who seem to be able to resist stress more easily—may have developed better stress strategies, or have better stress buffers (such as a good network of friends), than those who are less hardy or more reactive to stress. They may have had more experience of stress, or there may be aspects within their character (like a good sense of humour) that help them cope with stress better.

Exercise will work as a stress reducer for everyone. Some people may need to do it less than others; it is difficult to make a general rule. Otherwise, listen to your own body—it will tell you if anything is going wrong, and just continue exercising and relaxing, day in and day out. It really does work!

The physiology of stress

Sometimes it is helpful to understand a little more about the physiology of stress. Like each and every animal on this planet, we, the human animal, have a nervous system that "runs" our bodies without us ever thinking about it: it is called the Autonomic Nervous System (ANS). This organizes the heart, lungs, kidneys, muscle tone, hormones, digestion, etc., all below the level of consciousness. The ANS is divided into two separate halves: the sympathetic, the activity adrenalin-based half, and the parasympathetic, the relaxed digestive half. The sympathetic is the emergency response system: the "fight-or-flight" mechanism.

Imagine a deer or antelope grazing gently on the plains of the Serengeti: pure parasympathetic activity. It then smells a predator: its ears go up, the eyes widen, the head turns from side to side, it becomes very alert, its muscles are tense ready for "fight" or "flight"—totally sympathetic. These reactions are the affects of adrenalin that is now flooding through the animal preparing each part of its body, each organ, for this survival situation.

In such a situation, your muscles become ready to act instantly; your mind becomes more alert; your heart rate speeds up; adrenalin slows or shuts down your digestive system, speeds up your breathing, releases sugar for quick energy, and so forth: all perfectly designed to prepare your body to act physically in an emergency. The digestive system closes down, as you do not want to be digesting your lunch when you are trying to prevent yourself from becoming someone else's lunch. The blood retreats from the skin, to be available for the muscles. The muscles prime themselves and the heat rate speeds up, ready for instant action—fight or flight.

Back to the Serengeti: if the antelope runs away, or has to fight, that is fine! Most of the stress hormones (cortisoids) are then burnt off in the resulting intense physical activity. But if the animal does not have to fight or run, then eventually it gently relaxes, goes back to digesting its food and manages to digest some of the stress hormones as well: this is also fine. But . . . and here we have a problem . . . the human animal is NOT in the plains of the Serengeti, near where it originated. We have buses and bosses, trains and time schedules, school runs or spring-cleaning. We are continually under stress. On the Serengeti, we might only be chased once every two or three weeks, if we are unlucky. Now we get stressed three or four times in a day—if we are lucky!

So what happens to us, the human animals, is that the stress hormones and the by-products of adrenalin are *not* burnt off, or digested. They stay around, and then the next stress situation adds some more. These layers of stress eventually build up into a mass, or a block, which cannot be burnt off or easily digested. This physiological condition is called the "metabolic syndrome": a cluster of symptoms, including high blood pressure, insulin resistance, high cortisol levels, and high cholesterol, which can double the risk of heart disease and diabetes.

This build-up of stress also has a tendency to escalate the level of the next stressful situation, so that we also experience a build-up of emotional stress. This quickly spirals. All this means that instead of spending most of our time down at the parasympathetic end of the spectrum (Figure 1, solid double-arrowed line) with only a few excursions into stressful situations (sympathetic), as do most other animals, we spend most of our time at the higher stress end of the spectrum (dashed double-arrowed line) with only the occasional excursion into healthy relaxation. No wonder we're in such a state!

The result of this unnatural imbalance in our essential physiology is that, collectively and individually, we suffer from a large number of stress symptoms: not because there is anything particularly wrong with us, but because there is something seriously wrong with the way that we live our lives nowadays.

Our "normal" lives are not "natural" now. Our basic DNA differs from chimpanzees only by about 4%, so put a chimpanzee down in the middle of London or Edinburgh and it would probably not survive more than a few minutes before it was a gibbering wreck. Ever been shopping there on a Saturday in August or just before Christmas? Know the feeling? This is our basic physiology talking to us. It is stressful!

Therefore, we have to exercise more, to burn off most of the stress hormones, and to find more ways to spend more time just relaxing, so as to digest the stress residues and get ourselves back into physiological balance.

The combination of exercise and relaxation does this wonderfully; it is also essentially free, and instantly available. We have to find many more ways of doing things in a much more relaxed way. We have to pay much more attention to the physiological "costs" of living our modern lives, and especially in modern cities, and then compensate for these.

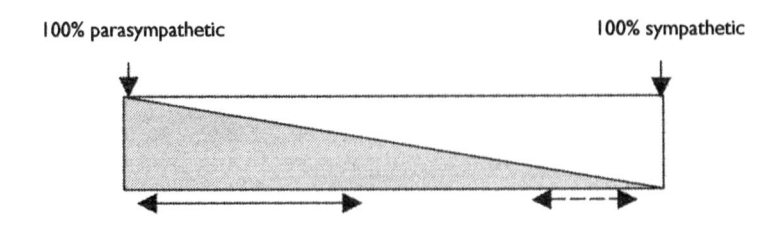

Figure 1. The parasympathetic/sympathetic spectrum.

We now tend also to live in isolated units (nuclear families) rather than in extended families and small social groups, where there was more support and a sense of "sharing" the burdens of life. All of this is very unnatural to our physiology and also to our psychology. Having only two adults locked up together in a small house, trying to cope with children, is very stressful in itself—more so if there is only one adult. And the children experience—and react to—the stress as well.

Self-help for stress

The main anti-stress self-help principles are laid out below in a twelve-point plan.

1. *Exercise more.* The important features are not what you do, but how much, and how often. Regularity is essential, and so is making it aerobic (getting out-of-breath and a bit hot and sweaty). Try to vary the pace and the type of aerobic exercise. There are some suggestions later on. Exercise that is enjoyable is also probably much better for you: a forty-minute stiff walk to the nearest hilltop is sometimes nicer than pounding away on a running machine in a gym for the same period. Playing football in the park with the kids is usually more fun (even if you lose) than bench-pressing weights with macho body-builders in the gym. Remember that these are all principles of de-stressing: so don't stress yourself too much doing any type of exercise. Just do it! Ideally, about five times per week, forty-five minutes minimum.
2. *Regular relaxation.* An absolute minimum of twenty minutes once a day or ten minutes twice a day. Look for deeper, regular breathing first, then an absence of "busy" thoughts, and then

try for an inner feeling of warmth and relaxation throughout the body. Try to keep wiping out invasive thoughts. Whether your relaxation method is called "deep relaxation", "heart coherence", "Autogenic Technique" or is some form of meditation, the method is relatively unimportant: the regular experience is essential. Lying on the sofa listening to Chopin or Mozart can also bliss you out, so can a Radox bath. Do whatever works for you!

3. *Manage present stress and conflicts better.* There are many simple ways of doing this, though they are not, by any means, usually easy. There are many different techniques, and again the method is not particularly important, but the principles are:

- *Identify what your stressors are.* External stressors can be pollution, excessive sun exposure, heavy workloads, emotional problems, bereavement, divorce, or separation, difficulties at home or work. Self-inflicted stressors are caffeine, hydrogenated fats, alcohol, smoking, and other recreational drugs. Internal stressors can be food allergies and intolerances, autoimmune diseases, high cholesterol, metabolic waste not being eliminated properly, blood sugar imbalances (and diabetes), hormonal imbalances, nutritional deficiencies, endogenous depression (from chemical imbalance), etc.

- *Conflicts.* With conflicts or emotional stress, try go to the source of the conflict: talking to other people does not usually work. Arrange a time and place and let the people involved know that it is about a problem you are having with them: approach them amicably; talk about some good things first, and then about the (difficult) behaviour or the conflict you are experiencing and how you are affected by it; finally, say what you would like, or need, to happen next. This does not guarantee that the conflict will disappear, but at least you are talking about it, saying you have a problem, and doing it in a way that is least likely to cause offence.

- *Prepare in advance for known (stressful) events.* Obtain good information; do not rush things; do not leave things to the last minute; do not skimp. Prioritize the important or immediate tasks. Know what you do well and stick to that. Take one day at a time. Learn not to be a perfectionist. Try not to escape from the present. Address any problems now!

- *Avoid debt!* Try not to overspend or get into debt (any further). Consult someone to help manage your finances a bit better or to consolidate your debts. There are plenty of experts and good advice is fairly readily available. You might have to get over some embarrassment about being in debt, or the extent of your debts, but it is best to be open and honest with those people who matter: partners, parents, bank managers, creditors, etc.
- *Talk to someone.* Ask for support. Get some professional help, be it from the Human Resources or the Health and Safety departments, a staff counsellor, an employee assistance programme (EAP), someone in the church, marriage guidance, your doctor, etc. Also, listen to those around you; they can often see your situation more clearly than you can. Whatever the cost to your pride, pocket, or principles, just do it. Life is complicated enough already without any inner turmoil, as well as more everyday stress and conflict to deal with. Try to develop a more positive attitude to yourself, your work and family, and the world.

4. *A healthy diet.* When we are stressed, or in distress, our diet usually goes to pieces and we focus much more on "comfort foods". Often our intake of alcohol and other legal "drugs" (sugar, caffeine, chocolate, and cigarettes) also increases. We are what we eat! And the road back to health usually means adopting a better balanced diet. Most people know the main principles:
   - reduce unhealthy (animal) fats;
   - increase healthy (Omega-3) fats (oily fish, nuts, seeds, some oils);
   - reduce carbohydrates considerably;
   - reduce sugar and salt intake; don't drink too much alcohol;
   - drink much more water—at least two litres a day;
   - eat five portions of fruit and vegetables a day;
   - eat less processed foods and pre-prepared meals;
   - eat more organic and home-cooked foods, if possible.
5. *Dealing with trauma and painful memories.* If there have been traumatic events and/or events that provoke anger, sadness, or other painful memories, these really need to be dealt with by working on them, talking through them, and eventually coming to terms with them, in some way. You will not heal fully

if you are still traumatized, or if old wounds are still upsetting you emotionally. These sorts of things, albeit in the past, can carry a lot of current stress. Which method you use: EMDR, emotional counselling, psychotherapy, etc., is relatively unimportant, but the process of emotional healing is totally necessary. Be as honest with yourself as possible about your need to heal.

6. *Enrich your relationships.* Talk more to those around you, spend more quality time with them, listen to them (really listen), and value them more. Discover more about their background, their (general and specific) thinking, their feelings, and their ideas. Ask about what affects them, or what troubles them. They will then feel that you are genuinely interested in them. Respect their views and how they cope—and how they cope with you. Empathy is a key concept. Then you can talk to them about what troubles you have, and open up and share a bit more. Now you know (about) them a bit better, you might trust them more. This can become the start of a much better relationship. You might also have to learn to say "No" to those who you feel are imposing on you, using you, or abusing the present relationship. Become more aware of your own limits and boundaries. When you do, others might respect your limits and boundaries better. Maybe there is one particular friend you can already really trust and relax with; when did you last spend quality time with them?

7. *Regular sleep and waking gently.* Getting into a regular routine of sleep is one of the most essential ways of avoiding stress. Always try to go to bed at the same time, and to wake up at the same time. Getting in to the habit of such a sleep pattern is very important, and not very easy. Try to avoid stressors right before bedtime: these include coffee, sugar, and alcohol. A gentle walk after dinner can be a good relaxant; so can a nice warm bath, or a massage. *Then* try to adjust the amount of sleep you get to the right amount for you: different people need different amounts: anywhere between six to eight hours is the most common. *Then* try "dawn simulators" or a light (on a timer) going on gently before the alarm clock wakes you. Try to spend a few minutes in bed before getting up: don't rush into the day already stressed. Don't worry if you wake a little early: learn to stay

lying down, reasonably relaxed, without getting anxious. You are still resting, even if you are not asleep.
8. *Focus on your health.* Your health is very important and it also is not a constant. It needs to be worked at—actively—in order for you to *stay* healthy. So, learn to take care of yourself, on all different levels, especially when you are stressed. Explore some of the other activities and possibilities that are around or available; there are probably many more than you think and some of them can be quite fun. Try something a little different, as you might have got yourself into a rut. Take a little time out, like a long weekend break, that can really refresh you (you may have some time "in lieu" available). Get away and regenerate yourself. One of the twenty-four-hour packages spent at a hydro hotel can be really nice (massage, jacuzzi, sauna, steam room, etc.), without breaking the bank. Consider also some of the more holistic approaches, alternative health concepts, or complementary medicine perspectives. Shiatsu, massage, acupuncture, tea-tree oil, green tea, or lavender oil baths can often help with stress and be very pleasurable, so treat yourself!
9. *Contact with nature.* We have often lost contact with nature and we do not realize how important this can be for us. The woods, the fields, the beach, the moors, the hills are all easily available, and wonderful. Go and take a walk. Get your hands in the earth, digging the garden or potting out some plants in window boxes. It is not an extra chore; it can be really relaxing. Allow yourself a breathing space: do something gentle that you enjoy in nature.
10. *Breathe! Breathe! Breathe!* Become much more aware of your breathing, regularly, daily, hourly. When we are anxious or stressed, we tend to breathe in and hold our breath. Eventually this adds to our stress and distress. Stop and breathe in for a count of five, through your nose, and then exhale for a count of seven, out through the mouth. You can visualize breathing in peace, strength, or whatever it is that you need, and then breathing out all that stress and anxiety and pain and distress. Let it all leave your body as you breathe out. When you breathe in, fill up your chest area and torso, up to the shoulders. When you breathe out, breathe out right down to the bottom of your belly. A hand on the chest or belly when you breathe deeply can

serve as a reminder. Try doing this regularly, even every fifteen minutes or so, just for a few in-breaths and out-breaths each time.

11. *Humour.* There is an archetypal story of a man who cured himself of cancer by locking himself in a hotel bedroom for three weeks with nothing but a collection of silent movies by Charlie Chaplin and Buster Keaton. He laughed his way back to health. Humour is very important for stress release. Find something that makes *you* laugh. Go out with people who you feel comfortable with, and with whom you can laugh and have a good (pleasant) time.

12. *Talk to someone.* This has been mentioned before. It is so important that it gets mentioned again. Not everyone finds this easy, but it does work. Trying to do it all by yourself (macho), or not wanting to bother other people (self-sacrificing), or thinking that other people are more important or have more worries than you (self-demeaning), or whatever—just does not help you one little bit. You are still stuck with the problems or difficulties that you have and are causing you stress. Many people are capable of listening, and just the experience of talking about some of the things that are worrying you can often mean that you provide yourself with some of the answers that you need. Take the plunge: just say to someone—a good friend, your partner, your (friendly) manager, a colleague perhaps: "I read this little booklet at the doctor's surgery on stress and I have just realized that I am a lot more stressed than I thought I was". See how they respond. It is a start, or it is a good first step.

Stress and modern life

Our modern lifestyles involve us in less physical activity than ever before throughout the five million years of human evolutionary history. Our patterns of life and work have never been more stressful. Stress levels have rarely ever been higher. The reason is that whenever we get upset or threatened in any way, our basic "fight-or flight" mechanism, based on adrenalin and cortisol, is activated. This has been mentioned before.

If we do not fight or run away (like one of the animals), because we are "civilized", then the stress hormones, the by-products and companions of adrenalin, like cortisone, remain unused and stay in our systems. Then they can start to build up and this causes us additional problems: more stress; increased heart-rate; tense muscles; aggressive emotions; startle-patterns; poorer sleep; increased weight; reliance on de-stressors (drugs and alcohol); and poor digestion—among other problems. Stress also restricts our ability to rebalance ourselves, internally as well as emotionally; our immune systems and self-regulatory functions can become seriously compromised. We suspect that as much as 70% of all disease and illness is linked to high levels of stress. So much for being "civilized"!

The threats that usually face us nowadays are essentially non-physical: there are no lions wandering in Hyde Park in London, down Kelvin Grove in Glasgow, or on Arthur's Seat in Edinburgh. It is much more likely that someone has upset us, we are worried about money, we are frustrated at work, our kids have left the sitting room in a mess, we are late and there is a traffic jam, etc. The hormones in our bodies are still being triggered by these stressful situations, by our stress or dis-(s)tress, but our bodies are not being utilized for physical action and so these hormones just stay in our systems. They can even be detected up to three weeks after a stressful event—and that is just from one event. How often do we get stressed like this? How do we deal with it, or not deal with it?

There are only two ways to eliminate these stress hormones from the body: burning them off through physical activity and digesting them slowly over time. And our digestive systems close down under stress: you do not want to be digesting your lunch when you are trying to avoid becoming something else's lunch. We can learn to start to channel the stress more appropriately; first of all into some sort of physical activity, so that it gets worked out of our bodies naturally, and then into ways that avoid building the stress up, or that release it more easily. However, the more inactive we are, the more the stress hormones will accumulate. The more the stress hormones accumulate, the more likely we are to react to situations in a stressful way; and so a vicious spiral builds up.

We need to consider, therefore, the emotional and psychological pressures that we are under. Our school reports said, "S/he must work harder". There is the "Protestant work ethic" that can make us prioritize our job before our family, and social value systems that prioritize other people (everyone else) before ourselves. At work, there are targets and quotas. The bosses put the managers under stress; they try to get us to comply with something that is essentially unrelated or meaningless to us: annual reports, share price, and profits. There are now regular newspaper reports making this sort of connection.

At home, mortgage costs have escalated astronomically. One full-time wage-earner cannot now provide for a family, with children, in a decent home. Many families now have to have two wage-earners. This creates problems in school holidays or if a child is sick. These families often have to rely on a grandparent or similar relation, and these often do not live very close. The stress is increasing remorselessly.

Many people have to do extra work at home, outside of their full-time hours. Home is not such a safe place any longer, and we have to pay for burglar alarms and fire alarms and higher insurance policies. We worry more about the children's schools, their diets, and whether they spend too much time in front of the TV or computer and away from us. We hardly have time for them, yet they are so important to us. And they want so much! They are also under stress: school-work, homework, and exams; peer group pressures; separated (often alienated) parents; powerful emotions, especially in adolescence; and the background pressure to become a little consumer. We (in the West) now also tend to live in isolated units (nuclear families) rather than in the extended families and small social groups of earlier times, where there was more support and a sense of "sharing" the burdens of life. Having only two adults locked up together in a small house, trying to cope with children as well as doing a full-time job, is very stressful in itself. And the children experience—and then react to—our stress as well. All of this is very unnatural to our physiology and also to our emotions and our psychology, our mental health.

Even when we go on holiday, the journey there is often stressful: airports are not people-friendly, flights can be early in the morning or late at night, and there are shuttle buses, taxis, or hire car firms to negotiate with, before we can get to our hotel and relax.

There is so much going on that is stressful, and that we have to cope with. Marital breakdowns, panic attacks, hysteria, road rage, teenage vandalism, drug-taking, and violence suddenly seem slightly more "sensible" reactions to situations that are essentially intolerable to our basic physiology and to our intrinsic ideas as to what life *should* be like: inexcusable, but understandable. All this sounds incredibly bleak and overwhelming. Yet . . . the remedies for stress are relatively simple, though not necessarily all that easy.

It is very difficult to work with the stresses of modern life as they are almost inevitably embedded in us: we grew up with them and we have been shaped by them. On one level this seems impossible to work with, but, on the other hand, not to challenge these forces around us and within us is to accept that change is not possible. This is not the case.

In the same way that the citizens and children of Beirut, Bosnia, Rwanda, and now Iraq will have to learn that the solution to their problems does not lie in having an AK47 or in killing their neighbours, we are going to have to learn that it is possible to overcome these social forces and to create a more stress-free life for ourselves. Our lives depend upon it!

Fitting exercise into your life

As explained, aerobic exercise is a very important tool in the struggle to defeat stress, and it is also very good for anxiety and depression. In fact, it is excellent for all forms of mental health. It is great for general health as well: it can help to cut down on the risk of your developing major illnesses and it can help you to live longer. Much of ageing is due to decreased mobility as a result of an increasingly sedentary lifestyle.

Regular exercise makes you feel and look better. It helps to release serotonin and endorphins—the "happy" hormones, responsible for the "feel-good" factor. It boosts your energy levels, reduces tension and anger, improves concentration, improves your sleep, increases heart and lung capacity, increases bone density, and has many other benefits for specific illnesses.

A little exercise goes a long way. You do not have to take out a subscription to a gym (that is how they make their money), run a marathon, or become a health freak. However, it is usually necessary to fit more exercise into your life—somehow—and then try to keep on doing it regularly.

The best form of exercise is aerobic exercise—where you get out of breath, and feel a bit hot and sweaty. Ideally, you should try to do some aerobic exercise about 4–5 times per week, or 5–6 times a week in more severe cases, with a minimum of 30–45 minutes each time. (This way the effects last longer, as after only twenty minutes the effects drop off quite quickly.) You can do this type of exercise any time, anywhere, anyhow: it really doesn't matter. It just works!

The really hard bit is adapting your life-style to include such exercise. And you do not really have much of a choice about this—because it works. It is therefore stupid to ignore something that is so simple and so effective. Even people with a disability, or in a wheelchair, or with a heart condition, can find ways of doing a workout. The trick, and the challenge, is to do it regularly.

We live, increasingly, in a sedentary, urban society. If we do not use our bodies, we get out of shape, unhealthy, and obese. We also get miserable: look at some of the faces around you! The remedy is relatively simple—get out of that chair, put the "sweats" on, and get out! You will be surprised and astonished at how much better you feel if you start to do this sort of exercise regularly. Even twice or three times a week makes an incredible difference.

There is often a difficulty, or a reluctance, in breaking the pattern or habit of our lives. Even if we are depressed, anxious, or struggling, something keeps us in that pattern or habit. We have to realize that this habit is the problem. It is not that *we* are the problem; it is the habit we have got into. It is a bad habit, because it gives us a problem. We have built an identity around that pattern: we think this is who we are. That is not true. That is what we do, not who we are. We are someone who has just got a little stuck in that pattern. And we can change that.

Here are a number of suggestions about how to change your pattern of how you fit exercise into your life—or the pattern of how you don't. Choose one, two, or more of these suggestions that might work for you.

- "Power-walk" (you do not have to jog) around the edge of the local golf course or park.
- Use an MP3 player or a Walkman to make it more interesting.
- Occasionally bike to work, or to visit someone on your bike.
- Get an exercise bike, treadmill, or stepper; put it in the corner of the bedroom or living room; and use it regularly—especially if it is raining outside!

FITTING EXERCISE INTO YOUR LIFE 53

- Instead of watching or listening to your favourite "soap" while sitting down—exercise while you do so.
- Join a Tai Chi or Yoga class once a week: there is almost bound to be one quite close to you nowadays. Maybe do this *with* your partner, friend, or flatmate, it will be something different to talk about.
- Shops such as TK Max sell simple Pilates equipment quite cheaply: get some and use it; there are often instructional DVDs that come with the equipment.
- Most evenings, try to walk around the block for half an hour before you go in and get ready for bed.
- Swimming 30–40 lengths (using different strokes) whenever you go to the swimming pool.
- Volunteer to exercise your neighbour's dog: make him/her very happy and get lots of doggy love while you get slim and trim—and happier.
- Get a local Ordnance Survey map and start to explore some of the local footpaths.
- Get a pedometer, clip it on your belt or waistband, and count your daily steps: try to build up towards 10,000 steps per day (most people do 3,000–5,000 anyway).
- Get out of the car on the way home from the weekly shop and power-walk the last two miles while the others drive home and put the shopping away.
- Double-dig the garden vegetable plot; clear out the garden shed, attic, or garage; make a compost heap (or turn it over); do something active around the house or garden.
- Get off the bus one or two stops early and walk the last few hundred yards or so.
- If it is raining, get busy with the housework: vacuuming (175 calories per hour), shopping (245), sweeping (280), cleaning the floor (315), painting (360), etc.
- If you are relatively immobile, get some mini-dumbbells and hand-weights for your hands and arms only.
- In the local newspaper there are usually announcements about where and when the local Ramblers' group meets. Go along once or twice and see what it is like, what they are like, and whether you like that sort of walking/social activity.
- A light foam exercise mat in front of the TV, and a Pilates or Yoga video or DVD, and you are away on a new course of exercise.

- Try to make a point of doing one good long walk (6.5–10 miles/10–16 km) every couple of months, ideally up and down some steep hills.
- Join up with a work colleague and exercise, play squash, badminton (or something similar), for forty-five minutes during a lunch hour or after work, once a week.
- Get a group of friends, church-goers, work colleagues to form a team together, meeting once a month or so, to (say) raise money for charity by doing sponsored walks, competing with other teams, digging gardens, washing cars, doing a half-marathon, etc.
- Work towards a long-term goal: power-walking a marathon (or half-marathon); doing the West Highland Way, the Pennine Way, or the pilgrimage route to Santiago de Compostella; going on a cycling or trekking holiday—along the Great Wall of China, or to Maccu Picu (Machu Picchu), or whatever takes your fancy—or your wildest dream!

Thomas Jefferson once said, "Walking is the best possible exercise. Habituate yourself to walk very far". Walking is relatively cheap, easy, and can even be quite fun. You might even get to meet some of the "joggers", "dog-gers", or "floggers" (joke) as you walk around the nearest golf course regularly every week.

Different types of exercise

There are several different types of exercise, done for different reasons. Check some of these out for yourself: they might suit you.

Aerobics for the immune system

There are specific benefits to different forms of exercise that are now being realized. Not only does aerobic exercise burn off stress hormones, but it helps protect you from diabetes and heart disease. It can also reduce the likelihood that you will get periodonitis (gum disease) or other inflammatory ailments, as exercise boosts your immune system and reduces inflammation throughout the body.

Tai Chi for stress

The slow, meditative practice of Tai Chi generally produces a mental state of calm, and results in reduced anxiety and stress. It is a low-impact form of aerobic exercise and thus suitable for older people, or those with some limb ailments or disabilities. Research studies (in USA) also show that it lowers blood pressure, benefits arthritis, and boosts the immune system. There are also some ongoing studies about the positive effects of Tai Chi on cancer patients.

Swimming for PMS

Apparently, there is hormonal flux experienced by women in their menstrual cycle that often causes them to skip high intensity exercise or work-outs. These effects are lessened with low intensity exercise, like long swims.

Pilates for back pain

"Pilates has a long list of benefits including improved body mechanics, balance, coordination, strength and flexibility," said Dr Cedric X. Bryant, chief exercise physiologist for the American Council on Exercise (Bryant, 2006). "While the ACE study shows that a Pilates session burns a relatively small amount of calories, it is still a valuable addition to any exercise routine offering the essential elements of building a strong core and increasing flexibility."

When you strengthen the core muscles of the back, the various parts of the spine are helped back into alignment: this can help back pain. When you strengthen the muscles of the stomach, you access a lot of lower body strength as well, and this helps to rebalance your body and benefits other movement.

Yoga or Alexander Technique for headaches

Many headaches arise from muscle tension in the back of the neck, sometimes due to storing stress there, and sometimes from bad posture. Both these techniques can help your posture and make it less likely that you will store stress there. The Alexander Technique has also been shown to be effective in reducing the disability of patients suffering from Parkinson's disease, and in improving pain behaviour and disability in patients with back pain.

Exercising together

Doing anything in a group is usually more fun than doing things alone. There is the added social factor, as well as the inducement of knowing that others are going to be there at such-and-such a time. Exercise becomes less "punitive", you can measure your progress alongside others, and get empathy for any difficulties that you might have. While joining a group can be a little daunting at first, most such like-minded exercise groups or local ramblers' groups and sports' clubs are fairly benign and friendly. It can also be a way of meeting new people and building friendships, especially if you have just moved into a new area.

The gym

There are many easy-access, low-cost gyms or local leisure centres nowadays. Many people buy a subscription to one of the more commercial gyms, and then do not use it fully. Pay session by session for the first few months and see if you like it. Do not go for the "introductory offer", or—if you do—make sure there is an opt-out clause.

The centre's staff are usually of a very high calibre. These gyms and community leisure centres nearly always vet the qualifications and experience of their exercise class leaders and group facilitators carefully, and there should always be information about what professional association they belong to. Different classes have different styles. If you do not like what you get from a particular group or class, then don't go back to that one: find another one that works for you. Or just use the facilities yourself.

You can treat the commercial gym more as a specialist centre, as joining one on a regular basis can be quite expensive, although you can often get a day ticket. You might want to develop a special workout, or get some specialist advice with a particular problem. The local authority leisure centres have almost as good facilities, are often cheaper, and they also have a number of different classes or other events that might also interest you.

At home

If you cannot get to a gym, or if you don't like them, there are very good videos and DVDs that you can use at home. Try getting an aerobics, Yoga and/or Pilates video (or DVD) from somewhere like Amazon, e-Bay, or a local charity shop. A towel and an exercise mat are the only other things that you really need, besides some regular time and some determination. You can also sometimes find a small exercise bike, rowing machine, hand weights, or something similar on e-Bay, at TK Max, in the large supermarkets, or in the local small ads, for home use. All of these can be woven into your life at home. You can work away at these as you listen to the radio or an MP3 player, or even while you watch your favourite soap on TV.

It really does not matter physiologically what type of exercise you do; your body doesn't mind. As long as you get out of breath and a bit hot and sweaty, you will be burning off the stress hormones and generating some more of the "happy" hormones, particularly endorphin. It is much more important to do the type of exercise that "works" for you.

You are going to have to do this exercise regularly, week in and week out. Therefore, you will need to enjoy what you are doing. If you feel a bit lonely and isolated, then it may be best to do something in a group or at a centre or gym, where you will meet people. If you are aiming just to get fitter and healthier, then do something that you really enjoy and/or take your MP3 player with you with some really fabulous tracks or an audio book that you have downloaded.

Relaxation

Besides doing exercise, it is really important to relax as well. However, only try relaxing first thing in the morning, or some time after you have exercised. Done regularly, this will help you to rebalance your basic bodily functioning (the autonomic nervous system), which is what gets overstressed. For most people under stress, it is very difficult to relax—for two main reasons: (1) they think they cannot afford the time; and (2) they are so stressed that they cannot relax easily. It is therefore necessary to build in a programme of relaxation (ideally once or twice a day for twenty minutes). There are many different ways to relax. Here are several suggestions:

- *Progressive relaxation.* You can get booklets, tapes or CDs of (usually) progressive relaxation exercises that tell you how first to tense, then to relax, progressively, all the various sets of individual muscle groups in your body (feet, calves, thighs, buttocks, etc.). As you do this, you tend to relax generally more and more. It is sometimes called "differential relaxation".
- *Autogenic therapy.* I often teach people the principles of a form of relaxation known as "autogenic therapy". This was designed

for people with hypertension. It works using a mental script and an image for the various parts of the body. The advantage of learning a system like this is that you can do it anywhere and without any special equipment. You can get a book that teaches you the details, or there are special autogenic therapists who can be found through the Autogenic Therapy Association website. It is medically recognized as being effective for hypertension (high blood pressure). It could also work for your stress.

- *Music.* Certain types of music are very soothing and relaxing: Mozart, Chopin, some Bach, Boccherini, etc. Try to get some CDs or tapes and listen to what works for you in the car, or at home, instead of listening to the radio. Alternatively, tune your car radio to Radio 3, or Classic FM, rather than the news or pop music. CDs of whale songs or Peruvian flute music can also be relaxing. Set some special time aside, possibly with a comfortable set of headphones, and chill out.
- *Warm water.* This is very relaxing. Go for Radox-type baths, a nice long soak, with a candle and some music in the background. Or get yourself to the nearest jacuzzi, maybe even in your lunch hour. Hydrotherapy is a very well-established relaxation treatment.
- *Massage* is an excellent form of relaxation. It does not particularly matter what type of massage, but aromatherapy massages are now quite popular and fairly readily available. They will usually cost £20–30 but it is an excellent investment to kick-start you into a better pattern of relaxation and self-care. Ask your partner for a foot-massage as you watch TV together. Sometimes a bit of self-massage helps: first work your fingers across the scalp; then into the back of your neck; then one shoulder after another; then those tense muscles at the top of the chest towards the shoulder and by the collar bones; these can all be massaged by yourself, taking only a minute or two, while at work, and without any embarrassment. Stretch and yawn before you go back to your task, refreshed and more relaxed.
- *Breaks* are also important. You (are supposed to) have scheduled tea breaks at work: so take them. Do not work on through them. You should have a half-hour minimum lunch break, by law:

take it! Get out of the office or workplace. Do not pass up on holidays, or time in lieu. If you work from home, take five minutes every hour—as a minimum—and a lunch break away from your work area. Arrange for quality time away: mini-breaks, long weekends, or whatever. Anything less than this is essentially counter-productive in the long term.

- *Do something different.* A really good form of relaxation is to do something completely different. It does not have to be specifically relaxing: it could be something like Pilates, Tai Chi, Aikido, or Yoga. Something physical is probably better than something sedentary, and these disciplines are more balancing than relaxing. But it could be a local drama group or a choir: something that will take you out of yourself, allow you to do something different, and help you to meet others as well.
- *Reading, watching films or TV, listening to music or the radio,* can also be quite relaxing—in relatively small doses: doing it too much can be a way of just "cutting off", and this is not very relaxing. It is best to have a regular routine and stick to it: reading the paper on the way to work, or watching the news or a favourite TV show at a set time.
- *Meditation.* Nearly every religion or culture practises some form of meditation. There have been a number of scientific studies to show that it has quite profound effects on both mind and body, if done regularly. It does not seem to matter particularly what type of meditation is practised: there is an example of one later.
- *Mindfulness.* Mindfulness practice, a form of meditation, is now becoming accepted within the realms of CBT, or they are adopting it because it has been shown to be effective. Some of the "Mindfulness" practised is in the form of a meditation; however, it can be extended into everyday life. One of the proponents of such a practice is a remarkable Vietnamese Zen Buddhist monk called Thich Nhat Hahn. Besides being nominated for a Nobel Peace prize, he has written a number of easily readable books (e.g., Hahn, 1995), now mainstream in the National Health Service.

Again, it really does not matter physiologically (to your body) what type of relaxation you do. The important aspect is to really "chill out", almost to the point where you are "blissing out" a little—that state where you are almost falling asleep or having daydream-type images.

Please remember that you are trying to move from the stressed-out "sympathetic" end of the Autonomic Nervous System spectrum towards the "parasympathetic" end of the ANS spectrum (see Figure 1, p. 38). This is going to take some time, plenty of practice, and regularity. I usually recommend that people should do about twenty minutes of relaxation 8–9 times per week.

The type of relaxation also needs to work for you. If you are a classical music enthusiast, that isn't a problem. For others, it might be something physical, something more social, or something quite solitary.

A relaxation technique

There are several different techniques and some suggestions have been given earlier. Specific techniques need to work for you. You cannot "fail" the technique, though the technique might "fail" to help you.

Before you try any relaxation technique, try to make sure that you are reasonably capable of relaxing. If you are over-stressed, or have just had an argument with your partner or boss, then you will probably not be able to use any technique effectively. Take time to cool down emotionally. Perhaps do some exercise, or workout, first, and burn some of those stress hormones off. Get yourself into a good state to use your particular technique, whatever it is.

If you do not have a particular one that works for you, here is a simple one. Sit comfortably in a chair, or on a cushion, with your back reasonably straight, and your head nicely balanced on the top. Feel comfortable and supported and alert: if you lie down, you might go to sleep. Now divide the time that you have available into four equal sections: e.g., 20 minutes = 4 × 5-minute sections. Don't go on for any longer than that.

Section 1: monitor your breathing

Close your eyes and just listen to your breathing. Don't change your breathing; just monitor it, observe it. After a couple of minutes, breathe into any area of your body that feels particularly stressed or tense. Feel the muscles of that part of your body lift and fall with your breathing. Imagine the in-breath as a wave, just warmth, relaxing and softening those tense muscles. Imagine the out-breath as a letting go of all your stress and tension. Just continue to do this, focusing particularly on your relaxing out-breath.

Section 2: extend your awareness

Allow your awareness to open to what is around you: any bird song; the noise of traffic; the smells (nice or nasty) from the open window (or whatever); the pressure of the chair against your back and legs; the clothes against your skin and the shoes on your feet; the warmth of the sun on your body; the coolness of the draught on your skin. Stay open and aware to whatever inputs there are. Keep breathing gently. Just do this for the whole time allotted for this section.

Section 3: focus on your self

Bring your awareness now to the person (you) that is sitting and breathing, and become aware of yourself—your self. How are you feeling? What is it like being this person? How are you feeling about yourself: all the different aspects of your self?

Perhaps you can imagine yourself as a pillar of light (or energy) with many different facets: a facet for the you who is at home, a facet for the you at work, a facet for you in the family, a facet for you with your partner, the facet that you show to your friends, etc. Each facet is slightly different, yet all are aspects of the whole pillar—you. What colours of emotion or feeling are there? How do these colours change between the facets? How do you feel about each of these different aspects? What aspects of yourself are not being shown?

Section 4: let it all go

Imagine a wind gently blowing all the stress and tension away, just as it blows the autumn leaves. Or try to imagine you are in a slow-moving train, and all these different images come passing by, and then they disappear. Focus on nothing in particular; hold on to nothing.

Occasionally there is a thought that may seem important: "It's Auntie Mary's birthday tomorrow and I need to send her a card." Or "The car tax was due yesterday. I must do something about that very soon." Put these thoughts into (say) a balloon and let them just bob around. Don't hang on to them now. You can take them with you when you leave this relaxation space. Deal with them one by one afterwards. Now go back to relaxing and letting things go.

When you have finished relaxing, don't jump up and run for a bus. Move slowly and gently for a few moments; drink some water; try to embody and carry with you something of the level of relaxation you have just achieved.

Do this sort of exercise regularly: daily if you can; ideally twice a day, for about twenty minutes. The technique is good in itself, but it is also a means to an end. The real trick is to build the more relaxed state into your everyday overall state of being through the regular practice. As you practise it regularly, make sure you become more relaxed generally. Then you will be able to cope with anything.

Air-travel addenda

In (say) a long transatlantic flight, give yourself a pattern of activity and relaxation throughout the flight:

- Settling in, ten minutes; relaxation exercise, twenty minutes; drink water; read your book, twenty minutes; drink water again and then do the sitting exercises in the in-flight magazine, ten minutes.
- Read/watch film/listen to your music/talk to neighbour, thirty minutes; relaxation exercise, ten minutes; get up, stretch, walk around, go up one aisle and down another, do a little stretching exercise for your legs and ankles, ten minutes. Meditate, ten minutes.
- Eat meal, twenty minutes; bathroom, ten minutes; read a book/ watch film/listen to music/talk to neighbour, thirty minutes.

- That is three hours taken up, so repeat or vary slightly for the rest of the flight.

Breaking up the time like this makes it much easier to cope with. Focus on the activity you are doing now! Don't think ahead, or of how much time is left.

Meditation and mindfulness

A very powerful form of relaxation is meditation. This does not have to be religious, or based on a particular faith. Essentially, it is sitting still, breathing regularly, and quietening your mind. When you do this, your body slows down and you shift more into the parasympathetic (see p. 38). Eventually, your mind will slow down, too, and you will become more peaceful and relaxed. This is extremely good for many medical conditions, such as hypertension (high blood pressure), or for reducing the stress that can aggravate many conditions, both medical and psychological.

Meditation position

Make sure you are not going to be disturbed: switch the ringer on the phone off, turn off the mobile, hang a note on the bedroom door, and tell others in the house you are going to meditate for (say) twenty minutes. Settle into a comfortable sitting position, either on a straight-backed chair, with your feet flat on the floor, or sitting cross-legged on a soft surface on the floor. Your spine should be vertical, your body fairly relaxed, your weight supported and balanced.

Check your body and breathing

Bring your awareness to how your body is feeling. Spend a minute or so checking yourself out, doing a body scan. Become aware of how your body feels: warm or cold, comfortable or uncomfortable, the feel of your clothes against your skin, and whether your belt, waistband, or collar feels constraining. Make any adjustments necessary. Then, become aware of your breathing: is it deep, shallow, or light; is it only in the chest or the belly; are you holding your breath at all, or is it flowing in and out fairly freely? Become aware of which parts of your body move when you breathe: maybe there is a slight pause at the top of the in-breath or the bottom of the out-breath. Maybe you are breathing in and out only through your nose, or only through your mouth. Don't try to control your breathing, just allow the breath to flow—in and out. Simply let the breath "breathe" itself. This is very peaceful. You do not really have to do anything else, just keep on doing this.

Either empty your mind or focus your mind

Sooner or later your mind will start to wander, or thoughts will come into your mind that distract your awareness and your peace of mind. This is very common, especially in the early learning stages. It is not a mistake or failure: it is just what the mind does. Congratulations for noticing that your attention is not on your breath. Just empty your mind of its thoughts, and/or refocus on your breathing. This will happen over and over again. Just keep on emptying your mind of thoughts and refocusing your awareness on your breathing.

Sometimes you might wish to focus or meditate on a particular topic, like world peace, a prayer for someone close to you, or "healing". As you breathe in, concentrate or focus these qualities inside of you; as you breathe out, send out these qualities into the world. Again, your attention may wander at times, or thoughts may cascade through your mind. That is normal: just refocus your attention and awareness on your intent. Make each moment count. Keep coming back to the topic or focus of the meditation.

All thoughts have equal value: there are not "good" thoughts or "bad" thoughts. Thinking is not "bad" and an empty mind "good". Do not get distracted by judgement or by content. Do not try to suppress or eliminate certain thoughts or topics. What matters is your awareness of your thoughts and when you are thinking, and what you want to do about it: judge it, hang on to it, or let it go. The last suggestion is the best one: our thoughts can distract us.

Length

Continue like this for 15–20 minutes (or longer if you wish). Fifteen to twenty minutes is the minimum time to get the maximum benefit. Try doing this once or twice a day, regularly, every day. The affect is cumulative, so you may not notice a huge difference after just the first few times. The effect is usually quite subtle, though—over time—it is powerful. After a while, you will really notice the difference if you miss doing your regular meditation. Just find a few moments and do it again.

Practice, practice, and more practice

You are gradually training your mind to become less reactive and calmer. You will find this has other, wider benefits. Your anxiety and stress levels will start to diminish. You will be able to concentrate more. You will feel more centred. You will have greater patience. You will become less judgemental. Each meditation is different. They vary considerably. Some meditations can be dramatic, visionary, or life-changing; however, these are fairly rare. In some meditations, you may fall asleep. Just observe the differences. Don't get caught up in the "glamour" of any particularly powerful meditation. Meditation really only works over time, when done with regularity.

> The man who sat on the ground in his tipi meditating on life and its meaning, accepting the kinship of all creatures and acknowledging unity with the universe of things was infusing into his being the true essence of civilization. And when native man left off this form of development, his humanization was retarded in growth. [Chief Luther Standing Bear, quoted in McLuhan, 1973]

Mindfulness

When we are stressed, we often become absent-minded, or we may be doing something (like reading a book) and realize that we have not been aware of doing it (or what we are reading): our mind has become distracted. When we are on automatic pilot like this, our body is doing one thing and our mind is doing another. Accidents and mistakes can therefore happen. Negative thoughts can build up and coalesce behind what we are doing on the day-to-day level. We are trying to find better solutions to our stress, but we are often constantly monitoring and judging (and therefore undermining) how we are doing. On a day-to-day basis, mindlessness is not very productive and is often quite harmful.

Mindfulness means paying attention, in a particular way, on purpose, in the present moment, and non-judgementally. It can be useful for anxiety, depression, better pain control, anger management, obsessive–compulsive tendencies, and self-healing, as well as for stress. The core skills of mindfulness are: "Be aware" and "Let go!"

Being aware is literally just that: being aware that you have a pain here; that you find this or that activity stressful; that you don't have the energy for "this" any longer; or that you are irritated by that person. Letting go is literally just that: letting go of your irritation, your pain, your stress, your boredom, anger, or fatigue; freeing your self from any attachments or fixed ideas, as these can "trap" us, or fix us into a particular position.

Practising mindfulness

You can start practising mindfulness by introducing "mindful" meditations into your regular routine of meditation. Let mindfulness (or awareness) become the focus of your meditation. In your meditation, done as mentioned before, become aware of every feeling or sensation, every thought or every noise outside—the ticking of the clock, the distant traffic, bird song. And then let these perceptions go! Expand and extend your awareness—and then just let any insights or sensations go: there is a continual emptying process. Try to stay in the moment: what am I aware of now? What now?

Then you can extend your mindfulness practice into everything that you are doing. How am I doing this? How interesting! What am I feeling now? How interesting! And then let all this go. The moment passes. You are doing or feeling something else. How interesting! And now move on to the next moment.

Next, you can go deeper into what you are doing. When eating a tangerine, become aware of the texture of the skin, its brilliant orange-ness, and the contrast with the whiteness inside; the feel of the skin being peeled away from the fruit, the tiny spurt of juice and scent, the separation of the segments, the explosion of taste as you bite into a segment, the smell, the discarded peel. You can become aware of the tree on which it grew, how many hours of sunshine it absorbed, the water and the warmth necessary for it to grow, the people who grew it and picked it, the country it grew in, and how it has travelled across the world to end up in your hand. What a depth and miracle of mindfulness there is in this one action! And now move on to the next action.

Or, when you are doing the washing up (or some other action), try standing at the kitchen sink, and just do the washing up. You might become aware of the bubbles and the warmth of the water, the scent of the washing-up liquid, the action of the sponge or mop on the plate, the change in the plate's appearance, the way some bits of food stick to it and others do not. Become aware of the sunshine (or weather) outside, the bird song or street noises, other people in the house, and so forth. All these are a part of the experience of doing the washing up (or whatever you are doing). Mindfulness practice enriches these experiences.

If you catch yourself thinking about tomorrow's shopping list, stop doing the washing up, write down the shopping list, then return to doing the washing up. Stay in the moment. If you do not like washing up, and want to finish it quickly so as to watch TV or eat dessert, you may become equally incapable of enjoying TV or dessert, as your mind will jump on to the next action. Focus on this one, just this one action in this moment, and you may find that you quite enjoy the process of washing up "mindfully".

The process of mindfulness

There is no end to this process. Each meditation, each mindful action, can build and grow. The further in you go into the territory of mindfulness, the bigger it gets. You will slow down a little, you will become calmer and less reactive, you will look at the wider picture and become more thoughtful. It is so simple, and it is not—

for a moment—easy. This is definitely "the road less travelled"—yet it is a very rich journey. We can even make each step that we take (literally) "mindful", so it becomes a walking meditation. We are not trying to get anywhere or trying to get to some specific end: we are just making every moment count. We are just enjoying the process of travelling; really enriching the journey itself. This is also a way towards finding what we really want out of life, and who we really are.

Symptoms of stress

Some of the most frequently experienced physical symptoms of people in anxiety or stress are headaches and migraines. There are many other symptoms of stress, but these seem to top the list. It is very easy to reach for an analgesic (pain-killer): there are plenty to choose from. However, these can also be symptoms of something starting to be seriously wrong. Would you ignore a little flashing light on your car dashboard display?

Headaches

Headaches and migraines are very different. Headaches are usually experienced as an ache or pain in the head, or as if there is a tight band around the head. You can usually carry on doing things with a headache, though you might need to use some medication. They may arise from a short-term problem: stress, worry, too much alcohol, etc. Headaches can also be a symptom of an underlying problem and so, if you experience constant or persistent headaches, go to see your GP.

Here are a couple of background checks: is the headache part of a hangover? Too much alcohol dehydrates you and destroys your reserves of vitamin C: so try drinking a couple of large glasses of orange juice, or have a smoothie, and the headache may well disappear relatively quickly. Have you had too much chocolate, coffee, etc? People who are sensitive to caffeine can easily experience headaches because of this. Again, caffeine dehydrates. Drink plenty of water. Drink plenty of water anyway: at least 1.5–2 litres per day.

The next thing to check out is whether you have been exposed to any sort of chemicals. Paint fumes, dry cleaning agents, cleansing products, petrol fumes, butane, etc., can all cause headaches. The air you have been breathing may have been mildly poisoned.

High levels of positive ionization, as found near high voltage electrical equipment, or from some types of neon lighting, or just before a thunderstorm, can also cause headaches. Short-wave radiation emissions (e.g., from mobile phone masts) can also affect some people. Your headache can be a reaction to toxicity: a form of warning signal. Try to change your working or living environment; make sure your windows are open, or closed (as the case may be); switch cleaning products; get a negative ion generator. These are all reasonable ways to try to reduce these headache symptoms. If they persist, the place you live or work in might have an aspect of what is known as "sick building syndrome". See what happens if you can get to work in a different building for a month or so.

Once all these possibilities have been checked out, you might need to consider some of the physiological aspects of persistent headaches. Maybe you carry particular tensions in your neck and shoulders: check out your posture. Put a cushion behind your lower back. Sometimes cold packs or heat pads around the neck can help to relieve any specific muscular tension; alternating these can be very effective: about ten minutes each and then take a thirty-minute pause. If the problem persists, you might need to consult a physiotherapist, an osteopath, a massage therapist, acupuncturist, or a cranio-sacral therapist. They are all very skilled and all have different perspectives on muscular tensions. One of these alternative health therapies might work for you. Alexander Technique, Pilates, Rolfing, or Tai Chi, are some disciplines that might help you with your posture. The trick is to find better ways to hold up this heavy head of yours rather than just muscularly, as this can constrict the blood supply to the brain: hence the headache.

The next level of investigation is more emotional and psychological. Maybe the headaches are "symbolic" of something: a pressure that you have not acknowledged yet; an unexpressed anger; an emotional pain; or unconscious distress. In order to discover the emotional or psychological component, you should try to "contact" the headache, and this means allowing the "ache" or "pain" to "talk" to you. This is a sort of internal dialogue. If you could allow that headache to "talk" to you, to tell you something, what would that something be? What would it say? Does the headache carry any sort of message for you? What is your body saying? Follow that.

Migraines

Migraines are something totally different. They affect about 20% of the population, and women are three times more likely to be affected than men. Migraines can last from between four hours and three days. Sometimes people experience symptoms several hours before the migraine actually starts: these can be a warning "aura" before the migraine starts, or feelings of tiredness, sometimes even bursts of energy, or food cravings. Sometimes there are flashing lights or zig-zag lines that move across your eyes. Sometimes there is a difficulty in finding the right words, or a feeling of numbness in parts of the face or body. Once the migraine starts, it can either be one-sided or felt all over the head. It can be a throbbing pain, made worse by any movement, sound, or bright lights—to the point at which you might not be able to work, and/or have to lie down in a darkened room until the migraine passes. There may be initial fluid retention, followed by diuresis afterwards. There might also be nausea. In severe cases, feelings of weakness can persist for a few days after the migraine has passed.

Migraines are usually triggered by a combination of different factors. The most common triggers are:

- *Lack of food*: missing meals and eating snack meals (especially sugary ones) can cause a drop in blood sugar levels that can trigger an attack. This is especially true for children.
- *Certain specific foods*: the most common ones are caffeine, chocolate, monosodium glutamate (MSG), and red wine. You need to work out which foods are good for you, or not.

- *Change in sleeping patterns*: too much or too little sleep can sometimes trigger a migraine. Try adopting a more regular sleep pattern.
- *Hormonal changes*: the oral contraceptive pill can sometimes trigger a migraine, so it can be a good idea to change your form of contraception for a while and see if the migraines go.
- *Neck and head pains*: muscle tensions caused by bad posture, driving, or doing computer work can create the conditions for a migraine.
- *Stress*: sometimes, after a stressful period (the first few days of a holiday, for example), one can experience a migraine caused by the preceding stress.
- *Travel*: migraines can occur after a long journey, possibly a stressful one, possibly with different foods, at different times, with dehydration (especially from long air journeys), and disrupted sleep patterns or normal routines.
- *Environmental changes*: bright lights, loud noises, strong smells, travelling, chemical influences, can all trigger attacks in some people.
- *Background stress*: this can aggravate any of the other triggers. A glass of wine by itself might not trigger a migraine, but it might after a hard day, taken on an empty stomach.
- *Combinations of the above*: migraines are often caused by an accumulation of these triggers. Once the threshold level of the migraine is reached, it will happen. This threshold can be raised by either internal or external factors or both.

Things you can do yourself for migraines are: to keep a detailed diary listing all the details of your migraine attacks (date, day of the week, time, symptoms, duration, type of treatment and when it was taken, the triggers that were present, etc.). You can use this diary to understand and moderate the triggers that affect you and reduce their influence so that your threshold does not get exceeded. This is the basis of effective self-management.

As you do this, you will be more able to identify your own particular triggers. Otherwise, if you have some medication, take it early, and carry a dose with you. Get more information from the medical websites or from specialist migraine sites.

Other anti-stress exercises

Seek a larger connection

We all need to feel a part of something larger than ourselves; whether it be a community group, a church, a sports team, an interest group or political party, a large close-knit family, or helping out with a charity or a fund-raising event. Again, the method is unimportant, but the wider contact is pretty essential for human, social animals. Maybe there are new belief systems, philosophies or spiritual practices that you would like to explore: join a group whose members are studying these. Maybe greater and deeper self-awareness will help: try a meditation or "mindfulness" group. Contact with nature is also very therapeutic, via the garden, the hills, the sea, wilderness holidays, or the local woods and fields. You might even want to consider a form of pilgrimage or a retreat at a significant point in your life: many people do this.

Anti-stress foods

Certain nutrients have been shown to help with stress. The "fighting five" are the vitamins A, C, and E and the minerals zinc and selenium. These disarm those "nasty" free radicals produced under stress. Foods containing such antioxidants include: plums, tomatoes, kiwi fruits, dark green vegetables (cabbage, kale, broccoli, spinach), seafood, sesame seeds, and pumpkin seeds. With continued stress, it might also be worth getting a nutritionist to check your levels of DHEA (dehydroepiandosterone) and cortisol: stress decreases the former and increases the latter, and a nutritionist can help you rebalance these. Vitamin C supports the adrenal glands and can be most easily found in black and red berries, kiwi and citrus fruits. The adrenal glands also need magnesium, found in grains, green leafy vegetables, soya beans, almonds, wheatgerm, cod, and mackerel. Cutting down on sugar (and alcohol) helps the liver to detoxify the body. Stimulant drinks (coffee and caffeine drinks) encourage adrenalin production and should be cut down or eliminated totally. Please do not drink *anything* with aspartame (a sweetener used in many soft drinks, and even in flavoured mineral water) in it.

Acting together

In some situations, you may not be the only person being affected by stress. In a family, the other members are almost certainly affected; at work, there may be structural or management problems that also affect others. It may be helpful to talk to others in similar situations to see if they feel the same. For example, you and your work colleagues together could talk to management, or to your union, to bring to their attention the pressing (and stressing) difficulties you are suffering from (see below). A family conference, with everyone sitting round the table, can also help to resolve things: maybe get an uncle or a grandparent to be there as well; their wisdom is often helpful. Tenants acting together can help to resolve difficulties with landlords, or local resident groups can resolve situations in the neighbourhood, or on the estate.

Self-help groups

There is a variety of self-help groups, usually created by people who have had similar experiences to you: some of these are local, some national, others are internet-based. Making a connection with people with similar difficulties can be very supportive. Try using a search engine to find a local group.

Information and advice agencies

There are a number of advice agencies and help-lines that may be useful. They usually give good information and advice, and can often refer you to a specialist in that particular field. They are usually professional and confidential. These include: Citizens' Advice Bureau; credit unions (for help with financial difficulties); trades unions and professional associations (for work-related difficulties); various help-lines for specific problems (consult the local telephone directory).

Different roles

Stress can put enormous strain on the strongest of relationships. Often we get locked into a particular role or pattern of behaviour. If one can step out of this role, things can suddenly seem different, or more possible. One way of doing this is to ask others close to you what their problems are, or what is giving them stress. It can be very upsetting, exhausting, and draining (for them) to be close to someone in stress (you): they may be feeling that they are the one contributing to the situation; you may also be feeling a bit guilty. Get talking with such people along different lines. Another way is consciously to try to "walk a mile in someone else's shoes". Try going back to an earlier way of being together, doing things together, when things were better. Try to step out of your present pattern of behaviour, your present "role": it is probably just not working for you any longer.

Stress at work

This is now being recognized as a "killer" and long-term studies show that people in stressful jobs are almost twice as likely to develop heart disease, diabetes or other stress-related conditions. Discuss your stress at work first with your work mates, then with your team leader or manager, and then with the Human Resources department or the Health and Safety department: both of the latter are supposed to be on your side. If you do not get proper help from them, take it up with your union.

Stress and life events

Most people who come to their GP with stress, or anxiety and/or depression, are suffering from a combination of stressful life events. This has happened, then that happened, then the other. An accumulation of very stressful life events in a relatively short period (e.g., 12–18 months) can really increase one's vulnerability to anxiety or depression, or can even bring it on, essentially due to an emotional "overload". These creep up on you and accumulate without you necessarily noticing. Yes, of course you know that it was stressful when "X" died, and that there was also "stuff" going on at the office. But you might not have realized that the depression six months later or the panic attacks were all connected to these events.

Several life events are suggested in Table 1, and some sample scores (rated up to 100) are given. If you want to calculate your life event stress score, please use the relevant column in the table and write in *your* stress scores for those events that you have experienced over the last (say) eighteen months, or the eighteen months immediately before the time that you became depressed.

The "Sample scores" are just the average ones, to be used only as a guide. It is "Your score" that is significant. For example, some

Table 1. Life event stress inventory (LSEI).

List of stressful life events	Sample scores	Your scores	Comments
Death of a spouse, partner or child	100		
Divorce	73		
Marital separation	65		
Imprisonment	63		
Death of a close family member	60		
Personal injury or illness	55		
Marriage	50		
Dismissal from work	47		
Retirement	45		
Change in health of family member	44		
Pregnancy	40		
Sexual difficulties	39		
New family member	39		
Business/work changes	39		
Change in financial situation	38		
Death of a close friend	37		
Change in amount of arguments with spouse	36		
Taking out a major mortgage	32		
Foreclosure of mortgage or loan	30		
Change in responsibilities at work	29		
Child leaving home	29		
Trouble with in-laws (or neighbours)	29		
Spouse begins or stops work	27		
End/change school, or begin college	26		
Change in living conditions	26		
Change in social activities	26		
Trouble with the boss	23		
Changes in work hours/shifts/conditions	20		
Holidays	15		
Christmas	15		
Changes in sleep/diet	15		
Minor violations of the law	11		
. . .			
. . .			
YOUR TOTAL SCORE			

Adapted from Holmes & Rähe (1967)

people might consider that their marriage was the happiest time of their life and everything went swimmingly. If that were true for you, you would then score considerably less than the sample score of fifty, because this is a measurement of life event stress. Others might have had marriages that were very stressful, so they might want to score more, though probably less than (say) a term of imprisonment (LESI Score, sixty-three). So you decide upon your particular score for a particular life event. Sometimes the anticipation of the possibility of such an event (like a term of imprisonment) is almost as stressful as the actual event. Fill in your scores after discussion with your nearest and dearest. They might know (better than you) exactly how stressful a particular situation was for you.

A space has been left for you to add in any life events not mentioned in the list, e.g., "tsunami", "getting caught in a war zone", "identity theft", etc.

A score of about 150–190 points counts as a mild life crisis, with a chance of illnesses such as headaches, fatigue, hypertension, body pains, ulcers, infections, etc. Two hundred to two hundred and fifty points is moving towards a moderate life crisis. Here you could expect a higher incidence of arguments between partners, reactions such as spending too much, getting drunk, inappropriate behaviour, etc. You might also experience greater physical symptoms, as above, as well as the onset of conditions such as asthma, psoriasis, shingles, etc.

If you score a total of between 250–300 points for stressful events over the eighteen months you are considering, your symptoms (often depression or anxiety, sometimes serious illness, or an increased incidence of minor illnesses) are probably resulting from an accumulation of such stressful life events. If you are suffering from depression, this form is sometimes called a "reactive depression" or "exogenous depression". This means that there is probably not anything wrong with you, but there was something very wrong with what had happened to you. In some ways, a depression like this can even be seen as a sort of safety valve. When your central heating boiler gets over hot, the thermostat switches it off. When you get overstressed, part of you might similarly switch off and you see yourself as depressed. Over 300 points counts as a major life crisis.

If you score more than about 400 points, you deserve a medal; you have survived and are still upright—just! (I counselled one woman who had scored more than 900 points—she came from South Lanarkshire, not Rwanda or Darfur!) Having discovered your score, make sure that you take appropriate measures to start to reduce the current stress in your life.

DEPRESSION

Self-help for depression

Between about 12% (one person in eight) and 25% (one person in four) of the population are treated for depression at some time or other in their life. The average age of onset is usually between forty and fifty, though almost any age is possible. Depression is more common in women than in men. It is much more common in lower socio-economic classes, and in more disadvantaged people. Periods of major depression can also recur. Anxiety is sometimes an aspect of depression.

Depression is more of a "state" or (technically) a "mood" disorder, and is only very occasionally severe enough to be considered a mental illness. Major (psychotic illness) depression has a prevalence of only about 4–5% of those already diagnosed with "ordinary" depression (i.e., present in less than 1% of the population).

Sources of depression

There are very many different ways in which someone can become depressed, and there are several different views on depression that are presented later. Often a series of overwhelming life events coming soon, one after the other, will result in a depressive reaction; or it can come (most frequently) from a build-up of general life stresses. If the source is essentially outside of the self, it is called "exogenous" or "reactive" depression. With other people, depression can occur after a particular illness (flu or a viral infection), or after a pregnancy, or as a result of the menopause, or as a side effect of medications, all of which indicate a more internal origin (endogenous). Some people are slightly more genetically disposed to having a depression. It can also be an aspect of their character that they have developed during the course of their life. For most people it is a combination of things that accumulate, with possibly one major event (like bereavement or a loss) that will trigger the onset of the depression.

Symptoms of depression

The symptoms of depression tend to fall into four main groupings: emotions or feelings; physical symptoms; thought patterns; and behavioural symptoms.

- *Emotions*: feeling like crying a lot; feeling alone (even in company); feeling sad, depressed upset, hopeless, despairing, or just numb; feeling anxious, irritable, or unreasonably angry; feeling lethargic; having no interest or enjoyment in things (even things that used to be enjoyable); low self-esteem and feelings of worthlessness and/or guilt.
- *Physical symptoms*: loss of energy, lethargy, tiredness, or fatigue; restlessness or agitation; changes in appetite (either poor or increased) and resulting weight loss or gain; difficulties in sleeping (either not falling asleep easily, not returning to sleep after waking during the night, early morning wakening, or, conversely, a desire to sleep a great deal of the time); headaches; indigestion; stomach pains; irregular periods.
- *Thoughts*: difficulty in concentrating or a slowness in thinking; indecisiveness; loss of confidence in self; having an unusually negative or gloomy outlook; thinking that everything is hopeless or that the worst will happen; negative self-concept, self-reproach and self-blame, even self-hate; recurrent thoughts of death or suicide.

- *Behaviour*: having difficulty in doing anything; neglecting everyday tasks, like regular meals and personal hygiene; putting off doing things, even things that one normally enjoys; having short occasional bursts of energy, and then usually not completing things; cutting oneself off from friends, family, regular support, or social activities; difficulty in maintaining regular work hours.

Standard treatment

The NICE Guidelines on depression recommend self-help first (Step 1), with counselling as the next intervention (Step 2), with possibly some anti-depressant medication as well (Step 3) in slightly more severe cases These first three steps cover most people with depression. The usual treatment for depression (once it has been identified) is therefore often a combination of self-help (exercise, relaxation, information, and social prescribing), with then some counselling or psychotherapy and/or possibly some antidepressant medication. This is reasonably successful, and nearly all patients really do get better within a medium time-period of a few weeks or months from seeking treatment. Time heals, counselling helps, and medication can relieve some of the worst symptoms. Self-help techniques are the much the most effective, cheapest, and easiest, and should be tried first.

There is a section on anti-depressant medication a little later. But it is worth mentioning that sometimes anti-depressant medication is prescribed too soon, or too often. This is not really the fault of the GP: patients usually want something to make them feel better quickly, and they may have already delayed seeing the doctor, or owning up to being depressed.

If anti-depressant medication is going to be a part of your treatment plan, then it is very important to take it exactly as prescribed. These medications are quite strong stuff, though they are not a miracle cure, or a replacement for therapy. What medication can do is to create an inner stability (take the depressed edge off) that will allow you to regain a sense of yourself, or to make use of counselling or psychotherapy.

Severe and enduring depression can indicate that there might be semi-permanent biochemical changes in the brain's functioning and these, while rare, are not so amenable to psychotherapeutic treatment.

Self-help techniques

There are a number of simple suggestions for self-help for depression. Remember that self-help is the first essential step of any treatment plan for depression, so you might just want to try out some of these to see if they help. However, it is the hardest thing in the world to change your life around when it feels as if you are wading through treacle, or at the bottom of a deep well. So some of these will not be easy to do, or to get started on, because you are depressed. Don't let it stop you trying.

Hope

The most important ingredient towards getting better is hope. This can come from the knowledge that these sorts of suggestions are generally quite effective, and so most people *do* get better reasonably quickly, and from the trust that the most important factor in getting better is your *own* attitude towards your recovery.

Exercise

Any activity that promotes endurance, flexibility, or strengthening is a natural anti-depressant. Exercise, and in particular aerobic exercise, improves circulation, brings increased blood flow and oxygen to the brain, releases endorphins (the body's natural pain-killing chemicals), boosts serotonin, and counteracts stress. Unfortunately, the most challenging aspect of depression is a general lack of motivation and low energy levels. The overwhelming sense of physical inertia can make it very difficult to do even the most simple tasks, much less get out and do some regular exercise. Aerobic exercise is becoming a much more recognized form of anti-depressant therapy. It is widely acknowledged that if you *can* discipline yourself to do some form of exercise regularly, you will *definitely* feel better for it. Even a brisk walk once a day is a very good start. Get a friend or family to help you with your motivation at first.

Diet

Good nutrition supports the optimal functioning of your body and brain. Try to eat a balanced diet of healthy foods. Eating as much organic produce as possible will help to minimize the intake of chemicals and preservatives, which can cause problems in sensitive individuals. Another part of nutritional self-care is cutting back on sugar, salt, sweets, and alcohol. Studies have shown that too much sugar (in any form) can foster anxiety, as well as depression. Alcohol can also have a negative effect. Eat the more complex carbohydrates. Drink plenty of water. Do not eat any "comfort" foods, or much in the way of ready-prepared and processed foods. Eat little and often: have bowls of fruit and nuts to hand: fruit smoothies are very good. There is a section on "Foods for depression" a little later.

Sleep

Try to develop a good sleep schedule—a regular time of going to sleep and arising—and stick to it. Sleep irregularities are among the early warning signs of anxiety and depression. A good night's sleep can really help towards curing depression. Prepare yourself: don't eat too late, take some very gentle exercise before you go to bed, have a bath, read a book for a little when in bed.

Be prepared

Make a list of things that you really must do each day and tick them off as you go: this can give you a sense of achievement. If you think of something pleasant and self-indulgent that you would rather do than one of your chores, then do it instead and just enjoy it. Then do the chore a little later.

Breathe

One of the most powerful ways to impact your involuntary nervous system and your emotions is through your breathing. If you are stressed, or startled, or angry, just stop . . . close your eyes and focus on your breathing. Inhale slowly through your nose, directing the air up into your chest as well as deep into your belly, fill your whole body with as much air as possible. Then hold this position for a few seconds. Next, exhale slowly through your mouth and try to empty your body of all that air—completely, like squeezing it out. Repeat this 4–5 times, and you will see how well this technique works. You will feel a bit better. Your feelings will have changed a bit. Not bad for a couple of minutes' work.

Laugh

Even when you are just making laughing expressions with the muscles of your face, your body starts to produce the various chemicals (endorphins) that make you feel happier. Watch films or TV programmes that are funny. Listen to jokes or read books that you enjoy. Most importantly, meet up with friends who make you laugh, or whom you can laugh with.

Keep a journal

Writing in a diary or journal is one of the best self-help methods that you can use. Put down any new sights and smells, thoughts or feelings, or write about new experiences of any kind. Note down everything that you have done during the day, but especially write about your feelings—and the variety and complexity of them. Write every day, if possible. It may help to write at the same time every day, maybe after dinner or before bed. Write for yourself only: do not show this journal to anyone.

Extend or maintain your social contacts

When we get depressed, we often cut ourselves off from our friends and family. Try to reconnect and make the effort to see these people again. They are the closest people to you. Tell them that you have been a bit depressed. It makes things easier than trying to hide it, or do it all yourself.

Voluntary organizations

There are several voluntary organizations that can give active support and help to people with depression. Depression Alliance is one of these. If your depression was triggered by a bereavement, an organization like Cruse may well be able to help.

Natural world

We have often lost touch with the natural world. Try cutting yourself off from the media for a while: do not read newspapers, or watch the news on TV. Give yourself a break. Spend some more time in nature. Whether it is watching a moonrise over a mountain peak, a sunset over the ocean, or simply taking a leisurely walk in your city park, or by a river, spending time in nature imparts its healing touch.

If you have a garden, there's always something to do in it, or just to enjoy it. Even in a flat you can do this: try repotting some houseplants, pottering with some bulbs, sorting out a window box or some patio planters, it all helps marvellously. Maybe a friend needs a bit of help with their plants or garden, so that you can enjoy their garden and their company as well.

A recent survey by MIND showed that when a walk in a country park was compared with a walk in an indoor shopping centre, 71% of people with depression reported a decrease in the levels of depression, 71% felt less tense, and 90% felt higher self-esteem after their green walk; after walking through the indoor shopping centre 22% felt their depression increased, 50% felt more tense, and 44% felt a decrease in self-esteem.

Prayer

If you believe that prayer can have an effect, take some regular time to pray, both by yourself and/or with other people. Meditation involves stilling the mind, so that we can then hear the "still small voice of God" within, and be open to any spiritual guidance. This is also very relaxing and a great aid towards reducing anxiety. Going (back) to church or a regular religious meeting can help reconnect with something that was important for you, and bigger than you, which can be very good.

Creativity

Try to indulge in some right-brain creative activity. Try to allow yourself to become lost in something creative or constructive. Creative activity can embrace many things: cooking, artwork, dancing, gardening, writing poetry or prose, doing jigsaws, and any form of craft, etc. It is the doing of these that is important—not how well you do them. As you do such activity, different parts of your brain (right-brain) are used, different connections are made: these are restorative. Sometimes it helps to paint some interpretive images of your depression, or write about them, or sculpt them, or make poems.

Do not judge

Try not to judge yourself or others, but particularly try not to judge yourself. Negative judgements and criticisms always debilitate, rather than give you any good feelings or help constructively with your situation. This is just not what you want or need. Do not go there: keep coming away from that place of judgement or blame! Try to replace negative thought forms with some more positive ones; try to suspend judgement.

Being in the "now"

Try to enjoy each moment as best you can. Focus your thoughts on what is happening right now—at this moment. Do not dwell on what is past, or on "if only", or what has happened, or what has not happened. What has happened in the past cannot now be changed. We can learn from events in the past, perhaps, but do not worry about it, or obsessively think about it. It is past. It is gone. It is over. Leave it in the past and stay in, or come into, the present.

The present is very important; the future is also important—but it is determined by the present, and by what you do in the present. Do not let your mind race forward in time to "what if", or what disaster might possibly happen: that is one of the symptoms of depression, known as "catastrophizing". Try to work out what your next step—the very next step (in a few minutes' time)—should be. Plan just a short time ahead, reasonably and appropriately, and then leave the planning and just start to do it. Take just one step at a time. See what happens, when it happens. The "now" is the most important time; here is the important place: right here and now. Stay in the present moment as best you can. Try saying, "At this moment in time, everything is (reasonably) all right." Keep on telling yourself this. Focus your thoughts on the little positive things you have around you, right now.

Look to your strengths

Everyone is good at something, or has some interest in something, or enjoys something. Find out what interests you, what you like, what gets you going, and what works for you. Get involved in that; forget the other stuff. Focus on, *not* what you cannot do, but what you *can* do, what your strengths are.

You will find that you do have a choice; see if you can choose something that works better for you. This way you can move away from your present depression and move towards more positive choices about health, prevention, collaboration, empowerment, wellness, and happiness. We all have this potential. We sometimes forget to use it.

Silver linings

Even the worst situations can have some sort of a silver lining. We will not often see it, or be able to benefit from it, if we are stuck in our depression. Then we only see the black clouds. As we begin to move out of the depression, or lift ourselves out, if only a little, or just for a moment, the chance of seeing that silver lining increases.

If we can understand a little more of our surrounding situation, or see things from another person's perspective, or whatever, then we may be able to use this more positive perspective. And so this helps the next step.

Get good information

This book is only one part of the information that you might need for yourself. Check out the local library, log on to the Internet, pick up some leaflets at your local Health Centre, ask your doctor, or whatever. If all these are telling you pretty much the same things, then you probably have all the information that you need. There may be a few bits and pieces that you are not sure of, and want to check out further, but don't let that stop you doing all or any of the above in the interim. You have the information: now start to use it!

There is a lot of good information available about the subject of depression, especially on the Internet. Check out Depression Alliance, or Depression Alliance, Scotland. The charity MIND puts out a leaflet, "Understanding depression"; there are also informational websites such as MoodJuice, or Living Life to the Full. Dorothy Rowe has written a couple of good psychological books on depression (Rowe, 1991, 2003). There are lots of other self-help books on depression—most of them are pretty sensible.

Working with depression

People in a depression often feel that everything compounds their condition. They are feeling low, so they don't want to go out, so they lose touch with their friends, so they feel alone, so there is no point in going out, and this all adds to their depression.

The depressive spiral

Continuous, automatic, negative thoughts that are typical of a depression can actually distort one's thinking patterns and perpetuate errors such as "all or nothing" thinking, "catastrophizing", "personalizing", focusing on "the negative", and "jumping to conclusions". These "thinking distortions" can result in, or even create, a low mood. This leads to decreased activity, which leads to a less rewarding existence. This leads to more negative thinking. Therefore, we go steadily downwards into a depressive spiral.

How to stop the depressive spiral

There are several ways how to stop this sort of spiral, the main ones being listed below. Try all of them and see which works for you.

1. Understand the problem. Identify your pattern; increase awareness of when you are doing it; begin to stop any behaviour habits that really do not work for you.
2. Forgive and forget the past. Instead, focus more on the present and the future, as this is much more under your control.
3. Challenge your negative thought patterns. Your thinking affects your feelings, so change your thoughts; try to replace negative thoughts with more positive ones.
4. Increase your activity levels gradually; especially your physical activity. Identify and work towards achievable step-by-step goals.
5. Use all your support systems, both personal and professional, and then increase these. A close, confiding relationship is very important. Try to share your feelings, fears, etc., as well as your hopes and pleasures.
6. Look after yourself. Try to increase your self-esteem; try to express yourself more assertively; say "No" and mean it; go for what *you* want and the way *you* want it.
7. It is a new learning process; it is gradual; there are no magic wands; there is a step-by-step progression from something that does not work for you towards something that works better.
8. If none of this works, consult your doctor. Get a counselling referral. Some anti-depressant medication might also be appropriate and helpful. Usually, the sooner that this happens, the quicker and better the response is.

However, the initial emphasis is always on self-help. No one can "make" you better.

Protection

Protective factors that *decrease* one's vulnerability to the symptoms of depression include:

- increasing one's self-esteem, based on self-worth, not based on achievements: "Who one is, rather than what one does";
- cutting the depressive spiral whenever possible (see above);
- stopping negative thinking patterns and practising positive thinking habits;
- focusing one the next single change—and achieving it—and not getting swamped by the amount you imagine that has to be changed;
- expressing one's thoughts, needs, and feelings more clearly, openly, and assertively.
- increasing one's network of friends, activities, and social support system;
- balancing stress better, including the demands made on you from others and those you make on yourself;
- getting a much better balance within your self, especially through more exercise and relaxation, but also in the general life–work balance.
- looking after your "self" better—at all levels;
- looking after your self—properly—on all levels.
- looking at ALL the factors that have conspired to put you into this place of being depressed: biological, psychological, experiential (things that happened to you), emotional, spiritual, and social and environmental (the people and things around you).

Don't let it stop you

There are many famous people who have had some form of mental health issue, or even mental illness, and who have still achieved a lot in their life: Hans Christian Anderson, Ludwig Von Beethoven, Winston Churchill, Kurt Cobain, Charles Darwin, Emily Dickinson, Thomas Edison, Steven Fry, F. Scott Fitzgerald, Betty Ford, Paul Gauguin, King George III, Johan Goethe, Ernest Hemingway, Victor Hugo, Thomas Jefferson, John Keats, Abraham Lincoln, Michelangelo, Florence Nightingale, King Saul, Robert Louis Stevenson, Sir Isaac Newton, Virginia Woolf, and many others: and it didn't stop them.

Don't let it stop you.

"This too shall pass"

This is an old Sufi (or Jewish) saying, also sometimes attributed to King Solomon, or even Abraham Lincoln. Nothing is really permanent: this also will pass away. You will get over this. Try to remind yourself not only that you can and will get better, but also that you can even become a better person as a result of getting over this. You will become more resilient and stronger; you will become more aware of yourself; you should understand more of what affects you; and you will have gained a number of "life skills". This "darkness" shall also pass away—there really is a light at the end of the tunnel, if you care to walk in that direction.

Foods for depression

Food influences our brain chemistry. Some foods promote a feeling of well-being, others can suppress positive emotions. Ironically, many foods that make us feel good are not especially beneficial to our health: we call these "comfort foods". Therefore, we need to find a healthy balance between what is good for us and what makes us feel better.

Nerve impulses in the brain are carried by neurotransmitters. One of those needed is serotonin and the SSRI-type of anti-depressants, such as Prozac, inhibit the re-uptake of serotonin, allowing it to remain available and thus produce a feeling of well-being. Your body manufactures serotonin. Vitamin B6 is necessary to the synthesis of serotonin and B6 can be found in certain whole grains (millet, buckwheat, oats) as well as shellfish (prawns, shrimp, lobster, and mussels). Ensure that you have enough B6 to make the serotonin you need.

However, we often crave carbohydrates and sweet foods when we are in a depression, and these also affect the chemicals in our brain—though in the short term only ("quick fix"; "sugar high"). So it is better to avoid these, and avoid putting on weight, and aim for the longer-term effects. Good blood sugar management is important in fighting depression. Try taking in complex sugars from complex carbohydrates and also from proteins, and a little of the more natural sugars (fructose and glucose) rather than the added sugar (corn syrup) in many processed foods. Check the labels carefully.

Protein sources of complex sugars are nuts, legumes, beans, tofu, eggs, fish, and poultry. You can eat these with a little carbohydrate (which also contain sugars) but this latter is processed more quickly. If you can increase the protein to carbohydrate ratio, you will eat less anyway as your appetite is largely controlled by the amount of protein you eat.

Complex carbohydrates are contained in bananas, barley, beans, brown rice, chick peas, lentils, nuts, oats, parsnips, potatoes, root vegetables, sweet corn, wholegrain flour and cereals, wholemeal flour and cereals, and yams. Once digested, these release glucose and sugars back into the body at a slower and more even rate than from simple carbohydrates. Carbohydrates should make up no more than 50% of your total diet, and refined sugars (simple carbohydrates) no more than 10%.

Low levels of another brain chemical, dopamine, are also linked with depression. This brain chemical is created from tyrosine, an amino acid found in protein type foods. It requires the vitamins B12 and B9 (folic acid) as well as the mineral magnesium for its production. Foods rich in tyrosine include almonds, avocados, bananas, cottage cheese, lima beans, peanuts (raw, unsalted), pumpkin seeds, and sesame seeds. Foods high in B12 include dairy and fish products. Foods high in B9 (folic acid) include calves' liver, soya flour, green leafy vegetables (e.g., broccoli), eggs, and brown rice. Magnesium can be found in sunflower seeds, green leafy vegetables, wheatgerm, soya beans, mackerel, swordfish, and cod.

Vitamin B3 has also been found particularly useful in managing depression, and this vitamin is found in fish, eggs, brewer's yeast, whole grains, and poultry. There is also a link with low zinc levels, often in post-partum situations. Zinc is found in oysters, endives, alfalfa sprouts, seaweed, brown rice, asparagus, mushrooms, turkey, and radishes.

Energy-producing snacks (yes, please eat between meals!) like those listed below help to rebalance your blood sugar throughout the day and thus help fight off depression.

- Almonds, chopped dates, and an apple.
- Natural low-fat yoghurt (sugar free) with ground pumpkin seeds and wheatgerm.
- Dried fruit (only once or twice per week) with a handful of mixed nuts.
- Crispbread or oatcake with cheese.
- Oat and wheatgerm flapjacks with dried apricots and chopped apple.
- Avocado dip with rice cakes or rye crispbread.
- Raw vegetables (carrots, celery, etc.) with yoghurt or sour cream dip.
- Cereal granola bars (sugar-free) with nuts and fresh fruit.
- Humous on crispbread or oatcakes.
- Fresh fruit salad with sesame seeds.

Some people with depression sometimes have food allergies. The foods that trigger these allergies can be identified quite simply nowadays. The commonest allergens are wheat, dairy products, and citrus fruits. Some depressed people are allergic to gluten. If you think any of this might apply to you, seek proper, sound advice.

Try to eat little and often; try to avoid comfort foods (often with a high fat or sugar content); please try to avoid any fizzy drinks (caffeine and sugar loaded: diet drinks contain aspartame—and you certainly do NOT want that in your body).

Please also remember to exercise as well. This stimulates all your systems and improves your circulation. You should also drink lots of water (at least 1.5 litres per day) and this helps to flush out your bodily system, which has got "stuck" with the depression, and that is when waste products and residues also get stuck.

What not to eat or drink

There are three or four things that it is essential to avoid with respect to foods connected with anxiety and depression. Making some changes with these can really help you to turn your life around—especially if you are taking too much of them. All have some chemical and/or mood addictive components, so it will not be easy to make some of these changes.

Caffeine

Caffeine, in small amounts, acts as a stimulant and gives you a boost. It stimulates the production of the amount of norepinephrine and dopamine in your brain. These stimulants make you more alert and awake: just the same as if you have a surprise, or a fright. Your body then produces adrenalin. Effectively, you are "shocking" your system chemically with caffeine. This uses up some of your supply of vitamin B1 (thiamine), the anti-stress vitamin. This type of stimulation therefore adds to your stress and reduces your ability to cope with (dis)stress.

A cup of percolated coffee has about 130–150 mg of caffeine, instant coffee has about 65 mg, a cup of tea 25–50 mg, a 330 ml cola drink, 45 mg, and other caffeinated fizzy drinks contain about 40 mg. A 200 g bar of plain chocolate contains about 80 mg of caffeine, 200 g of milk chocolate has 50 mg, a small cup ice cream has 50–90 mg, cold/flu/headache tablets contain 30 mg, and alertness tablets, 100–200 mg. How many milligrams of caffeine do you take in each day? Try reducing it gently.

If you take much too much caffeine, this can lead to an increase in anxiety and even panic attacks. Chronic caffeine takers (those who deny that coffee is addictive) can suffer from stomach cramps, constipation or diarrhoea, heartburn or stomach acidity, headaches, dizziness, spots in front of the eyes and ringing ears, shaking in the body and tingling in the hands and feet, and racing heartbeats. Caffeine can increase your tiredness as the short-term stimulant effects wear off. It can increase mood swings. It can also mean that it is difficult for you to concentrate *without* a cup of tea/coffee. Try cutting down on your caffeine intake.

Try stopping completely, or changing to decaffeinated, or herbal alternatives: green tea is very good for you. Drink much more water: this will, surprisingly, give you energy, as it helps to release stored up energy. Are you experiencing any mild withdrawal symptoms? Persist with cutting caffeine down and these symptoms should pass within several days. Make sure you are taking some vitamin and mineral supplements as well.

Alcohol

Alcohol, in very small amounts, can be beneficial to your health: perhaps one medium glass of red wine a day maximum (2–3 units). Anything more than that is not so good. People with anxiety or depression tend to drink alcohol to relieve some of their symptoms, as it can increase their confidence and pleasure for short periods of time. However, the effects are short-lived, and once the alcohol wears off a little, then the down-swing starts again. Thus, alcohol can actually lower your mood, as it acts as a central nervous system (CNS) depressant. Drinking alcohol also reduces the amount of vitamin C in the body and builds up lactic acid. Heavy drinkers can experience anxiety attacks, panic attacks, and the development of phobias.

Because alcohol is addictive, too much alcohol taken regularly can create an emotional and psychological dependence. This can lead to greater expenditure on alcohol, even to violence and abuse, family break-ups, loss of job, higher risk of accidents, and increased long-term health risks.

Sugar

Sugar comes in many forms. Your body needs energy and this is obtained from a type of sugar, glucose. This is found in both carbohydrates and in proteins. Some other carbohydrates break down quickly (simple carbohydrates), and these are found mostly in chocolate, sweets, beer, crisps, cakes, biscuits, white bread, pasta, fizzy drinks (corn syrup), etc. These cause your body to overcompensate as they process these sugars: this is experienced as a "sugar rush". The next effect is for your body sugar level to drop as these sugars get used up: "sugar blues" or hypoglycaemia. This can cause anxiety, depression, fatigue, irritability, palpitations, sweating, feelings of weakness, or light-headedness.

The more complex carbohydrates take much longer to break down. Consuming these is therefore much better for maintaining a healthy level of blood sugar, and it is easier on your body. These complex carbohydrates are found in potatoes, rice, oatmeal, wholemeal, and whole grains. Try switching your diet from simple to complex carbohydrates and feel the beneficial effects.

Junk food

If a fair proportion of what you are eating is processed foods and "ready meals", the assortment of extra salt, sugars, additives, and so forth can accumulate in your body. These types of food are fine occasionally: eating them all the time is really not a good idea—at all! I do not want to go into all the horror stories but (believe me) they do have some validity, especially for children.

Too much salt (sodium) is bad for you, though a little is absolutely necessary: it can lead to high blood pressure or hypertension. Most people should cut their total salt intake, probably by about half. A lot of salt is put into processed foods: check the labels (0.5 g of sodium per 100 g in food is too much; less than 0.1 g per 100g is all right). Don't add salt to food during cooking, add it later when it is on the plate—if you wish. Cut out snacks and crisps especially. Foods high in salt include pickles, smoked fish, soy sauce, stock cubes, tinned vegetables and sauces.

Please also avoid aspartame, the sweetener in so-called diet drinks: you really do not want know what it might do to you. But, if you dare to type "aspartame risks" into a search engine, then you can check it out for yourself. In all fairness, the jury is still partially out on this one.

Somatic aspects of depression

Depression and the body

Many people who are anxious or depressed feel out of contact with their bodies. When we become frightened, anxious, depressed, or distressed, we contract emotionally and also we contract physically. We shrink a little and tighten up. When we are feeling depressed, our heads drop and our chest area becomes more concave: we slouch a bit. We may not make proper eye contact. We will probably walk a bit more slowly, or do less physically. These contractions, although fairly minor, can accumulate, especially over time, and stop the healthy flow of pleasure, excitation, and feeling within our bodies. We then start to feel out-of-touch with ourselves, and also with others. Our ability to communicate with other people and to express our emotions is decreased. These types of physical reaction can actually enhance our depressive symptoms.

If these reactions turn into patterns that become persistent and chronic, then, even if our external circumstances change for the better, our bodies have become habituated into these contracted patterns. It then becomes very difficulty to feel genuinely better, as we have become "stuck" somatically as well as emotionally. Effective therapeutic work with anxiety and depression may mean looking at these habitual and contracted body-holding patterns, and trying to work with them also. Trying to cure depression just by changing our thought patterns makes things very difficult, even almost impossible, as our physical energy levels are still quite depressed, or even blocked by our muscular tensions.

This is where some knowledge of body-orientated psychotherapy or "somatic psychology" can be very useful. Working *with* the body can help the person release some of these blocks, find some of their stored or repressed energy, and start to use this creatively to change their thinking patterns and behaviour.

Breathing

Our patterns of breathing are very important in helping to restore our sense of vitality. Increased (deeper, fuller) breathing in the upper chest area is very important, if not absolutely necessary. Try taking a few deep breaths: breathing in through the nose and out through the mouth: hold for a moment at the top of the in-breath. Stretch and yawn a little if you feel like it as you breathe in. When you breathe in, fill your lungs, straighten up a little, and open up your chest and shoulders. When we take in more oxygen, we increase the circulation of the blood, and this increases our vitality. All this is healthy.

Straightening up and stretching will help us realize how slumped and contracted we have become, or how tense and tight we have grown. A regular massage can also help. This realization can even become quite painful as our musculature becomes aware again of how tense and tight it is, or how collapsed we may have become. Holding patterns in the neck and shoulders can then start to relax and loosen up a bit. An increased breathing pattern is like a massage from the inside: try taking such deeper breaths (say) once an hour. Only as we become aware of our habitual physical "holding" patterns can we start to change them.

When you breathe out, try to let go of all the stress, tension, holding patterns and anxiety. Breathe out through your mouth; give a little sigh; breathe right to the bottom of your belly and push out as much air as you can. Allow your shoulders to drop and sag a little. Hold that "empty" position for just a moment or two. Then you are ready for the next in-breath.

Try doing this standing up, as well as sitting. You can even stretch your back backwards a little as you breathe in, and then allow it to arch forward as you breathe out.

Exercise and relaxation

These have been mentioned before in the section on Stress. They are very important factors in the somatic management of depression. Please do not forget to do these regularly.

I often try to encourage people a little bit by giving them a calendar for the next month with squares for each day in which they can stick various coloured stickers or dots. Each week they will need (say): 4–5 red dots, each indicating a 30–45-minute aerobic exercise session; 8–9 green dots, each indicating a twenty-minute relaxation session; a couple of blue dots, each indicating a "leisure or pleasure" session; and a daily brown dot showing they have completed their daily, self-appointed task list of 3–4 "must do" items. This calendar can be kept on the fridge with a couple of fridge magnets, so that everyone can see how well they are doing in tackling their depression. This is an excellent way of forming a new somatic habit.

An increased healthy use of the body, breathing exercises, and, most importantly, increased somatic awareness, will all become very important factors on the way back to emotional and physical health. Find the forms of exercise that suit you best and you enjoy the most: walking, swimming, cycling, dancing, running, hill-climbing, aerobics, or whatever. Then start to do these more. Force yourself to do these regularly, even if you don't feel like it on any particular day. You *will* start to feel better when you develop and implement this sort of pattern.

As we continue to do these things more frequently and regularly, we start to become more aware of our bodies; and this leads us to become a bit more alive and a bit more vital. This is just the start of the process back towards a healthy, vibrant life, and an undepressed state that goes with this. It is a simple, but not an easy, road. It demands patience, persistence, and determination. And there are also considerable benefits as we start to feel more and more aware and alive and less depressed. It is also extremely effective. The "down" side is that we have to change some of our ingrained habits: we have to force ourselves to do a little bit more each day—even though we may not feel like it; we may have to change our diet a bit, drink less, eat more healthily, and relax more.

Other somatic methods

Massage work, Shiatsu, Alexander Technique, Feldenkrais (Awareness through Movement), Touch for Health, as well as some of the martial arts like Tai Chi, TaiQuonDo, Karate or Aikido, are all fundamentally beneficial. Bioenergetics and other modalities of body-orientated psychotherapy can be very useful in certain circumstances. There are many other aspects of complementary medicine and body therapies (like acupuncture, Bowen technique, cranio-sacral work, chiropractice, homoeopathy, etc.) that can be helpful in this process of working with the depression in our bodies and feeling better about ourselves.

Mindfulness practice is another form of body awareness that can be helpful in fighting off anxiety and depression. Some of the exercises in "mindfulness practice" are derived from the writings of a Vietnamese Buddhist monk called Thich Nhat Hahn (1992). These can be really helpful, especially in cases of "anxious depression" and are now fairly mainstream within CBT in the NHS.

As the body loosens up and some of the chronic tensions begin to ease, you may find that some of your more long-held or repressed feelings start to emerge. We can begin to discover some of the feelings and emotions that might underlie, or be associated with, our depression: anger, frustration, pain, loss, rage, abandonment, etc. These can now all start to emerge. The depression has been part of the "cover-up" of some of these deeper feelings.

Counselling or psychotherapy can be very useful at this point, as it can help to provide you a safe space in which to explore any negative feelings, and this can lead to an understanding of why we might have had to repress them in the first place. This then leads to further choice points, and the progression out of the depression can progress—onward and upward!

Different views of depression

Overview

Depression has been part of the human condition for many thousands of years, Plato and Aristotle wrote about it. Over this time it has been viewed in many different ways. In medieval days, it was believed that bad or noxious influences could infect the body and spirit with "melancholia" (Greek: black bile) or there was an imbalance in one of the four "humours" of the body (phlegmatic, sanguine, choleric, or melancholic).

More modern views tend to see depression as a medical problem, or an illness, which may be appropriate for your particular situation but is far more likely not to be, because very few people actually have depression as an illness. Depression is much more commonly a state or a mood, and this can be caused by a whole variety of very different factors—mostly nothing to do with medicine.

Biological components of depression

There are several internal (biological) sources of depression. Most common of these is a hormonal imbalance. This can be after giving birth (post natal depression), or during adolescence, or during the menopause (in both men and women).

There are also some illnesses where depression is often a consequence, like glandular fever or chronic fatigue syndrome. These have depression as a "biological" component, as well as the psychological one where your life effectively has been torn up for a while. Some viral infections can also have depression as a symptom (or a consequence) and so can some vitamin deficiencies. These types of depressions are sometimes called "endogenous depression".

Some scientists think that people who persistently are in a good mood have a higher amount of natural endorphins, serotonin and dopamine. This implies that people in depression might have—for some reason—lower levels of these neurotransmitters.

Parental or family sources of depression

Some people have been seriously depressed for most of their lives. Sometimes this can be traced back to the early loss of a parent, or a family disaster, or it can be traced to the fact that their main caregiving parent(s) were themselves seriously depressed, so they "learnt" to be this way, or they were not given (their parent could not give) the right sort of emotional care and attention that they needed as a child, which can also cause depression. This type of "learnt" depression can best be treated with long-term psychotherapy. Sometimes medication can initially ameliorate the effects of such a depression.

Additionally, there is some evidence that bipolar depression can run in families and therefore this (fairly extreme) type of depression has a genetic predisposition. Some people thus have bipolar depression as an inherited *potential*—which does not mean to say that they will inevitably have this type of depression. A milder form of this is sometimes called cyclothymia.

Traumatic sources of depression

Sometimes the onset of the depression can be traced back to shortly after a trauma, or a traumatic period, in one's life. This can often result in depression especially if the trauma has not been worked with or resolved in some effective way. Depression here can be seen as a symptom of what is now called post traumatic stress disorder (PTSD). Depression is relatively common in PTSD patients, particularly if there was a sense of helplessness, or of being trapped, in their particular traumatic situation. Again this can be treated fairly effectively with specialist counselling or therapy for PTSD (see the section on "Trauma and PTSD").

Depression as overload

One important view of depression is that it is a positive and protective reaction to almost overwhelming stress. In the same way that a thermostat shuts down a boiler when it starts to get too hot, depression can be seen as a shut-down of the person's emotional system, primarily because their psyche has become over-loaded through a build-up of lots of stressful situations or events. Your system is saying, "That's enough! I can't cope with anything else. Show me the underside of the duvet." So, this is a form of an emotional safety mechanism, and we sometimes call this "exogenous", or reactive, depression.

At least 60% of the people that I see can relate to this type of depression, possibly as many as 75%. It is very common. It means—significantly—that there is nothing essentially wrong with you: ust that what has happened to you has just been too much. This is also looked at in more detail in the section "Stress and life events".

Different psychotherapeutic views

Analytical psychology, developed by the psychologist C. G. Jung, sees depression as a damming-up of energy, which, when released, can help the person adopt a more positive direction in their life. It is thus a usually temporary hiatus, a gathering of forces before the next (positive) change is made.

Psychoanalysis (another type of psychotherapy) theorizes that inadequate emotional development in childhood keeps people in a psychologically dependent position, especially with regard to their self-esteem. This can lead to depression in later life. A "learnt helplessness" can result, similar to people becoming institutionalized in hospital.

Another psychological view is that depression is like being trapped in a prison-like state, or being lost in a dark fog. However, it is also a psychological defence against pain or fear. This is not necessarily a bad thing, as—if you can brave the pain and fear—you can then step outside of this prison, or cut through the fog, of your depression and find a new sense of self.

Cognitive behavioural theories focus on the development of negative thought patterns and interpretations: negative events (possibly in childhood) cause a basically pessimistic view of one's self and the world, which gets triggered by more recent events, and then reinforced by the various negative schema and interpretations that one develops.

Transpersonal psychology theories can see depression as a thwarting of the growth or emergence of the spiritual side of your essential nature, psyche, or soul. Other theories have it as an evolutionary adaptation, to back down in moments of extreme stress. Take your pick of the one that seems most relevant to you or invent your own. It is difficult to state whether some of these different views have a great deal of empiric (scientific) validity. These theories, while interesting, and while they may apply to some people, can also get in the way of taking effective, pragmatic action to help yourself, as you can become dependent on the therapist of that particular modality for *their* way out of *your* difficulties.

Bio-psycho-social model

The bio-psycho-social model is becoming increasingly popular in the USA and in Europe, as it recognizes a combination of factors in the formation of illness or disease and in its treatment. It is an adaptation of the medical model, but it seems to be more effective, and precludes a multi-disciplinary approach. It is recognized that one's state of mind can affect one's immune system, and this leads into the discipline of psychoneuroimmunology. Within depression (for example), it is recognized that the depression itself might not be the cause of the higher incidence of accidents or liver damage, but a depressed person is more likely to take risks, and also to become alcoholic, which can then affect the liver.

Social perspectives

The high incidence of depression in middle-aged women, and in people from lower socio-economic classes, gives the view that outside causes, unconnected with the self, can also be a significant factor in depression.

If the children have all left home and there are therefore much lower activity levels because you are not looking after them, your *raison d'être* can seem to have disappeared, just as a man, dependent on his role or status at work, can become depressed when made redundant or when he retires. This is an existential form of depression. You wake up one morning and say, "Is this it for the rest of my life?" Of course not, but since you have been focused on bringing up children, or working to pay the mortgage, it will take a while to find a new focus.

Another common source of depression is in people from a low socio-economic position: this is a modern euphemism for being poor. If there is nothing that one can do (immediately) about one's socio-economic situation, or financial situation, helplessness and despair can result. Low social skills, and the possibility that depressed people can also depress those others around them, start to compound this aspect of the picture.

However, there is another social or environmental component. If, as a result of emigration or "cultural shock", you find yourself in totally the wrong place, depression can easily result. Imagine you were a successful (say) doctor in (say) Croatia, or somewhere, but because your ethnic origin was in the minority there, when things got difficult you could not stay, and so—after great difficulties— you, and your wife and family, left your nice house, your family connections, and your country of origin, and ended up in a high-rise block of flats, in a foreign country, where you don't speak the language very well, on the outskirts of (say) Glasgow, with the stairwells smelling of urine and people dealing drugs on the landing, and no work, and little money, and the children being discriminated against in school, and being treated as an alien, sponging on the state, etc.—well, that is pretty depressing.

Other existential perspectives

Just imagine—for a moment—that you were born, or felt, a little "different": maybe you had a birthmark on your face; maybe you were gay or lesbian; maybe you were adopted; maybe you were extra-sensitive, or angry; or maybe you were just "different". This "difference" effectively separates you from the people around you, so you do not feel the same, think the same, want the same, or whatever. You may even hear, or see, or feel things differently. Oh, you try to pretend that you are the same. You get very good at that! It s a great survival technique—and it works. So, after thirty years or so, what have you got now? You have got a tough shell—it had to be tough. But you also have a hollow inside, because these gentler aspects have never been affirmed, or helped to feel all right. That is pretty depressing as well. This probably effects your self-esteem, too.

All these views of depression are real and valid. Some of them may not apply to you, but they are still valid. It sometimes helps to say, "Oh, I've got that." Then you have a "label" for your type of depression. It is then easier to go out and find one or two other people who have the same "thing" as you. Suddenly, you are not alone. This really helps. It may not cure the actual depression, but it certainly makes a difference to know it is not just something that is wrong with you.

Emotional expression in depression

Basic principle

One significant aspect of depression is often the lack of emotional expression. When we do not, or are not able, to express some of our emotions, they can build up inside of us. This can create agitation and pressure, a little like being a pressure cooker. Then, there is even less of an incentive to "take the lid off". Further build-ups of emotion can lead to these turning "sour" and "black"; we can even become bitter and cynical. We can begin to alienate ourselves from those around us, or we can even turn these emotions against ourselves and, instead of being negative to others, we can become negative towards ourselves: self-deprecating, self-hating, or even self-harming.

Further build-up of inner tension from unexpressed feelings can become untenable after a while, as we cannot hold all these feelings in forever. We can then either "blow up" into some form of anxiety disorder, or we can eventually collapse under all of this unexpressed "stuff". This is usually a collapse into depression.

At some point, we will have to start to express some of these feelings that we have been locking up for so long. Unfortunately, the resultant build-up or the turning sour of these feelings means that the initial stages of this expression can feel very nasty, as this is what tends to come out first—either as an explosion, or as a stream of blackness. We need to find a degree of safety.

Find a safe channel

The initial reservation about expressing one's emotions can help to keep all of one's negative feelings well locked in. However, this is also the initial "edge" that we have to get over. We do not necessarily want to open the floodgates wide, and risk getting swamped by all these feelings. So we need to find the safer methods first (more like sluice gates). We need to begin to let out some of these negative feelings in a way that is not going to swamp us, explode, or horrify others.

It is sometimes easier to use the safe space that is usually created by a confidential and therapeutic situation. Here one can begin to express some of the more unacceptable, negative feelings in an atmosphere of reasonable safety and confidentiality. Later, when these feelings are a bit more integrated, they can be mentioned to other people, when appropriate.

Another fairly safe way to express feeling is to start to write: write a personal journal, write letters to those people in your life that you felt that you never said half of what you wanted to say (but don't send them), write as a means of remembering, write as a record of the things that happened to you that you have never told anyone, or write to tell the real truth. Try it! It might not be your way, but try it out first.

Another quite safe way is through other forms of artistic expression: artwork, painting, music, movement or dance therapy, sculpture, or pottery. All or any of these can be the medium that works for you. If you feel drawn to one of these, try it out. It can be easier then to tell someone afterwards why you shaped things this way rather than that way. This can be the start of turning your art into a form of art therapy.

Try exploring your feelings

You can also try talking *about* feelings, rather than talking *from* your feelings. Talking about feelings is a first step, a safe way. Some people start by telling things in quite a removed fashion: "One often feels this way, doesn't one," or "It feels like this or that" (rather than "I feel . . ."). Try to find someone safe to talk to: a partner, a colleague, a good friend. Make a simple contract with them not to tell anyone else, not to interrupt too much, not to question, or dismiss, what you are feeling. Take it in easy stages. Arrange a follow-up session. You may not be able to talk much at first, but later . . .

Then try allowing yourself to feel some of these feelings when you are alone, totally by yourself: walking the dog, down by the river, on the beach, in a wood, in a car in a lay-by, in your bedroom. Pick up a stick or stone; throw it or hit something with it. Shout or make noises if you can. Hit your fists against the steering wheel. Allow yourself to cry, if that's appropriate. Curl up in bed and put your thumb in your mouth. Hit a cushion or pillow. Do whatever you need to do for yourself—without any censorship.

Giving your self the permission to feel some of these old, deep, locked-in feelings is not easy, but it is important. You will also have locked in some of your depth, your complexity, and your spontaneity. Furthermore, it takes energy to keep these feelings locked up. You can begin to liberate yourself this way.

As you become more familiar, or comfortable, with some of these feelings, then you can start to tell your confidante not just about them, but talking from them. You can allow yourself to feel the feelings as you are talking. Now you are feeling, in the moment, and with a degree of integrity between your inside feelings and what you are expressing.

Whatever works for you!

The important emphasis is to own what you are feeling, and to own that some of these feelings may not have often been expressed for many years. These may now need to be addressed.

There are some legitimate steps in the clear expression of feelings: "I" statements help; more open communication and assertive statements help; actively avoiding blaming thought patterns helps; owning one's own thoughts and feelings helps.

But whatever way you go, or whatever you try, has to work for you! This is *your* process and *you* will need to find *your* way through it. Essentially, no one else can help you with this aspect.

Emotional expression

Try expressing some of the safer feelings first: those of pleasure, appreciation, excitement, etc. In locking up our negative feelings, we can often also cut ourselves off from the positive ones. So dig deep, even though you are depressed, and try to express some of the easier feelings and the more pleasurable ones. Simple statements, such as "Thank you for helping me do . . .", or "I really appreciated it when you did . . .", make a big difference to other people, and (in due course) to yourself.

Sometimes, if you are feeling sad, it can help to watch a real tearjerker film like *Kramer v. Kramer*, or even *Bambi*; whatever helps to start those tears flowing. The other emotions can often follow once the sluice gates are open to one emotion. It is your responsibility to track these basic feelings; no one else really can.

Sometimes, the range or volume of emotions confuses us. We do not really know what we feel because we feel so much, and so differently to what we usually feel. We may both love, and sometimes hate, our parents, or our children, or our partners. So, if this is your situation, start with just one of these feelings. Allow your self to feel first one thing, and let that run for a little. Then switch to something else. Later switch back. Any release is better than none.

Sometimes, one's range of feelings has been flattened: this is quite common in depression, even to the extent that you feel as if you feel nothing. In this instance, start with that: "I feel flat; I feel nothing", and then continue to describe how that feels. Other feelings will creep in once you have started and if you let them.

Sometimes we have been avoiding feelings, or emotional expression, resorting to convention, or just to locking things up. Try to make a simple statements like: "I feel this . . . or that . . .". Try to avoid using phrases such as "I think . . ." or "One should . . .", as these types of statement take you away from what you really feel.

It is often all too easy just to say nothing, if that has been your pattern, so try to say something. Try to be as real as possible.

You could practise telling your feelings to someone else first: your hairdresser, a colleague, a counsellor, a neighbour, your partner, or a minister. Tell them what you feel about this or that before you tell the other close members of your family. The emotional charge is much less. Success and honest feedback is sometimes more trustable from strangers than from people you are already emotionally involved with, or who are involved with you.

Sometimes people are flooded with too many feelings, like crying that never seems to stop, or anger that does not die down. The doorway to one set of feelings is open and access to others is closed. Try to describe some of the other feelings, the non-dominant ones. Focus on these for a while. Balance will often come. However, this flooding can also be a symptom of trauma, and, if this is the case, you may need some specialist help.

Trauma work

Many new developments are happening in this field. With regard to emotional expression in therapy, the essential point is never to allow yourself to re-traumatize. All recall of events and appropriate emotional expression should happen within the person's emotional "comfort zone". This means working very finely, and very gradually, with a lot of precise attention from the therapist. People really do heal this way. And it takes time and care. There is no "quick fix"—despite what you might read elsewhere. There is a section on "PTSD and trauma".

A caveat (or warning)

There are some therapies that theorize that it is really good to get all your feelings out. However, by making this a maxim, this is effectively fitting the person to the therapy, and not the therapy to the person. If any sort of therapy, or therapist, insists in some way that you should be expressing your feelings, this is (perhaps) not a good therapy or therapist. The person in therapy—you—should never be forced to do anything that does feel right for you, at any time, in any way whatsoever. Vote with your feet: just walk away!

Emotional expression is good when it comes from within. When there is an upwelling, or a surge of feeling, or a bubble bursts, or it happens spontaneously, or . . . whatever. If you really needed to do a particular thing, or say a particular thing, then that is what you really needed to do. End of story, or of that chapter of the story! There may, of course, be consequences . . . but that is another chapter.

Basic working principles for depression

Avoid addictions

Sometimes, when in an anxiety or a depression, we can get into short-term habits or coping patterns that can become quite addictive. These can include work-a-holism, alcohol abuse, emotionally cutting off, over-eating, over-using stimulants, getting irrationally angry, etc. None of these will help you to cope better in the long run. It is not that any of these are intrinsically "wrong", for they may feel as if they help you a little—in the moment. However, they are also often a product of your depression—and they need to be taken seriously. They can actually make your situation worse in the long term. If you were able to feel better about yourself, then you would not be resorting to these addictive coping mechanisms. So, parts of the process of you working on your depression and out of your depressed state will therefore include you working off, or away from, these habits.

Sometimes these addictive habits include always being nice to people, doing it yourself because it is less hassle than getting others to do their share, not asking for help, etc. These can be just as destructive in the long run.

Identify your patterns

If you can recognize a particular pattern of yours, then you have a good chance of changing it. If you cannot recognize it yet, then you will not be able to change it. Try to see what patterns of thinking and feeling happen, or what takes you into a bad mood, or what you usually go for either to stop yourself feeling so bad, or to make yourself feel a little bit better. Ask yourself when this seems to happen: "Has this happened before?"; "Do I always react like this to this/that set of events?"; "Is this familiar?" These are good initial questions. If this is the case, and you can identify a pattern, then this gives you a potential choice of doing something differently when it happens again.

You might need to step out of your pattern for a while—maybe by looking at yourself through another person's eyes. This is where therapy (or a good, honest friend) can be really helpful. It is then easier to be able to say: "That is my pattern—and it isn't working for me any longer."

Set up an "alarm bell" system

Before you can make any effective change, you have to get to a choice point: a moment when you have recognized a pattern, and can then consider doing something different. You need a little internal "alarm bell". This can be quite simply set up. It is as much of a mental trick as anything.

> Examples: "Here I go again!" "I sound just like my mother/father." "I don't want to be like this any more." "I've just put myself down again"; or "I have just . . . blamed myself again"; or "I've just kept quiet again, and not said how I feel."

Such observations can set up the alarm, and, once it is set, it causes you to stop (like a red traffic light at a junction); then there is the possibility of a new choice point or going in a different direction. "I can try to do it differently this time."

The "I don't know" place

This is the place that you get to, after this alarm bell system has gone off, when you are stopping the old habit. It is often the place where you feel "I don't know how to do it differently". This is true. You don't. However, it is actually quite an important and valuable place to be. Here, you are recognizing something very significant: that you *really* don't know how to do it any differently. You have probably *not* been here in this place before. This is a relatively new place. It is different, and it might therefore be quite useful. It can also be quite scary, terrifying even. Stick with it, explore this space a little, and try to find new ways of dealing with these things.

All you know is that the old and familiar way works to an extent, but it is also somewhat dysfunctional since it is not working very well at the present. This is why you have stopped and set up an alarm bell system. Now you have chosen to try something different. There are potentially many new and different directions. Some of them you probably do not want to try: that is fine. Use your discrimination. Use your judgement. Choose one direction that seems a reasonable one. Then go into "explorer mode"—go in that direction just one step at a time. If it does not work out for you, you can backtrack a few steps and then try going in another direction.

Most of the time we avoid this sort of place because we are afraid of the unknown. We do not see the positive aspects, only those aspects that seem quite scary or terrifying. So, enjoy the new possibilities that can open up in this "I don't know" space.

Leave the past behind

As you go through these steps, you are now entering into totally new territory. This is the time to be in the present, not to stay with the past. Do not hang on to the past, those old thought forms, old patterns, and old attitudes. You will limit your future potential for change if you do. What happened before—perhaps, oh so many times—does *not* have to happen again. You can change and start to do new things, or do things in a different way.

This is starting to become something different. The time to let go of the old and the past, and the past patterns, and the reasons behind these patterns, is right now. Changing these patterns also means letting go of the past. So, now is the time to leave behind some of the old "stuff" that you do not want any longer, and change some of those outdated thought patterns as well. Behavioural changes can, and probably will, follow.

Examples

> "I did this or that because I did not know any better then: I did not have much of a choice. Things can be different now. I want to change."

> "I used to do it that way in order to survive. It worked then and so I continued to do it that way. It does not work so well now. That is why I am changing now."

> "I am changing the way I see and do things. I don't do 'that' any longer. I am not sure which way is going to be best, so I am exploring different ways cautiously."

> "In a moment of forgetfulness, I started to do things the 'old way'. Then I stopped myself and went to the new way of doing things. It wasn't too bad—only a momentary lapse. I am actually quite pleased."

Focus on yourself

Many times we may have ended up where we are because our concerns for other people have dominated our lives. While this is very admirable, and we have given and given to others, one of the problems is that now it seems that we have ended up with nothing for ourselves. This can be what is depressing and debilitating us. Resentment and bitterness can also grow here. The way out is to focus more on what you need. Yes, you!

Look inside yourself and see what sort of situation *you* might want to create for *your*self. This is possibly closer to what *you* need, and this is what *you* can give to *your*self. It sounds simple, but is not necessarily easy to do to begin with. You may need to practise a little. Some of the old "What about..." or "Yes, but..." scripts will get in the way, at first. Persist. Let yourself dream a little. How would you like it to be—for you?

Try this on for size: "I am going to do it my way, because this is what really works for me." See how this sentence makes you feel if you just say it to yourself. Then try it out—in little ways at first. This can be a hugely important change. It might even feel quite selfish at first, but don't worry—this has to be one of the new directions that you are going to try. This way you can restore yourself and help to become more yourself. Then you can choose to help others again . . . if you want to; when you want to; and in the way that you want to. Then this way will be the way it works for you—as well as for them.

Sometimes people become depressed because they spend all their energy looking after other people, and they have none left for themselves. Here is another sentence: "I need to look after myself properly, so that I can then continue to be available for other people." Sounds good, but it is not easy to break the habit of a lifetime. We shall come back to this point in a later section.

Look to the future

As you begin to make these changes, you can start to imagine a little more of what might be possible. If you cannot imagine it, then it probably will not happen, as you just will not be able to see this as a possible or legitimate direction. So maybe you can dream a little: "What if . . ."

What goals would you like to achieve? Where would you like to be; in (say) six weeks, in six months, in twelve months? What would you like to have changed? What would you like to see differently? Dream a little bit more. Follow the thought that flirts with your attention, "Oh, I wish . . .", or "If only . . .", or "I have always wanted to . . ." It really does not matter what that is, except that it comes from somewhere deep inside you. That is the important point, and that is the one to follow.

Take the next step

If you were to go in that new direction, what is the next step? What would it take to do that? Today can actually be the first day of the rest of your life. Remember the phrase, "Carpe Diem!"—seize the day. Try it out, and just see what happens. These dreams or goals will help you to set a new direction for yourself. You can then take at least one step in that direction. The journey starts with that one step.

> Example: I am depressed because my life does not seem to be going anywhere. I have thought of going back to college; of taking a course in . . . (whatever).

Good! That's a start. Ring up a college and get a prospectus. That is the next step. Get some more real information. Read it carefully and find out what course might suit you. Find out what the requirements are, how long the course is, how much it will cost, etc. Don't let the answers put you off. These answers can help you to formulate your next set of goals. "Oh, first I have to do this . . . and then I have to get that . . ." Take it one step at a time.

Find something that you can do well

Nearly everyone can do something (usually at least two or three things) reasonably well. Focus on these—and only on these. Do not castigate yourself for *not* being able to do that, or the other; or being no good at (say) mathematics, or car mechanics. That way you can stay depressed about yourself. Choose one of the things that you actually can do quite well, and develop that aspect of yourself more. It may turn into something quite unique and valuable to you.

Then choose another. Focus and motivation are important here. You may need a little bit of encouragement at first to overcome the initial aspects of the depression. But there is then a slow and steady progress.

Appreciate yourself

You have actually come a long way already. You should stop a second and appreciate yourself. Give yourself a pat on the back, or a gold star. You have done something significant. Give yourself a little treat—a reward. This is an important step. By doing this you become less depressed—and you stop the depressive spiral. "Today has not been too bad. I managed to do this and that." There may be a way to go yet, but this has been a really good start.

A bit about anti-depressant drugs

Doctors have been told to reduce the amount of anti-depressant medications that they prescribe. People have very mixed views about such medications. There are a number of different types of anti-depressant medications, and they tend to fall into four main categories, listed below.

- *Tricyclic anti-depressants* are used for moderate to severe endogenous (physiologically based) depression. They can help with improvement in sleep problems. They take about two weeks to have an effect. They can also be prescribed for panic disorders. Some have additional sedative properties. Names of this type (brand names are in parentheses) include: amitryptelinehydrochloride (Triptafen); amoxapine; doxepin (Sinequan); lofepramine (Gamanil); nortriptyline (Allegron, Motival); trimaprimaine (Motival); trazadone hydrochloride (Trazadone, Molipaxin).
- *Monomanine-oxidase inhibitors*. These are now used much less frequently. There are some dangers with respect to diet and interactions with other drugs. They are usually now used if tricyclic drugs do not work, and they can be used if patients are

quite reactive. You must NOT drink alcohol if taking this medication. Names include: phenelzine (Nardil); isocarbocazid; tranylcypromine; moclobemide (Manerix).
- *Selective serotonin re-uptake inhibitors (SSRIs).* Now, these are the most common form of anti-depressants prescribed. They are used for many different types of depression. They usually take about two weeks to have an effect. They are generally less sedating than other types of anti-depressants. Some have an anti-anxiety component built in as well. Some (a very few) carry slight risks of increased suicidal ideation (usually when changing doses suddenly, or in teenagers). Names include: citalopram; escitalopram (Cipralex); fluoxetine (Prozac); fluvoxamine; paroxetine (Seroxat); sertraline (Lustral).
- *Other anti-depressants.* Flupentixol; mirtazapine; tryptophan and venlafaxine have different bases. Some inhibit serotonin and noradrenalin re-uptake; others increase noradrenalin and serotonin neurotransmission. There are new anti-depressants being created that also work with dopamine levels.

It is common for these medications to be prescribed by your GP for a minimum of 3–6 months. With moderate to severe depression, it has to be stated that some form of medication might be needed— for a while.

These modern anti-depressant medications actually do work. But people do not seem to like taking anti-depressants, in comparison (say) with pills for high blood pressure. However, for some, they are a necessary aid to lift that depressed mood, so as to get to this point of objectivity, or to get to the ability to start to help yourself. Some people have also had these medications prescribed for years without any ill effects.

The most common anti-depressants

The way that the most common form of anti-depressant (SSRIs) works is that they help make more serotonin available to the cells in your brain. Serotonin is a natural neurotransmitter and is used in the transmission of messages from one brain cell to another. The SSRI anti-depressant prevents the re-uptake, or re-absorption, of serotonin back into the vesicles in which it is stored; serotonin thus stays around in the links (synapses) between the brain cells, so that the next time a brain cell fires, the transmission of that impulse is easier because more serotonin is available and this means essentially easier brain message transmission. It acts as a form of neurotransmitter lubricant. You are therefore less likely to get "stuck" in some depressive thought pattern or negative mood cycle. You can also create more serotonin from various foods (see the section "Foods for depression"). Noradrenalin and dopamine are other neurotransmitters that can also affect one's mood.

The SSRIs take about two weeks to boost you up to the right level of serotonin in your body. Taking just one or two capsules when you are feeling down is really NOT the way to take them: you should follow the instructions quite carefully. A few people occasionally suffer some side effects from some of these SSRI anti-depressants. These are usually not terribly serious, although sometimes your doctor will prescribe a different SSRI with less side effects.

These anti-depressants can therefore be seen as acting a bit like a buoyancy aid: they help to keep your head above the surface, as you learn to swim in this sea of emotions, moods, feelings, and weird thoughts. After a while, you probably will not need them any more. Then you can come off them, but please come off them slowly and very gently. If you do not, there is a small risk that you will "bomb"—disappear suddenly into a black hole of depression again, or even become suicidal.

If it is decided to come off the SSRI anti-depressant medication, the following guidelines are strongly recommended: (1) you MUST consult your doctor; (2) you SHOULD come off them very, very slowly. I quite often have to start seeing people again when they have come off their anti-depressant too quickly: they were feeling better so they stopped taking the tablets.

After a discussion with your doctor (make a twenty-minute appointment), the best way to come off this type of medication is to drop (say) one tablet in four—i.e., don't take the anti-depressant on every fourth day. Try this pattern for 3–4 weeks. Then, if everything seems OK, try dropping one in three (not taking a pill every third day) for about three weeks or a month; then drop one in two for another three weeks to a month. Now you are safely down to half your original dosage. At any time, if things start to feel strange or funny, you can easily go back up to the previous level where you were feeling all right. You have not "come off" the medication and therefore do not need to start again with the 2–3 weeks introductory period before they begin to have an effect.

The NICE *Guidelines on Depression* (CG23) now recommend that anti-depressants should NOT be prescribed immediately—unless there is very good cause. For mild to moderate depression, Step 1 in the recommended Stepped Care programme of self-help techniques, plus information, plus a combination of exercise and relaxation is recommended first, along with a period of "watchful waiting". Many people get over their depression within a few months like this without any intervention. However, some cognitive behavioural therapy and/or psychosocial counselling or psychotherapy is appropriate at the next stage, Step 2, if this first stage is unsuccessful. For moderate to severe depression, Step 3, a combination of counselling and then (possibly) some anti-depressant medication is what is now recommended.

However, the absolutely best anti-depressant known, and readily available, is—you won't like this—about 30–45 minutes of aerobic exercise (where you get out of breath and hot and sweaty) about 4–5 times per week. This method works by eliminating (burning off) a lot of the stress hormones (adrenalin, cortisol, etc.) that are generated through stress and in depression, and by helping the brain to produce endorphines (the hormones associated with pleasure). Do NOT substitute this method for your anti-depressant medication until you have talked to your doctor. Just do the exercise anyway. When you feel better, then you can decide about the medication.

Some people take herbal remedies like St John's Wort for depression. This can be effective, but if you take this you MUST NOT take any other medication, or any other herbal medicine. It can react violently with other drugs and herbs. For more information about St John's Wort: please consult http://nccam.nih.gov/health/stjohnswort/

Negative emotions

There are several main negative emotions that we often have to work with in these various emotional states, especially depression. The five "biggies" are: denial, guilt, shame, jealousy, and resentment. Anger is often seen as pretty negative as well, and this is dealt with separately in the section on "Anger management". There is also a section in the book titled "Self-harm".

Denial

If you are in denial, then nothing is wrong, and it is not your fault—which is rubbish! This attitude needs to change. Nothing else will change until this does. In fact, things will probably have to get worse—considerably worse—before anything will force you into accepting that something really is wrong, that you are involved, partially responsible, and therefore you probably need to make some changes. How long do you want to wait, and how much more do you want to suffer before this denial ends? Denial can take many forms: denial of illness, conflict, concern, hope, responsibility, etc. You may need to work on changing your attitude to yourself and others before you start to get any "goodies". Instead of "either . . . or . . ." situations: good–bad; right–wrong; etc., instead try to see things more as "both . . . and . . .". This can ease some of the rigidity and polarity and help you move forward a little. The most significant feature of anyone's treatment is the moment they come out of denial and say, "OK. Something really is wrong. I think I could do with some help here."

Guilt and shame

These two emotions are quite closely connected: "I shouldn't be like this, I have let everybody down"; "I must have done something wrong"; "I ought to have done better"; "I am no good." Guilt usually involves a judgement of our self, often set against almost impossible standards of perfection, or a belief that we have violated a certain set of rules. Shame is usually a view that we are not a very nice person, or we have done something that we suppose is wrong or dirty—sometimes a very long time ago. Once we get into the pattern, or habit, of seeing ourselves in these ways (guilty or shameful), it is quite difficult to break. Both are distortions of who we really are, a bit like looking at ourselves in one of those crazy mirrors in a fairground. We see ourselves as only shameful, or totally guilty. The steps that we need to take to get out of these patterns are usually as listed below.

- *Re-assess the seriousness of our actions.* We tend to feel (totally) guilty or shameful about *all* our actions, both large and small. This is quite absolute, quite black and white, no shades of grey. If we were to graduate our feelings, what would we feel REALLY bad about, or quite bad about, or just a little bad about—a twinge, say? Try to begin to categorize your feelings, and not let the small things carry the same weight as the big ones. In this analysis, you can use questions like: "Do other people consider this to be as bad as I do?"; "Why do some people consider it less seriously?"; "How would I feel if my best friend had done this?"; "How important will it be tomorrow, or next week, or next year?"; "If someone had done this to me, . . ."; "Did I know ahead of time that this would have these effects?"; "Do my

current judgements apply, if they are based on what I knew then?"; "Can I make amends in any way—and how much should these amends be?"; "Was there a worse action that I avoided by doing this?"
- *Eliminate those "shoulds" and "oughts"*. These were probably given to us as children, by our parents, teachers, church, or whatever. However useful and well-meaning they were then, how appropriate are they now for you as an adult, thirty, forty or fifty years later? What if you were to change the words "should" or "ought to" into "could"? "I could go to church this Sunday." "I could send everyone a postcard when I am on holiday." "I could go to this [event] because I have been asked." The thought-form or statement carries a totally different weight to it now and there is much more choice involved. Does it make you feel differently? Rules and strictures are (possibly) all right for a learning situation for a child, but, as we mature, we can respect our own individual choice and discrimination. We might not want to do this or that, and there is no need to feel shameful or guilty about it.
- *Change the blame*. Either try to change the way you blame yourself, often for something you were not particularly responsible for, or consider that you may be blaming other people and overlooking ways in which that you might have contributed to the problem, without really realizing it. It does not do anyone any good at all. Just stop it, please. It is almost a form of self-indulgence. "Somebody should be guilty; there isn't anyone else around, so it must be me." Or something like that!
- *Weighing personal responsibility*. "How much was I, myself, actually responsible for this?" Try to construct something like a "responsibility cake" with different sections or slices for all the people or things that might have been responsible.

In an example where you were a passenger in a car that crashed, which is the driver's section of responsibility, which the slippery road, which the oncoming car's undipped headlights, which the distraction from the music, which is your section?

In an argument about your mother-in-law coming to stay, which section is your spouse's refusal to hear anything negative about his/her mother, which section about you wanting to go off and do something else that week-end, which about having had a drink or two, which about having had a bad day at work, and which is your section?

- *Breaking the silence.* Shame is often the perception that we have done something wrong and shameful, therefore we need to keep silent about it. We feel that if anyone finds out, there will be this terrible reaction; we must therefore be such a horrible person, etc. The best way to work at this one—another distortion—is to challenge it. Tell someone. The chances are that you will get a different reaction to that which you fear most. You may need to choose the person that you tell quite carefully: tell them how anxious you feel; make sure there is enough time available. Your partner, your best friend, a counsellor, a doctor, a minister or priest, should, one hopes, respond to your "shameful" secret quite reasonably and responsibly. This more general acceptance from another person will help you to reassess your feelings about your shame and guilt.

Jealousy

The primary fear in jealousy is that you might lose something that you think is yours, or someone else has something that you think should be yours. Behind this feeling is a possibly some deep-seated anxiety, insecurity, or lack of confidence: there are probably also deep feelings of deprivation. To overcome these feelings the jealous person tries to feel better than other people, or to have more than them, or to keep what they have. There may also be a great fear of change. This manifests itself in a form of hyper-vigilance; the person's attention is always on what is happening around them, scanning what others have or are doing, trying to keep a measure of control over others. But ... "the more you look, the more you will see". There is more on this point later on.

Resentment

This is where anger at a person or situation is turned back inwards and repressed. The result is often a negative emotion like resentment. And this tends to stick: or you get stuck with it. There is a fairly straightforward process by which one can work through resentment, but it is usually quite difficult and some additional help may be needed.

- First, you have to identify what you are angry about and whom you are angry with.
- Then you need to find safe ways to start to express this anger. Try writing about it in a journal, talking it over with someone or in therapy, throwing rocks on the beach or in the forest, hitting a cushion, etc. All these can be good.
- With someone else, try to examine any of your irrational thought processes.
- Then try working on your self-esteem and self-confidence. These probably need a boost: look in the appropriate sections of this book.
- When you feel strong enough, look again at what you are resentful about: how much might be your responsibility? How clearly were you seeing the situation? Could you have done anything different? Spend some time reassessing the situations and the people you feel angry about.
- Hanging on to anger and resentment can give a (negative) form of strength or justification: how much do you want to change?

None of these really negative emotions is easy to deal with. They will take time. You may need some help. Most psychological therapists (counsellors, psychotherapists, psychologists) have experience of working with people with these feelings and thoughts. Working through these feelings can really change your life.

Working with negative emotions

This section tries to explain some of the deeper emotional dynamics that you tend to contact, and try to deal with, during counselling and especially psychotherapy. However, they are not all negative, as working with these emotions can lead you towards new growth, and even transformation.

The source of negative feelings

Frequently negative feelings can get locked up inside us, and then they can fester. One of our most vital skills is developing an ability to listen to the true story of our lives: the conflict between the things we feel—the things our bodies register—and the things we think we ought to feel, so as to comply with moral norms and social standards that we have been taught and have internalized at a very early age. If and when these thoughts and feelings are in conflict, they can and will turn negative.

Many of these negative feelings come from the basic, simple reality that our parents were possibly unable to love us in the way that we needed to be loved or respected as a child—I am being very careful with my wording here. If you were truly loved in childhood, then you will love your parents in return: this is natural. If you were truly accepted in the school playground, then you will feel respected and view others healthily as well. We need simple love, acceptance, and respect.

However, those around us as we were growing up may have wanted us to be more "this" or more "that"—either for their own needs, or because they truly believed that this would be good for us. They might have loved us or liked us, but they also wanted us to be different. Any sort of (conditional) love, acceptance, or respect has the effect of changing who we are. In order to get the love, acceptance, or respect that we need for our emotional survival, we become the "good boy" or the "nice girl", or whatever seems to be demanded of us. They have the power and, as children, we are dependent on them. So, in order to get their love or respect, we had to conform. However, any form of enforced or conditional love can do a great deal of harm.

This conformity becomes a trap. We need love and acceptance for our emotional survival, so we suppress the supposedly "bad" or "nasty" sides of ourselves in order to get it. These are not necessarily bad or nasty feelings—they are just the ones that are not accepted by those around us. They do not seem to accept or respect our differences, or uniqueness, so we adapt. In so doing, we lose contact with ourselves; we also lose the ability to express our true feelings and we keep our differences inside. Because they are unacceptable, they become "bad" or "nasty" feelings. However, these were also part of our uniqueness, and this lack (and subsequent distortion) impedes our creativity, our vitality, our integrity, and our authenticity. We conform instead to the mediocre and the mundane.

This sort of conditional love (where you get love and acceptance only if you meet certain requirements) was probably made up out of quite a mixture of different ingredients: expectations, denial, illusions, obedience, fear, the anticipation of punishment, gratitude (for crumbs), bias, bigotry, ignorance, etc. If you experienced any of these as you grew up, then you may well have some of the resultant negative feelings: this is almost inevitable. This list of things denies and obfuscates love, respect, and acceptance, which is essentially what we need to develop a healthy sense of self-esteem.

But what can happen to these negative feelings locked up inside ourselves? If they were ever to come out and get (say) directed back against our parents, people who we are/were totally dependent on, then we could not easily express these, they would not accept them, and we would become unacceptable. These people might not then love us, or might reject us further, and then we could not survive emotionally—possibly even physically. So, we internalize these negative feelings even more, for a very valid reason: survival.

This suppression eventually becomes chronic (long-term) and by this time we have also cut off a bit from the internal conflict (of trying to be "good" or "nice" but feeling "bad" or "nasty" inside) by anaesthetizing all of this "stuff" so that it has now become a set of sub-conscious feelings and thus is largely inaccessible. After a while, we just "know" (inside) that we are "bad" or "nasty" because we have all these "bad" or "nasty" feelings inside ourselves. We also forget about our uniqueness, as it was not accepted or respected and became quite painful whenever it emerged.

This becomes a form of rejection for who you really are, from those outside you, who want you to be "nice" or "good", and from yourself, who now feels that you are really "bad" or "nasty" inside. This rejection, or separation from yourself, can ultimately turn out to be quite harmful and corrosive.

We can end up thinking, "Oh, there must be something wrong with me." In later life, the beginning of a cure is when it actually becomes acceptable to get angry, or to feel a degree of self-esteem, and start to reject some of this old internalization. As you can see, the process of working with these negative emotions is quite complex. Layer after layer has to be peeled away. It is all relatively straightforward, but it is certainly not easy. However, eventually we start to get clear, or clearer about ourselves. The above sentence can then become, "There was nothing, and is nothing, fundamentally wrong with me."

Developing support

Some form of outside support, help, or therapy is often needed for this process, and at various stages or times throughout the process. The support can come from a "companion"—a friend, a partner, flatmate, support group or enlightened relative—who can:

- share with us the difficulties of not getting the right sort of love;
- share the shock and horror of getting the wrong sort of love as a child;
- act as an "enlightened" witness to our own feelings of what we needed and did not get in that early situation, or from those people around us then;
- help us to re-parent ourselves, sometimes allowing us to get the support and attention that we need;
- direct others (as in psychodrama) to help us understand those old patterns and re-pattern them into a new dynamic.

This type of support does not have to be from a therapist, but it does need to be someone, or a group of people, who have made this sort of journey themselves and who are essentially supportive of you embarking on this process. They should be able to set their own needs to one side and just "be there" for you. Support is often essential, just the support of someone being there for you as you struggle with all this, and how we grow best is with the right sort of support. There are sometimes deep and powerful feelings within us, not just psychological, not just negative, but often connected with our bodies, our aches and pains, and our illnesses, that need to be expressed and affirmed after the many long years of being suppressed and withheld. This "letting out" needs to be done in a supportive context where there is no pushing, or fixed concepts, or theories that do not apply to us, but instead there is just acceptance, and permission to let these feelings out when it is right for us and in the way that is right for us.

Working through these feelings

It is absolutely necessary to work through most or all of these negative feelings. If they did happen to arise from your parents being unable to love you in the way that you needed to be loved, then there are some inherently powerful conflicts lying under the surface. I am not saying here that your parents did not love you, but I am saying that they may not have loved you in the natural and healthy way that you needed to be loved, as a baby and as a child. They were probably not perfect, nor did they always get it right for you. It was not necessarily their fault, so they should not be blamed. They tried hard and did well according to their own lights. And it was also not your fault, yet you are the one who is suffering from some of this deficit, and you are the one who is having to carry the consequences.

And you may be caught by having to love them as well. Part of you, I am sure, does love them. But there is a part of you (because of the existence of these negative emotions) that may not be able to do so easily. So, they have to be worked through.

The traumatic events that tend to create these negative feelings may have occurred as the result of an incident or accident, or a circumstance in childhood that (say) took one of your parents away from you, or from a bad school experience, or a hospitalization or illness that made things very difficult, or from some other form of distress or abuse.

No one is really to blame in this sort of situation. But they also have a profound emotional impact. When we do not receive the right emotional "food" in childhood, then our "emotional body" cannot grow up properly and healthily. The result of this emotional lack creates an effect, such as low self-esteem, or the need for recognition and appreciation, for example. This process can be seen to be a little like the childhood disease of rickets. (Rickets is a distortion of the bones in childhood, caused by a lack of vitamin D, that leads to the leg bones being too soft when they are growing, resulting in bent legs or lameness.) So the "lack" of the "right stuff" in childhood causes a distortion throughout their life. Luckily, with the right sort of help, even later in life, our emotional bodies can pick up again, and start to heal, when we start to address these negative feelings and begin to work with them more positively.

Healing the wound

The first major point is to acknowledge these emotional "deficiencies"; that they exist and they have legitimacy. We feel this way for a very valid reason, even though the feeling is perhaps a negative one. This is a really good start. We cannot work with these feelings unless we make this acknowledgement. We also need to acknowledge that we may have repressed these feelings for a very valid reason as well: emotional survival. But the time has come now to stop that old pattern and to express these feelings safely and form some new patterns.

Some people decide to work with their emotional material through art, literature, poetry, or creativity, others in new relationships, or different lifestyles, some through helping others. But, for the working through to be effective and satisfying, the essential inner work has got to be done as well. There needs to be a prioritization of working through your inner feelings, your depression, your anxious states of mind or body, your negative thoughts, or your low self-esteem. Then you can start to express yourself much better; otherwise, you may be avoiding some of these issues by doing the art, getting into a new relationship, or repeating a pattern that does not work for you. Only you can tell. Focus on what you feel that you need to do for yourself.

Working through negative feelings is not easy. If we take the example of the negative emotion of jealousy, the jealous person needs to recognize, first of all, that their jealousy is a real problem, it is affecting their life, and then they need to work to change it. This is not easy because their focus tends to be primarily on other people—and what they might have that the jealous person does not have—and not on that person's "self" and the more positive gifts and benefits that they do have, albeit perhaps buried. If we are focused on other people and their "assets", we cannot see ourselves so well. Additionally, the jealous person is usually quite afraid of internal changes, wanting their external possessions or position (status) to change instead, and thus they want to stay in control. So, it is not an easy emotion to work with.

On a more positive note, it is (perhaps) quite a good strategy to try to realize that you yourself are worthwhile, worthy, and have nearly all the assets that you need. There is no real need to feel jealous of others, therefore. If one can turn away from the focus on other people, and look more at your self, this will benefit the process. The feeling of jealousy comes from feelings of quite low self-esteem. This has little to do with you, but is linked to your perception of yourself. Working through the section on "Self-esteem" might help the feelings of jealousy about what others have, and that you think that you do not have.

In working through these types of emotions, it is only a very strong-willed person who is able to manage to do this on his or her own. Furthermore, it is quite rare to have a good and close friend who can be there just for you and not get involved as well. This is why it is sometimes better to consult someone else professionally, like a counsellor or psychotherapist. This also helps to "contain" the process to that hour, place, and relationship, so that it does not leak out all over the place. There is nothing worse than struggling with feelings of (say) abandonment, only to be told by your partner that you are really a very needy person and this is putting them off, or, when dealing with authority issues, to be told by someone in the office that you are being bossy or rebellious. "I know! I know! I am working on it. Give me a break!"

In looking at these issues, within a self-help book, it is important to realize what one can do for oneself, and when one may need help from others, or professionally. The purpose and intent of this process is yours and yours alone: nothing can happen without this form of determination. Self-awareness is also absolutely essential, totally up to you, and only you will be the main beneficiary of it. Only you can possibly be fully aware of all the different emotions locked within your self. You were there when the "choice" was made to repress some of these feelings in order to survive emotionally: a valid, worthwhile, and successful choice as it turned out—it worked! But the situation that you are in now is a very different one. Your emotional survival—mental health, happiness—depends on a different "choice" being made. You may now realize that some of your resilience, your creativity, and something of your uniqueness also got locked up with those negative feelings. If you want access to these hidden aspects of yourself, then you will have to work through some of those repressed feelings that lie in the way. Unfortunately, you do not get something for nothing. You are going to have to do the work.

Thoughts and moods in depression

Basic concepts

Experiences that happen to us (initially often neutral) are received by our senses, and processed by our brain. There they are interpreted, or given a particular set of meanings, dependent on our way of thinking, expectations, or previous experiences. This is all before we experience any emotional responses.

Depending on the type of experience and the different expectations or meanings that we can attach to it, our subsequent emotional reactions can vary considerably. Essentially, our feelings are often created by our thought patterns, and our thoughts are determined by our moods. Dependent on our thoughts, and thus our feelings, we then decide to behave in certain ways. There is, therefore, a connection between thoughts, moods, and behaviour. Within cognitive–behavioural therapy (CBT), this thought–mood–behaviour connection is seen as fairly paramount, and as the essential key to any change. While this is true, it is—of course—not the whole story.

Internal belief systems, and sub-conscious thought patterns (like the one where you don't think that you are a very nice person) will determine how and what you perceive of the surrounding environment: events that are happening, or may happen; how you might respond to them; how you interpret your perceptions; and what conclusions you might draw from these.

Example: If you are feeling a bit low and negative about yourself, and a friend rings up and asks you to come to a party, you might refuse because your internal script says, "What's the point! I won't meet anyone who will like me ... because I am unlikeable." (The last phrase may not actually be self-vocalized.) However, in this example, you would also have just totally ignored the fact that your friend liked you enough to make the effort to ring you up and ask you to the party.

When we feel low in mood, our thinking also becomes more negative. Then we may reflect more on (bad) past events or negative experiences, or we might worry about possible (bad) events or negative future outcomes. Thus, we maintain that basic negative mood. The "depression" (negative mood) can also lead to pessimism (negative thinking). This means that we are going to be likely to view anything in the present or future negatively, and with a selective negative bias (the glass is half-empty) rather than a positive one (seeing the glass as possibly half-full). Taking things against your self, getting aggressive, or anticipating disasters are all very common forms of reaction (behaviour) triggered by this sort of negative thinking in depression. The original thought–mood connection also works as a mood–thought connection, and thus we get what is the beginning of a potentially depressive spiral. We will look more at this later.

Example: On a greyish day, you are feeling a little low because (say) you have just received a larger utility bill than you had budgeted for. Then you see an acquaintance in the street who doesn't seem to notice you. You can interpret this as either:

1. I am sad, flat and boring: s/he doesn't like me any more (low self-esteem); or
2. How rude of them, I am never going to speak to him/her again (anger); or
3. How typical! Everything is going wrong today. I wonder what (wrong thing) will happen next (pessimism); or
4. There can be a whole range of other reactions.

You have totally forgotten that your negative mood was caused by the larger than anticipated utility bill. What might you have thought about the meeting with your neighbour if you had been told that you had been overcharged for the last six months and that a substantive rebate was due?

Understanding the problem

If you can start to identify that you are feeling depressed, and recognize that this may well affect your thinking and your mood, then you can begin to do something about it. As you start to tackle your thoughts and moods, you may become aware that there is a variety of (sometimes conflicting) moods just under the surface. These might include feeling afraid, anxious, angry, ashamed, confused, depressed, disappointed, disgusted, embarrassed, enraged, excited, frightened, frustrated, grief, guilty, humiliated, hurt, insecure, jealous, lost, nervous, numb, out of control, panicky, enraged, remorseful, sad, scared, uncomfortable, vengeful, and so forth. All these feelings can come and go. We do not like feeling these moods, so they tend to get labelled "negative", and there is then a tendency to suppress these and cut off from them, or even to allow them to escalate and reinforce each other. Our conflicting emotions can become a quagmire into which we sink.

If you feel totally depressed, "and that is all there is to it", then it will feel as if nothing else is possible, and there is little or no hope of anything better. Your feeling, or mood (of depression), is swamping any rational or cognitive abilities and any other minor feelings. You might thus pass over (say) the pleasure that you would normally feel when your son's team won his football game, or other "normal" reactions to something nice happening. Our thoughts (cognitive input) need a level of detachment, an ability to recognize what is happening, the capacity to take a step back and look at our situation, and see anything other than the depression. We have to be able to say: "I am thinking this way because I am depressed. This is not total reality. There may be 'evidence' that supports these thoughts and moods, and there may be 'evidence' that does not support these thoughts, which I am ignoring because I am depressed."

As we begin to recognize that we are depressed (first stage), we can begin to step out of the depression just a little bit. Imagine you can see a dial or a scale showing your level of depression in front of you. Where are you on the dial or scale: 10%, 30%, 50%, 75%? This is a good second stage. Now you can begin to imagine reducing the needle of the dial, slowly and gradually. What might you need to do to be able to achieve this? Or you might want to envisage a scale with both positive and negative sides, and you now happen to be down one end (the depressed or negative end) of this scale. What would help you to move to a position of feeling slightly less depressed? Try to find one thing that would make you feel less depressed, focus on it and think about it, do it, and then check your internal scale again. This is the third stage. Awareness comes first, then a moment of detachment, then the possibility of a positive action.

A reality check

The sort of approach found in this book actually does work: most people do get better—mainly because this approach is reality-based and self-empowering. Essentially, it is up to you—and you can do it. It is important to remember this. A large number (a massive number) of people suffer from a depressive episode at some point in their life. That is their reality. There is usually just one "bad" episode. However, people really do get better. This is possible— honestly! It does take some time and effort though.

Your reality may be that you are depressed—here and now— and you do not know how to cope with it: that is all right. No one knows how to cope with it the first time. We just have to learn how to cope, and to keep on coping. And then—after a while—we get out of the "bad" patch. And things start to get better—bit-by-bit. That is the reality. That is what really happens.

While some of these things may not apply to you right now, where you have reached in your process, they do work, and they are often valid at other times. Check some of this out with someone else. They can sometimes see you better than you can see yourself. That will change soon as well. Soon you will know yourself—and like yourself—a lot better.

Thinking distortions in depression

When we are depressed, this affects our thoughts or our thinking. Our thoughts are often distorted by the depression, or rather the flavour of the thinking is distorted by the depressive feelings. Most of the time, it is the depression talking, rather than your "self". These depressed ways of thinking have a particular style or mood. After a while it is easier to recognize the mood and be able to say, "Oh, that's the depression talking again. That's not me!"

These depressed thoughts are thus often distorted, and when we are under stress or depressed, these distortions can become exaggerated: they are sometimes called "stinking thinking". This really is the depression talking. There are several categories of these types of thoughts. It is important to begin to be able to recognize them before you can begin to eliminate them. Many books and literature from cognitive–behavioural therapy (CBT) and other books on depression look at these types of thinking "errors". See how many bullet points you can tick.

- *All-or-nothing thinking*. This is thinking in absolutes: white or black, good or bad, all or nothing. Since you are depressed, it is therefore usually the second choice, the negative one. You may also tend to judge people (including yourself) or events in very absolute terms: "He's horrible", or "I'm an idiot", or "That was a disaster". You may condemn yourself completely as a person on the basis of a single event: "I failed then, therefore . . . my life is in ruins(?)", or "I've blown my diet completely", and so you then eat a whole carton of ice cream.

- *Labelling* is a different variant of this. Instead of saying "I made a mistake there", you label yourself, "I am an idiot", or label yourself as a fool or a failure. This is irrational, because you are not what you do. It is an abstraction that leads to anger, frustration, and low self-esteem. If you get angry with someone, then they become "a moron": you are labelling their character, rather than their behaviour. Why this works against you is that it is an absolute;. They are, or you are, totally bad: there is no chance of changing anything.
- *Negative focus.* In this example, you tend to focus just on the negative side of things. You ignore any positive possibilities, or misinterpret them. You focus on your inabilities and weaknesses; you "forget" any of the strengths or successes you have already had. Positive feedback or experiences do not count for anything. You constantly look on the dark side. There is quite an active mental filtering out of anything that contradicts this "world view". This is not your view, but it is an active part of the depression. It is the depression speaking; it is nothing to do with you, or, often, anything to do with reality.
- *Over-generalization.* This is where a single negative event is turned into a whole pattern of negative events that wear you down and defeat you. So what is the point? Words like "always" or "never" are often used.
- *"Awfulizing"*, *"catastrophizing"*. This is when you tend to magnify or exaggerate the importance of events, how awful or difficult they will be, over-estimating the consequences or chances of disaster: whatever can go wrong, will go wrong—in your mind's eye. A setback turns into a defeat. A molehill becomes a mountain. This is sometimes called "maximizing".
- *Discounting the positives.* This is where you discount or ignore anything positive, including anything that you do well, or insist that it makes no difference at all. This is also called "minimizing".

- *Jumping to conclusions.* This is where you make a negative interpretation of events without any evidence or fact. You might predict an "inevitable" negative outcome, or "know" that people are thinking bad thoughts about you. Again, this is the depression speaking; it is nothing to do with you. And again, there is no evidence for any of this; it is not real.
- *Personalizing.* You take full responsibility (unrealistically so) for anything unpleasant and for absolutely everything that goes wrong: even if it has little or nothing to do with you. If it is bad, it must be your fault. If it has not worked out, you "inevitably" spoilt it—and for others as well. This is also a distortion.
- *Blame.* This is similar. You blame yourself for things that you were not really responsible for, and/or you blame others and overlook ways in which you might have contributed to the problem.
- *Emotional reasoning.* "I feel like an idiot and therefore I must be one." "I feel bad about something, so there must be something wrong." You assume that your negative feelings are the way things really are. "I feel hopeless about my future, therefore my future is hopeless."
- *Living by fixed rules.* This is where you have exaggerated the usual social codes of behaviour into absolutes. They become "fixed rules", and your life seems to be led totally according to these. Anything different is either unthinkable or so laden with morality, guilt, or disappointment from others as to become almost impossible to consider. The more rigid these rules are, the more disappointed, angry, depressed, or guilty you are likely to feel.
- *"Should" statements.* Words like "should", "must", "can't", "ought to", and "have to" abound in your speech when you are depressed. You tell yourself that things "should" be the way you hoped they would be. Should statements that are directed against others can lead to anger and frustration; should statements directed against your self lead to guilt and frustration. Should statements coming from other people make you feel rebellious and you want to do the opposite. Should statements just do not work. Dump them into your mental waste-bin and empty the rubbish regularly.
- *There's nothing I can do.* The absolute collapse into impotency is awful: the despair and numbness. A variation of this is, "I make

myself numb and just focus on the everyday things. I can't do anything else." Again, this is probably the depression speaking; it is not really you.
- *Only seeing the dark.* This is slightly more of a perception than a thinking disorder, and it is quite close to "Discounting the positives". But a client said I should put this in, so . . . 90% of all matter in the universe is now known to be "dark matter". What we see in the night sky, all the stars, constellations, galaxies, everything is only 10% of what there is. So what do we look at? Do we focus on the "dark material", or do we allow the pinpoints of light to catch our attention?

The depressive spiral

This was mentioned earlier in the section "Working with depression". One of the ways that we stay in a depression is because we have continuous negative thoughts that keep us from feeling better. They have the effect of keeping us in the depressive spiral. These thoughts are semi-automatic: they seem to just happen. However, they can also be challenged: they have to be challenged, otherwise we will not get out of the depressive spiral and we will just carry on down.

Since they are *your* thoughts, you have to challenge them. But they are also *not* your thoughts, they are "the depression speaking". So, try to distance yourself from these thoughts. Challenge them. What is the evidence for this? Are there any other possible views? What would you have thought about this in the past, before you were depressed? What would someone else say—someone who you trust and who is not depressed? What would you say to someone else, if they said that to you? These types of challenges will help you to break the depressive spiral.

Please also remember that it is not just our thinking that keeps us fixed into our mood. Our behaviour patterns reinforce our thinking, and our thinking is reinforced by our behaviour. Just changing our thinking is often not enough; we have to make a physical change in our behaviour as well. Often our feelings will affect our thoughts, and these have an effect on our behaviour. You can envisage a triangular relationship between thoughts, feelings (mood), and behaviour. Each affects the other.

Common irrational belief systems

As you move through this pattern of self-examination of your emotions and your thought patterns (many of them negative), you will come across a few deeper belief systems. There is often a stronger emotion or feeling attached to these. These belief systems are more intransigent and more well held: they are also much more irrational. Each one of these beliefs needs to be taken out, looked at carefully, analysed and dissected, and then—usually—binned. Alternatively, you can try replacing them with something a bit more useful, more positive, more pragmatic or more constructive.

There are several of these common irrational belief systems, or beliefs, that underlie our thinking about our selves and about the world. They are often "learnt" early on in life and so become the unchallenged, often unconscious, basis of our thinking patterns. If these beliefs are held too rigidly, they are likely to lead to emotional distress later on in life, or they may even damage other people. These irrational belief systems are usually carried around in our heads all the time, and then come out into our thinking, often betrayed by such statements as:

- I must be successful, competent and achieving my goals in everything that I do. If I don't then I cannot consider myself as a worthwhile person.
- I should like to be liked or accepted by every significant person in my life for almost everything that I do. That will prove they love me.
- Things should be different. Things should be perfect. Then I will be able to cope.
- If something is, or may be, dangerous, then I feel anxious, upset, and preoccupied. If I feel these things, then something around me must be dangerous. It is their fault.
- I am unhappy, which means that I am out of control. That means I can't do anything to help myself. Someone must help me.
- It is much easier to avoid facing many of life's difficulties and responsibilities than it is to face up to them. I will just keep on avoiding things. It is also safer that way.
- It is too late. I should have done something about this ages ago. Now I have learnt to live with it, I suppose. It is easier to let things be. I can't change things now. They have been going on too long.
- No one has been "there" for me up to now. No one really cares. No one will help me anyway. I will just have to struggle on alone—as always.
- I can't ask anyone for help. This is a sign of weakness. I have to be strong for other people. Therefore, even though I need help, I can't ask them for it.
- The past cannot be changed, so if something once strongly affected one's (my) life, it just cannot be altered. I will always be like this. I am stuck being like this. I can't change.
- I should be a nice person, and then people will like me. I am not a nice person and people do not know how nasty I really am. If they really knew me, they would not like me.
- When people act badly, they are bad. When people act nicely, that means they are nice. People never really change.
- I know what is wrong. So why should I talk to someone else about it? They can't really do anything.
- I feel angry, therefore someone must have done something wrong to me. Therefore I am right to feel angry.

- People seem to stay away from me. They do this because they probably don't like me. Therefore they must sense how nasty I am and so they stay away from me. That means I really am nasty. They can see through me.
- I am depressed, therefore I am mentally ill. There is something seriously wrong with me. I need drugs and medication. I will never get better. People don't ever get completely better from mental illness.
- I am quite a weak person and I need someone else to rely on. I have found/got someone and I cannot survive without this person.
- The best thing I can do is to lie low and do nothing. I don't want to do anything or accept responsibility for anything. I can even get to enjoy this type of passivity or inertia.
- When people say nice things to me, they are just trying to be nice. Because really I am nasty. So they are lying to me, or trying not to hurt my feelings, therefore I can't trust them.

These points were expanded from original ideas in Ellis and Harper (1998), and in Powell (2006). Try to identify these automatic thoughts in the following ways, which were expanded from ideas in Greenberger and Padesky (1995).

- What was going through my mind just before I started to feel or think this way? Was I feeling positive or negative? Was there a particular memory or trigger? How was I feeling about myself? How familiar is this sort of situation?
- If this really were true, what does this say about me? What are the implications? What might happen to me, or what am I afraid might happen? What is the worst that could happen?
- What actual evidence is there for these beliefs? Who told me this, or first gave me these ideas? Did I think they were right? Why, and how? What evidence really is there against these beliefs? The people who seem to think or act differently: do I really like them or trust them? If I was feeling differently about myself, would that affect this belief system? Is it just a product of my negative feelings.
- If these other people really feel this or that about me, what does that mean? Does it mean they are right? Or that they don't

really know me? What are the implications of this, in general? What does it mean about other people in general? Am I really that different from everyone else, or is this just my feeling?
- Which thoughts have the "hottest" feelings attached to them? Automatic thoughts have associated strong moods, and these can provide clues to our emotional reactions. So which are these? What are the implications of this?

As you identify these automatic thoughts, these irrational belief systems, try to disempower them. Essentially, they are running your life. They are also probably ruining your life. They are not true; they cannot stand up to scrutiny; they are irrational; and no one really thinks that way about you. Given that, you can recognize that they do not work for you.

Try not to "feed" these irrational thoughts, as you then give them power. If you continue to listen to them, you will be harming yourself, and those around you; don't spin off negatively at that—just stop listening to them.

I was brought up in the Cold War, believing that Germans were like the enemy soldiers in the war comics, that there were thousands of slavering Russians with their hands on the throttles of hundreds of tanks ready to roll across Europe, that . . . never mind. The world has changed and I have now many German and Russian colleagues and some good friendships.

We have to learn to change these old thought forms: many are irrational; some we developed because we were (frankly) lied to; they were wrong. This is especially true where there were family secrets, prejudice and/or abuse. We therefore grow up with confusion: people whom we are told to believe and respect, or whom we admire or love, are lying to us. These infect our thinking patterns.

One part of healing the family dynamic, any prejudice, or abuse, is to expose these negative thought forms as lies. Another part is to restore the self-esteem and the lack of self-confidence that often accompanies this sort of conditioning. There is a triangle of thoughts, feelings, and actions that needs to be addressed. Thoughts can generate feelings and these can result in actions. Feelings can generate thoughts and actions can follow. Some people act on their feelings without thinking.

How to change your negative thinking

Remember, it's the depression speaking!

Often, our thoughts in depression are actually a symptom of the depression: it is therefore like the depression speaking to us, rather than a thought that arises from within us or one that is unique to us. This form of generic thinking in depression, the negative thoughts and distortions, must first be identified and clearly labelled. We have looked at some of these aspects in earlier sections.

You might need help from some other members of your family: imagine your partner saying something like this gently to you, or the children being encouraged to chorus, "That's the depression speaking!" whenever you start to practise "All-or-nothing" thinking, or start to "catastrophize". This can really help. Ultimately, you will have to learn how to do this for yourself, but initially some outside reminders can be useful. Essentially, you have to learn to differentiate between the depressive thoughts (those that are generated by the depressed state) and your more real, undepressed self.

Try to be flexible

"All-or-nothing" thinking is a form of thinking in absolutes. Some of the other forms of negative thinking or automatic thought forms are very fixed, or rigid. It is often necessary to consider what might lie in between the white and black; the all-or-nothing; the good and bad. Life usually is not this simple or this rigid. An in-between position is often more pragmatic and true to life. "Jumping to conclusions"—another form of thinking disorder—might also have to be looked at more flexibly, as might "Living by fixed rules". If you can look at yourself from the position that you might need to be more flexible, you can start to make steps in this direction. You may have to discard the "surety" of a fixed position, but (this is really a secret) it actually works better this way. Get to recognize when you might be getting stuck in such a fixed position. It does not really work.

It is really all right "not to know"

As the old patterns drop away, and before the new patterns consolidate and form, there will be a period of "not knowing", or you will get into the "I don't know" space. This is actually fine—AND it is not at all easy. The negative thinking is "wrong", but you do not yet know what the "right" positive thinking is, or whether it will work for you anyway. I have mentioned this phrase a number of times already, and I want to emphasize it here and now: "It really is all right not to know." It is actually quite a strong position to be in, if you can stand in it, especially if you know that you don't know. You have stopped doing the "same old, same old" and that is a positive step. But, since this has been a life-long habit, you will not really know yet what the other possibilities are. So it is, then, perhaps better to get into "explorer mode" and find out some new skills.

Be straightforward

All this negative thinking can also be quite confusing, to yourself and others. Try to keep things as clear and simple as possible. If you do not understand something, say so. If you do not know what to do, or where to go, try to feel all right—and open—about that. It is totally legitimate to ask, seek, or demand a clear answer, or to wait a bit, not knowing, until you do know or are clear.

If you think or feel something, however strange or weird, however much it might be condemned by others around you (or you fear that this might be so), try to say whatever it is that you think or feel—simply and straightforwardly. You may be surprised at how much others might actually agree with you, or understand something of what you are meaning, or what has been happening within you.

If you think you have a different opinion to other people, who seem to be expressing the same old stuff, try to explore this: say something like, "I am not sure about this, but there is possibly another perspective. I'm also not sure if I can explain it properly, but here goes. If you ... (and so on)." Just try it and see whether you can build up a different set of perspectives and a different set of responses to these.

The difficulty in being straightforward is that it can be very easy to blurt something out, or to be rude. All those feelings and opinions that have been suppressed or repressed for so many years just want to come out right away (like now!) and express themselves (in your face). Fine! Let these thoughts or feelings come out—but do it in a private "blog" or a diary. Do NOT bring that frustration out in the middle of a meeting at work, or at a large family gathering, unless you have thought it through and are prepared for the consequences.

Anyway, people will probably react more to how you are being straightforward, rather than to what you are saying. So try just to be calm and clear.

Your thoughts possibly come from another time

Your negative thought patterns probably come from another time: twenty or thirty or forty or so years ago from your childhood. You might have been brought up in a particular religion, or in a particular belief system, class, or political party that you now do not subscribe to, or in a different country with a different set of parameters and priorities. All of this can affect our thinking. Some of the "thoughts" that stem from this early conditioning are probably now not relevant, or are just plainly unhelpful. Believing that you will go to hell or heaven for eternity because of doing this or that does not help you very much in your present situation. Believing that this type of person, or those actions, or that situation, is bad prevents you from accessing the good that is also potentially present.

Many of our thought-forms are a result of coming either from a different time, or from a different state (in depression), or from the different world of your childhood upbringing. Some of these thought forms come from negative self-images picked up in childhood, and these have been latent—for the most part—until you got stressed and then became depressed. They are probably just as untrue or distorted as our old Cold War views of the Russians.

Try not to be so extreme!

Some of the various types of "Thinking disorders" are quite extreme. These have a particular flavour about them. You need to start recognizing the sound of, or the flavour of, such statements, or thoughts. If you can imagine a red light coming on, or an alarm bell sounding, whenever you get into one of these types of extreme thinking processes, it will help you to change your negative thought patterns. Soften these extreme thoughts a little: realize that—while you might be upset—you may not need to be so upset.

Think it all out carefully!

You (probably) need to make sure that you have thought things out properly. You won't have, but don't let that stop you trying. Remember, you are changing: your thoughts, your behaviours, and your feelings. So please take absolutely 100% (not 99.9%) responsibility for all of this. You are changing, and this is fine, or it will be, for you! For others, they see you as changing, moving (perhaps) away from them(?), doing something different, raising fears instead of providing security, and so forth. This can create a lot of worries or confusion within the family.

You may have to think things out, and explain things, a bit more carefully. You might need to take (just a little) responsibility for the effects of your (new) thoughts and actions. Please think it out very carefully! If you really want to/need to/must leave your family and go and paint on a South Sea island (like Gauguin did), try to make sure the rest of the family is reasonably provided for before you leave. If you want to stop being a doctor, leave your husband and family, and take up with a new lover and teach Reiki (or whatever), that is fine! But make sure there is someone else who is going to pick the children up from school, if you are not now going to be there. All actions have reasonably foreseeable consequences. You probably do not want to create more confusion. Things are confusing enough already.

Detachment is important

As you begin to change your negative thinking patterns, you might need to detach yourself a little from them. If you were cleaning out a long neglected pond at the bottom of the garden, you would inevitably get dirty and the old stuff in the bottom of the pond will smell a lot. It is a very dirty job; please believe me! However, you would not let that put you off. You would detach yourself from the muck and the stink for a little while. You would continue to clear it all out and cart the rubbish away, and soon the water will settle, and become clean and fresh. Then you get to take a long, hot shower. By this process, you will have created an asset, instead of a neglected area of liability. Detachment can be useful at times.

You can try to observe your process, as if you are watching it on a TV screen. We often say, "Never mind, it will soon be over." Or you can see these negative thought patterns as just one aspect of yourself: the quintessential you is not changing, a part of you is, just as if you take off one set of clothes and put on another, better fitting set. These little tricks will help with your detachment from these negative thoughts. They are not you, just a redundant part of your life.

Emotions are also very important

It is all very well to try to correct your negative thinking, but this is unlikely to be completely successful unless you have also worked on the feelings that frequently underpin your thoughts and belief systems. An earlier section of this book is titled "Negative emotions. Please do not ignore this section: it is extremely important. Working with your negative feelings can change your thoughts and perspectives. Changing your thoughts and perspectives can influence your emotions.

Don't compromise!

This is important! You possibly compromised yourself—emotionally or intellectually— in order to survive before this depression happened. This was perfectly legitimate, then. This might have happened in childhood, or many years later when you did not listen to your "inner voice" and took that job that wasn't right for you, or left that person who might have been right for you, or whatever. No one is saying that this compromise caused the depression, but it might have added to your internal stress levels, or your internal conflicts. Now you are in the situation where you are trying to get it right for yourself. So don't compromise now! Maybe later, if it seems appropriate, you could concede a little, but then you are considering the issues from a different perspective and may come to a different conclusion. For the moment, please do not compromise! Try to get it absolutely right for yourself now—as much as you are able to. If you have to do things in steps or stages, that is all right, but don't compromise on the basic direction—unless it turns out not to be working for *you*. Then change direction, but do not compromise your self.

THE PROCESS

Your inner process

What has been happening is that you have started on a positive road towards mental health, tackling your anxiety and/or depression. You have started to reduce your levels of stress and to tackle some of the residual stress, mostly through a combination of exercise, relaxation, and diet. You have also probably started to change your thought patterns, and you will almost certainly find that, as you do this, your moods and feelings will have begun to change as well.

You have started to accept that the negative perspective dominated by the depression is not a valid one. You have started to look for other possibilities. This is a positive change. You have begun to challenge the way that you have done some things previously, thinking that this was the only way possible. You have started to look at other possibilities. You have also begun to challenge some of the setbacks, the negative thought forms and feelings, and the inherent difficulties of depression a little, as well as challenging some of your own fears. This is all excellent progress.

We have also looked at some of the "nasties" that can exist in depression: these are called "thinking distortions" and "irrational belief systems" and "negative emotions". They have to change, since they can perpetuate the depression or aggravate the anxiety state, and as soon as possible. This sort of necessary change is a little like driving on the right when you go across to Europe, or if you hire a car in America. You suddenly have to learn to drive on the right, rather than on the left. The "old way" just doesn't work any longer; you are in a very different situation. You just have to do it, learn to do it very quickly, and then to keep on doing it.

Challenge is a necessary part of change. This is the start of the way forward, the way that will get you out of the depression. It is a little like picking yourself up by your own bootlaces, but that is what it is like. It takes an effort and lots of determination. You are ultimately the only person who will be able to help yourself out of this depression.

For the moment, let us press on.

Your process

You are definitely in a process and there is no quick fix. The process of "healing" is yours, and it is totally unique to you. There are various stages and dynamics to this process. While the outer manifestations might look like a depression, an anxiety state, a period of extreme stress, a breakdown, an illness, or a life-change, the inner process is the important bit. Focus on that!

It is probably best seen initially as a form of growth, rather than as a cure. A cure implies that there was something wrong with you, or that you were sick, or that someone has to cure you. We have seen that this is probably not the case.

In this growth process, which is also a form of healing (if you really wish to see it that way), one can shed one's symptoms, reduce anxiety, re-establish your self-esteem, regain joy in your life, and free oneself of depression, as well as heal old wounds, cure chronic illnesses, break out of addictive patterns of behaviour, and reduce that state of constant exhaustion. Though it is quite hard work to change, it is just as hard to heal. You will also be quite a different person as you go through this process or when having gone through this process. So, seeing this as a growth and healing process is probably a good idea at first. Be prepared to change, and even welcome it. Then become interested in what is going to happen next.

Rebuilding the self

As you do this inner work, you are starting to rebuild your self more towards your true self. You are recognizing that you do have choices. You are now choosing to do some things differently. You are exploring some of the complexities of your uniqueness. You are rebuilding your strength and your self-esteem, step by step. Your early difficulties might have prevented some of this development happening then, as a child: it can happen now; perhaps it is "catch-up" time.

This is the self-experiential aspect of your process of growth. As you grow and heal, and heal and grow, you start to feel a different person, more like the person that you feel you could have been. It is as if you start to come back on track in your life again. It is important to see everything that has happened to you as an essential part of this process—even the bad bits, or the bits where you got "lost". You may have married and had children. These are an important part of your old life, as well as a part of your new one. You are not going to throw everything away and start afresh; that is not growth or process.

When we rebuild the self, it is like trying to get the pieces of the jigsaw into the right pattern, so that they fit properly this time. We do not throw out the old jigsaw (because it didn't work) and get a new set of pieces. We reshape the old ones, the bits we have got, into a pattern that really starts to work better for us. That is the easy bit.

Undoing, redoing, and mourning

So there now comes a difficult and complicated stage in our process that often seems to go on and on, or the same old "stuff" comes around, again and again. This is the readjustment phase. "Stuff" that has happened to us has caused us to turn back feelings (guilt, shame, etc.) on ourselves. This has frozen us; we have got stuck. These are negative feelings and they affect us as we begin to tackle them. We may become self-punishing, or have developed low self-esteem. We may be very cautious, self-restraining, or fearful. We may have internalized some of the negativity around us, and so we now think we are "bad" or "stupid" or "worthless" or that we have "failed". These patterns or habits have to be undone: but they can only be undone bit-by-bit. We then have to redo them, again and again, so that new, healthier patterns and habits get formed in the place of the old ones.

We cannot undo everything, throw out all the old and replace it with only new stuff. That is impossible. We would not exist any longer. It is too drastic, random, and scary. It is also just not possible. We have to sift through everything that we have, that we are, making choices. We have to learn to individuate, or discriminate, to make the right choices for ourselves, unique to us at this point in time. We may be wrong and make bad choices, but we will learn from these mistakes and get better at what we choose. So this is an ongoing, gradual process.

We also have to mourn some of the old opportunities that were lost, as we need to recognize that we could not respond appropriately then. We have to find better ways of doing things now: ways that are less harmful or less constraining. We have to discover that we can remake these old choices in a better way now. As we do this repatterning work, and some of the grieving for the old and the lost parts of us comes through, a new sense of strength and solidity builds.

Discrimination

As children, we were told to do certain things and not to do other things. Now we need to redefine these and work out what is right for ourselves. We need to exercise adult discrimination. We need to be able to choose to (say) get angry, if it seems appropriate, or to criticize someone else, when necessary, or to challenge authority, if that seems oppressive. These are often difficult things to do as they go against our childhood conditioning. We now have to choose between the various things we were told. My father used to tell me, "Don't lend money to family or friends: you will lose one or the other or both." Sound advice and (unfortunately) often very true. But he also told me other things which were sadly bigoted, outdated, and very inappropriate. But which one do we choose? How do we know that one is right and the other wrong? We don't, except by trial and error. We have stand outside of the "authority" of these early messages and become our own authority. We have to learn to discriminate.

There is a sort of cost–benefit exercise that can be useful, in the first instance: list the advantages of expressing the negative emotion or choice in one column and then the disadvantages in another. Then weigh up the benefits by making a ratio out of 100 (e.g., 60:40). You are asking yourself, "Will it help me to feel this way? Will it hurt me to feel this way?" Both will probably happen. Is it worth expressing it or making that particular choice? You decide. The so-called negative feelings may actually be a healthy expression of your real feelings, a "true" position, and expressing them now may therefore be constructive: positive or negative?

Trouble-shooting

Sometimes it is not clear why a particular situation has upset you, or why your behaviour (that you felt all right with) seems to have upset other people. You can try to trouble-shoot by asking yourself the following kinds of questions.

- Did I identify the problem or event correctly? Is there possibly another way of looking at this situation?
- What really happened? What did I really do or say? What did others really do or say? What might someone else say?
- Could my "upset-ness" have come from another source? Was I/were they upset by *what* I/they said/did or by *how* I/they said or did that thing?
- Is my basic reaction right, but is the level of reaction somewhat distorted? Am I *too* (angry/upset, etc.)? Does the strength of feeling come from somewhere else entirely and is out of proportion to the present, or not really anything to do with the present situation?
- If I repeat or review this incident to myself now, can I find another possible interpretation? What might "X" say, or "Y" say?
- Am I reminded of any "type" of situation here? Does this fit into any sort of pattern? Are there echoes of an earlier situation?

- Are my negative thoughts, feelings, or actions taking a particular position (possibly defensive), or do they fit into a rationalization (I "should" feel/think/act like this)?
- If I could have lived that event over again, would I do it differently? If "Yes", should I or could I say this to anyone concerned?
- Are there any positive aspects? Do these negate my negative impressions? Can I stand up for the positive aspects *as well as* acknowledging the negative ones?

You may not get any positive or particularly helpful answers, but the exercise of asking such questions opens yourself up to lots of other possibilities. You can more openly review and view your situation. In the long run, it will be helpful to your process.

Alarm bell systems

What is necessary is to identify and then to challenge some of these distortions and patterns of thinking. Set up a little mental alarm bell whenever you notice one, or get someone close to you to help you identify one (or some) of these dysfunctional patterns that you have. This is the first and very necessary step. Then you have to stop thinking that way. You have to learn to stop. That is the hard bit. It is like a habit, or even an addiction. It is very hard to stop thinking that way. But to carry on thinking that way is to stay in the depression. What helps to stop is to try to replace the negative "thinking distortions" and "irrational beliefs" with something more positive. If you can do this, that is great. If you cannot, just stop the negative thought patterns, and then think about something else. Later on you may also have to tackle some of your habitual patterns of behaviour, your addictions, your ways to hide or avoid some of the deeper stuff, and so forth. You may well need some specialist extra help at some point.

Paradoxes

What seemed to be true is now false. What seemed to be wrong might now be part of the truth. Paradoxes surround us. This is a necessary part of the whole process of reconstruction and reconsolidation. There is not just one answer, one truth. And we will not find it by thinking about it. We seem to find answers—many of them partially true—in weird and wonderful places, or in mundane situations, or when we are sleeping or dreaming, or thinking about other things. Synchronicities seem to become more important than logical connections. Metaphysical responses seem more profound than absolute facts. It really is all right *not* to know. In this sense, knowledge (that which is known) can be limiting and constraining.

Trying to understand what is actually happening to us takes us further from the truth. It is also quite frightening and often very confusing. What we need to do—perhaps—is to trust this process of deconstruction, and trust that whatever emerges at the other end will be more appropriate for us now, and will see us through. But there is no telling—of course! We cannot "know" what will be right for us. We are in a process of redefining what we have been told is wrong. We have to risk breaking up the jigsaw that we were given in order to see whether we can get the pieces into a better configuration this time around—one that works for ourselves.

Life is no longer fixed any into absolutes such as right and wrong, good and bad, black and white, this is true and that is also true. There are both rights and wrongs on both sides. Black exists (of course) and so does white—and there are also many, many shades (and colours) in between—none of them absolutely right or wrong, but all different, all valid (to a degree)—and thus all very confusing. And so the wonderful dance of life goes on.

Untwisting our bodies

We have to remember to free or "untwist" our bodies, as many of these (negative) feelings and experiences have been somatized. We store these feelings and experience these emotions in our bodies. We can work on these cognitively and emotionally, but we also have to work on them physically.

Please remember to do some regular aerobic exercise. This is incredibly important for eliminating all those nasty stress hormones. Just get as hot and sweaty and out-of-breath as you can. If you can work out in any way at all, start with 20–25 minutes and work up to forty-five minutes minimum. That way your metabolism goes on working long after you stop. Do this as regularly as you can—at least 3–4 times per week normally, or 4–5 times a week if you are at all depressed. After you exercise, you can get in some decent relaxation: this double act, of exercise then relaxation, will really help you to rebalance your autonomic nervous system. Then you can start to have fun and unravel the twists in your psyche: try some long hot baths, or a sauna and jacuzzi, getting some massage, or doing some Alexander Technique work, or Tai Chi, Pilates, or Yoga. These types of disciplines will help open your body up to greater flexibility and new possibilities.

Untangling our psyche

We have also tried to identify some of the knots and distortions that can exist—and not just to our thinking and our emotions. Perceptions (right or wrong ones) lead to thoughts (accurate or otherwise) and these lead to feelings and emotions. We identify with these; we think this is who we are. These thoughts, feelings, and emotions may be negative or dysfunctional, depending on our perceptions; they may be distorted because of bad experiences; they may be confused and conflicting. Who we really are is something totally different. Our thoughts, feelings, perceptions, behaviours, are all performed by our psyche. It is this that we need to untangle.

But the self-examination process, untwisting or untangling our psyche (one hopes), will also have a positive aspect as to how we see ourselves, more clearly and how we feel about ourselves and our bodies. We can look at other ways of untwisting our thoughts. We have looked at ways of working with our feelings, of checking that our perceptions are reasonably valid or consensual, and of moderating our behaviour. So now we need to look a little bit further at how to untwist all this and work to contact the true nature of ourselves, and our psyches.

As these three areas (mind, feelings, and body) begin to sort themselves out, our perspectives, desires, and expectations will change. People often tend to move away from the traditional or conventional, the conservative and the materialistic points of view. They become more concerned about their quality of life, defining this more intangibly than an extra bedroom, or a bigger car. They tend to opt for healthier options, like organic foods. They tend to become more concerned with bigger problems and ethical issues, like the state of the planet, people who are starving, or injustice. They may concern themselves more with their spiritual development. All these are aspects that arise from untwisting our psyches.

Reconsolidation

This stage, or this part of the process, becomes quite interesting. It is like a paradigm shift. Things start to make sense in a different way. We begin to see the possibility of light at the end of the tunnel. There are occasional glimpses of clarity and an increasing sense of freedom, or of new possibilities. We are not just changing our selves, from the inside; we are changing things around us as well. We might decide to get a new job at about this stage, a more fulfilling one. Or we might decide to go back to college to finish that degree (or whatever). We may decide to go deeper into something new, or do something that we always wanted to do. However, this will not solve our problems.

This is also a repetitive and explorative process through which we solidify and reform ourselves. There is an increasing awareness now of being able to sense the new self and enjoy some of the new possibilities. And we will also realize that there are some bits that we still haven't dealt with. So, back into the process again!

Making reparations

This step, sometimes also the step of forgiveness, or the forgiveness of yourself, is one that people nearly always try to complete much too early. This is a mistake! Don't even think about going there for a long time! Wait until it happens naturally; perhaps even see it having happened in retrospect. Trying to do this step—the step that we all hope for—too early can lock you into a miasma of unexpressed feelings and confusions. You may need to repeat some of the above steps several times before you can find yourself back here again, ready to make any reparations that you feel are really appropriate and honest, without losing your integrity, or trying to assuage some guilt.

It is very difficult feeling negative feelings: it is (perhaps) the hardest thing that you will ever do. Do not run away from them by trying to make everything all right and nice. Some of the reparations might never happen anyway. The person(s) in the story, now "old" or past, may be dead, or may themselves have become a different person. They may not have realized, or may never be able to realize, what happened back then. Try not to look back, try to look forward instead—to when you can start feeling right with yourself. That is the best form of reparation: creating a new person, a new story, new possibilities, and a new and better You!

Avoiding relapse

There are three or four basic reasons for any relapse: (1) negative emotional states—like boredom, depression, or loneliness; (2) social pressures to revert to the "old" way, either direct pressures or perceived ones; (3) interpersonal conflicts, such as disagreements with your partner, or conflicts with relations; and (4) negative perceptions—about your ability to cope, inability to avoid distractions or temptations, or self-punitive thinking. The way to avoid such reason for relapse is to try to monitor any risks of the above and head them off by taking appropriate action: do a little planning ahead, develop some positive addictions (instead of negative ones), and try to control any slips from your new routines, perceptions, or habits.

The process of the process

There are various aspects to this developmental, healing process that have not been mentioned specifically yet. The process often moves through different areas of emphasis at different times. At certain times there is an emphasis on expressing old or covered-up feelings; there is, at times, a focus on old memories; at times there is a focus on the current (therapeutic) relationship; at times there is a focus about what is happening in one's body, or in one's intimate relationships, or one's working life and career; and at other times there is much more of a focus on the developing self, and what needs to happen next.

Your process is like a flow, like a river. There are many different aspects to a river. At times it can become quite stagnant, as in a marshy area, or flow into a quiet lake. At other times, it can be quite dynamic, caught up in a canyon, or forming a cataract or waterfall. Similarly, your process can get stuck on one level and continue on a different level, or in a different channel. It is very rare that it stops completely. Even a depression can be a different form of your process.

These different times of different focus interact with the different stages of the process in a sort of holographic weaving in-and-out, rather like a dance. This is just the way that it is; this is the process. The process can also happen in cycles or waves. One thing will happen, will complete, and then it changes, something else comes up—and then, here it comes again. This is a natural process. It is like floating on the waves, or dancing up and down, or winds changing direction. Enjoy the dancing! Enjoy the change.

The road less travelled

There are other, less negative, steps that come in at various points in your process. While there are short-term goals of eliminating negative thought, feelings, or behaviours, there are also positive developments of becoming more aware of yourself, and hence others, of increasing your compassion and sense of connection with others around you, of realizing that there are bigger pictures and wider horizons, and the possibility of being of service to others. An increasing sense of your own spirituality and inner contentment might develop. Paradoxically, this might also be paralleled with a greater sense of awareness that the only thing that really matters is what you are doing at this precise moment, or who is right here and now in this moment in front of you. To see them clearly, you have to be able to see yourself clearly. This is sometimes very hard, and it also carries its own rewards.

This may sound a bit philosophical and detached. We can be more detached, as well as becoming more involved. This type of spiritual path has no goal. There is no "Celestial City" on a mountain-top far away to travel towards in the hope of arriving at the Golden Gates with the sound of trumpets. The journey itself becomes the important thing, and the only real goal is to travel well.

This sounds nice and simple, and—to a certain extent—it is. However, it is not easy, and that is why this is "the road less travelled". It is a hard and sometimes very lonely road; but it is also a very rich one. The benefits can be beyond price, beyond your wildest imaginations. You find your real self!

Recovery

"Every person's experience of mental health problems . . . is unique, as is their recovery. . . . It is important to be clear that there is no right or wrong way to recover." This is from a book of stories of hope and recovery from people with long-term mental health problems, *Journeys of Recovery* (Carlton, 2002). The ordinary practical tasks of life and being involved with other people have a very good "grounding" effect, and the rhythm of daily doings can often provide a structure that helps to restore a sense of balance to people's lives.

At other times, it may be necessary to take time out and go quiet and deep inside yourself; maybe even go on retreat for a few days. This can be very restorative. Spending some time with other people, as in a therapeutic community, or with people in recovery, or a with a self-help or support group, can also help as, while their stories are not your story, there will be some common elements. It can make you feel less alone and more "normal".

Never ever doubt that you will recover.

Points to remember

- *Express your feelings.* This is a way of taking the internal pressure off yourself. It can relieve the pressure inside and your depression may start to lift. It will not disappear all at once and it might come back again for a while. But expressing your feelings—whatever they are—will help.
- *You and your feelings do matter.* You must begin to take yourself seriously. You can start to feel a bit surer of yourself. Your views are important. More often than not you may be right. You can make a contribution to the world. Those around you would be totally devastated if you were not here, with them.
- *Life is difficult, but it is not impossible.* Don't expect things to be easy, it makes difficult times worse. Confront difficulties; don't avoid them. Problems can become challenges. We all make mistakes at times; this is how we learn, so you can see these difficulties as potential learning experiences.
- *No one is an island.* We do need other people. They can help us and they can hurt us, but we still need them. Accept them for who they are. The people around you need you as well. And they need you for who you are. Try to accept yourself as well.

- *Look after your own needs.* We all need to take care of ourselves. You especially need to rebuild your strength, your happiness, and your self-esteem. Simple, but not easy. But this approach does work: it is not selfish, it is to the point, and it is needed—by you.
- *You are "in recovery".* If you had broken an arm or leg, you would not expect yourself to do all the housework, and nor would you if you had just had a major illness. See yourself as in recovery in a similar way. You will be able to pick up the reins (the control) of your life soon. For the moment you are healing, recovering from depression.
- *Keep your own ground and strive for balance.* Make sure that you know what it is that you want. Go for a balance of work and play; time to yourself and time with others; physical and mental activity; pleasure and leisure, activity, and rest.
- *Be flexible.* Nothing is all black or all white: it is just good or bad. "Both . . . and . . ." is sometimes a better perspective. "Should", "ought", and "must" are also not particularly helpful maxims. If there seem to be just two choices, both unacceptable, try to stay for a while in the "I don't know" place. "Good enough" is sometimes a lot better strategy than trying to get it perfect. These are all flexible strategies that might help.
- *Take full responsibility.* Take full responsibility for yourself, for everything. Do not blame anything: your parents, your childhood, society, what happened in the past, other people. They may have contributed, but you were also there. A "blame culture" or a "victim" mentality will not aid your recovery. You are also fully responsible for the process of your healing. No one will do it for you.
- *Consistency works.* A stop–start approach does not work so well. If you start something, try to finish it. If you have started something that now seems too big, break it down into smaller bits and try to complete some of these. "Little and often" is also quite a good maxim for recovery.
- *Glass half-full or half-empty?* Check whether you are looking at things from a negative perspective, or a more positive one. Try to find the other side of the coin, or the silver lining, or whatever. Things are not always totally black or bad: "discover the other".

- *This too will pass.* Sometimes it is just a question of time. When you are doing everything you should be doing, things *will* change for the better, but maybe they will change at a little slower pace than you would like. Patience! Do what you have already been doing, and "this too will pass". Your body and mind know how to heal – at their own pace.
- *It is never too late.* The rest of your life starts with today. You may not have done "this" or "that" before now, for very good reasons. You may not have realized what you now realize, you might now have done things differently, you may not have felt strong enough or clear enough, there were other people or things to consider. You can choose differently now, or tomorrow, if you want to: it is never too late!
- *Eat properly.* "We are what we eat." Eating properly, according to the recommendations given in the section "Foods for depression", can really help. Remember: "five-a-day"; "little and often"; "watch your portions"; "a balanced diet means a balanced life". Old maxims, possibly, but they often carry a degree of wisdom.
- *Breathe more; move more.* Find lots of different ways of increasing your vitality towards life. Pleasure is important. Increase awareness of your body and it will tell you what it needs. Breathe! Move! Do it more!
- *Stay in the moment.* Say to yourself, "Now what! What now?" Feel this exact moment, and become more aware. Pay attention to exactly how you feel, right now. Try to exercise no judgement, have no expectations, take nothing for granted. Just go inside and be with yourself. This is the best way to get unstuck from old patterns and stay in touch with what you really need.
- *Exercise, exercise, excercise.* I can't say this often enough. It really helps a massive amount. It works. Do whatever you can, as much as you can, when you can.
- *Many others have been here . . .* Many times, in the depths of depression and despair, we forget this point. We are not the only ones who have become depressed.
- *. . . and have returned to lead a fulfilling life.* Often, our life after depression can be more fulfilling than it was previously. In getting out of the depression, we may have addressed many of the issues that were limiting us, or holding us back.

- *Talking helps.* When we are depressed we feel very alone, and we also often feel that we don't want, or are unable, to talk to anyone else. "That's the depression talking." Don't listen to it. Find someone to talk to. It helps!
- *Every cloud has a silver lining.* Personally, I hate "old wives'" sayings like this. However, unfortunately, they often have a degree of truth about them. In this case, while being in a depression is by no means nice, it can have some benefits. You may take the time off that you need to get de-stressed. You may pay more attention to yourself rather than always looking after others. You may have come to realize that certain aspects of your life needed changing.
- *Negative thoughts are the depression "talking".* Most of the negative things you have been thinking about yourself and your life are a load of . . . codswallop. They are the negative thought forms created by the depression. Learn to keep away from them; don't disappear down the slippery slope of the depressive spiral.

Oh, one more!

- *Depression is not a mental illness.* It is an emotional state that you got into, and you can get out of it again.

ANXIETY

About anxiety

Introduction

Anxiety is the experience of having a feeling of unease, worry, or fear. It can be mild or severe. It is often caused by a situation of stress, either at home or at work, or—most likely—a combination or a build-up of such situations. About one person in twenty has a problem with anxiety at some point in their life.

Anxiety is not an illness. Most of the time it is a perfectly natural and normal way to feel. It often has a useful purpose. It is your body's natural alarm system, and it peps you up to deal with any difficulties you might have. It also keeps you alert and aware of possible difficulties. Some times it is associated with depression: i.e., you can be both depressed and anxious.

Anxiety becomes a problem when it gets out of control, or if people have a problem controlling their level of anxiety, or when the anxiety happens at inappropriate times. They may feel apprehensive, nervous, fearful, or tense. This can happen quite suddenly. They may have difficulty concentrating, or sleeping properly, or they may be waking early. Sometimes the cause of the anxiety is unclear and so people become more afraid, think they are going mad, or having a stroke, or something like that. While this is very understandable, these fears are almost certainly groundless.

Anxiety is a feeling, based on a perception of danger (real or imaginary), that prepares you physically to deal with the danger through the stimulation action of adrenalin. The anxiety you feel is real, and it is not in your imagination. The physical feelings and sensations of anxiety actually happen to you. They can be very strong. Many of the symptoms are somatic (feelings of choking, dizziness, feeling light-headed, face flushed, numbness or tingling, wobbliness in legs, etc.). Other physical symptoms can include heart racing or pounding, indigestion, chest pains, butterflies or cramps in the stomach, breathing difficulties, choking sensations, dizziness, blurred vision, blushing, wobbly legs, or a fear of dying. In serious cases of prolonged anxiety, there can even be gastrointestinal upsets and problems such as ulcers can be exacerbated. The chances are that if you have some of these, then they are symptoms of anxiety.

Anxiety can also cause a person to be much more aware of every sensation in their body, though these are usually misinterpreted and they think something may actually be physically wrong with them. Sometimes the physical symptoms are quite vague, or change, and so there is a difficulty in diagnosing that these symptoms are caused by an anxiety disorder.

However, anxiety—in itself—is not dangerous. You do not die of anxiety – these physical feelings will not hurt you in any way at all. You can learn how to cope with these feelings, and then they will become less frightening. However, you will have to learn to reduce your anxiety.

Anxiety can also affect you mentally, and in your behaviour. Anxiety can accompany some other conditions, like depression, or be the basis of, or add to, other conditions, like panic attacks, phobias, or compulsions. If you have taken some time off work, then you might become fearful that this will affect your job, or chances of promotion, or that you might be judged unfairly. This can increase low self-esteem and reduce your ability to judge a situation well. Your anxiety may thus escalate.

Anxiety can affect the way you think. Shakespeare wrote, "There is nothing good or bad, but thinking makes it so." There is a tendency to think in "all-or-nothing" terms, to jump to conclusions, to personalize, to focus on the negative, or to exaggerate what you imagine might happen: this is referred to as "awfulizing". Cognitive–behavioural therapy can help to identify these thinking patterns. However, it is hard to change the anxious feelings. And this is where a combination of exercise and relaxation can really work, as explained in the section on stress.

Anxiety can affect your behaviour, what you do and how important it feels to do it. Anxiety often drives you to do things right away, without hesitation, or impulsively, occasionally much too soon. Sometimes it can turn into repetitive behaviour (doing things over and over again), or what is particularly common is various forms of avoidance behaviour (not doing things) or avoiding other people, or crowds, or social situations that seem difficult—because they make you anxious. Sometimes people may become unable to go to work, or may want/need to have time off sick.

Anxiety can also be felt like a sudden "attack" in extreme cases. There is a sudden onset and feelings of breathlessness. Then it can be described as a panic attack or panic disorder. You are not having a heart attack, though it is quite a good idea to go to the hospital to have this checked out the first time it happens. There is a section about panic attacks a bit later on in this book. Your doctor may want to determine, with you, whether your anxiety is mild and the result of life stress, or a general anxiety disorder (also see later in the book), or of the panic attack sort, as these can affect the type of treatment s/he recommends.

Extreme or chronic (long-term) anxiety states can also develop eventually into obsessive–compulsive behaviour, or into phobias. There are sections about these "disorders" later in this book, too. Thankfully, people who suffer these are fairly few in number. I am not suggesting that one can overcome these "disorders" by using self-help methods; I just provide a little information, mainly so that people with anxiety do not start to get worried they may have one of these "disorders".

Finally, anxiety can be a way that people use to counteract their depression. If the depression is bad, and makes you feel as if you do not want to do anything, then feeling anxiety is a way of surviving the depression and making sure you don't "go under". It keeps you alive and functioning—just. But at what a cost!

Self-help for anxiety

The usually recommended treatment for anxiety (NICE Guidelines, CG22) is again a stepped-care approach: a combination of self-help techniques (exercise, relaxation, good information, etc.) at first, in Step 1, followed by a psychological treatment like counselling (Step 2) if that is needed, and possibly later some medication (Step 3), if the previous methods do not work. This combination of stepped treatments, starting with self-help, is reasonably successful, and nearly all patients really do get better, and reasonably quickly from the time of starting such treatment. There are further options, such as specialist referrals or psychiatric referrals (Step 4), for the relatively few more severe and enduring cases.

Treatment for anxiety thus involves, first and foremost, some exercise to burn off any excess stress hormones, and then some properly practised self-soothing relaxation therapy, combined with good information or "biblio-therapy". Second, it involves perhaps some psychological help (counselling or psychotherapy), and only very occasionally some anti-anxiety medication, either to be used very temporarily or perhaps in the form of an SSRI anti-depressant for longer periods. Understanding about anxiety is important, and it is often a major eye-opener that some of your other symptoms are possibly/probably caused by anxiety.

Self-soothing

Anxious people can start to prepare themselves with the various non-medical methods of working with their anxiety and these preparations can increase the efficacy of such non-medical approaches: essentially, the sooner you start to tackle this, the better. Some of this preparation work can be described as "self-soothing", "self-mothering", or giving oneself "solace". There are a variety of ways to do this.

The child's security blanket or favourite teddy bear are traditional childhood examples of transitional objects that provide solace and comfort. In an adult, such examples may take the form of a ritual cup of tea, listening to a favourite piece of music, reading a favourite book, tuning into this week's episode of your regular "soap", snuggling up on the sofa under a blanket, or just going to bed and getting under the duvet for a while. Focusing your attention on something else works quite well, too: people play computer games, or do jigsaws, or get involved in hobbies. You are not so anxious when you are doing something in a concentrated way. It is a temporary respite, though, as the anxiety comes back almost as soon as you stop.

Shopping is a slightly more expensive form of self-soothing. Putting on a favourite CD, wearing one's special sweater, or having a bowl of chicken soup are all cheaper and well-tried ways. What is your method of self-soothing? What works for you?

In the control of anxiety, it is very important to be able to give yourself a pleasant, soothing, relaxing experience quite quickly. Once this is done and you are not so anxious in the moment, then you can start to cope with the background of your anxiety much better. Take yourself off somewhere safe and soothe yourself a little, knowing, consciously, that you can do something very simple that is not only pleasant and safe, but also staves off the chance of further suffering. This is a very important first step. You start to realize that you have some degree of control.

Exercise

Any exercise that promotes activity, endurance, flexibility, or general strengthening is a natural anti-depressant, and thus also helps with stress and anxiety. Exercise, and in particular aerobic exercise, improves circulation, brings increased blood flow and oxygen to the brain, releases endorphins (the body's natural pain-killing and pleasure-making chemicals) and boosts serotonin and other neurotransmitters. The overwhelming sense of being unsure, or being anxious, can make it very difficult to sustain even simple tasks, much less get out and do some regular exercise—but this is one of the challenges you *must* overcome. Aerobic exercise is now a recognized and accepted form of therapy for anxiety. It is widely acknowledged that *if* you can discipline yourself to do some form of exercise regularly, you will almost *definitely* feel better for it. Even a brisk walk once a day is a very good start. Get a friend or family to help you with your motivation, or get a dog that needs exercise. Aim to build up to about 30–45 minutes of aerobic exercise about 4–5 times a week, or 5–6 times for more severe anxiety, if you can.

There are lots of suggestions in the section about "Fitting more exercise into your life".

You will almost certainly not be able to relax significantly until you have burnt off all the stress hormones in your body that have been generated by your anxiety, by doing aerobic exercise fairly regularly.

Relaxation

The simple forms of relaxation are usually the best. What makes you relax, or helps in the process? There are lots of suggestions throughout this book. Please choose the ones that suit you best. The section on "Meditation and mindfulness" describes possibly the best forms of relaxation for anxiety. But you really need to find something that works for you. There is more on "Relaxation" after this section.

The principles of healthy, anti-anxiety relaxation are to empty your mind (of worrying thoughts), stay in the moment (as most people worry about what has happened [the past] or what might happen in the future), breathe gently and a little more slowly and deeply, and focus on your deeper Self—what you really need or want. This technique, whether you call it relaxation or meditation, is very simple, almost incredibly so, but it is not easy, and—like anything worthwhile—will be improved by practice: just keep on doing it. It does work.

Medication

Most of the anti-anxiety medications (like benzodiazapine, or tranquillizers), while being quite effective, are not really recommended as they often have quite—sometimes very—addictive side effects, and so any treatment for anxiety involving medication is usually limited to the lowest possible dose for the shortest possible time. Several SSRI anti-depressants are licensed for anxiety, phobias, and panic disorders (see earlier section, "A bit about anti-depressant medication"). Obviously, some people become so debilitated by their anxiety that they might need some medical help to get them sufficiently out of a state of anxiety to a point where they can act coherently and address these anxieties, but this is usually only a very short-term solution and only in extreme cases.

Extensive studies have shown that for many people (at least 40%, as much as 55%, occasionally 70%), a placebo is almost as effective as the medication being tested. Medications and drugs can create dependencies, some are addictive, and some may have unpleasant side effects. The root cause of the anxiety is also not being addressed. So, please don't reach for a bottle of pills. There are other, better, ways: read on!

Breathing

One of the most powerful ways to affect your emotional state and the involuntary nervous system that is connected to anxiety is through greater control of your breathing. If you are stressed or startled or angry, stop, close your eyes, and focus your attention on your breathing. Inhale slowly through your nose, directing the air deep into your chest and belly. Pause a moment. Then exhale slowly and as much as possible through your mouth. Pause again. Repeat this 5–10 times and you will see how this simple technique works to reduce your anxiety.

Sleep

Try to develop a good sleep schedule—a regular time of going to sleep at night and arising in the morning—and stick to it. Sleep irregularities are amongst the early warning signs of both anxiety and depression. A good night's sleep can really help towards coping with anxiety. Prepare yourself: don't eat too late; take some gentle exercise before you go to bed; have a bath; read a book for a little when in bed. There is a later section about "Better sleep patterns".

Diet

Good nutrition supports the optimal functioning of your body and brain. Try to eat a balanced diet of healthy foods. Eating as much organic produce as possible will help to minimize the intake of chemicals and preservatives, which can cause problems, especially in sensitive individuals. Another part of nutritional self-care is cutting back on sugar (sweets, processed foods, simple carbohydrates, and alcohol), salt, and saturated fats.

Studies have shown that too much salt, as well as sugar (in any form), can foster anxiety, as well as, possibly, depression. Alcohol can also have a negative effect. Try not to eat comfort foods and especially not any ready-prepared and processed foods: the additives can build up quite quickly and affect your emotional state. Prepared sauces can be fairly high in sugar and salt: also check out the calorie content. Try to eat the more of the complex carbohydrates: oats, brown or wholemeal, fruit, protein, nuts, and seeds. Try to avoid the saturated (animal) fats and opt for olive oil, oily fish (salmon, tuna, mackerel, sardines, etc,).

Read the labels. Drink plenty of water. Eat little and often: have bowls of fruit and nuts to hand. Smoothies are good.

What not to do

It is usually not necessary—or advised—to take any medication for anxiety, though occasionally one of the tranquillizers are prescribed for a very short period of time, and analgesics (such as codeine) are sometimes self-prescribed. However, these substances are quite addictive and, if you overuse them, you might discover that you soon have another problem to cope with. SSRI anti-depressants are also sometimes prescribed. Other substances (like alcohol, cigarettes, and 'soft' drugs) that people often turn to when anxious are not really advised, even though some of them are legal. They also have their tendencies to be addictive, taxed, expensive, and any relief is of very short duration. Another very common way of coping with anxiety is "comfort eating", but this just helps you to put weight on: it does not do anything to remove your anxiety.

Things to avoid

Try to avoid too much tea, coffee, or caffeinated drinks, as they can make you more agitated. Don't smoke too much: it can have a similar effect, even though the initial "hit" is relaxing. Don't take too much sugar or salt for similar reasons. Don't drink too much. Don't eat too little—or too much. Try to avoid overworking and becoming overtired. Avoid too little relaxation—you are going to need to be strong, rested, and ready to go. Try to avoid staying in bed too long as well. It is also not a good idea to cut yourself off from people, friends or family, as a way of avoiding anxious situations. All of these are types of avoidance behaviours.

Conscious control

The next important thing is to start to address some of these anxieties directly. The anxiety may be real, but, in itself, it is NOT going to kill you. It is important to realize that there is really nothing to be afraid of in these feelings. You may have become afraid of the fear itself. So do NOT panic. Do NOT try to run away from, or fight off, these feelings. The solution is simple, but not easy.

You must start to sit with these anxieties: breathe gently, just let them be, let them pass away and change, and try not to let them affect you. Sometimes your anxiety is centred on the fear or the pain of possible suffering, or anticipation of another bout of depression, or of failing, or having a migraine, or of being alone, or whatever. Work with controlling this; work to control this. The trick is to keep breathing. Stay in control and breathe. Don't let the anxious thoughts continue to go round and round, or start to escalate; don't fight them; don't run away; just separate from them, disempower them, and breathe. It is easy to say, and much harder to do. But this is all you have to do, for the moment. Get used to being with the anxiety and not letting it control you.

As you begin to master the initial anxiety—and you will—then you can start to use your imagination. Imagine the fear or the anxiety getting smaller and smaller. Give it a form or a shape, such as a black dog, or a spiky orange shape. Then imagine this shape or object getting quieter, or smaller, or softer, or a nicer colour. Work to reduce your images of your anxiety. As you get better at this, you can deliberately start going into situations where you used to feel anxious. Just keep your thoughts under control, and keep breathing. If you have been having palpitations whenever you get in to a high place, or a small confined space, or in a situation where you are a little phobic, deliberately start to go back to these places, when it is nice and quiet, and just breathe. Stay a few seconds or a minute or two, and breathe. Take it one step at a time. Try to get back, as soon as possible, to doing all the things that you stopped doing because of your anxiety. You will feel a little anxious at first, but then it will pass. Stay in control. Don't hurry the process. Use whatever little tricks you have. Do it with friends, if that works for you, or alone, if it does not.

Remember—try NOT to leave a particular situation until the anxiety, the fear, or the panic has diminished and until you have felt that you are in charge of your feelings. Any moment of anxiety is another opportunity to practise these techniques. Plan your "targets" and be specific: "I will go to the supermarket and stay in there for at least ten minutes. I will buy at least five items. I will not go to the shortest queue. At any moment that I feel any panic, I will breathe properly and wait till my anxiety goes down." Practice makes perfect, and you will feel stronger and better each time. Don't just do it once, do it several times. Don't let yourself take things easy, keep at it. Don't procrastinate or put off tackling these situations, persist. Just keep doing these types of things until you master many of your anxieties. There may be a few setbacks, but you will recover from them. The anxieties may not go away completely, but they will become much less disabling, and you will become much more confident in dealing with them.

Keep a journal

Writing in a diary or journal is one of the best self-help methods you can use. Put down and record new sights and smells, new experiences of any kind. Note down the things that you have done during the day, and how you felt doing them. Especially, write about your feelings. Write every day, if possible. It may help to write at the same time every day, maybe after dinner, or before you get ready for bed. Write for yourself only. Try not to censure it. Do not worry about the spelling or punctuation. You are the only person who should ever read it.

The effect of having a journal is that: (a) you "ground" some of your thoughts and feelings—spending some time identifying them and then expressing them on paper allows you to get more in touch with yourself; and (b) you can look back and see what you were feeling then and how it has changed in the "now".

Natural world

Try to spend some more time out in nature: it is very relaxing. Whether it is watching a moonrise over a mountain peak, a sunset over the ocean, or simply taking a leisurely walk in your city park or by a river, spending time in nature imparts its healing touch. We tend to become much less anxious when we are out in nature; it is difficult to say why. It just works! Even spending a little time in the garden, or with some house-plants or a window box can be very relaxing and soothing.

Prayer

If you believe that prayer can have an effect, take some regular time to pray, both by yourself and/or with other people. Meditation involves stilling the mind, so that we can hear the "still small voice" of God within, and be open to any spiritual guidance. This is also very relaxing and can be a great aid towards reducing anxiety, if it works for you.

Different benefits

These self-help methods of consciously utilizing your own internal resources and maintaining a balanced life-style are also very useful and effective for people with other issues, such as chronic pain. They work by providing a solid basis for recovery, by increasing a sense of internal balance, and by adding to a growing sense of relaxation, harmony, and peace. This is also the basis of effective anxiety management. Physiologically, more beneficial hormones, some of them called endorphins, are being released into your body from your brain, and these really help you to relax. These can also act as an anaesthetic. In such a slightly more relaxed state, your body–mind's own resources and healing processes can start to become more optimized, your immune system strengthens, and your internal self-regulation is gradually restored. This is not any sort of New Age belief, but well-researched psychobiology, mixed with a healthy amount of common sense.

Relaxation

It is also very important to learn to relax as well. This helps you to rebalance your basic body functioning (autonomic nervous system), which often gets overstressed—especially with anxiety. For most people suffering from anxiety, or under stress, it is very difficult to relax, for three main reasons.

1. They are still so stressed (full of stress hormones) that they just cannot relax easily.
2. They (think they) don't have the time, or they think that they cannot do it "properly", or that it will not work, or whatever. This is just the anxiety talking. Don't listen to it!
3. They may be using their anxiety to keep themselves from disappearing into the "black hole" of depression.

It is therefore necessary to build in a programme of relaxation (ideally once or twice a day for twenty minutes each time) and this should either be done first thing in the morning before you get up (often the most anxious time), or sometime after you have done your daily exercise routine. The many and various relaxation techniques that we look at in a moment all have their own claims to effectiveness: visualization, relaxation, prayer, humour, biofeedback, Tai Chi, massage, and meditation are some of the choices. Most carry a significant feature: increased self-awareness.

Increased self-awareness

This is a method of tapping into the body's own resources, through increased self-awareness, especially related to your anxiety. This is also a method that can be applied to many different conditions. For anxious people, it is particularly effective. In anxiety management courses, promoted by various departments of many NHS Trusts, one of the first techniques is to look at different forms of breathing and relaxation, often using exercises that employ your imagination. These all carry self-awareness as an essential component.

There are many different ways to relax, and listed below are several suggestions.

- *Mediation and "mindfulness"*. These techniques are becoming much more fashionable as people realize their efficacy. There are sections earlier in the book in which these methods are described more fully.
- *Progressive relaxation*. You can get tapes or CDs of (usually) progressive relaxation exercises that tell you how first to tense, then to relax, all the various sets of muscles in your body. As you do this, you progressively relax more and more.
- *Autogenic therapy*. I often teach people the principles of a form of autogenic therapy, a form of relaxation that was designed for people with hypertension, and works using a script and an image for the various parts of the body. The advantage of learning something like this system is that you can do it anywhere and without any special equipment. You can get a book that teaches you, or there are special therapists (go to the Autogenic Therapy Association website).
- *Music*. Certain types of music are very soothing and relaxing: I find that Mozart, some Bach, Boccherini, Albinoni, etc., as well as more modern music, is good for me. Try to get some CDs or tapes that you find relaxing and listen to these in the car, or at home, instead of listening to the radio. Alternatively, tune your

car radio to Radio 3, or Classic FM, rather than the news bulletins or pop music.
- *Warm water*. This is very relaxing: hydrotherapy is a very well established relaxation treatment, dating back to the Greek and Roman times. Go for Radox-type baths, and a nice long soak in the bath with some lavender oil, a candle, and some gentle background music: keep topping up the hot water. If there are other people in the house, make sure they know you are going to be in the bathroom for at least half an hour, and must not be disturbed for any reason whatsoever. Or get yourself to the nearest jacuzzi, maybe even in your lunch hour. Some of the spa hotels do very relaxing one-night or week-end packages.
- *Massage* is also an excellent form of relaxation. It does not particularly matter what type of massage, but aromatherapy massages are now quite popular and fairly readily available. They will usually cost £20–£30, but this is an excellent investment to kick-start you into a better pattern of relaxation and self-care. Alternatively, ask your partner for a foot-massage as you watch television together. Sometimes a bit of self-massage also helps: first do the scalp, then the back of the neck, then one shoulder after another, then those tense muscles at the top of the chest towards the shoulder, and then those by the collar bones. These areas can all be massaged by yourself, taking only a minute or two, and without any embarrassment, even if done while at work.
- *Breaks* are also important. You have scheduled tea-breaks at work, so take them; do not work on through. You should have a half-hour minimum lunch break, by law; take it. Get out of the office or workplace. Don't pass up on holidays, or time in lieu. If you work from home, take five minutes every hour—as a minimum—and a lunch break away from your work. Arrange for quality time away, mini-breaks, long weekends, or whatever. Anything less than this is basically counter-productive in the long term.
- *Leisure and pleasure*. Reading, watching films or television, listening to music or the radio can also be very relaxing—in relatively small doses. It is best to have a regular routine and stick to it: reading the paper on the way to work, or watching the news or a favourite TV show at a set time.

Further relaxation: being at peace

As you begin to practise the combination of exercise and relaxation regularly, your basic body system (the autonomic nervous system) begins to rebalance itself. You might soon experience feeling more yourself again, the old self. I hope you are using some of the other methods of relaxation suggested, or ones that work for you. However, there is a way to go yet, as we want you to move towards a new self, a much more relaxed and peaceful self. Not only does your body have to rebalance and settle down, but so does your mind.

There are several techniques or practices that can help you to do this. They mostly involve a level of meditation, or mindfulness awareness, or mind-emptying practices. Several variations of these have been practised throughout human history and these principles are found in all the major religions and philosophies. The goal is to achieve a peaceful mind, not necessarily an empty one. None of these methods conflicts with any major religion.

A Vietnamese Buddhist monk, Thich Nhat Hahn, wrote, "Being at peace is not the same as being anesthetized. A peaceful mind does not mean a mind empty of thoughts, sensations, and emotions. A peaceful mind is not an absent one". He wrote a very good manual of relaxation and meditation exercises, *Peace is Every Step: The Path of Mindfulness in Everyday Life* (1992). He wrote another lovely little book, called *Being Peace* (2005), which is also recommended.

When you begin meditating, or practising mindfulness, do not suppress all your thoughts and feelings in order to try to create a peaceful mind. That sort of suppression will backfire eventually. The unwanted thoughts—the anxious ones—are also currently a part of you, and peace does not from having one part split off and another accepted. It comes more from the acceptance of all parts of your self. Try to be aware of all your perceptions; try to allow these to pass through your mind—and then just allow them to pass away, out of your mind. Holding on to them will not result in a peaceful mind. Some of the thoughts or feelings may be angry, some hateful, some shameful, some anxious, some confused. These are all parts of us; let us accept them and then let them go.

There may be some moments of wisdom, or perceptions of beauty; these are also parts of us, so let us accept them, too. And we will also have to let them go. There will be (initially) a lot of trivia; this will settle down eventually. It just takes some practice. We will soon realize that our perceptions of beauty (however nice they are) and our perceptions of all the other things as well (however disturbing they are) are all fairly ephemeral, insubstantial, passing, and limited. They are essentially perceptions: they are right or wrong, good or bad, but they are not reality. They are what we feel or believe. They are what we want, or do not want to happen. When we realize this, then we are getting closer to a true realization of ourselves and of reality.

What matters more than what we think or perceive is whether we are "being" in the moment, this exact moment, now. This is all that is real. This moment lasts for just a second or two, and then there is a new moment and then another new now. This passes as well. In this moment, there are no feelings, no real thoughts, no right or wrong, just an experience of being.

We need to practise being in the moment, sitting and watching things pass. It is a little like being in a slow-moving, gentle, railway train. After a while, it becomes quite peaceful. You may need to practise this, in whatever way works for you, on a regular basis, and probably twenty minutes a day is a really good start. Do it sitting down with an upright back. Perhaps light a candle, or make a little ritual out of it, if you want. A prayer or two for other people never did any harm. Then settle down and allow your mind to quieten. Become a little detached from the passing thoughts.

Occasionally there will be one or two that you want to keep hold of, such as the fact that it is (say) Auntie Mary's birthday tomorrow and you need to send her a card. In your mind's eye, put these thoughts into a balloon and let them bob around, like at a child's party, and at the end of the exercise you can gather them up and deal with them, one by one. For the rest of the exercise, just let these thoughts go. Stay in the moment. This is the first step towards being at peace.

Perhaps something small needs to be said here about the basic philosophy. For thousands of years people—from all religions— have been struggling with our basic "human condition": life is very difficult! Worrying about it gives you two problems immediately: life is difficult, and you want or expect something different. Of course, we would like things to be more like Paradise, or the

Garden of Eden, or some mythical time. But life just is not like that. Sorry! That is the world of myths and fairy tales, or dreams of winning the Lottery. Believe me, you think you've got problems! Win the Lottery, then you've got problems! However, in Europe, the USA, and the West generally, we seem to look for a solution that is something material, outside of ourselves, and immediate. There is a dream of an ideal place or time that we can get to if only we do this or that, or that someone can give to us. We become focused on a particular goal. The advertisers then try to sell us stuff that will make our life better, richer, bigger, etc., and so the myth perpetuates. In the East, there tends to be (or has been) a greater focus on enjoying things much more in the moment: instead of trying to get somewhere special, the goal is to try to "travel well".

You can practise all this further as you do things for your anxiety. When you are (say) doing the washing up, just do the washing up. Don't think about the shopping list, let it go. If it won't go, then stop doing the washing up and write down the shopping list. Then go back to doing the washing up. Be aware of all the aspects of doing the washing up: the bubbles, the water temperature, the plates, the scent of the liquid soap, the sunlight coming through the window, the background noises, the feel of the dish mop, etc. Do the washing up fully. "Be" the person who is doing the washing up, instead of trying to get the washing up over so that you can "be" yourself more in other ways.

Or, when you are walking, be aware of how you put your feet down, and lift them up. Become aware of the sights and smells around you: of Mrs Brown over the way who has just come out of hospital; of the roses in the garden of No. 32. Take those extra few moments on your way to the bus, or wherever.

When you are driving, make sure that you are aware of all the other cars, the traffic signals, and the pedestrians. Take pleasure in your awareness. So, you can take pleasure in walking, in being at peace when you do the washing up, or making the shopping list. This is how to start being peaceful, being peace-full, "Being Peace", more and more of the time.

It makes a big change from feeling anxious all the time! It is also a wonderful start to taking control over your anxiety in a gentle, non-stressed way.

Social anxiety

Shyness and social anxiety are quite common problems, often strongly connected with low self-esteem (see later). You can work on these symptoms yourself. They do not fall into the category of "social phobia" (see the section on "Phobias"), where you might need some external help. Many people, both men and women, experience some degree of social anxiety, especially in new situations. These feelings can become amplified or exaggerated if, or when, you are also anxious about other things as well. Anxieties about public speaking, performance, or interviews are very common.

Symptoms

The symptoms of shyness and social anxiety are a combination of cognitive, emotional, and physical. People experience significant emotional distress in the following sorts of situations: being introduced to new people; being the centre (or focus) of attention; being watched while they do something; meeting "important" people; being in social situations, such as parties, meetings, or conferences;

having to say something publicly. They fear being teased or criticized, judged or rejected, or making a fool of themselves. Many people experience a form of "shyness" in some form or another at different times in their lives, but these people do not start behaving differently, or avoiding those situations of social anxiety. They get on with their lives. They don't have social anxiety. The symptoms of social anxiety fall into different categories, listed below.

- *Cognitive.* You tend to carry a negative picture of yourself in your mind. Thoughts and perceptions can be: "I think I may embarrass myself in front of others. Then I will just die." "People will think that I am crap, so I just won't do that." "I am sure that people won't or don't like me, so I won't go."
- *Emotions.* "I feel fear in front of other people: this may happen, or that may happen, or I am not sure what will happen—so I had better either stay quiet and hope no one will notice me, or—better still—get out of this situation."
- *Sensations.* These vary, and can include heartbeat racing and pounding, chest feeling tight and painful, stomach churning, needing to go to the toilet, numbness or tingling in extremities, sweating, feeling faint, dizziness, blushing, stammering, and some of the other symptoms of general anxiety (mentioned in an earlier section).

These symptoms can then affect our actions, so we get a set of behavioural symptoms as well.

- *Behavioural.* Because of our thoughts and feelings, we might tend to avoid social situations. Because of this avoidance, we will not get any new evidence that we might be wrong, so we persist in these avoidance behaviours. These become a habit: "I don't like going out." This means that you probably cannot relax properly in any social situation: you might drink or smoke more, talk more quickly, etc. You might constantly rehearse what you are going to say; or only make very short social contacts, moving on quickly. You may not like talking on the telephone, or meeting new people.

Social anxiety is (supposedly) the third largest psychological problem in the world today—and possibly the least understood. People "know" that their fears are irrational, and do not make any sense, but that does not help much: they feel or believe something totally different. They can begin to avoid situations where they feel any anxiety.

This avoidance behaviour can eventually start to limit and constrain your life, as it keeps you from doing things, and from learning that you can cope and do other things. If a situation is avoided, then it can feel even more difficult the next time. Sometimes people get into the habit of "safety behaviours"—such as always going out with a friend—but these also prevent people learning to do things by themselves. Avoidance and safety behaviour is a form of fear of being afraid. You can even anticipate the fear and start to feel afraid.

Some people experience a more extreme form of social anxiety, and this is classified as a "social phobia". Just being told to do something different does not work: you have to experience doing the thing (that you fear) and only then do you discover that your fears are not justified. And you may have to do this gradually, and then over and over again. There is, therefore, a degree of desensitization to the phobic object(s) that needs to happen. This is probably best done with a specialist counsellor or psychotherapist. A few individual one-to-one sessions might be necessary at first to help understand the problem and perhaps the origins of it, and then you will need to start doing things that you have feared to do—in safe ways and in a step-by-step process. You might consider working in a small group at some point; a group of other people who also suffer from social anxiety.

Essentially, there is a step-by-step process of desensitization, or treatment, for social anxiety that is usually almost totally effective. In terms of self-help, some people go to public speaking groups, or book clubs, or something pretty safe at first. This then gives them a little more social confidence. So they can then go on to the next step. You can also do a lot more "checking". Most people with social anxiety rarely look to see how other people are actually reacting or responding to them, therefore their anxiety almost blinds them to their reality. They might find that people actually liked them, if they looked.

All these methods need to address the anxiety that lies behind social phobia. The previously mentioned techniques for working with anxiety will also work with social phobia. Please remember that this is not a disorder. It is just extremely common and can (fairly easily) be overcome.

There are a couple of support organizations for social anxiety and social phobia:

>www.social-anxiety.org.uk;
>www.socialanxietyonline.co.uk

While the recommended "treatment" for social anxiety and social phobia is usually described as CBT, and there is no doubt that you might need some help for the more extreme forms of social phobia, there is a lot you can do for yourself by re-learning and re-training the way you think about yourself in social situations that you fear. Self-help techniques have been shown to be reasonably effective for social anxiety.

Panic attacks

What are panic attacks?

Panic attacks are both a form and a symptom of anxiety disorder, and they are fairly common, occurring in 15–20% of the population. The symptoms of a panic attack are varied and can include a sudden onset of intense apprehension or nervousness, or actual fear or terror accompanied by a variety of physical symptoms, such as palpitations, pounding heart, or fast heart rate, sweating, trembling and shaking, difficulties in breathing, sensations of shortness of breath or smothering, feelings of choking, chest pain or discomfort, nausea or abdominal distress, feeling dizzy, unsteady, lightheaded, or faint, de-realization (feelings of unreality) or depersonalization (being detached from oneself), fear of losing control or going crazy, fear of dying, shaking, paresthesias (numbness or tingling sensations), chills or hot flushes, sweating, dry mouth, nausea, "jelly legs", visual difficulties, or that you cannot speak or think clearly, or fear that you might die, collapse, be having a heart attack, etc. If they occur very frequently, panic attacks can be seen as an anxiety disorder, or as accompanying anxiety disorders such as agoraphobia or social phobia.

Panic attacks are a fairly extreme stress reaction, perhaps more so than nausea, headaches, or diarrhoea, but also in some ways similar. They occur more frequently in women than men, yet also in healthy young adults. An attack can last for just a few seconds, more usually for about 5–10 minutes, or occasionally for as long as an hour, or be experienced as a series of short attacks. The experience may be very frightening, but—and this is most important—the panic attack is not dangerous in itself.

There is some evidence of an inherited potential. People who experience panic attacks also seem to be those who experience stress in their respiratory and cardiovascular system, rather than anywhere else. They can be affected by changes in hormone levels (as in menstruation or the menopause). Panic attacks are one of the symptoms that accompany acute stress, post traumatic shock, or sometimes agitated depression. They are slightly more common in people with asthma or diabetes, or if you have been taking stimulants (caffeine, amphetamines), or if you are withdrawing from tranquillizers. There is also a strong connection to the levels of carbon dioxide (CO_2) in the bloodstream.

While, especially the first time, it is quite common to *feel* as if you are having something like a heart attack, and indeed you may even be sent to hospital to make sure that you are *not* having a heart attack, the actual panic attack is relatively harmless in itself, although, of course, it is all very scary—after all, you are in a panic!

Very often, the panic attack can produce more fear and worry, so that the symptoms escalate and you get into an anxiety-spiralling effect, where the symptoms seem to feed on each other and increase. At this point, you have to stop the spiral, or somebody around you must help you stop it. This is actually quite simple to do, though not easy, since you are in a panic, and half-way up the walls, so to speak.

What happens?

The panic attack often involves quite strong physical feelings or body reactions, such as those mentioned above, or feeling breathless, one's heart racing, feeling suffocated or smothered, sudden sweating, tingling feelings, hot or cold flushes, clammy hands, shaking or trembling, ringing in the ears, upset stomach, nausea, faintness or dizziness. The emotional feelings involved might be a sudden rush of intense fear, or the person feeling they are losing control, or that something awful might happen to them. The thoughts that accompany panic attacks often include: "I am going mad"; "I am going to die"; "I am having a stroke or heart attack"; "I am going to embarrass myself"; "There is something wrong with me".

The fear of having such a panic attack can be almost as bad as the panic itself. Avoidance behaviours are quite common. If you are interpreting things as dangerous or horrible, they may seem more so, and then you are getting into a vicious spiral. However, don't panic! Panic attacks are treatable. It is possible to reduce the frequency of panic attacks by addressing one's general levels of anxiety and stress. It is possible to control an actual panic attack by taking a few very simple measures. Persistent panic attacks can also now be treated pharmacologically.

Panic attacks can last for a few seconds, or can continue for a longish period leaving one feeling shaken, tense and exhausted. People can really feel as if they are having a heart attack, angina, or a stroke and, the first time one happens, they often call out their GP or an ambulance. Once you have been diagnosed as having panic attacks or "panic disorder", this sort of medical intervention should not be necessary, as there are a number of other things that you can do for yourself—and anyway, there is nothing specifically wrong with you.

Panic attacks can sometimes be predicted, especially if they have happened to you in similar circumstances. Sometimes, however, they are unpredictable, and within a few seconds you can be in a state of panic. On occasion, you can wake up suddenly from sleep in the middle of the night in a state of panic, which is very frightening as there is no warning of an onset. The fear of dying during such nocturnal panic attacks is quite common.

Breathing

Hyperventilation is a form of very shallow, quick breathing, rather like panting. It is very common, if not endemic, in panic attacks, and, indeed, one's breathing holds the key to undoing and being able to control these panic attacks. This is dealt with in more detail the next section. One point: the commonly known about, short-term, "paper-bag" breathing technique is now not usually recommended, or is even actively discouraged. In the next section, we explore a much better and safer technique.

Behaviours

Behaviours associated with panic attacks include the inability to sit still, fidgeting, snapping at people, pacing up and down, having to leave the room suddenly, and frequent yawning or sighing. Sometimes, as mentioned, the fear of having another panic attack makes one limit one's actions, and then one either avoids places where an attack might be likely, such as busy shops, crowded places, etc., or one starts to avoid doing certain things for the same reason: exerting oneself, being alone, going to the cinema, having an argument, etc.

Avoidance behaviours.

Sometimes these behaviours can build up to a point at which they really begin to constrain or limit your life. You may be limiting your activities, or not doing things that you normally do, or doing them a lot less frequently. At this point you might even be becoming a little afraid of being afraid, or "phobic" (see the next section), as in agoraphobia, or even of becoming panicky in a certain situation, as in driving. There are various treatments for these different behaviours.

Examinations and tests

The main tests are to ensure that you are *not* having a heart attack or that there is not something else wrong with you. Some family background may be asked for; you may be asked about your alcohol and caffeine intake, and whether you have taken any over-the-counter or herbal medicines. You might receive an ECG (electrocardiogram) to check your heart activity, or possibly an EEG (electroencephalogram) if there is any risk of, or history of, seizures. There are no specific tests for panic attacks.

Working with panic attacks

If you experience reasonably frequent panic attacks, there are some very simple things that you can do to reduce the likelihood of having them, to prevent one happening, or even to stop an actual attack. The panic attack is your normal physiological fear reaction, but taken to an extreme and usually happening in an ordinary situation. The whole system (sympathetic part of the ANS) has become oversensitive, probably as a result of stress, trauma, or tiredness, and is now being triggered much too easily and too often.

Reduce the related problems

Many people who have panic attacks find that they are generally overstressed. If the panic attacks are related to your general level of stress, you *must* try to do something about this first. Aerobic exercise, relaxation tapes, meditation, and some cognitive therapy can all be very effective.

Some people have a drinking problem. The alcohol itself makes you more likely to have a panic attack, then you have a drink "to steady your nerves", and so a spiral begins. Try to stop this; get some help.

Depression, as well as anxiety, can also cause panic attacks, so this needs to be addressed, either by self-help techniques, counselling, or psychotherapy, or by medication, or by a combination of these. Some people have experienced a severe trauma, which is still largely unresolved. This can also precipitate panic attacks and some form of treatment (medication), as well as some form of therapy, is almost usually advisable in such cases, to start with.

Become more aware

It is really necessary to become more aware of when you might start to feel panicky, or when you start to get over-agitated: only then you can begin to do something about it. Even if the onset of a panic attack seems to be almost immediate, there is nearly always a build-up, even if it is a short one. Set up a mental alarm bell: get friends or family to give you some feedback; become more aware of the possible triggers to a panic attack; remember that there might also be background factors like lack of sleep, general stress levels, too low blood sugar, poor breathing patterns, and/or situations where you feel less secure.

When you start to become anxious, your breathing gets a bit shallower and faster, and you breathe out less than you breathe in. This has the effect of reducing the CO_2 that you breathe out and this starts to accumulate in your bloodstream. At some point down the line, the part of your brain (the hypothalamus) that monitors things like blood sugar levels (hunger) and blood fluid levels (thirst) gets triggered by these increased CO_2 levels and it thinks you are suffocating. So, it informs the rest of the brain that there is an emergency and switches on the alarm signals! A panic attack!

Remember that the panic attack symptoms are the body's normal fear reactions that are being exaggerated. There almost certainly is not an emergency. Nothing worse will happen. Stay in control. Accept the feelings you have; run them through you and do not let them run you. Stay with the present—what is happening *right now*. Do not run away, do not try to avoid the situation, or try to escape. Accept what feelings you have—*even the fear*. Do not let your feelings control you. Try not to fight the feelings of fear or panic; feel them. They will not kill you; breathe them in and out, allow yourself to feel them in your body, ground them, then rise above them.

Do something

It is important to do something, just one action that triggers you coming back into being in charge, and being in control. This might be to apply a little pressure at the pressure point on the inside of your wrist (either side of the tendons, where a travel sickness band has bobbles), or to make a deep, long out-breath, or just to sit down. Then consciously relax any tense muscles. Focus on basic relaxation techniques. Imagine the anxiety going down, bit by bit. The fact you have done something puts you back in control and the panic starts to lessen. All this becomes easier and more effective each time that you do it.

Breathe out

In a panic attack, it is very common to struggle for the in-breath, or to take very high, short, fast breaths. It is important—indeed absolutely necessary—to breathe in gently, hold it for a moment, and then breathe out very deeply—in order to change the oxygen/carbon dioxide balance in your blood stream. This should stop the attack within a few breaths. Focus on the out-breath first, and then the in-breath will follow. Force the air out of the open mouth and imagine you are fogging some glass—even try to give a little sigh with the out-breath. Then allow the breath to come back in, slowly and gently and breathe down right into the abdomen. Hold it for a moment at the top of the breath, to allow the oxygen to be absorbed into your bloodstream, and then breathe out strongly again, right down to the belly. Repeat this for a couple of times. Practise this regularly. Then you will know how to cope in a panic attack.

Things to avoid and not to avoid

There are some things to avoid: becoming over-tired, allowing your blood sugar levels to get too low, exerting yourself too much, especially in a stressful situation, caffeine, and alcohol. The feelings can be also maintained by continuing to worry about anything, including having a panic attack, over-breathing (hyperventilation), and avoidance of situations that make you nervous.

Don't avoid situations that make you feel afraid. Gradually take yourself closer, or more often, into the situations that give you these panic attacks. Choose "safe" times and ways to do this: discuss the situation and your fears first, practise, and then follow through on the agreed plan of action. This is called "graded practice".

Tips to prevent panic attacks

- Reduce your general levels of stress. There are a number of suggestions in earlier sections of this book.
- Take regular exercise and try to relax regularly as well. This combination is one of the best "stress-busters" known to both modern medicine and all humankind.
- Avoid caffeine and fizzy drinks. Try to reduce levels of sugar, tobacco, and alcohol. Avoid other drugs and stimulants.
- See if you can find ways to express yourself better: you don't have to be assertive, just to be clear. Take a few moments to work out what you need to say, then say it.
- Do not worry about having to sit down, or leave the room, or leave the store quite suddenly. Just make a simple statement of a few words, "I am sorry, I just have to leave for a few moments. I'll be back a bit later." Grab your things and get out.
- Develop various coping strategies: sit close to the door, use the acupressure point in your wrists (same as for travel sickness), be clear about your timing (so you know when you can leave).
- Try not to bottle up your emotions. Talk to a friend about how you are feeling, or another close family member, or give someone a ring, or write in your journal.
- Learn to breathe properly. Use your diaphragm (just below the ribs). Put one hand on your belly and one on your chest. Breathe in slowly (count to four): both hands should rise, belly and then chest. Breathe out slowly (count to four): both hands should fall, chest then belly. Focus on expelling the out-breath.

- Eat regularly (a little and often), drink 1.5–2 litres of water per day, avoid processed foods with high salt or sugar levels, avoid all fizzy drinks, keep your blood sugar levels stable.
- Join a local support group or an internet site for people with panic attacks; if there isn't one locally, start one up and tell your GP and other local doctors. You won't feel so isolated or alone, and you can discuss strategies and share feelings.
- Listen to your feelings: these are different from your thoughts. Ignoring them can cause internal stress. Ask yourself, "What do I feel about this?" There may be several different feelings.
- Don't set yourself unrealistically high expectations, avoid too many "should" or "must" statements, don't try to be "best", consider the more realistic concept of "good enough".
- Learn a relaxation technique (like the Autogenic Technique) and practise it regularly.
- Use imagery and "take" yourself to that ideal beach, or a meadow of flowers, or beside a mountain stream. Keep that image in the forefront of your mind as you relax.
- Challenge some of your negative thought patterns: "I can't do this"; "I can't stay here"; "I am going mad"; or "Something dreadful will happen". You can, you are not, and it won't. Only you can change these thought patterns—and they are not your thoughts, this is the "anxiety speaking". These thoughts are symptoms of your levels of anxiety.
- Try some positive thought forms, such as affirmations. "I am calm and in control." "I have the power to change this." "I feel strong and positive."
- Become more aware of the signals, and counteract them earlier. If you feel an attack coming on, think positively, sit down, breathe more easily. Take a few minutes.
- Don't depend on others being there, reassuring you, or doing it for you. It is better to rely on yourself. You can cope. You can change this pattern. It is relatively easy.

Phobias

Panic attacks plus

For some people, their levels of anxiety are much higher than those people with panic attacks or social anxiety, and their anxiety (or fear) becomes centred on, or central to, one or two specific areas. These people suffer from what are called "phobias", and they can experience irrational terror, dread, or panic whenever they are confronted with the feared object, situation, or activity.

The person experiencing the phobia may be able to recognize the irrational nature of the fear, but that doesn't stop it, and they cannot really seem to do anything about it. The level of anxiety caused by the phobia can become so disruptive or so extreme that they start to avoid a situation where they might experience that fear. They become afraid of having the fear. This is called "avoidant behaviour" or "avoidance behaviour", but it is really the fear of becoming afraid. Many people who suffer from a phobia therefore develop an overwhelming desire to avoid the source of fear, so much so that this desire (or fear) then interferes—sometimes quite seriously—with their ordinary, everyday family life, job, and social relationships.

Physical symptoms often accompany the intense anxiety of phobias and include blushing, profuse sweating, or trembling, as well as general symptoms of anxiety, including difficulty talking, nausea, or other stomach discomforts. Phobias can take a number of different forms, or be "attached" to a number of different areas, some of which are listed below.

- Social phobia, sometimes called "social anxiety disorder", is an excessive fear, often of being extremely embarrassed in front of other people. The most common social phobia is fear of public speaking, or of being in a public place and of something embarrassing happening. People might have a persistent, intense, and chronic fear of being watched and judged by others, or of being embarrassed or humiliated by something they themselves do. Their fear may be so severe that it interferes with their work, or school, or other ordinary activities. They might worry for days or weeks in advance of a dreaded social situation. Social phobia can cause diminished self-esteem and depression. To try to reduce their anxiety and alleviate depression, people with social phobia might abuse alcohol or other drugs, which can then lead to addiction. Some people with social phobia may also have other anxiety disorders, such as panic disorder or obsessive–compulsive disorder. About 5% of adults suffer from social phobia. Social phobia occurs twice as often in women as in men, although (unusually) a higher proportion of men seek help for this disorder. The disorder typically begins in childhood or early adolescence and rarely develops after the age of twenty-five. For more information, visit www.social-anxiety.org.uk.
- Agoraphobia is the fear of being in a situation that might trigger a panic attack and from which it is difficult to escape. People who have severe agoraphobia become virtually housebound. Others avoid open spaces, standing in line, large shops, or being in a crowd. This can be treated the same as all the other phobias, but it is a little more difficult logistically, as the people helping you might first have to come to you, as you cannot get to them.
- Specific phobias relate to specific objects or situations, such as flying, heights, needles, spiders, or snakes. They are generally

more common in women than in men, and tend to emerge during childhood. They are (largely unfounded) fears of particular objects or situations. Specific phobias can be attached to an almost an unlimited number of objects or situations. A diagnosis of a phobia can be made if any exposure to the feared object or situation causes high levels of anxiety (often experienced as a panic attack).

Causes

Phobias usually arise from a combination of external events and various internal predispositions. In a famous experiment, a psychologist, Martin Seligman, used a technique to establish phobias for snakes and flowers. The results of the experiment showed that it took far fewer "shocks" to create an adverse response to a picture of a snake than to a picture of a flower, leading to the conclusion that certain objects may have a genetic predisposition to being associated with fear. Some specific phobias can be traced back to a specific triggering event, usually a traumatic experience at an early age. Some phobias, like social phobia and agoraphobia, have more complex causes that are essentially not known.

There is some evidence that phobias are "connected" to an oversensitization of the amygdala, a part of the mid-brain's limbic or emotional system. The amygdala releases hormones into the body, sometimes stress hormones and these can trigger the "fight-or-flight" system.

Treatment of phobias

Various forms of treatment seem to be effective for the very different phobias. These can include medication (to reduce the "startle" reflex), or specific forms of short-term psychotherapy, sometimes based on cognitive–behavioural therapy (CBT). CBT can be particularly useful in treating social phobia. When used for specific or social phobia, this treatment is based on a procedure known as "exposure therapy", which involves helping people choose to expose themselves to the fear object, realize that this is not quite as frightening as "perceived", and then become gradually more comfortable with those situations that frighten them.

Therapy can also include anxiety management training and "cognitive restructuring" to help people identify their misperceptions. Supportive therapy such as group therapy, or couple or family therapy, can help to educate relatives about the disorder, and some people with social phobia can benefit from social skills training.

Phobias are very treatable, once diagnosed: because as many as 85% of those who seek treatment for phobias should be able to resume normal activities following their treatment. Recovery can happen after only a couple of months, but can take longer, depending on individual circumstances and the severity of the disorder.

Some children have severe and specific phobias: these should be taken seriously and not dismissed. Children often have phobias about the dark, being alone, water, insects, spiders, bees, heights, choking, snakes, particular colours or foods, dogs, birds, mice, and other animals. These phobias can interfere with their normal life, education, or sociality. Effective treatment is available.

List of phobias

There are some quite interesting lists of phobias: these can be found on various websites (e.g., Wikipedia). There are usually then links that can be found to various self-help groups and further information. I have mentioned agoraphobia—fear of open places—and claustrophobia is a fear of confined spaces; however, many people suffer from emetophobia (fear of vomiting) or haemophobia (fear of blood) without perhaps realizing that, technically, they have a phobia. So don't get too worried, unless this phobia is actually running your life in some way.

General anxiety disorder

So far we have been discussing fairly mild levels of anxiety and what can be done with them. However, some people suffer from what is called general anxiety disorder (GAD). They are affected by levels of unrealistic or excessive anxiety, and seem to worry about nearly everything; essentially, they worry all the time. For example, they may have consistent worries about financial matters, even though their bank balance is perfectly healthy and there is no sign of any major debts, or they worry about their health, even though they have had a recent check-up and nothing wrong was found. Their level of anxiety is much higher and *much* more persistent than most people. This might have lasted for a long time, but maybe recently it got worse. The reason this description is included here is so that people who do *not* have GAD can eliminate themselves. However, if you do have GAD, you will be able to do quite a lot with the basic self-help techniques that are listed for anxiety.

There is more of a psychological basis to GAD, and, while the symptoms of GAD seem to have no particular cause, they are certainly more intense than reasonable. The symptoms include chronic anxiety, exaggerated worry, restlessness, tension, and irritability, problems in concentration, difficulties in going to sleep, or remaining asleep. In addition to the psychological symptoms, people with GAD often experience some physical symptoms. These can include fatigue, muscle tension, muscle aches, difficulty swallowing, twitching, irritability, hot flushes, trembling, headaches, dizzy spells, twitching, muscle tension, aches and pains, stomach upsets, and sweating. Patients with GAD often feel anxious, shaky, easily upset, and often report that they feel on edge. They are sometimes even unaware of the levels of tension and anxiety that they experience; they seem to be able to blank it out, as it is (or has been) such a part of their everyday existence.

Anxiety that is based on general levels of stress or depression (already described), or on a real situation, such as financial worries from having lost one's job, is *not* a sign of GAD. The essential feature of GAD is an unreasonable or persistent worry that is *not* related to any other source or anxiety. If someone is experiencing chronic or excessive worry about events that are quite unlikely to occur, there may be a cause for to consider that that person may be suffering from GAD.

The level of anxiety experienced by people with GAD is very difficult to control consciously, and can cause considerable complications in their daily life, at home, at work, and in social settings. Most people with GAD claim that they have felt anxious for most of their entire life, and other family members would usually support this. The disorder can emerge during childhood or adolescence; however, onset of the disorder in an adult is also quite common. One of the relatively common features seems to be a parent who was also depressed or anxious. GAD is not a mental illness; it is a psychological disorder that can—surprisingly—be relatively easily treated.

Simple as the causes are or the remedies might seem (it is certainly not rocket-science), they are also not "easy" in that they—the remedies—demand persistence, perseverance, and patience, as well as a degree of bloody-mindedness. More on this later.

The current "expert" working hypothesis is that GAD is probably caused by a combination of both biological factors and fairly extreme life events. Many people with GAD have also suffered from other medical disorders at some point in their life. There seem to be some resultant changes in the brain chemistry of people with

GAD, especially particular abnormalities in the levels of the neurotransmitter, serotonin. There does not seem to be a specific genetic component; however, anxious behaviour can easily be "learnt" from being brought up by an anxious parent and this can sometimes condense into GAD or give someone a propensity in adulthood towards GAD.

While ordinary levels of anxiety are among the most treatable of all mental health issues, and self-help techniques and counselling are usually very effective for this, the treatment for GAD often involves the use of some medication, especially in severe cases, as well as some psychotherapy.

The most commonly used anti-anxiety medications are the benzodiazepines such as Diazepam, Alprazolam, or Lorazepam. Other drugs, such as Buspirone, can be helpful for some individuals with GAD. SSRIs and newer anti-depressants also show some benefits. Anti-psychotic drugs can be useful in very severe cases. The main problem is that anti-anxiety drugs, like Valium or Temazepam, are basically quite addictive, so alternatives (possibly slightly less effective) have to be used. Once you, and your health professional, have established a medication that works for you, don't stop taking it. Do NOT stop taking it as soon as you feel a little bit better, or you might relapse.

If you think that you, or a member of your family, suffers from GAD, it is therefore important to consult your/their GP, and possibly get a further psychological or psychiatric referral, just to ensure you get the best possible diagnosis and treatment. There is also quite a lot of self-help information available and you might want to consult this, or the various listed websites. Type "general anxiety disorder" into a search engine.

Other anxiety disorders

There are several other "disorders" based on anxiety. Social anxiety disorder has been mentioned; this can also be found in the more serious condition of social phobia.

Obsessive–compulsive disorder (OCD) is also based on levels of extreme anxiety. If you think you suffer from OCD, get a referral from your GP to a Department of Clinical Psychology. OCD is a treatable condition, but you will probably need some help to get over this.

All of these anxiety disorders can be likened to an old-fashioned pressure cooker. Once one's anxiety levels start to increase, then they seem to gather their own momentum. The "pressure" builds up and up. At some point, the anxiety will leak out. Whether it will appear in the form of panic attacks, or social anxiety, or phobias, or OCD depends on the person's "psychic makeup".

It is important not to get "hooked" on the symptom; the problem underlying all of these is an increase in the basic level of anxiety. It is this that needs to be "treated".

SELF-ESTEEM ISSUES

Introducing issues of self-esteem

In the Bible it says, "Pride goeth before destruction, and a haughty spirit before a fall" (Proverbs, 16, v. 18). In Ancient Greece, one of the great sins was that of hubris—an overwhelming pride or arrogance that meant that you thought that you were like a God—so the Gods punished this "sin" and brought about your downfall. This was one of their belief systems, anyway. In the Middle Ages, the prevailing Christian view of man in relation to God ran along these lines, written by Thomas à Kempis:

> But if I abase myself, and bring myself to nought, and shrink from all self-esteem, and grind myself to dust, which I am, Thy grace will be favourable unto me, and Thy light will be near unto my heart; and all self-esteem, how little so ever it be, shall be swallowed up in the depths of my nothingness, and shall perish for ever. [Kempis, 1427]

However valid these views may have been then, they are not really so relevant for us, in relation to other people, at least six hundred years later. These are all pretty much "either ... or ..." views in that there is a basic polarization: pride = fall, etc. What seems to work better nowadays is more of a "both ... and ..." perspective:

where two seemingly opposing views are both held as reasonably valid. Thus, we can *both* relish our accomplishments *and* tread a reasonable line to stay clear of excessive pride or narcissism. If we hold a different opinion, we may be seen as *both* "eccentric" *and* "interesting": that is not necessarily a bad thing.

One of the major components of depression, possibly even a source of depression, is low self-esteem. Robert Frost, the American poet, said, "Depression occurs when one looks back with no pride, and looks forward with no hope". However, low self-esteem has other much more negative effects.

If you have low self-esteem, you might not be willing to risk anything in trying to learn something different. If you have too high self-esteem, then you don't think you need to learn anything new. It is a tricky and narrow road to walk. There is little doubt that most people would benefit from an improvement in their self-esteem. There is, therefore, a section following on "Low self-esteem", what to do about it, and how to become more assertive, and stand up for your "rights".

Low self-esteem

Low self-esteem can be a subtle and corrosive destroyer. It is characterized by negative statements that you make (or believe) about yourself. In your early life, usually up to about two years old, at least, you had self-esteem coming out of every pore of your body. It was your world: everything in it was there for You. Anyway, that is how you perceived yourself then. Some time after that, as you progressed through childhood, you began to lose this self-esteem, or this perception was taken away from you, or it slipped away, or was eroded or corroded, as you realized that other people also existed. Some of these people around you even had rights—sometimes it might have seemed that they had rights over you, or they seemed to be more important than you. This is often (unfortunately) a necessary part of growing up—at least to a certain extent. I happen to believe that most parents overdid this process a little bit and might have denied their children certain rights, such as respect and, thus, self-respect. This inevitably erodes their self-esteem.

However, there is one way, and one way only, to get your self-esteem back. It doesn't come as a gift. It isn't found somewhere outside of yourself. You can't earn it back, or win it in a lottery, or find it around the next corner or in a cornflakes packet. You have to start to reclaim it back—for yourself—by yourself!

You need to recognize that the particular negative statements that you carry about yourself have a particular flavour or style. Some of them are characterized by, "I should..." or "I ought to..." or "I am always... like that". In these statements, you may have exaggerated the "negative" aspects and got your potentially "positive" situation out of perspective. You may have over-generalized your faults and thus consider yourself an absolute failure. Sometimes this is because you have made just one mistake. You may consistently ignore (or not even take in) any positive statements about yourself: "They are just saying that to be nice." You may "know" that people are thinking "bad" things about you, even without checking with them (or anyone else): "They must be, because I am 'bad'" (or whatever).

You may also see things in very "black-and-white" terms: you are either "good" or "bad", and, since you are obviously not "good", since you make mistakes, or have uncharitable thoughts, or have heavy thighs, or whatever, then you must—absolutely inevitably—be "bad". This is not good or constructive thinking.

This recognition process is not easy. These things have built up, or you have constructed this view about yourself, over time. Originally it might have been for very good reasons. It might have helped you survive a very difficult situation: a critical mother (perhaps), or a repressive home or school situation. If you wanted or needed affection (and you might have wanted that desperately), you would then have had to "agree" with the predominant message, "You are the source of the problems in the family."

Or your father might have wanted a boy—sorry, you are a girl, "not good enough". Or your father might have wanted you, his son, to have all the advantages that he never had, and to succeed where he didn't. Sorry, you are human. You are still his son. But maybe not the imaginary super-son that he wanted to fulfil all his ambitions. But whose problem was this?

In such instances, s/he (your mother or father) could not accept you, their child, just for what you were. That is painful. To survive this pain, you had to, or chose to, adopt a position of low self-esteem. "I will succumb to your (obvious) disappointment in me."

There are other ways of losing your self-esteem: critical messages from the school or the playground, a trauma, accident or event that somehow sets you apart, the loss of a beloved grandparent, some physical defect, scar, or birthmark, or a sudden weight gain, or something similarly traumatic, or perhaps just a slow, cold, corrosion.

It is going to take some time to exorcise these early messages, whatever they were, from your psyche. You have been carrying them around and living according to these "rules" for many years. However, these messages were ones that you had to, or chose to, adopt. They are not actually messages about who you are. They are thus not necessarily true.

Please remember that these thoughts and feelings have become YOUR perception of yourself. They have nothing to do with who you *really* are. In the same way that your parents could not see you as you were—they only saw that you were not what they wanted you to be—you are not seeing yourself as who you really are. You are only seeing one particular aspect of yourself, from one particular (poor) perspective.

If you are going to develop any sort of positive self-esteem, you really need to start to fight back and claim it back. You need to develop a new perspective. You need to challenge this eternally negative or self-critical voice. You need to "dump the critic" and consider some different thought forms. Please, do not discount your capabilities here. You can do this, if you really want to. But you are going to have to break that mould; that one of low self-esteem. You have going to have to be much less modest, and talk more openly about how you feel, and what you want. We know that "You shouldn't blow your own trumpet", but you are going to have to do this a little bit more (or a lot more) than you ever did before. You are going to have to find a way of feeling good about yourself. This will seem like having to cross a socially unacceptable line; you have never done this, or dared to do this before. Unfortunately, there is no other way.

But keep working steadily with this. You will need lots of practice, at first. Develop ways to check out your negative thoughts, and get some other (or more objective) feedback. Label these: "John thinks I am ..."; "Peter thinks I am ..."; "Mary thinks I am ..."; and so on. This is a crucial part of the first step. Now you are going to have to do something a little bit more.

Your negative thoughts and feelings about yourself have created a pattern of behaviour of putting yourself down (or not putting yourself forward) and a thought form (something like, "You are not good enough") that reinforces this, with a whole raft of secondary feelings built up to support all of this.

Sorry! But it is wrong, and it is a lie—and you must really try and see this—because it is only one, usually very small and sometimes quite distorted, aspect of who you really are, the complete "you". You developed this way of thinking, behaving and being, probably because you needed to survive a difficult emotional situation. That situation has now changed, but you haven't. There is a different way of thinking and behaving available—at your fingertips. But you have to want to reach out for it, knowing somewhere that the old pattern, now pretty dysfunctional, is capable of being broken down and disappearing, and a new pattern establishing itself. Others have done it, now you can do it. As the L'Oreal TV commercial says, "You're worth it!"

I am deliberately making this sound quite simple: it is—but it is by no means easy. It is quite an entrenched pattern to break, and you may really need some help and support from your friends. Or you might need a little professional counselling, or some self-esteem classes, just for a while, in order to implement these changes fully. You can also get involved in a self-esteem group so that you can get together with some friends and change your life. Maybe you can run one of these for others in due course.

The old pattern is quite embedded. You will need to fight it specifically. You may need to start to say to yourself: "I am a worthwhile person because ..." and then choose one, just one, particular thing that you can do, or something is good about you, or that you can do well. Build on this. This could be something successful you have done, or something you worked hard at, or a natural quality or kindness. Work hard to get a foot in the door. "At least I can do this reasonably well. That means something." Then choose something else. You can gradually build up a succession of positive statements. These will slowly begin to replace the negative statements that you have developed, and held on to, about yourself.

These positive statements are as true, if not more so, than the negative ones. This is the first step. It has to be done. Only you know yourself well enough to be able to do it. However, you can also ask your close friends. They might see something you cannot see—yet!

To a certain extent this type of self-esteem is conditional, as it is dependent on various things that you have done, on parts of your persona, on your opinions, etc. And, however well this works, this is still conditional self-esteem. Conditional self-esteem has some benefits, as it affirms some of your talents and skills; it may motivate you to work hard, and to do your best, or to try to be a nice person. But conditional self-esteem also has its disadvantages; it is vulnerable to circumstances. What happens if you are not as productive and successful as you think that you should be? What happens if the firm is taken over, or closes, and you are made redundant? Or if someone close to you leaves? Does this mean that you are now worthless? Or inferior? Of course not, but it certainly feels that way. Your first steps towards better self-esteem can thus easily be corroded. Our culture or society is based on a very few "winners" getting all the glory—and there is an implication that the rest of us are thus essentially "losers". We admire the winners, and yet we know (somewhere inside) that we will never be one of them. The "star", or "hero" culture reinforces this and is only useful for selling magazines and TV programmes. We live vicariously: in our imaginations we are, or want to be, like them, especially if we buy this product, or support this team, or pop group, or whatever. This is quintessentially quite depressing.

We are thus continually reinforcing our lack of self-esteem. So, then we need a new washing machine, or a car, or a holiday, or a new girlfriend/boyfriend to make ourselves feel better. So it goes on and on. The advertisers and the magazines love it. However, we can turn this situation around. We can start to disengage our self-esteem from these superficial needs, or conditions. We can start to feel independently "good enough". We can start to see that everyone, even the rich and famous, have their weak points (even though this sells more magazines and TV shows). We can step out of this "good/bad" image and say, "Yes, I like them ... but I am not like them." We can start to see that we might—just possibly—not want to be in their shoes. Oh, we'd like their success, but not their problems. Dream on! The two go hand-in-hand. You cannot have one without the other. Stick with yourself. What are *you* good at? What works for you? What doesn't? What do you feel? What does this make you want or need? How can you start to get it for yourself?

Unconditional self-esteem

Unconditional self-esteem is not so vulnerable; it is just a little harder to get your head around what it is. You can start to try to respect yourself just because you are "you": a unique human being. On the one hand, you are ordinary, like most other people. And, moreover, there is also no one else exactly like you on this planet—and never has been. This is a pretty amazing thing, actually. You can start to try to respect yourself for no other reason than you have decided to change your life and to stop living with low self-esteem. You can start to try to like yourself just because you need compassion and support, and not because you have (or have not) earned it. You can start to try to admire yourself because you are the best expression of "you" that you have managed to come up with—yet! Certainly there are some rough edges still, but hey! All these concepts are totally independent of any outside circumstances: they are unconditional. They actually do boost your self-esteem. See if you can think up some others.

Such thoughts help to build a new feeling about yourself. You can start to look at different areas of your life, away from the "comfort zone" that you might have built for yourself. You could possibly change many different aspects of yourself—just because you wanted to. It is your life; you can live it your way. Here are some of the areas of possible growth or change: personal friends; job or career; family; leisure time; financial; education; tidiness, timeliness, and efficiency; health; image and self-image; appearance; living situation; etc. Try to change one of them at least. A success in one area can then lead to a change in a different area. It really is one step at a time, and then another step, and another. You get to decide what you want to change: that is the way things are going to happen from now on.

Exercise

Imagine, for a moment, that you have a cloak: the Cloak of Unconditional Self-Esteem—a bit like the Cloak of Invisibility in the Harry Potter books and films. Try putting this cloak on and wearing it for a few minutes. How does it make you feel? What does "unconditional self-esteem" do for you? What is different? What might you want to do differently? Explore this for a moment or two.

Then choose one of the above areas—just as an exercise, still wearing this cloak—and take a few minutes to consider: if you were going to make some changes in this area, what would they be? The changes are all designed to help you to be more yourself. They are not selfish, putting you before other people. They are not self-effacing, putting other people before you. You and others co-exist equally. You like some things, they like other things. No problem. Now, consider what changes you might like to instigate.

- Fed up with doing the chores? Then imagine having a cleaner come in twice a week. Or imagine putting up a rota for other members of the household to do some of the chores. How would you feel if that happened?
- If you had (say) £2,000 for a total makeover (as Trinny and Susanna sometimes offer on TV), what would you do? How might you feel about yourself then? It isn't an impossible amount.
- If you could change places with someone for a week, what different things would you do? Then bring that experience back into your present life: what changes might you make now?
- If you were put in charge of the office for a week, what changes would you make there? Have you tried making one or two suggestions? Even anonymously?
- If you could be more yourself, that "unique you", what would you do differently; how would you be different? How might this feel?

Now choose another area and try imagining some changes in that area. Then try a third. Fine, end of exercise. Keep the cloak on for just a few minutes more. Nice, isn't it?

Now—what is stopping you making some of those changes right now? Who is stopping you? Please try to avoid the (almost inevitable) "Yes, but . . ." response. Please also remember that I am trying to make this simple, but I do not presume, for a moment, that it is going to be easy. However, it is possible. You are still wearing the "Cloak of Unconditional Self-Esteem". How could you be more like You—or like what, or who, You Really Are? You can take the cloak off now—if you want to. Or you can imagine that you can wear it a little more permanently. Or, maybe, it is now just "Yours". You decide!

Self-esteem strategies

Here are some basic self-esteem strategies. Some of the advantages of, and the ways to attain, something of this unconditional or self-determined self-esteem are listed below.

- You will be able to enjoy life more, when you are not worrying so much about yourself. If you are all right, then you're all right. You will not have to continually defend yourself against that critical inner voice that tells you you're inadequate, or whatever. Life gets easier. If you start to like and accept yourself more, you will have a greater capacity to like or love others. Indeed, some people would say this is a prerequisite to liking other people.
- This is a step-by-step learning process. Keep going with it and you will achieve it. It is not a "win-or-lose", "pass-or-fail" situation, like an exam. It is more like learning how to ride a bike, or swim, or cook. With more practice, you just get better at it. You are not trying to boost your self-esteem with any unreal statements. Stick to the truth! If you are not so afraid of failing, then you can become more adventurous. Try to conquer your fear!
- With just a little more self-esteem, you can start to feel more equal to people. As a person you are as good as them. You can try to walk a bit taller, be a bit bolder, and act a bit more confidently. You have your own special attributes, *and* so do they. This way, you step out of the "good/bad", "inferior/superior" polarity. You are right and they are right. This way you can become more independent.
- You will start to see things much less two-dimensionally: good/bad, black/white, up/down, either/or. Things can

become both "this" and "that". This gives everyone many more possibilities and much greater flexibility.
- You will expand yourself with these possibilities. You will grow. You might start to explore the things that you have always wanted to do, but never perhaps had enough self-confidence to do before.
- You can start to face any shortcomings that you do happen to have much more openly and honestly; using these suggestions as a method of, or guide to, self-improvement. This is better than hiding them, or not wanting to look at them, because that might erode what little self-esteem you have.
- You will also be able to hear, and accept, any guidance or criticism much better, because your self-esteem will be more grounded and self-determined. You will become less defensive. You can begin to feel better about yourself, and you can enjoy life more, as you will not constantly be worrying whether you are "good enough" or not. You are "good enough".
- Greater self-esteem will *not* mean that you become self-centred or insensitive to the needs of others. You may fear that, but you have a very long way to go before you ever cross that line. Actually, you will probably become more considerate to others as you happen to know what some of the "downside" is like.
- Life won't seem quite so critical or fragile. You will probably be able to face the rise and fall of things going well, or not so well, more philosophically and with greater equanimity. Disappointments will not destroy you—they haven't done so already—and you will be able to build on some of your successes.
- You may begin to realize that you were responding to the world from quite a hurt and wounded place. This is not the only place to view it from. Those hurts and wounds, while valid and true and in need of healing, are not your only reality. You can step beyond them to a better viewpoint.
- In relationships, you can start to become more of an equal, instead of being almost totally dependent on whether s/he loves you or not. This opens many new possibilities in the relationship: you might agree to disagree, instead of one person being "right" and the other "wrong", for example. Or you might, just occasionally, say, "No!" or "Why not?"

- You will start to feel stronger about speaking up whenever you think something is going wrong, or sharing your perspective, which might just be equally as valuable as anyone else's—or better.
- Practise in small, relatively safe ways at first: in the family, in the group in the office, with your friends. Then allow the positive feedback to build your self-confidence. If there is negative feedback, don't let that stop you. Just try again.
- This process is the process that begins to heal these psychic wounds of low self-esteem. You don't have to do anything else.

Improving self-esteem

Basic principle

One of the main reasons behind a general lack of self-esteem or self-confidence is that these naturally occurring feelings have been eroded over a long period of time. If this erosion started in early childhood, it is possible that even the concept of self-esteem or self-confidence might seem strange or alien. There is really only way to get it back: one just needs to claim it—or reclaim it. Listed below are a few techniques gleaned from other (sometimes famous) people's suggestions, adapted from a series of women's magazine articles.

- Look confident, even if you are quaking inside.
- Try looking after yourself, being nice to yourself, giving yourself a treat on a regular basis, being luxurious with yourself.
- Be realistic about what you ask for, then stick to it.
- It's better to be honest, even outrageously so, than to lie or evade. People always know.
- A truly confident person doesn't rely on the assessment of other people.

- Doing something you really want to do gives you a fantastic sense of self-worth.
- Many people have "the impostor syndrome"—where you feel someone's going to expose you for who you really are. Try just to be true to yourself.
- As a child you have no armour, so when bad things start to happen you start to think something's wrong with you. It seems there's no way out. A large part of confidence is banishing the feeling it must all be your fault.
- Learning to develop a "mask" or "professional persona" is a good short-term measure. Later on you should drop it. You will want to be accepted for who you really are.
- Learning jujitsu, or some other martial art, gives a woman a fantastic sense of confidence. You can think, "I can flatten this bloke if I want to."
- The courage to take risks comes from knowledge and experience. This means you have to take risks carefully and learn from your mistakes. The first time is the worst.
- Most successful people will acknowledge they could not have done it by themselves. Confidence alone is a great start: confidence backed up by other people is unstoppable.
- No one should ever tell anyone that they cannot do something. It is very provocative and they are inevitably proved wrong.
- The more you experiment and practise, the more you will feel sure about yourself.
- One way of dealing with anxiety-provoking situations is the "Don't Panic" rule. Take a deep breath; don't panic; and you will "wing it" somehow.
- Recognize when you are having an off-day and don't try to change it. Go home and get cosy.
- Whatever you are up against, there is always a way to succeed or get through.
- Never assume you are going to be great. Don't try to be fantastic. The key to success is not to put too much pressure on yourself. Just give it your best.
- Other people may look relaxed or confident, but most of them are feeling just like you, and so they are faking it.

- Eventually you will have to learn to stop worrying about yourself, and become more concerned with other people. This makes you very good company.
- If you find meeting new people difficult, there are ways of making it easier. When you go out, always wear something you feel good in. Don't get stuck in a corner; just circulate—you'll look confident even if you aren't feeling it. Have a couple of opening gambits.
- It is important to stretch yourself. Imagine your epitaph: "She tried everything, took it all in her stride, and gave it a go."
- Confidence comes from knowing you will cope, that you will get over any mistakes, that you gave your best. In the end, that is all that matters.

Using some of these strategies, which have all worked successfully, can make you start to like yourself a little more, to believe in yourself a little more, to acknowledge that you have a "self" and that it is a worthwhile one. This leads on to the next major step.

Earlier, it was said that you, and only you, can reclaim your self-esteem. This is true. But what is this self-esteem? You may not have had it for a long while. You may not know what self-esteem really is. It is not just one thing. It is made up of a number of components. You will have to reclaim each of these components.

Claiming your body

It is now generally accepted that we have the right not to be enslaved, not to be assaulted, not to be physically oppressed or endangered in a relationship, or at work. It is our body, and, within reasonable limits whereby we do not hurt or endanger others, we can do what we like with it. We can be advised not to smoke or eat too much, but we cannot be prevented from doing so. We can donate a kidney to someone else. There may be consequences, and it is we who shall suffer them. Similarly, if we go skiing and break our leg, mountain climbing and exhaust or hurt ourselves, or tattoo or pierce our body, it is essentially our right to treat our body how we like. We should not really need to reclaim our body. Some people are enslaved in the sex industry; others are treated brutally at home, or endangered at work. These people need to get help and support to restore the basic situation of self-autonomy.

Claiming your space

Just as you have a right of determination over your own body, so you have the right to your own space—whether it is physical space, psychic space, head-space, or whatever. You exist, so you have the right to a proper space to exist in. You have the right to breathe, to stretch, and to take up space. Just claim it. As a citizen of a modern state, you also have the right to have a space to live in. You may need to claim this, but you do not have to be homeless. There are, of course, homeless people, and people evicted from or fleeing from their own home state, and they also need our help. They have the right to claim asylum. You have the right to your space as well.

These are largely accepted rights and you do not have to apologize for existing. You also do not have to be sorry that you are here, alive, a member of the human race. The planet is actually a richer, more varied place with you (and others unlike you) on it. You have as much need for the right to a space of your own as anyone else on the planet, and that means a safe space, somewhere where you feel safe. If you do not have this, you should have it. You need it. Try to claim it.

You should have a room in a house, or a space or place in the house that you live in, that you feel is rightfully *yours*, so that you can go there and not be disturbed. You can go there and feel comfortable; you can go there and do whatever you want to do, or just do nothing, where you feel "safe" or "at home". We all need this sort of space. You might need to claim yours.

Claiming the right to speak

You also have the right to hold any political, social or other opinions *and* the right to a basic freedom of speech, as long as you do not promote the oppression of others (racism, terrorism, or similar). You will certainly have your own unique perspective on things, as no one can see things exactly your way, because they are not you.

Your views and perspectives may have never been fully or clearly formulated, expressed, or heard. That does not make them any less important; it actually makes them more important. You could try to find your voice and speak them out. It could be very interesting to hear what you have to say, as your views are important—they matter. If they are not heard, you may feel ignored and, also, others may miss out on something different, something valuable. So just speak out what your views are—clearly and simply. Choose a moment when no one else is speaking and just say them. Claim this right—the right to speak—as well.

Claiming the right to be heard

Are you *really* less important than anyone else? They seem to be able to claim the right to be heard: they speak up. Why not you? Why is your voice any less significant? Or do you not happen to claim this right for yourself?

Part of reclaiming one's self-esteem is also reclaiming this right to be heard. You may have been shouted down in the past. You may not have dared to speak out—in the past. But this is now, the present, times are different and things are changing. You can now claim your right to be heard, and to speak out.

The growth of Internet "blogs" and chat rooms, people's petitions and charters, radio phone-ins, letters to the newspapers, and so forth is all part of people claiming the right to speak out, to share their views, and to be heard. Don't exclude yourself. You have a valid point of view and someone out there will almost certainly want to hear it, may well be affected or influenced by it, and may even want to respond to it. If others can do this, why not you?

Claiming your ground

You also have the right to stand on firm ground. Everyone needs to be a degree of surety, of security, of consistency. Chaos is not all right. Domination is not all right. You may need to determine what your ground is, as no one else can really do this for you. So, when you are standing on it, then claim it. Find the place or space that works for you. As a child, you probably had a "special" place that you went to at times just to feel yourself. Why not as an adult?

Don't shift about just because others seem to want to be were you are standing. It is not just to do with physical ground, it has also to do with intellectual or emotional ground. Don't always defer to others: why are they any more important than you? If you claim an intellectual position, defend it until it is proved to be untenable, then adopt a better position. If it is a moral ground, and you think you are right, then that is what you believe. Stick to it, until you are proved incorrect.

You are there and I am here: we are both present. That is your position and *this* is my position. We may be close to each other, *and* there may be subtle differences. Maybe we can agree, and maybe there are subtle differences, so we may have to agree to differ, or even disagree. Your being "right" does not make me "wrong". My having a valid point of view does not deny the value of what you say or feel. Try to claim the validity of both: your ground is valid as long as my ground is also valid.

Rights with, not rights over

All of these rights that you are claiming, or reclaiming, are not rights over someone else, but rights with someone else. In the past, someone else's rights might have superseded yours, or you might have felt that someone else was more important or needy than you, and so you gave over your rights in favour of theirs. Maybe you had to, because the situation was oppressive. If people laughed at what you said in school, or ignored what you said at home, then you might have learnt to shut up, thinking that your views were not valid. Just because other people—then—could not or would not listen does not invalidate your views. Expressing your views does not invalidate theirs. And now you are reclaiming your rights. These are not rights that are more important than anyone else's—except to you. They are rights that you are claiming—equal to anyone else's rights. The only difference is that that you have not been claiming them for a while.

Other people may have to adapt to this new situation. They may have to make a little room for you—because you are now more "present". This should not diminish them in any way—it just levels the playing field. It may mean some changes, but it does not mean disastrous changes. These are not bad changes, they are changes that make things more equal—ultimately better for everyone. Other people may not want to change, they may not like the "new you"—tough! You like the new you. You are now claiming your space, your ground, your right to speak, your right to be heard, and all your other rights. This is who you are NOW. Now you are reclaiming all these rights and, with them, your self-esteem.

This just takes practice

Like everything, it will take a while to do this and get it right for you. It sounds simple: it is, but it is not easy. There are a thousand scripts telling you that "You shouldn't do this"; "Other people won't like you"; "You are selfish"; "You should think of others"; etc., etc., etc. It is time to ignore these a bit. Don't listen to these scripts. You have listened to them for years, and you have ended up where you are now. You do NOT need to do this again. This is a habit that needs to be broken. You are stopping doing this now. Reclaim your self-esteem. Now!

The rest of your life starts now. Yes, you will listen to the old scripts again, at times, but their power over you is broken. You have now reclaimed your right to choose. Sometimes you may choose the old way, that doesn't totally serve you (you are human and fallible), and sometimes you will choose the new way, and this does serve you, and ultimately everyone else. You decide for yourself.

We embody what we think and feel

Are you still carrying the cares of others? Are you putting yourself last—again? Are you being a little bit quiet or mousey in the corner? What would you look like, or feel like, if you stopped doing these things? How would you like to stand, or move, or look?

Just check out how you feel about yourself. How are you holding your body? Are you standing up straight? Are you nervous or jerky? Could you look a little less depressed, or anxious? What happens when you embody some of these changes? What would a calmer, stronger, more confident you look like? Think your body into this sort of state of being, just for a moment. Now do it for a little bit longer. Walk about like this for a little. Do you begin to like being who you are just a little bit more?

Take a deep breath—in your upper chest area. Allow your back to straighten, and your shoulders to drop, and gently reset the upper part of your body. Take in a couple of deep breaths. Shift your shoulders about a little and reset them. Hold your head up a little more. Turn your head from side to side, to straighten out your neck. Then look straight ahead. Stretch your jaw out, yawn a little, then allow it all to reset. Take another deep breath, and breathe out. Try relaxing into this new position.

Now choose—choose how you would like to stand, to move, to appear to others. Try it out for a few moments. Think how you would like to be, then become it. Do what is right for YOU! How does it feel? Would you like to go on feeling this way, being this way, doing things this way? You can! But you have to choose for yourself. You have to embody this new self. And you have to keep on doing it.

Rebuilding your self-esteem

Now, write down a list of positive statements about yourself from other people's perspectives: for example, "My mother likes this about me"; "My workmates say this about me"; "My partner says this about me". Then write a few from within yourself: "I like the paintings of (say) Gauguin, and the music of (say) John Williams, and the books by (say) Jane Austen". Post these statements up somewhere to remind yourself: by the bathroom mirror, on the fridge, on the back of the bedroom door, etc. See what difference this might make. This is you actually doing something for yourself by defining yourself. Defining yourself can lead to redefining yourself, or rebuilding your self-esteem.

As with any New Year Resolution, it is now up to you to start practising these types of statement.

Another basic principle

If you are not very sure of yourself, this next exercise could be for you. So the basic principle here is to ensure that the "you" that you are, and the "you" that you feel, and the "you" that you are working from, are all one-and-the-same "you", that this "you" is working in an integrated way and is becoming the "you" that you know or remember. You are becoming the "you" that you like (or, at least, feel comfortable with), and so you are becoming the "you" that you really want to be. This sentence is not really that confusing: try reading it again.

> *Exercise*: Ask yourself these three questions:
> "What am I feeling right now?"
> "What do I want or need right now?"
> "How can I get that? What is working for me, and what is not working, in my surroundings?"

Try not to judge your answers. Sometimes they might seem trivial, or ridiculous, or impossible, or just plain selfish, but that is what you are feeling, or this is what you want—at this moment in time. So just accept it. It might change later; feelings often do. If it doesn't change, then you probably really do feel this, or really do want this, or really don't like that. That is really important information.

As you learn to accept these aspects of yourself more, however quirky they are, you will learn to accept yourself. As you learn to accept yourself more, so your self-esteem will start to grow. As your self-esteem grows, then you will begin to be able to start to communicate some of these thoughts, feelings, wishes, or injunctions to other people. But don't worry about that now—that comes later. Stick to the present exercise.

Try to keep on doing this exercise. As you do this, and as you keep on doing it, you will start to build up a much clearer idea of who you really are, what you really feel, what you really want, and what you really don't want. This is essentially a process of clarifying, and of strengthening, and of "centring"—you are consolidating who you really are. This is a really good first step. It is quite important that you practise this; and just keep on practising it. "Practice makes perfect!" Repetition makes it better, clearer, and stronger. And the reason that this is important is that, somewhere along the line of your life, your self-esteem and self-confidence got eroded. This is just part of the process of getting it back—claiming it back. It is an essential step. It is grounded in reality. It is who you really are—for the moment, anyway. You get to change things later.

Asking for what you really want

Whether you realize it or not, you also have the right to ask for what you really want or need. Check out the "Rights charter". Many people have a problem in asking for what they really want—and we are not just talking about "things" here: it could be for help, or a little more understanding. What you really want might be (something like) approval, more attention, more time, time for yourself, forgiveness, safety, variety, rest, peace of mind, trust, etc. These are often the important things. This is especially true for people under stress, in depression, with anxiety, or low self-esteem.

Many people have a problem asking certain people for what they really want: it is sometimes difficult to ask from parents, colleagues, friends, partners, boss, children, colleagues, etc. Many people have problems in asking for what they want when they need help, are embarrassed, have an idea, feel selfish, feel guilty, feel vulnerable, feel stupid, are in a position of lesser power, or are afraid the answer will be "No", etc. Check out your own fears, both about the other person and about your self. And don't let these stop you asking.

The most effective way for you to ask for what you want, and an important skill you may need to practise, is to formulate a clear and assertive request. You may want to prepare this a little in advance. And you may need to determine certain facts in order to do this effectively. We shall look at the process of becoming more assertive in the next section.

Getting what you need

This is a little more difficult. Once you have become clear that you really do need this, or that, and that it is not a whim nor an impossibility, then you become more subject to outside forces. It *is* difficult to get a glass of water in the middle of the desert, but not impossible. You enter into a new process—one of getting what you want. This can be very different from doing what you should be doing, or doing things for other people. Some persistence, perseverance, and a little patience here might actually see you achieving this and overcoming some of the obstacles to this goal.

Becoming more assertive

Basic principle

Becoming assertive is communicating our thoughts and feelings, openly, honestly, clearly, and without violating any other person's rights. It is the healthy alternative to being aggressive, or to being passive. Being assertive means that

- we are able to say what we think and feel;
- we are able to ask for what we want;
- we can say "Yes" or "No" clearly and firmly;
- we can express a range and depth of emotions;
- we can express personal opinions;
- we do not feel constrained by other people's proclivities.

This means that we can start to communicate more effectively in our relationships—all without restricting ourselves unduly through fear of criticism, censure, or lack of confidence. This is improved self-esteem.

Being unassertive

We are usually quite unassertive (compliant, conforming, submissive, obedient, reserved, repressed, or quiet) because we have learnt or been forced to be so. Young babies are naturally self-assertive; their survival depends on it. These babies—and you were one once—tell those around them exactly what they need. But, as children, those around us also gradually shape our behaviour through the messages they give us, and the general level of encouragement (or lack of it), as well as by more overtly repressive or deprived circumstances. Lack of self-assertion can become chronic. In the long-term, being unassertive depletes our self-esteem, and the more we become unassertive, the more we lack a sense of identity. This can result in a corresponding lack of sense of purpose, faith, good feelings about the world and ourselves, feeling in control, trust, *joi de vivre*, etc. Negative feelings, depression, anxiety, or stress can result, and, furthermore, these can have physical and psychological repercussions.

Becoming more assertive

This is really the only way out of the unassertiveness that probably reinforces your low self-esteem. Becoming more assertive can improve our sense of identity, our self-confidence, our pleasure in ourselves, our lives, and the relationships around us, and our general mental and physical health. It can reduce feelings of depression, anxiety, and stress. It can save energy, and can give pleasure. It all sounds very simple, but it is not necessarily easy. It usually takes time, practice, a safe place to start, and possibly some help. However, it is well worth the effort.

Practical steps

There are several practical steps that you can take take, listed below.

Step one   You have to understand the theory and the underlying principles of this approach. Most of this is stated above, so you have already taken the first step(s).

Step two   You have to recognize what the differences are between the passive, the aggressive, and the assertive styles of communicating, in yourself and in the people around you. See what you like and dislike in yourself and others; see what you admire, and would like to be like. This will give you some good clues as to how to be different, or more assertive. You are probably already fairly aware, somewhere, what might work for you and what might not. Try to follow that.

Step three   You have to identify one or two situations where you feel you would really like to, or need to, become more assertive. You need to choose these carefully, as they need to be relevant to, and possible for, you. It is going to be a test of these new principles, within your self. You can create some simple checklists to help identify those situations where you feel quite uncomfortable, or where you would like to feel more assertive. You might want to choose a relatively safe arena in which to start, where the possible repercussions might not be too dramatic, or where it is relatively safe. Don't put your job or marriage on the line. Check it out with someone you trust. Devise a "fall-back" plan. Try to have a reasonable lead-in statement.

Further suggestions

- Practise a little first: you might want to prepare what you want to say, role-play it, or rehearse it a little. Try things out with the help of a friend, or a therapist/counsellor. Don't worry too much; it will always be different to what you imagine. You can probably imagine the worst, and it is usually never as bad as *that*. Also allow yourself the potential to make small mistakes and your ability to learn from these.
- Don't be put off by your fears about the reactions of others. Sometimes you just think or "know" that there are going to be repercussions, as other people have come to assume that you are like "so" or "such". However, they may be getting a surprise some time soon, so don't let those fears stop you. You may

also be quite surprised yourself soon, as people often quite like self-assertion in others.
- Transfer the results of the above into a real life situation. Don't raise your expectations too high, but don't assume total failure. Get some feedback; modify things appropriately—maybe you could have been more assertive, or could have said this rather than that, or in a slightly different way—and then just repeat and continue to become more assertive. This is just the start, but, one hopes, it is the start of something increasingly positive.

Watch out for negative thought patterns

There are internalized statements, which all carry a similar (familiar) flavour. Such statements prevent or inhibit us from asserting ourselves.

- It would be very selfish to say what I want.
- I'm not good enough, so why bother to push myself, or try for another situation.
- If I get assertive, I'll just upset someone else. So I will stay quiet.
- I might really embarrass myself, and then that will be worse.
- If they say "No", it will prove that this has all been a huge mistake.
- I shouldn't have to say all this: people should know what I want.
- I am almost bound to make a mistake, so I won't bother trying.
- I have been like this for so long, I haven't the energy to change now.
- The present situation is all right; why rock the boat?
- They will just laugh at me, or get angry.
- Nobody likes me. Why bother trying to make a relationship with them anyway?

Identify your negative thoughts

What negative thought patterns do you have? They are effectively stopping you becoming more assertive and liking yourself more. Try to get them clearly identified, written down and clearly labelled as "Negative". These thoughts (and the fears behind them) are what are stopping you. You have been stopping you, through these negative thought patterns and fears. They are not really you. They are just negative thoughts. So, start by making a list, and keep on adding to it when you identify a new one. Then see that all these thoughts are really obstructions: they are stopping you becoming "you".

Now comes the hard bit. How can you stop them stopping you? Where is the little switch inside you that you can turn and say, "Enough! No more. I've had it. I am going to live my life the way I want to"? There is no such switch, so you must now work quite hard to clear each one of these negative thoughts out of the way. For each thought, write out a challenge to that negativity: find a different statement, a more real or relevant one, a more positive one, one that you can stand behind.

Check out the "Rights Charter"

This is another concept that identifies a number of basic "rights", based on the presumption that we are all equal and that we all possess these same fundamental human rights. Many people either ignore these (if they like being in charge, or in control), or have forgotten that these rights exist (or apply to them). The essential goal of assertiveness is to reclaim your rights without violating the same rights of others. Check them out!

The "Rights Charter"

There are a number of basic rights that are very important, yet often forgotten, ignored, or not implemented, and all of these can really affect your self-esteem. These rights are slightly different from the fundamental human rights referred to later, in the section on "Legitimate needs". Essentially, we are all equal and we all possess the same rights, as listed below (adapted from Powell, 2006).

- I have the right to be treated with respect, as an equal human being.
- I have the right to acknowledge my needs as being equal to those of others, and important for me.

- I have the right to state my own opinions, thoughts, beliefs and feelings, which may well be different from others.
- I have the right to make reasonable requests, for these to be considered seriously and implemented wherever possible.
- I have the right to express my views, to have them listened to, and to be taken seriously.
- I have the right to make mistakes; and to learn from them.
- I have the right to say, "I don't understand"—and to have things explained properly.
- I have the right to determine what I am responsible for, and what I should do to exercise this responsibility.
- I have the right to decide not to take responsibility for other people, or their problems, and to engage on whatever level if appropriate for me.
- I have the right to say "no", to withdraw consent, or to change my mind, habits and even patterns of relationship.
- I have the right to be 'me', without being dependant on the approval of others.
- I have the right to enjoy my life, to enjoy my own company, my body, and my way of doing things, and to set my own priorities.
- I have the right to privacy, and to do what I want to do, when I want to do it.
- I have the right to choose. I can choose to be passive, or to be illogical, or not to care, or not to conform. I can choose to stay as I am now, or to change as and when I want to.
- I am an independent, mature, competent, powerful and potentially successful person, who can . . .

Copy these "Rights" out, change them slightly, or add to them in order to make yourself feel that they are really yours. Put them up somewhere (alongside the mirror in the bathroom, or on the fridge) so that you (and others) can see them regularly. Say them over to yourself frequently. They do help. They are important. They can help you improve your sense of your self. Without these, you may be belittling yourself and seeing yourself as something of a "nothing".

WHAT WORKS?

An overview of what works

There are a number of well-tried things that can really help towards becoming more assertive and gaining greater self-esteem and feeling better about yourself.

Body position and non-verbal behaviour

Many unconscious body positions and movements give off a passive signal; others may adopt, as a form of compensation, more aggressive body attitudes. There are also assertive body positions and abrupt or assertive movements. These forms of non-verbal behaviour include eye contact, facial expressions, speech patterns, body posture, and the use of your voice. They also include how you stand and sit, how you move, how you hold your shoulders, or use your hands. Become more aware of what is being communicated by you, and to you, non-verbally. See if someone can take a video of how you are when you talk to people. How do you come across when you are asking for something? If you can deliberately make some small and quite subtle changes in your body language, you will find that you get very different responses from people.

Experiment with these! Practise so that you start using the ones that you want.

Listening skills

While these may not actually be a direct step towards being more assertive, they can really help you to understand what people are saying and thus give you the space to say, more easily and appropriately, what you happen to think and feel.

These listening skills tend to fall into counselling categories labelled: attending skills; postures of involvement; appropriate body language; eye contact; a non-distracting environment; following skills; door openers; minimal encouragers; open (infrequent) questions; attentive silence; reflecting skills; paraphrasing; reflecting feelings; reflecting meaning; and summarizing. However, this is not a counselling course, and most of these skills are fairly self-evident, or can be found in books on listening or counselling skills. They can be practised gently in relatively safe situations, such as with a friend in a "co-counselling" set-up, where you each talk almost without interruption for fifteen or twenty minutes. This is described in greater detail in the section on "Relationship difficulties".

By doing some of these things when you are listening to someone, you are changing the dynamic of the relationship between you at that precise moment. You are not being passive; you are now listening actively. One or two of these small changes will change the dynamic that you have with other people quite significantly. You do not have to do all of them. The intent with which you listen to others will have changed. That is probably enough!

Assertive skills

Listed below are some basic assertiveness skills. These can really help you to come over as being more assertive, more confident and with a reasonable self-esteem.

1. *Being specific* (KISS—Keep It Short and Simple). Try to be as clear and precise as possible. Say whatever you want to say just as

specifically and as simply as you possibly can. Avoid rambling, padding, justifying, qualifying, excusing, or whatever. These can be part of any follow-up statement later: keep it—your essential statement—as short and as simple as possible. There is a degree of power, strength, and clarity in such simplicity.

2. *Repetition.* You may have to keep repeating what it is that you want to say a number of times in different ways—until it is clear to you that the other person has (or the others have) *really* heard you and *really* understood you. People can be stupid, or they might not want to hear, because that means that they might have to do something to accommodate your reality or feelings. Try saying whatever it is you need to say in different ways and at different times. This can help you stick to what is really important for you, without being distracted by their arguments or their objections or obfuscations. You can then relax a little because you now know exactly what it is that you are saying, and that they have (somehow) heard you. You can also avoid any irrelevancies, different logic, emotional appeals, arguments, objections, or other distractions. This is all about clarity and determination.

3. *Self-disclosure.* This skill is where you can disclose a little of what you are feeling with a relatively simple statement such as, "I feel a bit nervous about saying this", or "I feel slightly guilty, or selfish, in saying what I want." You have chosen to do this. You are in charge. The advantage of this sort of self-disclosure is that it usually reduces your levels of anxiety. Things are now out in the open more. You have said it. It also gives a basis for greater honesty and clarity. It can possibly encourage some reciprocation from the other person. It is also quite a subtle power position in that you have been fairly open and honest and this can put the ball into the other person's court, as they usually then need to make a similar response on a similar level. Try always using "I" statements.

4. *Negative inquiry.* This is where a possibly negative criticism from someone is turned into a piece of constructive feedback. For example: "You'll find that difficult, won't you, because you are quite shy?" is replied to by, "In what ways do you think that I am shy?" You are thus inviting further information in order to find out whether the criticism is constructive, or just manipulative

and harmful. You are also subtly but assertively questioning that particular judgement of yourself and even opening the situation into an improved channel of communication.

5. *Negative assertion.* This skill involves agreeing with someone else's (possibly true) criticism, and then perhaps qualifying it. It means accepting that you have some faults, and then adding in one of your virtues or positive aspects. You do NOT just passively accept their negative statements as being the complete picture or truth about yourself, you add in something from your side or from your perspective. This something might be an admission of a negative aspect, but you are taking control of the agenda. It takes a little self-confidence to do this, and a certain level of self-awareness, and a small belief in yourself that you are NOT just what the other person says you are. Part of what they might say is perhaps true, but you are much more than that. This is how to show it. "Yes, I am very sorry that I handed this piece of work in late, but—if you look at it carefully—you will see that I have added in this, and that, which really seemed to be needed, and this obviously took me a little more time. I couldn't check this with you as you were away that day, but I did check with X and s/he said, 'Go for it'."

6. *Workable compromise.* When there is a conflict between what you want and what someone else wants, it is important to remember this skill or principle. A workable compromise is something you can *both* agree to. It is not where one person wins and the other loses; it is more a negotiation to a situation that both parties can live with, and where both feel listened to and respected. Compromising on a solution in a difficult situation does NOT mean compromising your self-respect or self-esteem. If the situation seems polarized, "either . . . or . . ."; "win/lose"; "black or white", then hold out, maintain the in-between "I don't know" space for a while, and don't be pushed into accepting something on "their" terms or because of "their" deadlines. You do need to be sure of your ground—that your demands, or your needs, or your position is a reasonable one. Then try to stay in the undecided position (not black, not white) until you both can find an acceptable middle way that works for all parties. Don't try to get there too soon. Don't leave it too long. But it will mean being clear about and able to sustain some,

possibly considerable, degree of tension while the issue stays unresolved.
7. *"Both ... and ..."*. This is something that is often forgotten about. It is very different from "either ... or ...". This skill first gets us out of the false duality often presented or imagined in either/or statements: "He is right, therefore I am wrong." Many people still think in black and white terms. Tabloid newspapers also seem to encourage this perspective. A more open approach allows *both* you to have a clear position *and* the other person to have their point of view without necessarily negating either of you. Both points of view can be valid: "I can be right about this, and you are right when you say that". It also puts you firmly in the picture without necessarily threatening the other person's position. It can even go much wider: you can *both* want this *and* see the potential dangers of it; or "We both agree to doing this and now I also happen to want that".
8. *Something unique*. Finally, add in something unique to yourself; just a little thing. Take a pause and see if there is something else that you might want to say. A little flavour of "you". This is, after all, you being affirmative.

These reminders are just a start. I am trying to be supremely pragmatic. There are several more assertiveness training skills and they can often be explored best in some sort of self-esteem group, or something similar. There is a necessary level of experience and confidence building that is needed and this cannot be got from just words on a page, a CD-ROM, or a one-day course.

There are also lots of other self-help types of books on several of these topics. Local Health Boards and specialist groups (like MIND) also put out pamphlets and booklets, which can help. Some large work organizations run courses that are open to their staff: you may be able to get a place on one of these, especially if you are going into a new area of work.

You might need to search a little for the right forum in which your assertiveness skill-building can happen. Some members of the new(ish) profession of "life coaches" could be helpful here. There are plenty of commercial courses and sites, so, as always, get good information and preferably a personal recommendation from someone before you part with any money. Don't be shy about "doing it your way"!

What works for me

This section contains some ideas, concepts, and exercises to try to help you to establish what works uniquely for you, and what might not. It follows on from the Self-esteem section and other earlier sections, and it can also stand alone as a set of techniques to help you get clearer about what it is that you want for yourself. If only some of it works for you that is great! If something does not work for you, bin that idea and use something that does work. Focus on what works for you—and only on that. This really continues the process of self-empowerment. You have to be the person who empowers himself or herself. This information can only offer you ideas and suggestions; you decide what works for you.

Take time out and the head-space that you need

Often what does *not* work is when we do not have enough time and space for ourselves, even to find out what it is that we feel or need. We can all too easily get caught up in other people's rhythms and routines, and what they expect of us; we can also get caught up in our own busy patterns that prevent us thinking or feeling too much. We might also take, or make, any excuse to just stop! Things will probably not change or improve for you very much until you prioritize this sort of regular time and space for yourself.

Some specific time set aside for self-reflection, relaxation, leisure, or meditation is usually fairly essential. Twenty minutes once a day is usually the absolute minimum to make any significant difference, ten minutes twice a day is slightly better, twenty minutes twice a day is much better, even ideal. It is usually possible to find this sort of time by making some small changes in your normal routine: getting up a little bit earlier, eating lunch by yourself, pulling into a lay-by before you get back home, sitting quietly upstairs in the bedroom while the others are downstairs, taking the dog out for a walk, some gentle gardening, going to bed half-an-hour later, or whatever.

Please try to ensure that you get this sort of "time out" regularly, and then do it fairly religiously, for at least a month or two. Then you will be able to see what a difference it can make.

What do I really want

There are three essential questions that we have met already. You may need to keep asking yourself these three questions and eventually the answer to the question, "What do I really want?" will come to you. The three questions, if I may remind you, are:

- "What am I feeling right now?";
- "What would I like or need right now?";
- "What works for me and what doesn't work in my immediate surroundings?"

The answers to these questions, if you keep repeating them over and over to yourself, will eventually come to you, and these will really help you to identify what works for you, and what does not. They are based on what you are feeling right now, and this can change moment-by-moment: what this feeling generates, and then how to fulfil that need, are all unique to yourself. So, please keep on asking yourself these questions. Remember that you are probably coming from a position of depression, anxiety, or a lack of self-esteem. Things are already quite difficult for you. Asking these questions, changing some of your thoughts and perceptions, and doing these little exercises helps put the "you" back into you, and the "you" then comes, much more clearly, back into the picture. You start to get your life back!

Finding your own inner voice

Often we listen to the voices of others too much: "You should do this", or "You can't say that". What would happen if you listened more to your own inner voice? If you could hear that inner voice, what would it say? Sometimes, we do not give ourselves the space and time to find out what *our* inner voice is saying, let alone ever saying it out loud. Sometimes you only find *your* voice in times of silence, such as when taking time out, as mentioned above, or by asking yourself some of the above questions, or just by sitting quietly by yourself.

If you start to practise this, an increasing sense of yourself can mean that, in odd moments, you suddenly "know" what it is that you really want. It is then surprising how clear your voice can be, how simple what it is that you really need to say can be, and how extremely difficult actually saying it can be. Just hang on to what it is that you want to say, and be aware of these difficulties, and then the right moment will present itself. You will then find yourself saying what it is that you need to say.

What we are describing is a very different experience to "hearing voices" that often say things that you do not like or want to hear, be it God or schizophrenia. This is much more a sense of an inner "knowing": knowing what it is that you want to say, and what it is that perhaps you just have never really said before. Remember this is part of a general self-empowerment process. You are just saying what works for you, and what it is that you are feeling, wanting, or needing right now.

Try to focus on the fact that this, just this one thing, is what is absolutely true for you, right now, and that it is all that you really need to say. It does not matter whether people particularly like it or not; it is the truth. It is your truth, and maybe it has not been said clearly or properly enough yet—if ever. So just let the words come out, just let them be spoken, now. They will come out, at the right moment. It often then gets easier after that.

The tyranny of niceness

It is really good that we want to be nice to others, and that we can be nice to others, and it is also fantastic when people are nice to us. However, "having" to be nice to others can eventually become something of a tyranny. It can become a trap for our selves. Only ever being nice to others means that you are not allowed ever to be nasty, irritated, or annoyed with them, or whatever. This can mean that, while you may have these feelings, you cannot express them. This means that you can get depleted, exhausted, run down, possibly even angry inside, and, eventually, of very little use to yourself or anyone else.

Perhaps we feel that we should *always* be nice to others, but this is when it can start *not* to work for us. We can start to feel resentful: "When is anyone nice to me?" The trick, and the way out of the trap, is to be nice to yourself first: most importantly, you can start to try to like yourself, and so to look after yourself really well. Once you do this, you are then much freer and much more able to be nicer to others—when it is right for you to do so.

Which bit of "no" do you not understand?

Sometimes what works for you is just what works for you, and what used to work for you just does not work any longer. Other people can therefore sometimes have a considerable difficulty in hearing, or accepting, that you have changed, or circumstances have changed. They can even seem to be unable or unwilling to hear you say effectively "No! I don't want to do that any longer." If they really cannot, or do not want to allow you to change, that is when you might need to say something like: "Which bit of 'no' do you not understand?", or "Sorry; but my 'no' means 'no'",or, simply, "I can't do that. It just doesn't work for me any more."

People might take a little bit of an offence at first, especially if they are expecting you not to say "No" (because you never have done), or to say "Yes, of course!" (because you always do). But they'll get used to the change eventually. If it doesn't work for you, you cannot go on doing it, and by stopping now you will probably become a nicer and happier person, and so others may even learn to appreciate the changes that you are implementing.

Getting rid of addictive patterns

What can really work, is to use this opportunity to get rid of any other addictive patterns that you might have been using to get through the depression, reduce the anxiety, or boost (artificially) your self-esteem. These can include abusing alcohol, smoking, comfort eating, over-spending, over-using caffeine or sugar, gambling, etc. You may need additional help to eliminate some of these behaviours, and there are plenty of specialist self-help groups (often based on the Alcoholics Anonymous 12-Step Model). But it is really good to try to get this stuff sorted out now, as soon as possible.

Self-awareness

Increased self-awareness

Increased self-awareness, which also includes increased somatic awareness (the awareness of what is happening in your body), and part of what is now often being called mindfulness, are an essential part of the road to full recovery, better self-esteem, and healthy emotional self-regulation thereafter. This type of awareness has been mentioned before in various ways throughout this book.

Essentially, it is a commonplace inner experience; readily discernible, ever changing, and unique to you. We encourage you to do everything that you can to increase this level of self-awareness, as the process of doing this will mobilize your body–mind's resources to their maximum potential. You will then start to get better, stronger, to like yourself more, and to start to heal any psychic wounds. Increased self-awareness is a very good heuristic (a device to understand the unknown). These are possibly also the unknown aspects of your self.

Increased attention

This is one of the important prerequisites. You will need to spend extra time "listening in" to your inner self and your body. Several ways may have already been suggested: progressive muscular relaxation, meditation, mindfulness practice, deep, regular breathing exercises, the Autogenic Technique, asking yourself various questions, etc. These all require you to set aside some special time regularly for this purpose, and to give yourself some increased attention. You are important to yourself, and you need to know and understand yourself better, and this is the only way. In the early stages, this special time probably needs to be quite substantial—twenty minutes at least, once or twice a day, if possible, and consistent, i.e., every day. Later on it can become more of a constant and regular checking-in to your self, and later still, an awareness (alarm-bells go off) of when you are not in contact with your self.

The perilous question

You will also need to move towards any specific problems ("What is this migraine trying to tell me?", or "What does my body want me to do?", or "How do I reduce my levels of stress?") rather than avoiding them, or cutting off from them, or trying to block them out of your awareness. I call this approach, "the perilous question" as it comes from the Arthurian legend of the Holy Grail. The Grail Castle is in a wasteland, and the King is wounded. The wound will not heal, nor will the wasteland flourish, until someone asks the perilous question. And the perilous question is, "How can this wound be healed?" You have to acknowledge that there really is a problem—a wound that needs healing. When you do this, and when you ask the perilous question, "How? How can this wound be healed?", an answer nearly always comes, although sometimes it is not always the one you want to hear!

General well-being

Again, as mentioned before, all of these methods need to be seen within a holistic context. You are trying to change some major aspects of your personality—your whole basic body–mind system, and to help it to achieve a more sustainable method of self-regulation, rather than just focusing on fixing one tiny part of it. You will not be very effective in the changes that you want to make if it is a matter of two steps forward and one step back, because you might also be stressing yourself out, stuffing yourself with junk food, or popping a variety of pills. You probably need to consider the whole picture: both your physical health and your mental health, your resilience and your desire to learn, your ability to cope, and your basic strength. This might mean starting to tackle habits like drinking, smoking, being overweight, eating habits, social life, and what you do with your energy.

Breathing

Your pattern of breathing is a wonderful gateway into your subconscious. It is a vital component in increased self-awareness and somatic awareness. It helps you to rebalance yourself. Just listen to your breathing: allow it to adjust to a natural, even, deep, effortless breathing "wave", with a similarity of pattern and flow to waves on the beach coming in and going out. Let your chest rise and fall as well as letting your belly move in and out. Breathe right down to the bottom of the abdomen as well as expanding the chest, so that the shoulders rise slightly. Spend some time, a lot more time than usual, just breathing consciously and effortlessly. Other things will follow.

Practise this full, whole-body breathing at odd moments throughout the day: on the bus, in the office, at home, when on the computer, or when out walking. You only need do it for four or five breaths every half-hour or so. Do it as often as you can. It is best, when sitting, if your back is reasonably straight and upright, or, when lying, lie flat on your back. If standing, make sure your knees are not locked upright. Various disciplines teach different types of breathing: childbirth classes, chronic pain groups, relaxation, Yoga, Chi Gong, neo-Reichian therapies, etc. Healthy breathing is essential for good physical and mental health.

Different selves

As you do all this work on yourself, you may become increasingly aware of the various different aspects of your self. We are different when we are with our parents than when we are with our children; we have a different relationship and are, in many ways, a different person, with our friends, or our partner, than we are with our employers or employees. We wear different hats all the time. Sometimes the "professional" hat can conflict with the "personal" hat. Sometimes we even have hidden, or secret, aspects of ourselves.

The process of self-awareness is to become clearer about all these different aspects. These may then begin to integrate, or strength from one aspect may flow over into another (weaker) aspect. This form of growth is common, healthy, and normal in the process of self-awareness.

Dreams and images

The body operates in terms of impressions, sensations, and particularly images, which sometimes also surface in our dreams, or in odd moments of reverie. Pay a little more attention to these images; explore them, write about them in a journal or dream diary, talk from them occasionally, rather than about them, paint them, play with them, bring them out in amateur dramatics or a theatre group, or something. They are an important part of your inner life. They may seem incoherent or chaotic at first, because you have not been paying attention to them. The more attention we give them, then the more we realize that they are an aspect of our "holistic" self.

Special times

You will definitely need some special times daily, and maybe a special space, like a quiet, undisturbed bedroom, in order to increase your level of self-awareness and your somatic awareness. As mentioned, about twenty minutes twice a day is a good allocation. You can break the twenty minutes up into different parts: ten minutes for relaxation, ten minutes of awareness. Many people find that this sort of relatively minor adjustment is the only definable extra time commitment that is really significant. The importance of these special times is that you give them to yourself regularly, that there is some routine in this. You are saying to yourself, "I am important enough to give myself twenty minutes of my time."

Letting go

It is sometimes necessary to let go of old patterns of life, habits, ways of being, dysfunctional relationships, emotions, mental rigidities and prejudices, views and belief systems, muscular tensions, physical and emotional stress, perfectionist attitudes, workaholic tendencies, etc. This letting go is different from giving up or dropping out: it is consciously creating a space for something new and better to come in. There is an implication that this letting go is not permanent or final. Some of the better-functioning aspects of the above can be picked up again later and reintegrated, if you want to. Letting go does naturally create some anxieties, usually just before you let go: afterwards, there is often a great relief. Letting go is often necessary and important in order to experience and recognize the more positive aspects that you are trying to connect with and introduce.

Facing yourself

This is the hard part. We often have to face up to aspects of ourselves that we really do not want to look at. We may have been actively avoiding these aspects for years. We have known about them, but not wanted to look at them. This can be part of the "dark night of the soul" or the "valley of the shadow". And it is hard, very hard! However, there is often the understanding that it is necessary, that things will not improve unless this is done, that maybe, just maybe, there is a form of redemption on the other side.

Probably you might need some help with this process of facing yourself. Help will be there, eventually. You may have to find it, or find the right person to help you. This could be a counsellor or psychotherapist. The issue(s) that you might want to address might be something like an addiction, or that you have hurt or abused others, or that at times you are not a very nice person, or that you have seriously cocked up somehow. Owning up to this, living with this reality, making amends where possible (promises don't mean a thing), facing your self and others with what you have done, and continuing to do this from now on, are all part of this process of increased self-awareness.

Special techniques

There are several special techniques that have been mentioned at various times: Alexander Technique, Tai Chi or Chi Gong, Autogenic Technique, mindfulness, etc. All of these can contribute to increased self-awareness.

Remember the goal is not to put your self into the hands of another (alternative) professional, who will do different things to you that you cannot do yourself. The goal is to attain a state of independent mental and physical health and well-being where you do not suffer from these problems. This state can then become sustainable and self-regulating. Some special techniques may be useful initially to help you on the road towards better health. You may decide to continue with them for a while. Ultimately, you should not need them.

Some of these special techniques can also include therapeutic touch, biofeedback, massage, reflexology, acupuncture, homoeopathic medicine, 12-Step addiction programmes, cranio-sacral work, progressive relaxation, various forms of meditation, eye movement desensitization and reprocessing (EMDR), etc. They can also include studying something that really interests you: joining a painting, or philosophy, class; going on a writing course; studying some of the Ancient Mysteries; doing a residential week of sacred dancing, or massage, in a community; or whatever.

Legitimate needs

This section contains a list of totally legitimate needs. These are the kinds of things that we *all* need—every person on the planet—and, for many of these, we even have a right to expect, or claim, them. It is up to us now to own these legitimate needs, and to claim them in everyday life. There is an assorted mixture of environmental, social, and personal conditions, activities, and experiences, all of which are important for our physical and psychological health. Some have been incorporated into the United Nations' Universal Declaration of Human Rights and the European Convention on Human Rights.

- *Physical needs.* From the moment you are born, you have the physical need for clean air, pure water, and wholesome food. Everyone on the planet needs this to survive and remain healthy. You also need suitable shelter and clothing, and the ability to stay warm. You need to be able to feel safe, in your own space or place. You also need to be able to keep yourself healthy: exercise and relaxation are important. We all also need degrees of stability, peace, and freedom in the physical, social, and political environment around us, in order to stay healthy

- *Emotional needs.* We need to be able to be happy. We need security, nurturing, intimacy, and tenderness. We need people paying attention and being interested in us, as well as just caring for us. We need outlets for our emotionally expressive and creative feelings, and, later on, for our sexual or intimate feelings. We need to be treated kindly, fairly, and honestly, so that we can learn what these qualities really are. We need to be able to communicate, and to learn when not to. We need some humour in our lives. We need to be able to learn from our mistakes, without too much criticism.
- *Social needs.* As humans and social animals, we need the company of others. We need to love and be loved, to have friends, and to feel respected and valued. At times of stress or distress, we need sympathy, compassion, and generosity. At times of achievement, we need recognition, appreciation, and congratulations. At times of difficulty, we need understanding, help, and maybe even to be forgiven, in order to learn forgiveness. We need to be able to interact with others, and we also need to be able to be by ourselves sometimes. We often need to feel that we are part of a group, or groups, and that we can trust others. These needs can help to determine who we are, in terms of our social identity. We need to be able to work together, and to co-operate, which sometimes means accepting leadership of others or over others.
- *Creative needs.* We need to do creative and useful work. It may also need to be remunerative. We need to feel that we are making a positive contribution to society. Our minds need information, stimulation, and challenge; we have an innate need to understand people and the world around us. We need, and have the right to, education. We need variety, recreation, and play. We have a drive towards accomplishment, and need to exercise this. We need to grow and experience change. We also need times of quietness and peace. We need the freedom of ideas, and to be able to express these openly and honestly. We have the right to freedom of thought and speech. We need authentic and consistent responses from others. Conformity can be restricting but chaos does not work, and neither does anarchy make for contentment.

- *Moral, ethical, and spiritual needs.* These are personal to each of us, but we all need to feel there is some value to our life. We need to feel that there are rules and a degree of order, value, and rightness; we also need a degree of autonomy, self-determination, and to make our own decisions about our own lives. We need to establish, and live by, our own standards of behaviour. We need to believe in ourselves, in people, in a natural order to things, and in the power (or rightness) of love. We need to experience power, both use and abuse, so that we can learn how to accept one and reject the other. Nearly all of us also seem to (or need to) believe in something larger than ourselves: a higher being or power—by whatever name one calls it.

Not having these needs fulfilled (being deprived of them, not owning them or claiming them, or repressing them) can mean that we get to feel less than who we really are, or less than we should be. We limit our own potential through limiting our own self-image and cutting our selves off from some of our legitimate needs. It can mean that we feel depleted or deprived. This can mean that we eventually become depressed, ill, anxious, angry, or feel bad about ourselves. So we have a degree of responsibility towards ourselves to make sure that we fulfil these legitimate needs. We may even need to challenge the conditions around us, or others, or old patterns within ourselves, that prevent us from so doing.

There is a form of hierarchy with these needs. As Figure 2 shows, starting at the nine o'clock position, these are the arrows that carry through from one sector to another, and then into the middle, and then out again. If the needs in one sector are not reasonably fulfilled (which is quite likely), then it is unlikely that we will be able to fulfil totally all the needs in another, later sector. However, it is not an absolute hierarchy. We may well be able to survive and grow with only some of the needs in a particular sector being fulfilled. Later we can come back and complete those unfulfilled needs. The arrows lead us around to the start again. The list of needs given here is not complete, nor is it absolute. If you come across a particular need that you have, add it to the list in the relevant sector.

Please consider what needs you feel are unfulfilled or incomplete. Make a checklist or inventory on a sheet of paper using three columns, headed "Yes", "Partially", and "No" for all these needs being fulfilled or not. Be as scrupulously honest with yourself as

PHYSICAL NEEDS

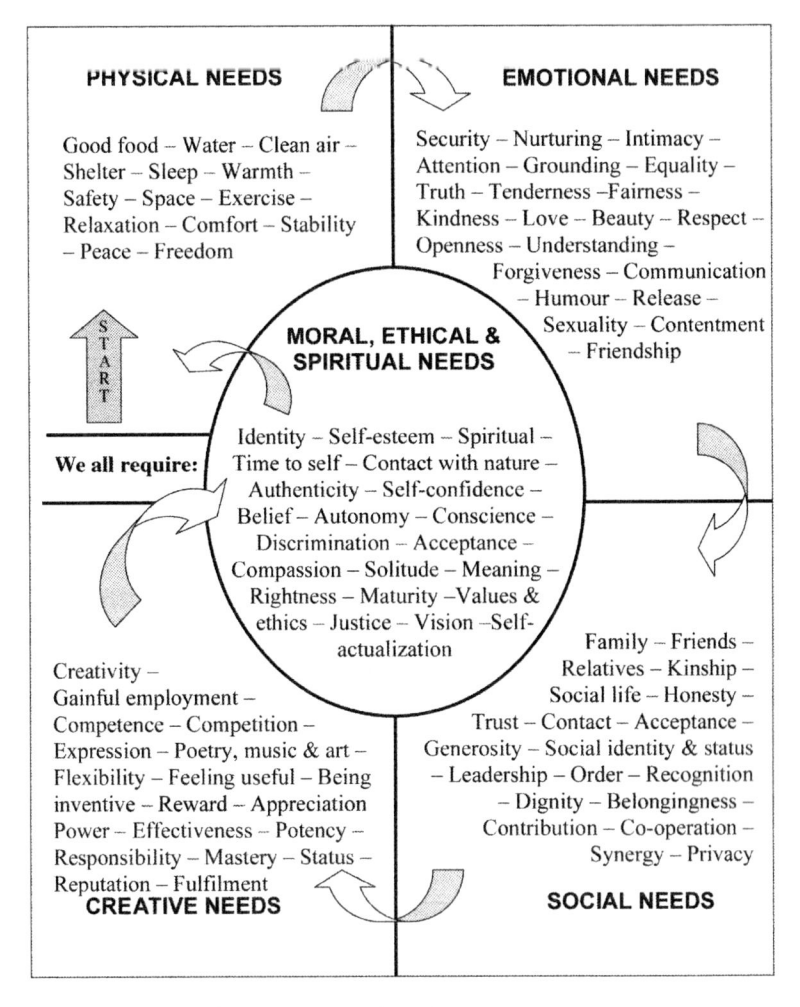

Good food – Water – Clean air – Shelter – Sleep – Warmth – Safety – Space – Exercise – Relaxation – Comfort – Stability – Peace – Freedom

EMOTIONAL NEEDS

Security – Nurturing – Intimacy – Attention – Grounding – Equality – Truth – Tenderness – Fairness – Kindness – Love – Beauty – Respect – Openness – Understanding – Forgiveness – Communication – Humour – Release – Sexuality – Contentment – Friendship

We all require:

MORAL, ETHICAL & SPIRITUAL NEEDS

Identity – Self-esteem – Spiritual – Time to self – Contact with nature – Authenticity – Self-confidence – Belief – Autonomy – Conscience – Discrimination – Acceptance – Compassion – Solitude – Meaning – Rightness – Maturity – Values & ethics – Justice – Vision – Self-actualization

CREATIVE NEEDS

Creativity – Gainful employment – Competence – Competition – Expression – Poetry, music & art – Flexibility – Feeling useful – Being inventive – Reward – Appreciation Power – Effectiveness – Potency – Responsibility – Mastery – Status – Reputation – Fulfilment

SOCIAL NEEDS

Family – Friends – Relatives – Kinship – Social life – Honesty – Trust – Contact – Acceptance – Generosity – Social identity & status – Leadership – Order – Recognition – Dignity – Belongingness – Contribution – Co-operation – Synergy – Privacy

Figure 2. A form of the hierarchy of needs.

you can be. This form of self-awareness is really essential. No one else knows or can tell you what you need. Some people who know you very well might be able to guess a little. But you are the real expert—about yourself!

Unfulfilled needs

Some of these unfulfilled needs may even be behind some of your more dysfunctional behaviour patterns. Often, we try to find someone else to give us what we never got earlier in life: and when it doesn't work with that person, then we are likely try with someone else, or somewhere else. We can repeat this pattern over and over again, desperately trying to get a basic need met that should have been fulfilled many years ago. And we do it now in ways that are increasingly inappropriate or dysfunctional: "Maybe this time . . .", or "This person seems the right person". But we are often setting ourselves up for a disappointment. This is a tragic mistake. Often, we just repeat the pattern of *not* getting our needs fulfilled.

Most of the time, now that we are adult, we must, we need to, find out how to give these things to ourselves, how to fulfil our own needs instead of being dependent on others to fill them. That is a hard one! You have to do it for yourself. Your friends can possibly help you with some areas; your partner may be able to help you with any needs at work or other issues, but probably not about needs at home (as they may be part of the problem); sometimes a parent can help you a little with difficulties with other people—but we are also trying to get away from the purely parental view and work out what we need for ourselves. But that is about it!

A good place to learn how, where, and in what way to get your needs fulfilled properly, and to practise exploring this area at first, is probably in a course of counselling or psychotherapy. "Life coaching" is a new area of work that might be able to help a little here as well.

Expressing your needs

All the above "needs" are very different from "wants", although sometimes this can be just a matter of language. At one end of the spectrum, these needs are paramount: they are needs that can mean life or death, happiness or misery. At the other end of the spectrum, we can do without some of those needs for a considerable period of time, even though we might still need them. "Wants" are on a different scale: we will probably not die, or suffer much, without a new washing machine, or without pistachio ice cream, which is what we might want. We may need a better working environment, and we may want a new job with more money.

Only you can also put these needs, or wants, into words. You need to be able to formulate an assertive statement. This means telling others clearly what it is you need, which is significantly different from asking for what you want. It works best if you can specify fairly precisely all the aspects of what it is you need. This can almost become formulaic. "I need ... [specify] ... from ... [the person you need it from] by ... [the time, date, or frequency that you need it] in or at ... [a place or manner] with ... [any other things or conditions]." Try to fill in an assertive statement outline like the one above. Distil or work these five main points out into a brief statement, suitable for the situation and for the person you are talking to. Try to eliminate any ambiguities. Maybe it could help to write it down, practise saying it (in private), or discuss it with someone else first.

You may also need to give the person you are talking to some degree of rationale, or reason, to help them understand your need. You might need to say what you are thinking, and/or to indicate how you are feeling, and why this does not work for you. Put this section in first. This forms a fairly complete package, a whole message. It also helps others to understand and respond more sympathetically or co-operatively. You may find that it works more effectively. The "whole message" perhaps comes best in three parts: I think ...; I feel ...; I need ... Often, indicating a positive result is helpful as well.

> Example: "I think that I do more than my fair share of the work around the house. You do not do any housework. I feel resentful when I am doing housework and you are reading the paper. Therefore I need you, A***, to help me more around the house, putting things away on a daily basis, and especially when you see me working. Essentially, I need you to help me—and not just reluctantly, I need you to want to help me. We both live here; we both go out to work. When we are both at home, we can, and should, share some of the housework. Then we can both sit down and relax afterwards and enjoy being at home together. This would make me feel a lot better."

The following list gives some possibly useful hints.

- Try to make sure that you are speaking to the right person, the real "source" of your problem.

- The first thing is to get this other person to agree to a time and place for the conversation that you need to have with them.
- Approach them positively, rather than negatively. Present the "problem" in a constructive way.
- Try to keep the "change" that you need them to make small enough to avoid a huge reaction (i.e., one step at a time).
- Try to keep the change requested as simple and specific as possible.
- Don't blame or attack the other person, just describe their behaviour that gives you a problem; try to describe the effect that this behaviour has on you.
- Express your own thoughts and feelings as factually as possible.
- Use "I" statements about your own situation and feeling: pointing fingers and "you" statements will create defensiveness.
- Be specific: stick to the clear, demonstrable facts; try to avoid exaggerations.
- Keep your voice, tone, and language moderate, even though you may be feeling agitated and charged.
- Watch your body language; maintain eye contact. Speak firmly and clearly.
- Listen to what they have to say in return. You may have been seeing only one side of the problem.
- Try to let them know that you have really heard them: by summarising their points.
- At this point, you may be able to start to discuss the differences that you have between you. Restate your original points, in summary, and restate their points, in summary.
- Don't get distracted from your goal.
- You may need to be prepared to offer a compromise.

All of this sounds quite simple, but it is usually not at all easy. It can even be quite difficult—especially the first time. It may also take some practice. You might want to run through the main points with a friend beforehand, using the above checklist as a guideline, in order to get some feedback on how things seem and how you come across, both to the friend and to yourself.

It can also be very rewarding, and (since it has not happened yet) it will probably take you quite a lot of effort, maybe even a row, a few tears, and a bit of emotional pain, before you achieve it.

Maybe you will also have to say this a few times in different ways and on different occasions to a few different people. Maybe you will also have a number of different things to say to a number of different people, in a number of different ways, in order to get things generally working out better for you. All this will radically improve your self-esteem. It is really worth the effort. Success builds on success.

Asserting yourself

One of the reasons that we might have low self-esteem is that we have often become tied up and constrained by a mass of rules, conventions, and internal (often parental) scripts that essentially do not work for us. Indeed, these tend to favour others, or to discriminate against us. We need to challenge these "rules" and assert ourselves just a little. Things then usually work better for us.

Challenging the rules

Rules—traditions, rituals, laws, policies, regulations, scripts, codes, conventions, guidelines, patterns of behaviour, etc.—are usually there to be adhered to, and it often works best if everyone actually does stick to these rules or whatever. It provides a basic stability to society. However, sometimes these rules do not work for an individual, or in certain circumstances, or under certain conditions, and then we have to bend or reinterpret these rules. It is another "both ... and ..." process. The rules are important, and if they do not work, they need to be bent. And that might mean for you, here and now. You might have to challenge, bend (or break) one of these so-called rules or scripts to make things work for you.

If the rule, or whatever it is, is really not working for you, then you need to make a decision: whether to continue to follow the rule and continue to suffer in some way, or not to follow that particular rule or script or what you think you should be doing, and either try to change it or to get it changed. This is how rules, laws, codes of behaviour, and the scripts that we get from our parents, schools, or society actually do get changed. Somebody decides that this is not working and needs changing. Often this is an ordinary person, just like you. But it does mean asserting yourself a bit, saying "this just doesn't work for me", and then (possibly) having to accept some comment or criticism afterwards. This is also sometimes how an "ordinary" person becomes an "extraordinary" person.

Obviously, one needs to proceed slightly cautiously, as the rule or the convention may be there for a very valid reason: maybe that reason is now outdated, but then again, maybe it is not. Please proceed cautiously, but also with determination. Try to shape it into what works for you. This should not necessarily be taken as an inducement towards breaking the law.

There may often be consequences or reactions to breaking the rules, and you should be aware of, and prepared to accept, these if you do decide to break these rules, or to go against what others are doing (or not doing), or to assert yourself a little. But rules—even laws—that do not work can often become tyrannies. That means they do not work properly any longer, and so need changing. It sometimes takes a little courage to step across that line and break that rule or change that script. And sometimes that is the only way things will ultimately change for the better.

You can ask "Who made these rules?" and "Why?" as part of the process of discrimination, determination, and deciding what to do, or what not to continue doing. These questions do not really help the actual process of self-determination, or the process of change. Sometimes the rules were made for very good reasons, which just may not apply here, to you, or now. This rule bending or breaking can also be a significant part of the process of assertion and self-empowerment.

Just because it is a rule, it does not mean to say that it works for you. It may only work for the person maintaining that it is a rule.

It might even be their way to hang on to power, status, a way of doing things, or to protect themselves from change. Maybe things need to change. Maybe you need to claim, or reclaim, a sense of what works for you, and say what that is: assert it.

It is usually best just to challenge the rule first and then give the other person, or people, a chance to change it for themselves. Maybe they did not realize how much it did not work for other people. Maybe they were stuck in tradition, or whatever. The challenge can be often quite difficult and you may need some support from friends, other workmates, family, your union, the ombudsman, a grass-roots organization, etc. Something external might be necessary or helpful. Please also refer back to the section on expressing your needs clearly.

This whole journey that you are on is essentially about gaining knowledge, skills, and experience. That is ultimately all we ever do, and, indeed, why we are here. It does not really matter what you do (as a job) or the place from which you start. For you, the starting point may be this place of low self-esteem. For others it might be a place of grief, or depression, stress, or anxiety. It is all about gaining awareness of your self and following your own path with that. And to do that effectively, you need a little more power. So . . . All Power to the Person! You!

Two "Ds", three "Ps", and an "A"

The two Ds are Discrimination and Determination. You, and only you, can—and you need to—*discriminate* between what really works for you and what does not work for you. You may need to discriminate between what you need and what you want; between what you like and what you do not like; between who you think is "right" and who you think is not. Only you can decide.

You might also need to *discriminate* between your needs (which you may undervalue) and the assumed needs (often "wants") of others, which you might have over-estimated, or overvalued, especially if you have issues of low self-esteem. You may be surrendering some legitimate needs of your own, for fear of hurting or offending others, or of depriving them of what they want. You are actually depriving yourself here. And you are also the only person who can change this situation. You may need to hone this tool of discrimination.

You may also need to *determine* what it is that you want; what (new?) direction you are going in; when you are going to change; and what you might want to do with the rest of your life. You may need to determine your priorities. Some of your needs may be being fulfilled; others may be being ignored (by yourself or others): the priority then is for a broader perspective, or for more of a balance. Sometimes it is important to prioritise others: their needs become paramount (especially if they are very young, or ill). And at some later point, the balance will need to be redressed, and your unattended-to needs will now become more important. But only you can *determine* when this balance needs to shift.

You may also need considerable determination to get through this process. Another word for determination is Perseverance or Persistence, but that is one of the 'Ps'.

The three Ps are Patience, Persistence, and Positivism. You might need to exercise some *patience* (which is very different from passivity). This could be patience with your self, with other people, and with the time it takes to change things around and get over this bad patch. Patience is not a bad thing. It is just an understanding that some things that are worthwhile take a little time to achieve.

You will also need to *persist*, as, once that you know what you want and what works for you, it may take some considerable time and effort to implement these changes more fully, completely, or significantly. It does not happen overnight and you may have to repeat some things more than once in order to get them properly implemented. Other people will need to be considered, or negotiated with—sometimes—and that often takes time, patience, and determination (perseverance), so you will need some persistence.

You will also need to become quite *positive* that this is what is right for you, that this is what really works—for you, and that this is what will make things, not just better for you, but also better for those around you. You are moving towards a more positive future for yourself, and for those that you care for. This is what will work better for everyone. This is what fits in better with the changes that have already been made, with your whole process of recovery and growth.

Do not be put off by any fears and anxieties (your own or others). They have been around a long time, and you will have considered them fully. As they have done in the past, they are now still demonstrating the capacity to prevent yourself from fulfilling yourself. They will still continue to be around, this time and the next time, and so on, and you are also learning to master these anxieties and to get beyond that stage.

The A is for you to Appreciate yourself. You can appreciate and congratulate yourself for surviving, for getting here, today, to this place. You really did survive; you made it. Congratulations! You really deserve a medal or two, or three, so you had better get used to wearing them. Then you can also reward yourself again—give yourself another medal—for any of your successes in these directions of fulfilling your needs as you continue along your road to recovery and fulfilment.

You really do need to give this sort of appreciation to yourself. Do not rely on others doing it for you. They haven't done much of it up to now, or at least not so that you have noticed. It is also very nice when other people do notice and appreciate you for what you have done. Say, only to yourself, "Not before time", and out loud, "Thank you for noticing."

These are just little signposts on the path to improving your self-esteem. They work, if you pay attention to them. If you do not then you are really no worse off. It is just that you will not implement what you want to change in your life this time around.

Responding to criticism

Basic principles

Please remember that we might, at first, get quite a lot of support as we become more self-assertive. However, one thing that happens, unfortunately quite often, is that—as we emerge from our depression, or position of anxiety, or our lack of self-esteem—we might encounter some form of criticism.

This may not be genuine criticism; it might be that we are just hearing things this way. However, it might also be more intended— but that does not make it correct. The other person might not like what we are trying to do, or trying to change. They may be unconsciously critical, because we have been depressed, or because we are now trying to assert ourselves, or they might have got used to us being in an "inferior" position. Or we may be so used to hearing criticism as a form of hurtful rejection that we cannot (yet) hear it in any other way. Or the criticism may be accurate, and we might need to hear it, although we might still not be quite strong enough to hear or challenge this sort of "constructive" criticism head-on— if that is what it is. Listed below are some techniques to use in dealing with this sort of criticism.

Acknowledge the criticism

This technique is basically accepting or acknowledging the criticism without necessarily agreeing with it totally. The criticism might be constructive, but we might not be able to hear it as such—yet. The purpose of the criticism may be to stop any further criticism (coming from you) immediately. Attack is sometimes the best form of defence, and so this could usually work quite well. But, when someone criticizes you in this way, and if the criticism is in any way accurate, there is a tendency just to shut up and back down. That is the old way. However, instead, just try to follow the following relatively simple steps.

1. Say something like, "Thanks for telling me that you feel this way about me."
2. Try to paraphrase the criticism into your own words so that:
   (a) you feel a bit more comfortable with the criticism, and;
   (b) the critic is clear that you have heard them properly. "You mean that you think I do . . . and . . ., and that this has a negative effect on you. Well, I am sorry that you feel that way about me."
3. Thank the critic, if this is appropriate, and also indicate that you can benefit or learn from this criticism. "Thanks for telling me. Sometimes I am probably something like that, and now I am aware of this I will be trying to change the bits that don't work. I am sorry if I have caused any difficulties."
4. It is probably best not to admit that you are totally in the wrong (unless you really are), and just acknowledge that there is some accuracy and that you can benefit from this. Going into a full apology, or a grovel, or a total melt-down will not do much for your self-esteem.
5. Ask for any further information. Constructive criticism can be very useful, and even if it was not expressed very positively originally, you can often turn it round, disarm the negative aspects, and turn it into something useful. "Of course, I am always glad to hear some constructive suggestions about how I can do things a bit better. From what you said, it seems there is something here that I can improve on. Thank you for helping me with this. Do you have any further suggestions?"

6. If the criticism was wrong, or not very accurate, then explain yourself, if this is appropriate. Correct the other person's misconception. Try to give something of your reasons, or your perspectives.

Responding to criticism

One effective way to respond to criticism that might be negative is to use a somewhat assertive style. This style does not attack, surrender to, or sabotage the critic, it just gently disarms them. When you respond assertively to a critic, first you may need to clear up any misunderstandings, and then:

- you acknowledge what you consider to be accurate (though it may be biased);
- you state your perspective or point of view, which might well be different;
- you give your reasons;
- you ignore the rest.

Thus, you put an end to the unwelcome attack without sacrificing your self-esteem. This is very important. Much of the loss of self-esteem has come from unwarranted criticism. Being able to respond to criticism is therefore very important for people with low self-esteem. There are three secondary methods that it may be helpful to use in order to respond to criticism assertively. These are: acknowledgement (already mentioned), clouding, and probing (see below). Remember also that criticism is usually uninvited and unwelcome and that most critics do not deserve either an apology or an explanation. They will just have to be satisfied with being told that they are right—in this instance, or about this particular point. Remember also that valid criticism about something you might have said, or done, or not done, does not, repeat not, invalidate you as a person.

Acknowledgement

Acknowledgement of the criticism will not protect your self-esteem, if you acknowledge something that is not true about yourself.

Acknowledgement only works to protect your self-esteem when you can agree sincerely with what the critic is saying—even if you may dislike intensely the manner or the force of the criticism. So you may want both to acknowledge and to change the criticism: "You are always late." "Well, it is true that I am late today, and I have been late a few times this month because there have been difficulties with the route to work. But I am not always late."

This means that you need to be just strong enough to be able to filter out the truth that is in the criticism from any malice or bias. This can be quite difficult and it may take a little time. You might need to get away somewhere and think this out quietly to yourself first. Rehearse what you are going to say and then come back and face your critic. You might want to ask for a little more information. "When you say that I am always late, what do you mean exactly?" Or "When you said this was wrong, precisely which bits were wrong?" This can give you more information, or it can put the critic in their place. When you cannot agree fully with the critic, you might want to try "clouding" or "fogging".

Clouding

Clouding involves a token agreement with a critic. It can even be used when the criticism is neither constructive nor accurate. When you use clouding to deal with a criticism, you are saying to the critic, "You might be right about this bit, or that bit", but you are also stating implicitly (to yourself and others), "But you are not right about the rest." You therefore "cloud" by agreeing in part, in probability, or in principle.

1. *Agreeing in part.* When you agree in part, you find just one part of what the critic is saying to be accurate or valid, and you acknowledge that part only. Often criticisms, especially if they are expressed very emotionally, contain blanket statements ("You're no good"); or exaggerations ("We'll lose the house!"); or inaccurate statements ("You are always late!"). You need to filter these out and pick just one accurate or factual statement to respond to.
2. *Agreeing in probability.* You agree in probability by saying, "It's possible that you are right." Even if the chances are extremely

unlikely (like a million to one against), you can still say honestly, "It's possible".

The essence of clouding is that you are appearing to agree, and—to some extent—you are agreeing, and the critic in the other person will have to be satisfied with that. The unspoken, self-esteem-preserving message is, "Although you may possibly be right, I don't really think you are totally. And I intend to exercise my right to my own opinion. And I'll continue to do things (at least partially) my way." You are thereby maintaining your own integrity.

3. *Agreeing in principle.* This clouding technique acknowledges a critic's logic without necessarily endorsing all of their assumptions about you. It uses a conditional "if . . . then . . ." format. Again, you are appearing to agree with the critic, but you are also indicating to yourself and others that, although the basis of their criticism may be absolutely correct (driving too fast *is* dangerous), the application of it to you at this moment in time may not be appropriate—you may not be driving "too fast" at 60 mph on a clear, dry, motorway. So the critic is probably being over-sensitive or over-cautious in this particular instance.

Clouding is a legitimate defence against what seems to be inappropriate criticism. Such criticisms usually come from someone who has their own power issues, and there may also be issues of rank and/or relationship that get in the way of any fuller response. You do not have to feel bad just because you are being criticized, especially if the criticism is inaccurate, or overstated, or inappropriate. The sort of criticism here is not "constructive", but is often laden with negative emotion and can even be an indication of the critic's own insecurities. So, who is the person with problems? Once you have used a clouding technique, it is probably better to stop, to take a break. You have used this technique, now think things out a bit.

Stopping

Stopping does not mean that this issue is over. It just means that you have chosen not to go any further with it for the moment. It is your choice to end this now, and this can be quite empowering in itself. Stopping also leaves any of the unsaid statements more clearly unsaid. You are not "being stopped", you are choosing to stop: that is a big difference.

If, however, you find yourself being quite confused about the criticism, and not understanding what, why, when, how, or where the other person is really coming from, another totally legitimate response is to use the probing technique.

Probing

Probing is where you begin to check the accuracy of what the critic is saying, or the purpose of their criticism. It is best to use this as a last resort, as it can be slightly more confrontational than the other options, acknowledgement, clouding, or stopping and their various sub-sets. It is also best to be quite polite about this. A typical probing statement might be, "Excuse me, but I am not sure exactly what you mean. Could you explain this a little further please?" You have not taken on the criticism, whatever it is, and you have also put the ball back into the critic's court, so to speak. It is now up to them to make possibly a more reasoned and understandable approach to you. Once they have done this, you can still use either of the other techniques. You can also use this probing technique to gain a moment of thinking time. There may even be some information in their criticism of you that is totally valid, that you were unaware of previously, and thus needs some thinking about.

Summary

So, now try to use the following ideas to give yourself a clear idea of what response to make to any criticism. This may take a little time and/or practice before you feel any more confident about facing criticism from someone and not losing your self-esteem. However, it can be, and is sometimes, worth it! While criticism is often seen as negative, someone else is also telling you how they see you, often in no uncertain terms. While this is inevitably their perspective, and says quite a lot about them, it is also their "truth" as they see it. So, someone else is telling you their truth—possibly about how they see you. It might hurt, but there might also be a piece of valuable information buried in that "truth".

Remember to take that important and essential preliminary moment and try to remove any of your old self-esteem issues from the circuit. Your self-esteem is your affair; you are dealing with it, but, at this moment, deal with it later. Someone else's criticism, at this time, is something else, and this is what you are dealing with now. They are not necessarily connected. Put your feelings firmly to one side and try to listen to what the other person (the critic) is saying to you, about something that you may have said, or done, or not done. This does not have anything to do with the rest of you at this moment in time.

Essentially, you are protecting your true self from other people's opinions. Try to imagine a "force field", like an upright glass dome, surrounding yourself. Nothing can get inside this dome or force field unless you want it to get in. If there are any adverse comments or criticisms coming in your direction, then they wil bounce off this force field, or splash against the outside of the dome. Since it is a part of your energy field, you control all aspects of it: if you want to let your child or your cat in, of course they can come in; however, that sarscastic comment or snide remark stays out, and probably says more about the person making that statement rather than anything relevant about yourself.

FAMILY ISSUES

Bereavement and grieving

One of the more difficult situations that people in a family will face is when one of their close relatives dies. Sometimes partners or friends die, and this is tragic, even more so when children die. Families stretch across several generations and it is more likely that we will have the experience of an older family member, such as a parent or a grandparent, dying.

Someone has just died

This is one of the most difficult situations that we can experience in our lives. We are often quite unprepared, and it is often very difficult to deal with emotionally. When someone has just died, everyone is supposed to be sad, but we really have a whole mixture of feelings. There may be feelings of panic, weepiness, the inability to cry, sleep difficulties, or physical symptoms (such as heart palpitations). There may be a sense of agitation or anxiety symptoms. There may even be anger underneath all these feelings. Often, there is a deep depression or despair, which usually passes with time.

Some people also seem quite unemotional, and this may be a form of self-protection; they may not be uncaring—just not showing it. Others may have odd experiences, occasionally feeling as if they are having conversations with the deceased, or thinking they saw or felt them still present for a few moments: these experiences are not unusual. There are some practical things that have to be done. Please use the following as a sort of checklist.

- First, if possible, prepare for someone's death well in advance. After all, we are all going to die at some time. Talk over some things well in advance with your parents and/or your partner. Do they want their organs donated? Have they made a will? Do they want a funeral or cremation? Any special requests or bequests?
- Once someone close to you has actually died, do you want to see the body? It can be quite distressing, but some people also really regret not doing this later. You decide: there is no right or wrong—just what is right for you, now. How about some of the other members of the family—including the children? (It is possible sometimes to over-protect them.)
- In discussing funeral arrangements with the undertakers, have someone else who is close to you present. Do not get pressured into an expensive funeral that you do not really want: simple funerals can be very beautiful. What would the deceased person have wanted? What do you want? What would be best—for you?
- If possible, try not to make major life changes immediately after someone's death. Perhaps enough has changed already. Give yourself some time and space to get over the death: be easy on yourself. You may have to move house, clear things out, or change jobs, but try to do it gradually and in your own time.
- Try to look after your own health (and welfare) as much as possible. You may have been caring for the person who has died; now care for yourself. You are still alive. Make sure you stay that way. Grief can make us neglectful or careless of ourselves. So eat well, rest properly (even if you are not sleeping well), and take extra care of yourself physically. Take some time off work.

- Give yourself plenty of time. There are many adjustments to be made. These all take energy.

Emotional health and support

There seem often to be great difficulties for people in about talking about death and dying: people often do not want to talk about these things very much. Having a strong emotional reaction to someone's death is perfectly normal and healthy, and yet other people can find your strong emotions quite difficult to deal with. The process of adjusting to someone's death is called grieving, and, as a society, we sometimes do not do this very well.

Many people are brought up to think that if they "pull themselves together" and "get on with their lives", things will be all right, or that this is the thing to do. We get swamped with euphemisms. This can make it very difficult for people (you?) to show their real feelings, to speak about things to others, to cry, or to ask for help. In times of difficulty, it is actually better to speak to other people than trying to do it alone; it is healthier to allow yourself to feel and be sad than to pretend nothing has happened. Crying is important because it helps the body relax and helps the mind get rid of anxiety. It gives you space to think about all the frightening and confusing feelings that grief usually brings: despair, guilt, anger, revenge, fear, loneliness, relief, and shame.

Talk to others about what you are feeling. Do not shut yourself off, or bottle things up. Go to the doctor, get some counselling, talk to close friends, or to other people who have suffered a similar bereavement. It helps, really it does. If one particular person doesn't seem able to help, or it doesn't work for you to get help from/with that person, then try another. There is also an organization for bereaved persons, Cruse, made up of people who have gone through this process and know how it is different and difficult for everyone.

Factors that can influence

- Much will depend on your relationship with the person who has died: what was the actual connection (friend, parent,

sibling, child, etc.)? How close were you? When did you last see them? What was the quality of that contact recently? How might you have liked it to be different? Are there regrets?
- Much will also depend on the circumstances of their death. What was the manner of their death? Was it expected? Was it a sudden death, or one following a long illness? Was there a lot of pain involved for the person who died? Was it a suicide? Was it a peaceful death? What was the age of the person? Does this death carry a considerable loss factor (e.g., a young person, just before a wedding, birth, etc.)?
- Your previous experiences of bereavement are relevant. Have you experienced anything like this before? Was this death very different for you? Were other losses very painful, and does this death recreate some of those feelings? Are you still recovering from another loss or bereavement?
- Your views on death may be significant. Have you really thought about this before? What are your beliefs about what happens after death—if anything? Are you scared of dying or of others dying? Do you believe that you should not be feeling this way because of other people's views, or because others seem to be coping all right, or because you were not that close, or because you have to be strong for someone else, or because you think it is time to get over this?
- How much emotional first aid did you get (love from others, a shoulder to cry on)? It is also important that you should have someone who can listen and ask questions and not just comfort. Did people help you to confront your fears of the new and the unknown. Without help, you can feel increasing unease, restlessness, and anxiety, and if another crisis or event occurs you might react violently without really understanding why. How much time did you take off work? Sleep is important, and if you are having difficulty sleeping, your doctor may prescribe sleeping tablets for a short time. Later, try to set new goals for yourself—make new friends, take up new hobbies, and find something to give you new meaning in life.
- If you feel "stuck", or sense that regular, skilled support might help, then seek some counselling. With support from one's family, friends, someone from Cruse, or a trained counsellor, it is possible to move on. Other people's reactions can sometimes

be unhelpful, always harking back, or even avoiding contact with the bereaved person. This is usually because they do not know what to say or how to handle their grief, or yours. They do not realize how isolating or painful their avoidance can be.

The process of grieving

There are several stages in the process of grieving that most people usually need to go through. It continues for a while, sometimes long after the death and funeral. These are all quite common stages. There is also a sequential aspect to these stages, in that if you do not complete one stage properly, there may be a tendency not to be able to progress well on to the next stage.

1. *Shock and disbelief.* It is often hard to make sense of information about someone's death, at first. You can hardly believe it. Sometimes people feel quite numb, feel nothing, or even want to deny that the person has died. It can be quite an adjustment to get used to someone not being alive; you may expect that person to come in at any moment.
2. *Being overwhelmed.* Sometimes we are overwhelmed by the amount of feelings, or the conflicting feelings that we have around someone's death, usually someone who was significant for us. There may be reminders everywhere. Physical symptoms might include: anxiety, emotionality, sleeplessness, inability to concentrate, loss of appetite or "comfort eating", feeling sick, or a feeling of lethargy. Sometimes it is as if you cannot think about anything except the person who has died, or how you will cope without them. There is a struggle between accepting and denying the reality of what has happened.
3. *Low mood.* Bereavement involves a lot of natural sadness. This can affect how we feel about anything and everything else. Most other things can seem unimportant in comparison and there is little motivation or interest in your usual activities. Do not worry. This is natural grieving. It will pass. If it does not, then there may be some strong feelings that are being repressed.
4. *Strong feelings.* Bereavement often involves very strong feelings: anger, rage, guilt, loneliness, frustration, emptiness, etc. Our

belief in the "rightness" of life may have been threatened; that person may have always "been there" for you—and now they are not. Your belief systems may have been thrown in turmoil: there can be anger at God for letting this death happen, or anger at the person who has died. There may also be feelings of guilt: "I should have done more." There may be feelings of relief as that person's suffering has now ended. These can seem incompatible.
5. *Disorganization and reorganization.* There is a massive amount of disorganization, as well as the low and despairing feelings of bereavement. It can seem as if these feelings will go on forever. However, slowly and inevitably, life is reformed and nominally reorganized.
6. *Adapting.* This stage takes time, a great deal of time, much more time than the people around you often seem to want to allow you. "Time is a great healer" has to be balanced with "It's time to move on." If you are still in the midst of your grief, then you are not yet ready for this stage. However, it will start to happen anyway. Some people try to hold it off by keeping things unchanged, such as the room of a child who has died being kept as a "shrine". This may give the bereaved some comfort, but they may also be trying to hold on to that person by holding on to things as they were. They may not be allowing themselves to adapt to the death and bereavement. It is very natural, but it is not very productive. It also means that, in some way, the one who is grieving may be giving the impression that the dead person is more important than the living.

Moving on

Moving on and adapting does not mean forgetting about the person who has died, or betraying the very special place that they had in your life. It just means that your life continues, albeit in a different way to the way that it might have continued if that person had not died. There will be special times when your grief is brought back into focus again. Special dates (anniversaries, birthdays, etc.) can be triggers for remembering, for grieving a little—and can also be celebrated. Sometimes something surprising will bring back the memories, and the grief: a smell, a chance meeting, a location. However, the grief usually does lessen with time, and passes more easily. The memories can still be kept alive, but more as an acknowledgement or a testament to that person's life.

Accepting the loss

A healthy grieving process will include the opportunities to go through all these different stages: to be able to be in the low moods; to express all of the strong feelings; to feel the pain; to adapt to the new situation; to accept the loss; and also how to retain the memories healthily. It is surprising how many people will find that they will empathize with you; you will find that you are not alone. Please try not to feel guilty or disloyal: you have not done anything wrong by trying to get on with your life, by meeting other people, by very occasionally not remembering that that very special person is no longer here.

Please try to use the sympathy and support that is being offered from those around you. You might not want it all, but it is being offered to you in your grief and bereavement. Friends, family, ministers, counsellors, all really want to help you, and their help will make a big difference in how well you handle your bereavement and grief. You may need to talk it through with various people. A temporary distraction, a shoulder to cry on, a stranger in the train, a listening ear, can all be useful for momentary relief: family, work colleagues and friends tend to stay around longer. It may need to be talked out again and again.

It is impossible to say how long the grieving process will take. It is important to give oneself time before letting go of the past and starting a new life. Some people take years before they are ready to do so; most people take one or two years for a family member. Take the time that *you* need. And take it one day at a time. Here also are some other suggestions to help you to cope better.

- Don't clear out a bereaved person's belongings immediately. You may not want to erase the evidence that they existed, even if seeing these things currently gives you pain.
- Don't, however, make a shrine of their belongings and never let anything be touched. This is not letting go of them, and can

- become unhealthy over time. There is also no good time to clear things out, but you will find one.
- Don't be ashamed of being happy occasionally. It is allowed. This keeps you sane and normal. Life goes on.
- Keep in touch with other friends and family. Accept invitations. Invite old friends and people to visit whom you have not seen for a while. You may not enjoy it much, at first, but they may enjoy seeing you again. Even if they cannot make it, they will enjoy being asked.
- Don't worry if you seem to "fall apart" when you are alone. This is often when the grief is strongest or the loss hits the hardest.
- Don't resort too much to alcohol, cigarettes, or other substances in order to "get through".
- When you start to feel better, don't assume you have got over the death for ever. A sudden reminder can bring the grief back again. However, this will pass as well.
- Don't assume that because you do (or don't) want to talk about the person who died, everyone else feels the same. We all cope with loss and grief differently.
- Don't rush into a new relationship just to fill the hole in your life. Some people do. It is not necessarily the best thing for your self, or what is most respectful to the person who has just died, or for those others who cared about that person. It is better to wait a bit.
- If it feels appropriate, acknowledge the absence of the person at birthdays, celebrations, or special holidays. It may be important for you, or for others.

Family and friends can really help

- by spending "ordinary" time with you, helping you to normalize. Doing ordinary things, going places occasionally, including them (and you) in social events and activities, mostly by just being there, or by just being available, and staying available;
- by talking, and especially by listening, to the bereaved person. It is often difficult to always say the right thing, so don't try too hard. Sometimes it helps just to be spontaneous, or sometimes by admitting that you just don't know what to say. Sometimes the bereaved person needs to talk, to repeat, to meander, to remember—over and over. It should pass;

- by not taking the bereaved person's feelings personally, especially anger or irritation. They may be angry that you are alive and that the friend or relative, partner, or child who died isn't. Just sit it out;
- by *not* assuming anything about the person, but by asking and listening. By not buying into any set views about the deceased: "He was a bastard"; "She was a saint". What was the person really like? What is it really like for the bereaved, now. This can help the bereaved person identify and formulate their new reality;
- by dealing with any other crises or difficulties and supporting you that way. People with young children, money difficulties, employment issues, other relationship difficulties, etc., may want some help and support with these, rather than with the bereavement.

"Normal" bereavement issues

The survivor needs to "actualize" their loss—to move beyond the initial state of unreality. They may need to talk, to do something, sometimes over and over again, before it fully hits them that the deceased person has really gone and will not be there, ever again. The survivor also needs to be able to identify and express the wide range of feelings that exist with respect to the bereavement: the problem emotions are often anger, guilt, anxiety, and helplessness. The survivor may need help, or facilitation, in their ability to live without the other person. Did he do all the bills and drive the car? Did she always cook? Who decided what? How are they going to live without the other?

With a parent who has died, the surviving child (or children) has to come to terms with the lack of contact they may have had, or just with the absence—the cornerstone that has always been there. The survivor may also need a form of emotional relocation now that the deceased is not there any longer. In what place will the survivor now put the deceased, so that s/he can move on with their life. Nobody can fill their place, but the deceased may need to "occupy" another space emotionally, so that someone else could eventually adopt a similar place.

Grief needs time, more time, much more time, than is usually thought necessary or possible. Allow for individual differences. Everybody is unique and different. We also react differently. Some people were taught to hide their grief, anger, or distress. They may have become very good at this. Don't buy into this withdrawal or defence pattern. They are still in grief, or even in shock. They may use alcohol, sleeping tablets, work, etc., as a distraction: see through it. Occasionally, even speak to them about it.

Keep in contact, and keep providing the support. The bereaved person is still a person, especially now they have lost a significant other person. Stay in touch, it means so much! Do not read this as a set of rules, but more as a set of guidelines, or possibilities, or suggestions.

Complicated grief patterns

- Grief patterns in a bereaved person can be complicated if the relationship with the deceased was complicated, especially if it was ambivalent, and even more so if there was unexpressed anger or hostility. If the relationship was quite narcissistic or dependent (if the deceased was, in some way, an extension of oneself), the grief pattern can become complicated as the survivor's identity is in some way threatened too. Bereavement can reopen old wounds—especially if there was any former abuse: the abused often has low self-esteem and can blame themselves in some way.
- A complicated set of circumstances also complicates the grieving. Sometimes there is a mystery as to what happened; maybe the person's body is not discovered for a long while. Examples of this are a soldier missing in action, or a victim, one of thousands, of an earthquake or other major disaster,.
- If there is a history of bereavement complications or depressive illness, it is more likely that the present loss will also become complicated. Loss of parents early on in life can also complicate later losses.
- Some people just do not do grief well. They have great difficulty with emotional extremes, withdraw or shut down, or become hysterical and distraught for overlong, and this compli-

cates the usual pattern of bereavement. People's view of themselves can also hinder the process: being the "strong" person for others may mean that you cannot break down and grieve.
- Social complications can arise. In days gone by, the death of a "disgraced" (socially negated) person meant that no one could publicly acknowledge their death. Some people react similarly, from their religious convictions, to suicides (socially negated loss). This can cause complications for other involved people, as a child can adopt his or her parents' responses, thus not allowing their own. We have already mentioned complications that can arise if there is no social or wider support.
- Sometimes there is a situation where the person is not actually dead. They may be on a life support system, or they may have Alzheimer's or dementia, or may just be missing. To a certain extent, these people are *not* the people you knew and loved and they are not "there" for you: there will, therefore, be grief and loss.
- These complications can take four main forms (or combinations of these): (1) chronic (long term); (2) delayed; (3) exaggerated; or (4) masked. There are other complications if the loss is of a special type: suicides, sudden death, infant death and sudden infant (cot) death, miscarriages, still births, and abortions, AIDS, death of child before their parent, or where there is a multiple death situation (war, aeroplane crash, tsunami, earthquake, flood, etc.).
- Whatever the complication, the grieving process needs to be allowed to flow. Ultimately no one can properly help you with this; you need to do it for yourself. It is slightly easier in a culture where grief is allowed and openly expressed.

The "dying" process

During the first wave of the AIDS epidemic in America in the 1980s, and as a result of the hospice movement, a lot of work has been done on how to be with someone while they are dying. This is perhaps the hardest thing to do, to be with a loved one while they are dying. Part of you will desperately want to do something, anything. Part of you will want to run away and hide until it is all over. Part of you may even want to go with the loved one, so as to reduce your pain. Part of you may be extremely angry with God for letting this happen, especially if it is a child or a relatively young adult. Part of you will be devastated with grief, cannot bear the pain of the other person, and so forth. All of these are perfectly "normal" human reactions.

However, the dying person will also have their own needs of you: often these are just to "be there", "do nothing", "don't fuss", "be normal". That is possibly what *they* want. Ask them. Find out. Then you have a choice.

You can react, or you can give them what they want. They may be sad, but resigned; they may be scared; they may want to remember the good times; they may want to know that you will be all right and how you will cope when they are gone. This might be what is important to them.

There are various support systems and groups that can help with the dying and grieving process, and these are listed in the relevant section at the end of the book. The work and writings of Elisabeth Kübler-Ross (e.g., 1997) on bereavement are excellent and are fairly readily available, and there are other recommended books in the self-help books section.

Having to care for others

Basic principle

This section has been included because some people in depression often seem to have someone else that they feel they have to care for and, sometimes, people who have had to care for others can get very depressed themselves. We have been emphasizing how to care much better for yourself. Now we need to consider the other people in your life as well. We might also need to consider the possibility that, since you have been looking after others, now you may also need to look after yourself a bit more so that you can continue to look after these other people.

Reactions

When we discover that we now *have to* look after someone else (perhaps a parent or partner), either suddenly as a result of an accident, illness, or trauma, or gradually as a result of age or deterioration, it is useful to have some awareness of what might be some of the usual initial reactions. Forewarned is forearmed. There is now plenty of information out there for carers. However, many of the principles and the methods can also be applied to parents who are having to care for children, and even therapists who have to care for their clients.

Emotions

Various emotions may be aroused because of the cared-for person's situation, injuries, inabilities, or because of their suffering. These emotions can be very difficult to cope with. The cared-for person may have very powerful feelings, or difficult behaviour patterns. You, the carer, may also have strong emotional reactions, or your feelings may be also related to the emotional needs of the sufferer and/or your personal identification with them. It can get very messy.

Carers can experience many of the emotions associated with the high states of arousal that these events can engender. These may include anxiety, anger, guilt, shame, depression, resentment, helplessness, volatile emotions, and sleep difficulties. There may also be excitement, challenge, love and compassion, and lots of positive determination. There may be repetitive images, concerns, and even obsessions, and/or a marked change in character as you begin to deal with this new (and often unwanted) situation in yourself (as the carer).

These symptoms are usually part of the increased level of arousal associated with the increased level of demand on the caring part of our selves. It is important to recognize that these emotions in the carer are mostly quite normal reactions to an essentially abnormal situation. You have to acknowledge they are there, and also try to find a way through them. You are not a "bad" person for having them.

Roles

Roles change and various different thoughts and attitudes about this are quite common. This person (for example, your parent) may have been looking after you when you were a child, and now this role has reversed: you have to look after them.

You may also have married someone, and now discover that you have to care for their child at times. Since it is a new role, we can often become very concerned about whether we are doing enough in such a situation. This is called "carer's guilt": "Could we do more? Could we have done better?" In such a situation, we may need to discover more about ourselves, what is really needed of us, and what our limitations might be. We may have to say, "I can't do any more." This can be a good thing to say. The situation may be complicated in that we may also be grieving for any lost roles, in both the cared-for person and in ourselves.

Relationships

Sometimes the intense levels of emotional arousal and the changes associated with increased demands of caring for others can lead to difficulties in your relationships with other people, in the family, at work, and with friends. You now have less time available because of the increased demands of the cared-for person. You may be preoccupied with this new level of demand, and seem somewhat shut off from other people, and your other loved ones. You may become less open to other people's needs. You may need someone to be looking after *your* needs, and caring a bit for you. Again, these are perfectly normal changes or reactions to an unusual or even abnormal situation. However, you may need to look after yourself, before you can look after someone else.

How to cope better

The main thing to do is to give yourself a gold star (or three, four, or five) for doing what you are doing, and to keep on appreciating yourself for both caring and for coping. Relatively minor and momentary glitches need to be balanced with what you do, all the time, every day, and what you are doing well. Please don't punish yourself for a moment's inattention, especially when you have just done a twelve-hour stint, seven days a week, for the last six months, or three years.

Three basic principles

1. *Increase your self-awareness.* Be aware more clearly of who you are, what your needs are, what you can and cannot do.
2. *Find your centre.* Try to feel this greater sense of self somewhere in the centre of your body. If you had to touch the place where it is located, where would that be?
3. *Be clear as to your ground.* What was the deal when you took on this extra caring role? Do you have to hold down a full-time job as well? Is there anyone else who could be/should be helping?

Sensing these three essential aspects of your self, in whatever technique, form, or image that works for you is the first major step. This is something that you can do anyway, anywhere and any time. Without these points you will not have a clear sense of whom the "I" is in any such statement as "I am feeling ... [this or that]".

- Recognize the possibility of the feelings, changes, etc. occurring as a result of you doing something very different, or much more demanding, than what is/was usually experienced in your everyday life. These feelings are an important part of this new situation for you.
- Do NOT label any of the above feelings or experiences as evidence that there is something wrong with you. Recognize that they arise out of the change or abnormality of the situation that you are in and it is the *situation* that is probably the source of these feelings.
- You are an individual and you will react individually. There is no set plan; there is no correct way to respond. Some people need to talk, others do not. Some people are stoic, others are oppressed by not being able to talk. Your own experience is what is important for you. If others you know of in similar situations *seem* to be coping better or differently, then you don't know the half of it *and* they are also different from you. Try to avoid such comparisons.
- Check on your own limitations. Your abilities and your situation are unique to you. What can you give, and what are you just not able to give to a situation? What works for you and

what does not work for you? If doing this, that, *and* the other exhaust you, try to find an alternative: only do this, or that, and then let someone else do the other.
- Try to get some special time to yourself, when you are officially "off duty". This is very important. Use these times to relax, to unwind, to enjoy yourself. There should be no guilt about using this time just for you; indeed, it is absolutely necessary if you are to continue in this caring role. If you can use this special time successfully, you will return to the caring role or duties much more refreshed and able to be more efficient, more patient, and more compassionate. This is really fundamental, and it is often the most ignored. You need to have a life as well.
- It is also often necessary and/or advisable—as well as being quite helpful—to speak about or share some of your experiences on a fairly regular basis. If you have any colleagues, or know of other people, in a similar situation, you might be able to work out an arrangement with one of them so that you are able to see them, or speak to them on the phone, to discuss some of your experiences and concerns.
- There may be a local voluntary support organization, or a local group for carers. There may be support staff or respite care accessible through your doctor, the hospital, or through social services. There may be Internet websites, chat rooms, etc., that have special information or that can guide you towards such support facilities. Don't try to do this all alone: get appropriate support for yourself, and allow yourself to talk about the situation you are in.
- As the carer, you have as much right to knowledge and information as the cared-for person. You need to be able to recognize changes—for better or worse. You may be able to access information and resources that the cared-for person cannot access. You may have greater need to know about new developments in treatment, etc.
- Carers now have rights, but you may find they are not being exercised yet, fully enough or ideally enough, everywhere. However, the basic principles are currently in place. There are a number of pieces of legislation and related documents available. For details of some of these try: www.carersnet.org.uk/acts/acts.html

There are also new rights about carers' pensions: Stephen Timms, Minister for Pensions Reform, said recently:

> It is important that carers are aware of their entitlements and take the steps to receive the maximum benefit. The reforms, which this Government has introduced, ensure that carers and people with long-term illness can benefit from building a larger pension. We want people to act now and not miss out. [Press release 11/01/06]

Since 2002, 1.9 million carers and 2.2 million disabled people have begun to build up their entitlement to additional state pensions for the first time. Many carers can, and will, now receive their extra state pension fairly automatically. However, it is still important for people to make sure that this applies to them. For example, unpaid carers in particular may need to take action and apply for Home Responsibilities Protection to make sure that they don't miss out on these benefits. These things are usually not given freely; they sometimes have to be claimed.

Finally, there is just one Commandment for being a carer: Look After Your Self, so that you can continue to look after others.

Information for carers and families

Basic principles

The close family needs to know if a member of the family is ill, depressed, or anxious, having mental health issues, or in treatment. It just does not work trying to keep this sort of thing a secret. They can be told in a matter-of-fact way, appropriately, slightly after the event, but they should be told. Often they can then help with extra support.

There are many "old wives tales" and much social discrimination or prejudice about anxiety and depression, and people associate this with "mental illness". All this has to be debunked or "de-shamed". The vast majority of people who are being treated for anxiety, depression, low self-esteem, anger management, etc., are not, repeat not, mentally ill in any way whatsoever. Yes, they have depression, or anxiety. They are almost certainly not ill, or going mad, or needing to be hospitalized. Yes, some of the stress, or distress, of their lives has resulted in these symptoms, but believing that they need to "pull themselves together and get on with it" really doesn't help. Certainly there may be organic factors, but there is probably not something "wrong" with them. Yes, sometimes these states will occur, but will they be ill for the rest of their lives? Absolutely not.

The family needs to know that certain basic steps have been taken: an accurate diagnosis has been made; the GP has been informed; a referral has (or has not) been made and why; what the reasonable prognosis is; probably details of "best treatment" options have been given, etc. One person should be delegated to act as the main channel for information to keep other people informed, so that the individual, their doctor, or whomsoever is not pestered by different family members, and to ask questions, etc., on behalf of other family members.

The family needs to know that social isolation, on top of any of the current difficulties, makes things a lot worse. Invite the person to normal family events: if they don't show up, come late or leave early, do not take offence. Do not make any extraordinary demands on that person. If the person is irritable, down, unhappy, or unusually elated, it is probably a symptom of the depression, anxiety, or whatever. It is not necessarily the "true" person talking. Don't overreact, don't assume, and don't expect normalcy.

The family needs to know that the most important thing that they can do is to treat the person *as* a person, not as a patient or an object, something to be discussed in whispers that stop as soon as the person comes into the room. The wider family needs to know that there are almost certainly things they can do to help, and there are things that they should not do. These probably need to be laid out clearly and simple in some sort of simple family conference, a time and place where questions can be asked, requests and offers made, other ways suggested. This conference should be repeated every so often while the issues or problems with that family member are present.

Don't carry any blame as a family either: whatever happened was almost certainly not *your* fault. There is a lot of nonsense talked about "depression in the family": "Auntie Mary was like that"; "We should have done more when s/he was a child". You did what you did—probably the best you could do given the circumstances—and they reacted the way they did. Maybe you could have been different—sometimes. But then you would have been a different person. You are human, you make mistakes, you can have regrets. A lot of this is being wise after the event. It doesn't really help that person in this moment. Please don't go there.

There may also be a genetic component. Some conditions do have a genetic predisposition: red hair, blue eyes, sickle cell anaemia, a depressive tendency, a propensity towards schizophrenia or bipolar disorder, or both. Other family members may need to be aware of this. There is not much that can be done except for greater awareness and an earlier diagnosis. Every person reacts differently. There is no guarantee that this will inevitably happen.

All families behave differently. Each family has "rules" about how that family operates; these rules are often unspoken. For example, when family members are angry with each other, can they express this or do they have to keep it to themselves? How emotional can family members be with each other? How do decisions get made in the family? Who has input and who is expected to "just go along"? Are there limits on how much or in what ways children can argue with their parents? Are family members allowed to talk to people outside the family about family problems? What happens when one of these rules is broken: is the rule-breaker still considered to be a member of the family?

The family should know that a sudden onset of a mood disorder has a reasonably good prognosis: it is highly likely the person will get better in time. A slower onset, over time, or with a number of episodes, spread over years, has a somewhat less positive prognosis. And people still get better. Very few people do not get better. However, full recovery ("back to their old self") often takes time. Their "old self" may also be somewhat dysfunctional, and so there may need to be some changes. Not everyone likes changes; make sure you don't become part of their next problem.

The family should also know that modern medications are pretty effective, and although some have side effects, these usually do not last very long. Some of these medications can be taken for a considerable time period without any ill effect, and "doctor's orders" should nearly always be followed. Please don't interfere and give conflicting advice. It is fine to give observations, such as "You are noticeably more irritable". It is fine to express your concerns, but keep them as yours; don't make them into an accusation or a demand.

The family should perhaps know that often the person with the problems does not fully know themselves, or know whether they are all right or not, whether they are getting better, when they will get better, whether they will be better by Christmas, or what they want for their birthday, or whatever. There is often a lot of confusion built into the experience of such problems. Please try to keep these types of interrogative questions to a minimum. Let them know you have these questions, but don't try to get answers from them. Do not allow your fears and insecurities to impinge on their process.

The family should know that different behaviours can sometimes be experienced. The person might want more time to themselves, or to be doing more exercise, relaxation, Tai Chi, or Yoga as part of their treatment, or there may be some anti-social behaviours—such as excessive drinking, anger, suicidal ideation (thoughts)—that are a part of the problem that is being treated. These might all mix together a bit. The difference is that things are now more out in the open. Please do not judge. This does not mean you have to condone anything that does not work for you. Try to keep an impartial distance. Say what works for you and what doesn't. Maintain clear boundaries. Things will work themselves out eventually.

The family should know that there may well be some things that the person might not want them to know. The person may be being treated for something that is very difficult to talk about to another family member, but that is easier and therapeutic to talk about to a relative stranger. Or, in a moment of *non compos mentis*, they might have done something they are now deeply ashamed of. You, the family, probably do not need, or want, to know about this. Please don't feel excluded. The person concerned is trying to work these things out.

The family should know that they might have been affected by this person's problems, sometimes more deeply than they realize, so some of them may need help as well. This is totally legitimate and not really a sign of weakness or of any disorder in the family. Knock-on effects do happen. There are often family support units, or sometimes the family can become involved in the therapeutic process as a family.

Very occasionally, and this is extremely rare, the family may need to make a decision that might adversely affect the person in treatment. The person concerned may not agree, but may need to be confronted with the fact that everyone else agrees that this course of action really needs to happen. Such things could include an enforced period in hospital under the relevant Section of the Mental Health Act; a decision to cut off contact from (say) a partner or the children until the course of treatment is completed and successful; a period of separation because of the accumulated difficulties and stress; a temporary splitting of the family; or even prohibitions against contact because of potential violence or abuse; a cutting-off of support or funds or a restriction of the person's financial autonomy (because of compulsive overspending); etc. This sort of decision is extremely distressing to everyone concerned. It should be discussed in full, over time, with *all* the people concerned, and, hopefully, also with the person's GP and/or therapist, or specialist treatment team.

The family may really need to know a point of contact, someone they could call on if or when things take a turn for the worse. There are a number of legitimate ones: spouse, flatmate, college, work, GP, clinical department, therapist, police, court, etc. Other ones may also be arranged, with the full knowledge of those persons concerned.

Whatever has happened may be an episode that might be repeated. Some long-term planning, a sorting out of this or that, being clear about what might happen if things get worse, can be useful. Some sort of risk assessment, or contingency plan, usually is helpful.

However, families are often incredibly supportive and really helpful in a crisis. People often say that they really value the support they got, are incredibly appreciative, or realize that they never really "knew" that family member until this crisis came along. People will accept help—as well as honesty—from a family member that they would not accept from anyone else. So families can be great—please use them.

For help from outside the family, to support the family, try using a search engine to look for "Family support system [your area]" or "Family support network [your area)": there are an increasing number of family support systems being set up by local councils and voluntary organizations in local areas. These have plenty of good information and some resources; more importantly, they are often staffed by people who have been "there" themselves and now just want to be of help to others.

Parents at home, parents at work

This section is written for fathers and mothers who both work. It is really hard doing both—almost superhuman, almost schizophrenic, almost masochistic—except that we do not have a choice about it. We want to be creative and fulfilled at work, and we want to be at home with our children being the best parent that we can be. The split is not your fault. It is one of the more insidious products of the Industrial Revolution. Your problem is how to balance both sets of needs. You are not alone. You deserve a medal—each.

There is no right way or wrong way to be both a parent and a good employee. The balance will change over time anyway, as your children's needs change as they get older, and as you find different ways to satisfy the demands of employment. For some people, it is really important to be there with their children when they are babies, but someone has to go out and earn money, and that is often the father at this stage. Later, many families find that, if the father is made redundant, for instance, the mother comes into employment in her own way. If the father can come to terms with the changing role, then this can work. Ideally, the family will find some sort of a balance.

Below are some hints and suggestions.

- Working is good for self-esteem, so satisfaction in one area can offset difficulties in another.
- Getting away and being able to cut off for a while is good; you come back refreshed, whether this is to home or work. Don't think about work at home, or vice versa. The trick is to be fully present (100%) wherever you are, at work or at home.
- Make sure there is a good support system at "the other end". If you have to stay at home, perhaps because your children are sick, make sure someone else knows how to pick up on the few essentials at work that cannot wait. If you have to stay late occasionally, make sure there is a fallback system for the children at home. This applies to fathers as well as mothers.
- There is power in numbers: talk to people in similar situations, join forces at work with other men/women with children, put pressure on the company and on the community to ensure your needs are being met properly, with others, help to start up a playgroup, nursery, crèche, or child-minder service.
- Try to make things local: the commute is the killer. Try to live round the corner from the school, or work close to home.
- Just before you get home, or get to work, stop for a moment: put the "other place" completely behind you, compartmentalize it, discharge whatever you have to get rid of, do a little self-care, and then walk in to the office, or the home, fully present, fully "you", ready to partake wholeheartedly.
- If you have a partner, share housework and childcare responsibilities 50:50. It is perfectly all right for one to specialize in the garden or the cooking because they like it or are better at it, but make sure that it doesn't polarize. If you can work different shifts, it may benefit to do so, and then one is at home while the other is at work (for part of the time anyway), but then make sure you both have quality time together as well.
- Be as well prepared as possible. Make lunch-boxes up the night before, work out contingency plans, do risk assessments, educate neighbours or grandparents, have spares in stock, tell the children what to do when/if certain things happen.
- Create your own life plan, style, work–home combination; it is your life. Never assume that someone else's way will work for

you. You need to figure out what works the best for you, and for all of you, and then check it out.
- Have a regular family conference. The best time is often between main course and dessert on that special meal on Friday or Sunday night. Get into the habit of talking things through all together: what worked last week, what is happening that is special this week. Plot everything on the calendar on the kitchen wall, alongside the list of phone numbers. If anything changes, it gets changed there.
- If you do not have a lot of time to help out at school, or whatever your child is involved with, make sure the time you do have is spent when your child is present.
- Don't be afraid to ask for special arrangements, or unorthodox work times. They may work out better, and you won't know until you ask. Going in at 6.30 a.m. may mean leaving at 3.00 p.m. to pick up the children; this can be absolutely fine as someone is then on duty for the early deliveries or when the Far East calls. Having a two-week holiday before Easter may be cheaper than in the summer.
- Resist too many extra-curricular activities or overtime at work. Do just what is in your job description: that is what you get paid for. Do not subsidize your employer. But do occasionally go to the Christmas Party or the Summer Barbeque, with your other half and maybe the children as well, and invite your manager home to dinner with the family.
- Don't let your boss push you around. You are entitled to a home life. Often they will want you to do as much as you will say "Yes" to. You need to set the boundaries; you need to decide the limits. Going beyond these means that your work—and home life—will ultimately suffer. Then there will be a problem. Be clear about what you can and cannot do; people will respect you for that.
- Be equally clear at home. If the end of the financial year is coming up, then you cannot pick the children up from Scouts or dance class this month. They will have to get home differently—with a friend, or by bus, or something. Next month you can reciprocate when you are freer. You can only do this once, maybe twice, in a year.
- Pace yourself at work and at home. Find what works for you and then stick to it. If you are getting overloaded, then you are

probably trying to do too much. Maybe this means that you need some help. It is the wise person who realizes this early. Maybe only work three days a week, or get a lodger or an au pair to help with the children if you are a single parent, or perhaps your job really needs an assistant, or a review of the job description or the other parent's responsibilities are now necessary. It is not always that you are the one who is failing.

- Work for someone with children of their own. It helps.
- Remember also that the firm chose to employ you. They know you have children and chose to continue to employ you, knowing that at times you would need to go and resolve a particular situation at home or at school.
- Make the most of your time at home with the children. Spend hours playing with them on the carpet with Lego or whatever: these times are fleeting. They don't ever come back. Take them to the pool or the park regularly; they will remember you teaching them to swim, or those games of football all their lives. Keep the family rituals, the high-days and holidays, as sacrosanct as you can. Be there!
- Don't try to be perfect! Try to be reliable, try to be "good enough", try to be competent; try to be "you"!

Single parents

It is even harder for you very brave people, harder than anyone will ever know—except perhaps another single parent. You are (more likely than not) a mother; more likely than not you will have (perhaps fought for) sole or joint custody; and, more likely than not, you are also having to cope with some deep bitterness around the break-up or divorce as well. What more can be said? Nearly all of the list of suggestions given above still applies to you. Especially the bits about making it local, getting support from others, not being afraid to ask for special arrangements, talking to others, etc. The only bit that doesn't really apply is sharing the housework, so the children will just have to do more, and become much more self-reliant quite a lot earlier. It is a great pity, but it is also the reality of the situation.

Relationship issues

There is no way that we can cover all the very complex issues around relationship difficulties in one or two pages. These are, or should be, learnt skills, built up on a solid basis of love, respect, and mutual benefit. However, here are some guidelines for when things get a little rocky.

Don't question

Don't question that you ever loved each other, that you still love each other, and also that, currently, there are some serious difficulties preventing you exchanging that love freely and easily.

Pain

Because you love(d) each other a lot, and are/were very open to each other, you are also capable of hurting each other very deeply. It just goes with the territory. If one person in the relationship (A) feels hurt, the other person (B) *must* acknowledge that. This does not inevitably mean that person B has actually hurt person A, but A definitely feels hurt. Try to explore that tension between you. Try to understand some of the dynamics. Try to tease out the point where (perhaps) B actually did do something to A, *and* A somehow feels much more hurt by that than is actually justified by the nature of the event or offence. Maybe it touches on an old, unhealed wound. So A feels *really* hurt, and B feels that s/he didn't do *that* bad a thing and cannot understand why A is making such a fuss. So then A feels that his/her pain is not being acknowledged, etc.

The psychiatrist R. D. Laing wrote a wonderful book, *Knots* (1970), that investigates some of these confusions in depth.

Trust

There has almost certainly been a breakdown of trust somewhere between the two of you. This is serious, and potentially damaging, but it does not necessarily mean that the love between you has gone totally. One may feel betrayed because the other has had an affair, and the other may feel betrayed that the first no longer loves them because of a single indiscretion. And so on! However, trust does not come back easily. It has to be regained slowly and consistently over time. Any further serious breaches of trust, especially after a seeming determination (on both sides) to reform and change, might prove fatal to the essential core of the relationship: it depends on many factors.

Help

Both of you will almost certainly need help from an outside party, as well as from friends and relatives. Unfortunately, those closer to one than the other may well take sides, which is not helpful. Try to see a couples counsellor or similar—together. You both have a problem here in that the relationship that has supported you both is in difficulty. It does not matter who thinks what, or where the "fault" (if any) is, you are walking on the edge of a precipice and need a guide.

Listening

Perhaps the best thing you can do together is really to listen to each other. So often we get into our habitual patterns of relationship that just do not work any more. S/he says, "Why didn't you do this?" He/she feels attacked and disrespected and so walks out. S/he then feels ignored and abandoned. And so on. Here is an exercise. Try it out.

> Person A talks for an agreed length of time (say ten or fifteen or even twenty minutes) about the issues in the relationship that work, or don't work for them, using the topics below if you like, or other more specific issues, like sex, money, attitudes, the other's attitude to the children, how fast the person drives, or how much they drink. Don't make it all negative, put some positives in as well. Please use 'I' statements: "When you do this or when that happens, I feel...".
>
> Person B is not allowed to interrupt or say anything—except as a question for further information ("Who is Mary?" "Is John the new boss?"). At the end of the agreed time period, B repeats back to A (in about five minutes) as detailed a synopsis as possible of what A has said ("I heard you say that... and you feel this... and that... You said... and..."). Then you both take a short break and try NOT to discuss what has been said up to now. Then restart.
>
> Person B talks for the same period and then A repeats back their synopsis. The exercise is then over. You then need to set up another time when you can talk about the content of what each person has said. The reason that this can work is that both A and B have now been listened to, and know that they have been heard. It is a very good start.

This exercise comes from co-counselling, or reciprocal peer counselling. It creates a basic evenness within the relationship. Essentially, it is a grass-roots, low-cost, self-help method of personal change. It is a simple refinement of "You tell me your problems, and I'll tell you mine". It is not a discussion; the aim is to support the person in the "client" or "speaking" role to work through their own issues in a mainly self-directed way. The other person, in the listening role, is just "there" for that person during that time period.

Relationship questionnaire

There is another relatively simple technique, a measurement of relationship satisfaction, that can also be used as a guide or tool to improving your relationship. Copy out Table 2, and each person—separately—should then fill in their own rating for each of the categories given.

Make sure that you do this separately, then come together and compare results. The total maximum and minimum score possible is between −39 and +39 (both very rare); however, for most people (about 60–75%), some of the positive and negative scores will tend to cancel each other out and the normal grouping of totals is somewhere in the centre of this range, about −18 to +18.

- If both of you have totals that are positive, that is great—and there may also be a few issues (those that score negative) that you need to work on to improve the relationship a little more.
- If one person's total is positive and the other's is negative, then I suggest that you both enter into some process (perhaps rela-

Table 2. Measuring relationship satisfaction.

Aspect of relationship	Score*
	−3 −2 −1 0 +1 +2 +3
Intimacy and closeness	
Affection and caring	
Communication and openness	
Pleasure, laughter, fun	
How good you feel in this relationship	
How good you feel about the other person	
Respect and consideration	
Solidity and support	
Resolving conflicts and difficulties	
Trust and reliance	
Management of finances	
Duties around the home	
Being with the children (if relevant)	

*Scoring system: −3, very dissatisfied; −2, moderately dissatisfied; −1, slightly dissatisfied; 0, neutral; +1 slightly satisfied; +2, moderately satisfied; +3, very satisfied.

tionship counselling) to try and sort out this disparity. (NB: the person who scores the relationship as negative may not be the one who actually has the problem.)
- If you both have negative totals, then you are definitely going to need some help to try to turn this relationship around before it is too late. Get into proper relationship counselling.
- Using this "test" as a guide or a tool, you can also ask yourself and each other, "How could we make this category's negative score become more positive? What would you need? What would I like?" and this should give you some definite material to work with. Maybe use the co-counselling exercise above to do this.
- Try completing the relationship satisfaction table in three months' time, and see if there is any significant change.
- Work *with* each other in the interim. Both parties should try to make positive changes.

Building positive bridges

It is very easy to criticize and to feel negative, angry, indifferent, or despairing when the other person doesn't seem to do what you want them to do. Then they get angry because you are being negative, angry, indifferent, or despairing, and so you both get into a rather vicious negative spiral. Try building positive bridges instead.

"Do you remember that day in ... when we laughed until our sides ached?" "I loved it when we did ... and ...". These types of positive bridges, what does (or did) work rather than what doesn't work, can lead you away from the brink of the precipice. It is important to remember that you both loved each other, and probably still do.

You can try instead saying, "When you do ... rather than ..., it works for me and makes me feel positive towards you again." This is a positive statement, which, one hopes, might lead to a better outcome. The other person needs to steer away from their dysfunctional behaviours, as much as you need steering away from your sensibilities which have "red buttons" on them, towards a much more positive pattern: a positive bridge.

Instead of working at cross-purposes and creating dissonance, you can try working together (at co-purposes) and trying for a bit more harmony. People who stay together in a relationship tend to live longer than single people, especially more than those who were in a relationship. Splitting up may therefore shorten your life.

Sometimes relationship difficulties have something else behind them. It is not just that the two of you are not getting on. Something else might be wrong, and this is affecting the relationship. It can actually be quite a relief to discover this. But you will never discover what this is unless you start talking about it.

What type of love?

There are several different types of love: we have love for our parents; we have love for our children; we love our dog or cat, possibly because they "love" us. With our children, it is an almost unconditional love, as we will love them (probably) whatever they do. Love can often be confused with need: I need to love and be loved; you seem to fit that need; therefore I love you and you love (or need) me.

There can often still be "love" in a relationship that has, as a basis, "I'll scratch your back, if you scratch mine". What many people find in this type is more a form of interdependency: "I'll do the garden/cooking, if you do the cooking/garden." This has worked for thousands of years, and can continue to work very well, but it is not really "love" in itself. And, when it goes wrong, it starts to become conditional or co-dependent: "I'll continue to do this and this for you, as long as you don't disturb me or challenge me about that."

Scott Peck (2006), an American psychotherapist, wrote about love and relationships in a well-known book, *The Road Less Travelled*. It can be quite nice for each of you to read this book, chapter by chapter, discussing it as you go through it. This can help define what each of you mean, or want, about the type of love in your relationship with each other.

Sexual difficulties

There might be sexual difficulties that are not being talked about properly. Most of us have sexual difficulties at some time in our lives and these can be caused by a variety of factors such as stress, difficulties at work, poor self-esteem, or even an undiagnosed medical problem. Some medically prescribed drugs can affect one's sexual functioning. There may be some underlying complex psychological difficulties, or even confusion over sexual orientation—for instance, choosing the right time and place to "come out". Sexual difficulties that can respond well to psychological or psychosexual therapy include, for women, difficulties with vaginal intercourse or penetration (vaginismus), orgasmic difficulties (anorgasmia); for men, erectile difficulties (impotence), painful intercourse (dysparuenia), premature or retarded ejaculation; and for both, sexual phobia, sexual orientation issues, loss of sex drive, or loss of desire for partner.

Loss

Maybe you have lost one significant relationship (perhaps a parent or a child) and you may be emotionally grieving. Sometimes this can affect other relationships (such as with a partner) for considerable periods of time. If your partner is having a problem with this, it might just be a bit more their problem than yours. Perhaps some form of couples' counselling, or (for you) bereavement counselling, might be appropriate.

Life changes

At certain times in our lives, such as childbirth, menopause, death of a parent, retirement, etc., we have to change, quite radically, the perception that we have of ourselves. This means that we also change. This is normal and natural. If, however, our partner (or children, or parents) are effectively saying, "You've changed; you are not the same person that we knew and loved", then again there may be a problem. The problem may be slightly more theirs than yours, even though it has a considerable impact on you as well. You are trying to adapt to the new change, they do not want you to change. However, there is nothing wrong with you, other than you have (naturally and normally) changed according to changing life's circumstances. Their expectation may be that they want "the same old you". This could be a conservative or fixed outlook on life. This sort of change can also be applied to one person developing a serious illness, (re)starting work/college, children leaving home, or one of you becoming attracted (for a while) to someone else. Again, some form of couples' counselling may be appropriate, or, otherwise, some in-depth discussion about what these changes might mean for both of you.

Underlying emotions

This can be like a minefield. Perhaps (at the Christmas Party, say) your partner sees you laughing and joking with people at your work. They get a little envious or maybe even jealous, if it is with a member of the opposite sex. This makes them a bit cold or abrupt with you. Their reactions drive you a little further away, perhaps more into the company of these "friends" at work. A whole negative cycle can start. This just *has* to be talked out properly. Again, a counsellor can act as a mediator, or you can try the co-counselling exercise presented earlier.

Behaviour patterns

Sometimes long-established behaviour patterns have a detrimental effect on the relationship. It is not just a matter of changing the pattern of behaviour; sometimes the person's whole perception about themselves and others has to change as well. How we were parented affected us; it may model or affect how we relate to a significant other, or how we parent. These aspects can all impinge on the relationship we are in now.

How we manage these changes or these issues is extremely significant. We can hope to keep out of the areas of divorce and separation, but even if things are rocky just for a while, they can still be profoundly upsetting and distressing. Even a temporary loss of love, lack of trust or respect can have a long-term, corrosive effect. If the "problem" is caught relatively soon, and dealt with reasonably appropriately, much later distress can be avoided.

Relationship difficulties

Is it over?

When this question comes up in your mind, try not to react out of despair and panic, anger or rage. A relationship is much too valuable a thing to throw away in a moment, and the other person, whom you have loved and probably lived with for a while, is also much too valuable to be thrown away at a moment's notice because of your pain, fear, or panic. You are probably feeling hurt and betrayed, as well as being in despair. The other person may indeed have hurt you deeply or even betrayed you in some way. However, if you are hurt, betrayed, in despair, or panicking, this is possibly not the best space to be in to make important decisions about this relationship and about the rest of your life. Give it just a little time longer to let these feelings settle, and only then start to consider whether the relationship might really be over.

The pros and cons

When people try seriously to decide if their relationship is over, they often find themselves weighing up some of the pros and cons of whether this relationship is working for them, and whether it is still worth staying in it. On the "pro" side, they tend to put all their partner's positive character traits, the happy memories, and the advantages of being together. On the "con" side, they list all the things they do not like about their partner, the painful memories, and the reasons why living together sometimes feels impossible.

The problem with this system is that it is rather simplistic and that they are not measuring like-for-like. For example, how many negative points does it take to counteract her being an excellent mother? And how many happy memories over long years does it take to outweigh a one-night stand? So, unfortunately, there is no simple yardstick, no formula, and no conclusive test to help you decide whether your relationship is over. All you can do is to ask yourself some very difficult, soul-searching questions, feel some of the very painful feelings, communicate with the other person a lot more, and see what eventually balances out.

Is love enough?

Love means different things to different people and at different stages of their lives, so, can this four-letter word with so many different complex meanings really be relied on in the decision-making process? For example, one woman may spend years in an abusive relationship, saying, "I love him", while another will walk away from a seemingly idyllic marriage because she's no longer "in love".

Love can also sometimes blind us to the reality of what we really have. We might love this or that about the other person, and ignore many of their other lovely but less obvious qualities. And although it is difficult, we can choose to love someone, and we can choose to stop loving that person. We may feel that we truly love the other person, but they might experience this love very differently—as selfish, abusive, or cold. As well as being a feeling, love is something that we do—and that other people experience. How about "hard" love, or "cold" love, or "possessive" love?

"Ouch" sometimes works

Instead of reacting to something negative that your partner says or does (or doesn't do), how about saying "Ouch!" The reason why this sometimes works is that you are probably giving them a very different signal: you are not getting into the old "blame game", nor are you nagging or exploding or going quiet, or whatever your usual pattern of negative reaction is. You are just saying "Ouch! That hurt." You are not saying, "You hurt me." But you are indicating that whatever they did (or didn't do) had an impact. You are not retaliating or being reactive or provocative; you are just saying "Ouch!"

Do you still like your partner?

Before you can love someone properly, you also have to like them. If you enjoy being with your partner, agree with how they think and behave, and share the same dreams in life, you are doing pretty well. If your partner is also someone whom you respect, trust, and feel affection for, you have some of the basics for love to grow. If they are kind and if they respect you, that is another bonus point. Is all this "like" strong enough to carry you over some of the difficulties you are having with "love"?

Can you communicate?

All relationships hit some pretty serious problems at one time or another. The key to overcoming these is proper communication. Within your relationship, there needs to be a genuine capacity for sharing and expressing your thoughts and feelings in a way that feels all right for you both. Both parties need to make efforts to communicate properly: one cannot communicate with someone who is imitating a brick wall or a hedgehog. There also need to be built-in ways to resolve conflicts and for you both to address any unmet needs. The co-counselling technique mentioned earlier might help. Couples therapy might help. Wider family conferences can help break the nuclear family "one *vs.* the other" locked-in positions.

Is change possible?

If there is a particular issue that makes you want to leave, you first need to consider whether it is possible to make the changes needed to resolve the problem. Is the problem something that you can let go of, or is it fundamental to your happiness? Could you stay if "this" and "that" happened? How do you make these changes become possible? If the problem is something that you could possibly let go of, under certain conditions, you then have to ask yourself whether you can make the necessary changes *and* whether your partner can do the necessary changing.

If your partner does not agree that there is a problem, then they almost certainly will not change. They may therefore need to be confronted with the probability that it is over for you. If they do agree there is a problem, and that changes have to be made, and show a willingness to change, then you then have to decide whether you believe that they have the capacity to change and the perseverance to see these changes through.

Please remember that, while they might have committed the overt offence or betrayal or whatever, it takes two people to tango, and that you have both been dancing for a while. If they are going to start changing, how about a little reciprocation, or a few changes, from you just to help ease the process. Have you even asked them what they might like you to do—as well as what you want them to do. Sometimes these processes are reciprocal.

Is it too late?

There's no doubt that some situations can and do get better with time. Even the most painful betrayals can become less significant, if there is an ability to forgive and move on. But if either you or your partner has been hanging on to a grudge for years and there is no indication that the pain has eased at all, you may decide that it is too late for a resolution, or that there have been too many "lapses", or that the coldness or anger or whatever has gone on for just too long. Another indication that it may be too late to save the relationship is if one of you has already started to develop a life that excludes the other. This might include a change in career or lifestyle, or starting another relationship that you don't want to end. If this is the case, then, even though you have not made a verbal decision to end the relationship, it may be that emotionally you or the other person has already effectively left.

However, that is not the end of the story. There is a whole mass of communication that is needed in order to work out all the details of the ensuing separation: money, goods, property, children, pets, etc. You have had a whole life together and now it is starting to unravel. Do not cut and run or change the locks unless there is an emergency and you have been seriously advised to do so by any professionals involved. There are surprising benefits to be had from seeing a process through and making sure all the details are dealt with. It means that you can discuss things in the future, or even discover that, while the relationship is over, a friendship may develop.

Rebuilding the relationship

There are several things one can do to rebuild a relationship before it has gone too far and before it ends in divorce, acrimony, or just cold silences, all of which can turn out to be pretty expensive. These fall into three different areas, listed below.

1. *Stop coming from your pain.* Most acrimonious exchanges occur when one partner is coming from their painful feelings, and, instead of the other partner being there for them, helping them, soothing them, and responding appropriately, he or she also comes from their own painful feelings. This doesn't work. Instead, both parties need to try to: (a) recognize that this is probably what is happening; (b) try to create a language cue, or a signal, or a way of stopping this painful exchange; (c) then take a step back and see if you can come from a different place. If you can both start to build this habit into your relationship, over time, rather than continually "kvetching" or nagging, or blaming each other, then you will be taking the first step towards rebuilding a much better relationship.
2. *Building positive bridges.* The above, by itself, is probably not enough to restore or rebuild a relationship. You both have to

start building positive bridges: "Thanks for taking the dustbin out to the roadway"; "Thanks for remembering to pick up my suit from the cleaners". These bridges also need to "touch" the other person, so you have to ask or find out what aspects of themselves and what they do, that they want appreciated. If they respond to the above, "It's just what we agreed I'd do" then you are probably not "touching" them. If you'd asked them, "What would you like me to appreciate you for?" and they said, "Clearing up the garden leaves, because I really don't like that job", or "Ironing your shirts, because I hate ironing", then you might be getting somewhere when you start appreciating them for that. The bridge must be a positive one, and it must touch them. And if you do not know what they would like to have appreciated about themselves, do not be surprised that things are going wrong. So go and find out!
3. Get back to the "I–Thou" relationship. This is the relationship with the person that you fell in love with some time ago. Yes, they have their faults, or have grown fat, or drink too much, or whatever, but the essence of that person is still inside them, and that is the bit that you fell for and probably still love. Try to relate to that part of them again, from the essential part of you that is deep inside you and still loves them deeply. You may not have been coming from that part of yourself, because of all the other "stuff" that has been happening, but if you can contact that part of yourself, and then reach out for contact to that part of themselves . . . well, the relationship still stands a chance.

It is also probably true to say that, unless these three basic changes can be made, the relationship is unlikely to survive its current difficulties. There may still be a window of opportunity. Instead of working at cross-purposes, you can start working together (co-purposes). Sometimes it is necessary to make some external changes as well, to get out of the old patterns. Maybe this means that you need to sleep—for a while—in separate rooms, so that when you come together it is out of choice and desire, rather than out of routine. It may be necessary for one person to move out for a while, to give the other person some space and time. Sometimes marriages work better as intimate friendships, and the piece of paper (certificate) got in the way. If there is a separation, don't necessarily see it as a trial separation. Try seeing it as refinding the right space and type of contact. You may need to woo the other person all over again. It can even be quite fun.

The honeymoon is definitely over. Statistically, this usually takes at least three years. Another very difficult period is when the children start to leave home. Additionally, significant life events can put a real strain on the relationship. These events are often unexpected, thus causing additional strain, and can include accidents, injuries, illnesses, financial difficulties, or loss—of a job, a child, the home, or trust. There can also be difficulties such as infidelity, violence, sexual abuse, alcohol, or criminality. Now the real work starts.

You have chosen this person, and maybe even decided to have children with them. This creates an intimacy, which is important to maintain. This also means you are now committed to some sort of 20–30-year relationship with that person, as a co-parent, at least. There is probably going to be at least a weekly phone call, maybe a lot more. It is very difficult to cut and run from this sort of a commitment, and, if you do, the grief and pain that you will cause to people whom you love and who love you is phenomenal. As a counsellor and therapist, this is what I hear, and get to talk about—at some considerable length.

Therapy will not and cannot solve any couple's problems. It should, however, provide a forum—a relatively safe space—in which the couple can check out their boundaries and responsibilities, improve their communication and negotiating abilities, and increase the flexibility of their responses with and to each other.

Divorce and separation

Divorce or separation can be one of the most emotionally destructive situations that you ever find yourself in. There are also—often—children involved. Once you are absolutely committed to a divorce or legal separation, couples therapy is probably not appropriate for you; it is possibly too late for that. What you might need then are some pointers, some advice, mostly about what *not* to do.

In some places, it is court-ordered (mandatory) for divorced parents to have to attend a seminar on the implications of their divorce: how the children can be affected, what parental actions are appropriate and what are not, how to separate your feelings (as divorcing parents) from the feelings of the children, etc. Couples then need to produce a certificate of attendance at such a seminar for the court, prior to the divorce being heard. Modern divorce ought to be about careful negotiation and considerate mediation. Unfortunately, our legal system is not very good at this, as it is essentially adversarial and they just cannot seem to get out of that way of thinking. If you can avoid arguing things out in court, or having the court decide, or negotiating only through solicitors, really do so. Please! It will also be a lot cheaper and easier and probably much less acrimonious.

Try to work things out first between just the two of you, or maybe use a relative, or a mutual friend, or a professional acquaintance as an arbiter. Then each of you can go to your own solicitor with a roughly agreed set of arrangements, so that these can be checked over and then formalized. Please remember, there are not just two parties in a divorce (especially one with children): there may be several more involved people, as grandparents get used for additional childcare, or get excluded by one parent moving away, or by taking sides, or by having to become involved financially. Try to find a set of solutions that works for everyone. You will, perhaps, only do this by asking them what they need, and this includes the children as well. A family conference can be useful; probably more than one might be needed.

If your feelings about your ex-partner are those of hurt, or of bitterness, find somewhere to work on these separately, or find someone else (like a counsellor or psychotherapist) to work them out with. Please remember that your ex-partner may also be hurt and angry, or may feel abandoned and betrayed too. Both of you are probably hurting, and both of you may need some help. In divorce situations, there are no rights and wrongs; there are no winners, only potential losers. You both had something great—and now it is gone. Try not to take out your pain and distress on the other person; it might mean that you are not allowing yourself to feel it. In the long term, this may be to your disadvantage.

With respect to the children, they really are the innocent parties. They did not do anything wrong, they just came along—at your instigation (lest you forgot). Yet they are also the ones who probably will get hurt the most in any divorce situation. Please bear this in mind. There is a distinction here between the ones who feel the most hurt (possibly you and your ex) and the ones who will *be* the most hurt, probably your children.

If one of you has another lover, please be aware that you may be heaping hot coals on the head of your ex-partner. Maybe this is intentional. Just the existence of a third party is pretty inflammatory, irrespective of any rights or wrongs of who left whom, or who met whom, or when. One person is alone and their "other" now has another. Do not necessarily feel guilty, just be aware of possible feelings in your ex-partner!

Here is another point to consider: in the splitting up of property, pensions, holiday homes, etc., are you still considering a 50:50 split just because there are just two of you (adults), or are you considering (as well) the children as being significant beneficiaries with respect to college funds, inheritance, etc. The property they currently live in may be a significant part of their future inheritance. Discuss it with each other before you go to your solicitor(s).

The final, general, point is that frequently one party in a divorce situation will end up feeling depressed. This does not mean that they are mentally ill in any way whatsoever. It just means that the stress of the situation has landed here, with them, rather than anywhere else or with anyone else. An understanding GP, some fairly extensive counselling, some (possible) medication, a good solicitor, and a reasonable time lapse usually manages to correct this situation. Still, it is not a very nice place to be. Nor is it a nice place to put the other person into. Please don't rub it in by saying things such as, "You're so negative these days", or, "I can't talk to you, you are so depressed".

Dos and don'ts with children

- It is almost certainly not appropriate to blame or insult the other parent in front of the child, or children. The child has its own loyalties, and evidence shows that any bad-mouthing usually bounces back eventually on to the person who is doing it.
- It is not appropriate to say: "S/he's the one who left us." You do not want the child or children to feel abandoned. That is *not* what is happening. Furthermore, to the child's mind, if one parent can up and leave, then so can the other parent at any moment. So you are not helping them to feel secure. They need to be told something different—and probably closer to reality.
- You will probably need to reassure the children that you are not going to leave them in lots of different ways. Talking with them is one of the best. Telling them that you love them is another. Not getting angry with them is a third. Building a secure space: their room, their time, etc., is another. Waiting for their loaded question—it will come—about what happens if you die, or are you angry with them, or if you like (your new partner) a lot,

does that mean that you will want to go away and live with them and leave the child with someone else. Get the picture? The evidence suggests strongly that the child will have such fears anyway, and the fears will not go away for quite a long time. A few words now and then are not enough. Actions speak much louder than words: consistency speaks volumes.
- It is also not appropriate to change the way you speak about the other parent: "That man ..."; or "Your father/mother ..." instead of "Mummy" or "Daddy", as this is objectifying and alienating. Use the same pronoun or name as you have always done. The child still has the same relationship with that parent. Try to keep something constant.
- You may need to do something specific and positive about your own bitterness, or lack of self-esteem, or pain around the relationship break-up. Going into therapy or counselling is probably a really good idea. Speak to your GP in the first instance and s/he should be able to arrange a few sessions on the NHS. Don't be put off by not getting the right therapist immediately. You could also try insisting on you and your ex-partner getting some sessions with Couples Counselling or Relate in order to try to manage this time of separation and have a place to talk things over. Get granny, an uncle, aunt, or good friend to babysit these joint sessions. It might save considerably on the lawyer's bills as well.
- It is not appropriate to share with the child/children too many complex details, such as the financial settlement, lawyers' letters, legal terminology, court decisions, argumentative letters going to-and-fro, etc. The child has got quite enough to cope with. Almost all adult information is confusing for the child, especially the "stuff" around a divorce or separation. But don't patronize them. If they ask something specific, tell them. Answer questions such as "Why are we getting rid of the rabbits?"
- Try to make arrangements for childcare that are simple and regular. Stick to them as much as possible, but without being too rigid, as in "No you can't take part in this [e.g., major school trip] because you'll be staying with mum/dad then." This sort of rigidity just creates additional stress and distress for the child. However, both of you probably need to work or have a

degree of surety about arrangements. It is *not* all right to ring up on Friday evening and say, "I can't take the children this weekend. Something has come up."
- While it might seem fair for you and your ex-partner to have the children 50:50, this might not be the best arrangement for the children. They might prefer something different than being treated a little bit like "Pass the Parcel", or having their time split down the middle. They will want somewhere of their own, their special space, in the absent parent's new flat/house. They will want very special times with that person. They will want to see that person regularly. They will want as little disruption as possible. They will want to feel safe. They may well want to feel special to that person. Try to think things out from their perspective as well as your own and that of the other parent. Do not let too much of your bitterness, anger, or despair creep into these types of arrangements. Ask the child sometimes how it is working out for them.
- When you negotiate with the other parent about childcare, money, or whatever, please do it well away from the children, and especially not at the hand-over, with the child in the car seat. Negotiate preferably face-to-face, but, if that is not feasible, on the telephone, and with both parties giving this quality time. It is very important stuff. Text messages saying, "I can't give you the maintenance cheque this month!" are not appropriate.
- If your ex-partner bad-mouths you in front of the children (when you're not there) and they then tell you about it, don't retaliate. They are probably just telling you because they want some reassurance, or because they are confused. They don't need any further distress. Just say something neutral such as "That's not so", or "That's his/her opinion. It doesn't make it correct". Speak about this to the other parent quietly and firmly at a later moment.
- Don't believe everything your kids tell you—especially about their other parent. Much will be a (sort of) test to see how you react. "Daddy made pizza last night. It was great" is probably best reacted to with "That's nice. You like pizza", rather than "The lazy so-and-so never lifted a finger in the kitchen when we were together, and couldn't boil an egg without help."

- Your children will probably feel that the reason you are getting divorced is something to do with them. They usually do. You cannot stop them feeling that way easily. Telling them once or twice that this is not so is not going to make their belief go away. They will feel partially responsible. "Mummy and daddy were in love, they got married, then they had me/us and then they got divorced." The logic is damning. You will both need to work hard on this one.
- If you slag off the other person, then—to the extent that your child identifies with that person as their parent—you are slagging off a part of them. Your child may not say anything, but inside they will be hurting.
- When things get divided up, it should not necessarily always be on a 50:50 basis. There are actually more than two people involved. For example, the single parent with custody and, thus, the children, needs a bigger house than the other parent without the children. Unsurprisingly, this costs more. Why should the parent without custody have space for "another" at your expense? The "other" (new) man or woman may also be earning. Get as real as you possibly can! Some of the lawyers' formulae are frankly archaic and dysfunctional. Try to get the grandparents (on your side, at least) involved in any discussions. Argue your case in court, if you have to. 50:50 isn't always fair. As a counsellor and psychotherapist I have heard much too much bitterness about this point not to say something.
- Any sort of revenge is not a good idea: it just hurts people more, people who are hurt already, including you. Let the other party "win their spurs", or possibly "hoist themselves by their own petard": i.e., let their actions speak for themselves. They will be forming a new relationship with the children that will establish something (or not) for the significant future. You do not have to do anything. They will be judged by their actions by the children.
- Clarity, clarity, clarity! S/he will think you are doing things to get back at him/her; you are probably not. S/he will accuse you of wanting more, of changing the rules, of being vindictive. Just stay quiet, don't protest, don't argue back, don't get too angry. Just state what you (and the children) really need and keep on stating that. No other argument is needed or is necessary. If

s/he doesn't respond, so be it. Actions speak louder than words. The "broken record" technique is probably the best strategy.
- Extreme cases of alienation between the parents may cause, or force, the child to take sides. This can even result in what is now being described as Parental Alienation Syndrome (PAS).
- Children do not want parental acrimony; they want an improvement in the parental relationship, especially where and when it concerns their needs. When they don't get it, they start acting up, and possible long-term mental health damage starts, and then it just gets worse.
- Try not to go to court. Please do not even think about it! The only people who win in court are the lawyers. There are lots of studies that show that parental disputes and divorce settlements are much better settled out of court. Damage to the children is minimized when post-separation disputes are resolved through family mediation, and especially the type of mediation that is child-inclusive. This type of mediation, now being increasingly practised in Australia, is much better than the child-focused type of mediation, as it allows, or requires, the children to have their say. More information is available from Cafcass, the (England and Wales) Family Court support service, whose role is shifting towards helping parents solve their own disputes out of court.
- Divorce affects everyone: you, the children, and also the grandparents and other relatives, the neighbourhood friends, the children's relationships in school. Please take *their* feelings into consideration as well. Involve them. The children will love to go and spend some quality time there, with those other people, in a safe space that hasn't changed. Try to allow this; it may also give you both a break. Ask the grandparents (and other family members) not to take sides. Try to maintain the friendships that the children feel are important.

OTHER ISSUES

Anger management

Basic theories

There is some instinctual basis for anger and aggression as a necessary part of survival. However, despite the prevalence of aggression and violence throughout all of human history, aggression is not inevitable, anger and violence *can* be managed. Anger is both an emotional reaction against pain and it also carries with it (because of the increased adrenalin output) a natural anaesthetic: by getting angry you cover the pain. Other theories propose that aggression arises from environmental factors, especially if our basic drives are blocked or frustrated, but the hypothesis, that frustration always equals aggression and aggression always stems from frustration, is much too simplistic. Much investigation has centred on how the level of arousal affects aggression, as arousal often triggers a strong emotional response. There is also little doubt that past experiences and social conditioning have a powerful effect on aggression. Nearly all these effects can be modified to a degree by emotional and cognitive processes. This gives hope for the effective management of aggression.

Symptoms

The following characteristics are common for anger-prone people with difficulties in anger control and management:

- high levels of tension;
- high impulsivity;
- poor empathy;
- low tolerance of frustration;
- self-defeating anger;
- low self-esteem;
- problems with assertiveness;
- difficulty in coping with stress;
- desire to dominate.

Behavioural characteristics can include:

- disproportionate outbursts of anger (where the person over-reacts to minor issues);
- limited repertoire of responses (with few alternative coping strategies);
- overt or threatening behaviour (often unaware of non-verbal threat and impact);
- physical violence.

Such people may tend to keep their anger in and then explode, or keep it in and somatize it into (say) high blood pressure or heart disease, or they may get angry frequently, or get angry in certain situations only. People who get angry frequently, or are full of anger, are sometimes categorized as having a "Type A" personality, and this is often associated with health risks from heart attacks, angina, hypertension, high cholesterol, etc.

As well as being quite dominant and aggressive in personality terms, people with such issues can have a number of different (internal) beliefs or attitudes, some of which are listed below:

- a tendency to attach blame to others or project blame away from themselves;
- negative thoughts towards others, and other groups, comprising suspicion, hostility;

- poor social relationships;
- applying negative stereotypes, thus decreasing social contact and increasing chances of conflict;
- fixed or irrational beliefs without much evidence;
- exaggerating the significance of (often minor) events;
- having a high expectation of themselves (and others significant to them);
- being unrealistically perfectionist;
- being quite rigid and inflexible and seeing this as a virtue;
- being judgemental and thinking they are right.

Anger management training

What we think about and the actions that follow are very important in the management of aggression. However, it is probably beneficial to address some of the emotional issues and behaviour patterns as well. Relaxation techniques can play a large part in reducing the level of physiological arousal. Role-playing can help us understand that there may be better ways to resolve a situation of anger than the one we are used to. Examining the consequences can help to change our expectations and frustrations that often fuel anger. It is also sometimes valuable to see this type of "learnt behaviour" as addictive in order to try to prevent any relapse into old patterns. These techniques can be done best in a specialized anger-management training group.

Groups

Some people are just not suitable for, or just do not want to involve themselves in, anger management training. If there is no inclination or ability to understand what lies behind one's anger, then there is little point in trying to work with it. Sometimes aggressive behaviour is the result of a head injury resulting in brain damage, which is not amenable to anger management training (AMT) or anger control training (ACT). People suffering from substance abuse, or who have an active and untreated mental illness, often do not have the dedication, or the regular commitment, needed to work on themselves in this way. If the person is potentially violent, then they are probably also not suitable for an AMT/ACT group. There are some other contra-indications for AMT/ACT: serious previous convictions might prejudice other group members; an uneven mix of genders is usually not a good idea; mixing victims and perpetrators is usually not done; certain levels of intelligence and literacy are usually required; etc.

Despite all these constraints, the numbers excluded from such group trainings are relatively few and thus many people can benefit from an AMT/ACT group. These groups usually last about twelve weeks. After an initial referral, which can come from a variety of sources, there is usually an initial interview with one or both of the group leaders. This helps in various ways: to establish a therapeutic connection, to explain what will happen and the nature and goals of the group, to assess the client's specific needs, to evaluate their skills, strengths, and weaknesses, to make a risk assessment, to explore the client's motivation and commitment, to reduce any anxieties, and—most importantly—to establish a "contract" for working together and with others.

Self-help techniques

There are a number of things that you can do yourself. First, it is necessary to realize what your anger is like and what tends to cause it—this is especially important. Self-awareness is not easy, especially with anger. You will have to work on this, and probably ask your family and friends for some help as well.

Next, it is necessary to start tackling the physical symptoms of anxiety that underlie most anger. Then you begin to can tackle your angry thoughts and the angry behaviour using better problem-solving techniques, better ways of communication. Finally, take a look at some of your long-term belief systems. That is a lot to do! You might need some professional help. Be prepared for this; good intentions are often not enough.

There tends to be a "vicious cycle of anger" that is fed or perpetuated by problems with other people, difficulties and practical problems, frustrating events or situations, and stress. The cycle looks something like that shown in Figure 3. Each stage can affect every other, and then your anger can spiral out of control. Angry behaviour can cause consequences and reactions from others that

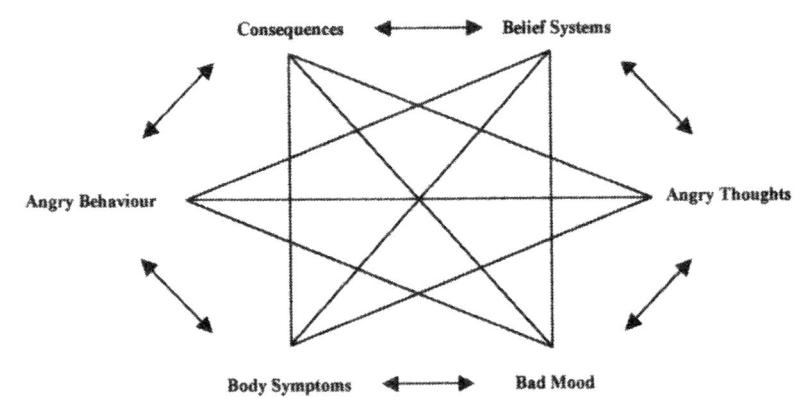

Figure 3. The cycle of anger.

feed our beliefs and inspire more angry thoughts in the person. Bodily symptoms can make us feel out of control and then our "bad mood" just becomes worse. There are other connections and consequences as well: all of these interconnect.

Now try to draw one of these diagrams for yourself. Put a "balloon" (such as is used in a cartoon to enclose speech) alongside each stage and put in some of the things that you think or feel, the things that trigger you, and some of the angry behaviours that you display. Check this out with members of your family, colleagues at work, or friends. This gives you a picture of *your* anger pattern.

You can also use the checklist below and overleaf to help identify aspects of your anger. Tick the ones that sometimes apply to you. Perhaps you can link some of these to the various places shown in Figure 3, and get more of a sense of what you do.

How you feel

- ☐ Angry or enraged.
- ☐ Flashes of anger.
- ☐ Restless or uptight.
- ☐ Slightly irritable

Bodily reactions

- ☐ Heart pounding, racing, skipping.
- ☐ Tight chest, breathlessness.
- ☐ Stomach churning.
- ☐ Legs weak.
- ☐ Head pounding, buzzing, full.
- ☐ Tense muscles.
- ☐ Hands shaking or in fists.
- ☐ Becoming hot, sweating.
- ☐ Needing to go to the toilet.

Angry behaviours

- ☐ Shouting or arguing.
- ☐ Hitting someone, or something.
- ☐ Walking out suddenly.
- ☐ Getting drunk/smoking/taking drugs.
- ☐ Becoming very defensive.
- ☐ Acting recklessly.
- ☐ Pushing or shoving or stamping.
- ☐ Saying something rude or unkind.
- ☐ Bottling it all up or sulking.
- ☐ Bursting into tears.
- ☐ Hurting yourself.

How you think

- ☐ Mind goes "blank" or "empty".
- ☐ Poor concentration.
- ☐ Obsessively thinking about . . .
- ☐ Thinking negatively about others.
- ☐ Overwhelmed with problems.

Common thoughts

- ☐ "I'll show you."
- ☐ "If I don't do something, I'll explode."
- ☐ "They've made a fool of me."
- ☐ "S/he's ruined everything."
- ☐ "You deserve this."
- ☐ "They've let me down again."
- ☐ "I can't trust anyone. I'll just have to . . . (do it myself?)"
- ☐ You're selfish/bad/stupid . . .

This sort of self-awareness is essential to any form of anger control, and so is being open to honest feedback from other people. Just doing this first stage will constitute a major step towards your own anger management.

The next stage is to take a detailed and serious look at what causes your anger, from both outside (people, events, situations) and inside (thoughts, feelings, worries, and memories). Your anger can vary considerably depending on these. What *really* winds you up and *really* gets you going? Are you using anger to cover some (usually) old pain; could you be saying *"Ouch!"* instead of *"You bastard! You've hurt me"*? Is the level of your anger commensurate with the other person's "offence"?

It is also very important to note here that it is probably not really "those" people or "these" events that make you angry; it is you who gets angry with these people and events. It is really important to understand that your reactions are your responsibility, and thus they are (or can be) under your control. If you do not realize this, you will never be able to control your anger because it is "them" that are making you angry. This is a very difficult step to take, but an essential one.

You might have grown up in a situation where there was a lot of anger, and thus you feel fundamentally angry, possibly rightly so. Some situations are terrible and are caused by other people's greed, stupidity, prejudice, hatred, and so forth. While you may have a totally legitimate right to feel angry, you now have the problem of what to do with your anger now, especially if the situation is presently a different one. Some families are poor at talking things through, or at handling emotions. Some societies and cultures that we grow up in glorify anger, war, fighting, and the taking of revenge; others disparage it. Either way, you are the person who is angry now, and you are the person who is now having a problem with your anger (as well as those around you).

Getting angry—and doing something angrily—is often unhelpful. Being angry in this externalized way means that you do not learn to handle the situation, both internally and externally, to the best of your abilities. The belief that getting angry makes you feel better is a myth. If you let your anger out (except in a very controlled way or safe situation), then it can easily get out of control. You are then out of control, because you cannot control it. You can easily cause harm to others, and also cause harm to yourself. It is much better to understand your anger, just to allow yourself to feel it—however difficult that is—and then find ways of controlling it, or expressing it safely. It is all right to say, "What you have just done or said makes me feel incredibly angry. I'd like to hit something now, but I can't do that." It is not acceptable to get angry and hit something, or someone. You might find that you can continue the conversation in the first instance, but you almost certainly will not be able to if you react in the second way.

Why we get angry

There are certain situations that would make almost anyone angry: we discover a friend or partner has betrayed us in some way;

someone breaks something precious, or steals something; someone does something that seems deliberately hurtful or appears to be ignoring us; someone walks out on us, or seemingly abandons us. These can all be major triggers for our anger.

There can also be an escalation of many small things, and then something else takes us to our limit, and we are angry about the last small thing, but the level of anger is more to do with all the other preceding things. Essentially, we are quite frustrated—maybe most of the time.

But sometimes we find ourselves getting angry and we do not really know why. It is possible that we grew up in a situation where it was considered usual to get angry, or where people did not handle their anger at all well, possibly due to alcohol or background violence.

We may find that we often get angry as a result of some of the things listed below.

- *It is a shock.* When someone does something unexpected or out-of-character, it can take time before our feelings of anger recede. We feel let down, or betrayed, or confused as to why that person, given our image of them, could do that thing.
- *We are vulnerable.* At certain times, for example, just before an exam, when we're pregnant, or we have been sick, we expect a little consideration from others. If we do not get it, we can get hurt and angry.
- *It is deliberate.* "They must have 'known' that would hurt me, or upset me, and they didn't ask, or say anything, or whatever." If something was done deliberately or maliciously, it is much harder to accept.
- *The person (who hurt us) is not sorry enough.* Well, that can be fixed.
- *It has happened before.* "I have said, over and over, that I really don't like it when you do that. How many times do I have to say this? I feel powerless, exhausted, frustrated."
- *It brings back memories.* Occasionally old hurts are reopened by current events. Sometimes the level of anger relates more to the old hurt than to the current transgression.

Anger has an impact on the aspects of our lives listed below.

- *Our relationships.* Many relationships are seriously damaged by ongoing anger. At home, it can mean someone living in terror, or there are daily arguments. In the office, it can be a form of bullying, especially if the angry person has status or rank. Feelings get suppressed, which is a form of oppression. Physical and emotional distance is created. Other problems begin to escalate.
- *Our health.* Our bodies become increasingly stressed. This negatively affects our heart, blood pressure, muscular tension, digestion, and immune system.
- *Our emotions.* Anger can keep us in the past, it can affect our self-esteem, and it can make us much more negative than we normally want to be.

It is therefore necessary to start controlling our anger, rather than letting it control—or destroy—our lives. This sounds simple, but it is not easy. We are almost certainly going to need some external help. The problem is that the people around us are either fed up with, or terrified by, our anger. They cannot—and will not—help us. So we need help. And this acknowledgement is not a bad thing. It—quite nicely—links us to other addictive behaviours (see the section on "12-step programmes").

We need to address these issues, as soon as possible.

Controlling anger

Many of these techniques can, and should, be used in conjunction with each other. Some complement others and none really conflicts with another: all can be effective. See which ones are effective for you:

- *Modifying expectations.* Much anger is attached to your high (and possibly commendable) set of expectations but these high expectations can also result in frustration. "Everyone in this family should . . ." "These people should not . . ." "I should have done . . ." Who said this? Why and how come? How useful is the "should" in these cases? If you can modify some of these expectations, some of your anger will dissipate. Try modifying these thoughts and expectations.

- *Angry thoughts.* These need to be recognized and paid more attention to, even challenged. They can arise from some thinking errors, like "taking things personally", "ignoring the positive", "perfectionism" (similar to high expectation of ourselves and others), and "black and white thinking". These thinking errors need to be corrected; then our angry thoughts can become more balanced and reasonable.
- *Keeping personal anger/mood diaries.* Keeping one of these can really help boost your self-awareness and can provide information about the frequency of your anger, or the situations which provoke it. It can also help you to log successes and coping strategies, as well as providing a monitor for changes over a longish period.
- *Relaxation techniques.* These are very useful ways of reducing the general background risks of anger. However, they should be done regularly and in conjunction with other things. Lying down on the sofa, listening to music, reading, pottering, doing "fun" things, using imaging techniques, can all be useful. Learning some relaxation exercises will probably help considerably; Yoga or Tai Chi classes are also useful and fairly widely available. There are also relaxation tapes readily available with sounds of waves, waterfalls, or whale songs.
- *Risk assessment.* As in modern Occupational Health and Safety work, we should make proper risk assessments about our anger. We need to discover in what situations we are likely to get angry, how often these occur, what the triggers are, what may make the anger worse, and then what we might be able to do to control our high-risk angry thoughts and feelings. How can we avoid these situations, lessen the frequency, and what can we do to reduce these risks?
- *Controlling the physical symptoms.* The sooner you manage to notice the physical and emotional symptoms, the easier it is to correct them. Good self-awareness is thus very important. As soon as you feel the anger rising, go and do something different. Get outside, have a breath of fresh air, duck your head in the water butt—whatever works to control your rising anger.
- *Incorrect beliefs.* Some people have incorrect thoughts or unhelpful beliefs about anger, such as "I can't control my anger. My father was angry and I inherited [learnt] my anger from him."

"If I don't let my anger out, I will explode." "If I don't show that I am angry, people will take advantage of me." "Only a saint or a wimp doesn't get angry." "Getting angry means that something might change." "It's a way of getting rid of anxiety." "I am justified in getting angry, they are plain wrong/bad/stupid." "Why shouldn't I get angry, people have hit on me all my life." None of these is totally true or very helpful; they are rather like pieces of rubbish. Drop them, bin them, and learn to keep getting rid of them. There are some other unhelpful ideas, as well: "Getting angry is bad behaviour." (This just punishes yourself.) "Getting angry is destructive." (Sometimes it isn't, when attached to a genuine grievance.) "If I get angry, I will destroy the other person." (Highly unlikely: more your fear than any reality.)

- *Exercise.* This is a very important method of controlling anger, as it allows you to discharge a whole mass of stress hormones relatively quickly. These hormones build up in the body and can really wind us up. Aerobic exercise is what really works and it must get you out of breath and quite hot and sweaty; only then does it burn these stress hormones off and allow proper relaxation afterwards. The form of exercise can also assist anger management: belting a squash ball into a corner is very satisfying; using a punch bag can exorcise some of those aggressive feelings; pushing oneself to get "the burn" can discharge some of the frustrations that build up; getting to the top of a hill or mountain can give one a great satisfaction.
- *Controlled breathing.* This is another useful technique. When we are angry, we tend to speed up our breathing and gulp air. This can affect the oxygen–carbon dioxide ratio in our bodies and this can create anxiety. Try slowing the breathing down (in-two-three-four: out-two-three-four-five) and focusing on expelling air (and tension) on the out-breath. You might need to practise this a bit beforehand, when you are not angry.
- *Changing angry behaviours.* Having kept the mood diary for a while, try to identify what happens in a situation where you get angry, and discuss this with someone not directly concerned. See what other things you could have done in those situations: leave the room for a while; take an extra minute before responding; do some relaxation; ask the other person why they

said that, and try to understand their situation; ask yourself why you are getting angry and how rational is it, or is it worth it; ask the other person to talk about the difficulties you are having, rather than any specific item which is making you angry; try using calm thoughts or images. Having identified other possibilities, try making some changes to your behaviour in those situations.

- *Problem solving.* Once you are a little more rational about everything, try some improved problem solving techniques. First, write the problem down, being as specific and as precise as possible. "I am broke" doesn't help much. "My monthly expenditure is £150 more than my income and I owe £3,000" is much more specific. Next, write down *all* possible solutions, and I mean *ALL* of them. Do not censure anything at this point (e.g., for the example above, include robbing a bank, selling the house, or getting another part-time job). Ask friends and family for suggestions. Get some information and ideas from advisers and experts (such as your bank manager), some from friends, and some from fantasies. Make the list as comprehensive as possible. Then, and only then, start to go through it, eliminating some (for the moment) and choosing one or two of the best solutions. Put each of these at the top of a separate sheet of paper and write down all the steps you could take to achieve this solution. Go into "What if . . ." scenarios; who could help; how could this be done; what might go wrong? Try to come up with an action plan with various options. There is little else you can do. In the past, you tried to problem solve this situation your old way, including by getting angry: it didn't work. The problem is still there. Now try following the above plan in the hope that this will work this time. Things cannot get worse.
- *Long term beliefs about your self and others can influence your levels of anger.* A comment or a casual aside from someone might trigger a long-term belief that leads to anger. Reading in the newspapers about an instance of (say) cruelty that is happening in (say) Germany or Japan might lead to an angry reaction because of beliefs derived from old wartime experiences, even if they happened to a father or an uncle. Try moderating the belief: "That was then; this is now."

- *Reduce stress.* Modern life is very stressful and we simply have not evolved to cope with these levels of stress very well. Anger is one of the more inappropriate reactions to stress. If this is true for you, then you really need to reduce your stress levels, either at home or at work, as much as possible and find ways to beat the stress before it overwhelms you again. There are some tips on how to do this elsewhere in this book. Try to ensure that you are not putting yourself under additional stress or pressure through your own expectations or "shoulds". Notice the build-up of stress as early as possible and then take some preventive actions: be nice to yourself, give yourself time to rest properly, eat properly, to enjoy yourself, to do a hobby or get out in nature, to spend time with friends or family, etc. Whatever works for you!
- *Communication skills.* Anger is usually not the best way to communicate well with other people. Misunderstandings can easily arise and lead to angry situations. People can take general comments personally, or can diffuse personal comments by taking them generally. There are lots of ways to improve one's communication skills, especially if your anger is getting in the way:
  - Slow down and listen to the other person. An instant reaction is probably wrong reaction. The first things that come to mind are probably more our minds talking than a proper response to the other person.
  - Try to understand what they are trying to say. Ask if you don't. Only when you are clear about what they are saying can you give a proper reaction. Most cynical or cutting remarks come from this place of misunderstanding.
  - Don't jump to conclusions about what the other person is saying. Don't try to mind-read. Let them finish speaking properly. Be aware that your own thoughts and assumptions may be colouring the picture of what you think they are saying.
  - Understand their feelings, because the other person has feelings as well. They may be angry with you for being angry with them. Maybe they are reacting to you because your anger makes them afraid, hurt, or unappreciated. Your anger may be demonstrating to them that you are hurt, afraid, or unappreciated: they may feel for you.

Such communications have the effect of moderating our angry responses and giving us the opportunity for more time (and thought) before we "fly off the handle" or "go ballistic".

- *Learning to let go.* This is one of the harder skills. Only you can do this, for yourself, and not for anyone else. You are letting the anger go, for your benefit, because you want to, and because it works better all round. As you begin to let this slip away, you will feel worse to begin with; it feels as if you have nothing. Then you will gradually begin to feel better about yourself, and about your self in relation to others.
- *Self-critical views.* These are the hardest to deal with as any (potential) criticism from outside hits a very raw spot. This means that no one can say anything to you, which is a pity, because there are some things you might actually want or need to hear. Because of the soreness caused by self-critical views, you may react angrily.
- *Cognitive coping strategies and self-calming statements.* There are a number of cognitive or "thinking" strategies (such as distraction, humour, rationalizing, self-praise, focusing, etc.) that can be useful in an anger situation. By practising these beforehand, one can often avoid getting into the "anger cycle". More details about these can be found in various CBT books.
- *Anger management groups.* See if you can find one of these locally: they may be run by the NHS department of Clinical Psychology, or the Community Psychiatric Nurses. People with similar problems come together regularly to discuss problems with anger, to look at anger management situations, to role-play, to take a reaction inventory, to look at aggression, to check behavioural observations, and to have personality assessments. They are remarkably successful when well led.

Living with an angry partner

Unfortunately, sometimes it is not you who is angry, but the person that you live with. Some people come from angry families, have been highly exposed to anger, and thus "learnt" at an early age that anger has some benefits. When they are frustrated, they get angry, and then they get their own way. What they have forgotten, or did not fully experience, is the downside of living with an angry person: the fear, the threat, and sometimes the violence. This is what you are experiencing.

With respect to any violence whatsoever against women, at any time, in a relationship, please contact the Women's Aid national helpline, immediately. Ring 0808–2000–247, or visit the website www.womensaid.org.uk. There is also some good information and advice in the anger management and the relationships section of the BBC website (see Sources of information: Anger management and violence towards the end of this book).

There is *no* justification for this type of anger against someone that you are in a relationship with. It is *not* your fault. You should *not* have to suffer this, neither should you have this inflicted upon you. You *both* need to do something about this if the relationship is to have any chance of surviving. However, if you do not do something—like saying "Enough"—then nothing will happen.

> Anybody can become angry, that is easy; but the man who gets angry at the right things, and with the right people, and in the right way, and at the right time, and for the right length of time, is to be commended. [Aristotle, *The Nicomachean Ethics*, *IV*, Chapter 5]

Sleep issues

A lot of people have difficulty with sleep, especially during times of stress, anxiety, and depression. Additionally there is perhaps a difficulty with perception, as there is a myth that we all need between seven and eight hours' sleep every night. The amount of sleep a person needs varies considerably at different times in their life: a newborn baby may spend fifteen hours asleep per day, but as children grow older they require less sleep (eleven hours average for five-year-olds and maybe 8–9 hours for teenagers). When people reach the age of about thirty, they may require fewer than eight hours, and as they get older, this can reduce even more. Many seventy-year-olds require less than six hours' sleep. Sleep also varies with physical activity, illness, habit, bereavements, etc. If we are worried about our sleep, we are more likely to sleep less.

There are two types of sleep: rapid eye movement (REM) when we dream, and non-REM sleep. We have different periods of these several times during the night, and the periods of non-REM sleep normally get progressively deeper. We need both types of sleep. As we age, so our sleep pattern changes. Disturbances in sleep, or the type of sleep, or when we sleep, are quite prevalent. Insomnia is surprisingly common: about 35% of adults are definitely affected: possibly many others do not report such problems. The type of sleep problems that occur might be getting to sleep, staying asleep (sleeping for too long), waking early (or waking and not being able to get back to sleep), and poor quality sleep (restless, light, or disturbingly full of dreams). Which is the one that affects you?

Listed below are a few suggestions to help to address the many issues that lie behind any sleep difficulties.

- Check that your surroundings are conducive to sleep: not too warm or too cold, a comfortable bed (try a pocket-sprung mattress), not too much light, or too noisy, and that there aren't issues with neighbourhood noise, traffic, or a noisy boiler or radiator that comes on at a particular time (say 6.00 a.m.), and wakes you up.
- Is there a problem (anxiety, stress, etc.) that is stopping you sleeping and does *this* need to be addressed properly, rather than trying to sort out the symptoms (sleep disturbances)? Are you worried about not getting "enough" sleep? Is the problem with your expectations of sleep? Has someone close to you died, or been in trouble, recently? Are there problems at work? Is sexual frustration an issue? All of these things can disturb your sleep.
- Check that your food (and particularly caffeine) intake is not affecting your sleep (too much coffee, fizzy drinks, chocolate, etc. can keep you awake), or that you are not becoming intolerant of certain types of foods (MSG in Chinese food, spices in curries, etc.)
- Too much alcohol can also affect how well you sleep. Nicotine is a stimulant: try not smoking for a while before you sleep.
- Try not to worry about not getting enough sleep. It is probable that you are getting enough, but the amount is less than you expect. Don't take naps during the day to catch up, as this will affect your natural rhythm and only add to your problem. Remember that our need for sleep is very individual thing, and it changes as we get older.
- Check that any medications you take are not affecting your sleep. Ask your GP and, if so, adjust the time that you take them. Mention any herbal remedies or other things that you take.

- Sleep can also be affected by disturbed routines, changing shift patterns, chronic pain, or not enough exercise. Major new events or life changes—house, job, baby, new partner, a family bereavement, new bed—can all have an effect on our sleep that can take a while to settle down.

Effects on sleep

When we get older, our sleep patterns naturally change. Often it means that we need less sleep, or that we start to doze more often during the day. Sometimes, when we are very stressed and worried, we sleep less well; we will probably need to do much more physical exercise to burn off the stress hormones before we can relax and go to sleep properly. If we have been travelling a lot, especially long air flights, our sleep can be disturbed for a few days afterwards. There are also some genetic conditions (e.g., Fragile X Syndrome) that can affect sleep, and sleep disturbances can also be an early indication of something more serious (medical, emotional, or psychological).

Sleep disturbances

Occasionally, and usually only in those who are middle-aged and overweight, people develop a medical condition called sleep apnoea, in which the larynx (air passage in the throat) closes when they are asleep, so they have to wake up a little in order to continue breathing and yet not sufficiently to be conscious that they are awake. Your partner would probably be able to tell you, as you might seem to stop breathing for a few seconds and then suddenly start breathing again for a little while. This pattern repeats itself throughout the night and means that, while you might not wake up, you are not getting good or proper sleep.

Other health conditions, including high blood pressure, can also affect your bladder so that you have to get up often in the night, or can affect your breathing, like allergic rhinitis (nasal congestion), both of which can disturb your sleep.

Other sleep disturbances are categorized in the terms of "night pains", "daytime dozing", "general insomnia", and "daytime fatigue", to mention only a few.

There are some instances in which sleep disturbance might have an emotional component, such as in what is known as "restless legs", or it might occur as an aftermath of trauma, or it can occasionally be a symptom of early heart disease (especially in women), or even as a symptom of other psychological conditions like a major depression, psychotic episode, or schizophrenia. Don't panic! You (or those around you) will almost certainly know if you have any of these.

Problem solving

Where your sleep is being affected by problems, the following techniques might help. Get out of bed and sit somewhere warm, quiet, and comfortable with a pen and paper.

1. Write down the problems you are thinking about.
2. Taking each problem, write down everything you can possibly think you might do to solve the problem.
3. Choose the most helpful solution and write down all the steps you are going to need to take to do it. Write as much as you can.
4. Write down any obstacles and how you might tackle them.
5. When you have finished, say to yourself firmly, "OK. That is it for now. I can't do anything more about this at this time of night. I am not going to let myself worry about it till the morning. I am going back to sleep."
6. Then spend at least twenty minutes winding down, reading a book or listening to some gentle music (possibly on headphones). When you start to feel sleepy, go back to bed.
7. If you still find yourself worrying, keep saying to yourself, "I've dealt with my worry for now. Worrying about it now will not help. I'll deal with it tomorrow."
8. If you don't drop off to sleep within about 20–30 minutes, do not stay in bed. The importance of this is discussed later. Get up and repeat the above steps.

Medications

Doctors are increasingly reluctant to prescribe any sedatives such as Temazepam, Diazepam, Mogodon, or Valium for sleep disturbances, as these medications are quite addictive. Some of the antidepressants (such as Trazadone) have a sedative effect and can sometimes be prescribed for sleep disorders. A good alternative remedy is lavender: either lavender blossoms encased in a sachet or in a little pillow, or as an essential oil, with a few drops put on the pillow.

Emotional issues

If your sleep is still disturbed—and you have done all of the above—then it is highly likely there is an underlying emotional issue that is affecting you more than you realize. A few counselling or psychotherapy sessions might help bring this more to the surface. Make sure you have gone through the above checklist first; it might save you some time, energy, and money.

Towards better sleep

You have to retrain your body into a much better sleep pattern. It takes at least three weeks. This can be done in a number of ways and the right routine and combination will depend on you. It has to work for you, otherwise it is pointless.

- You will first need to develop a different routine. Try not to eat too late in the evening, try to plan your evening so that there is a gentle wind-down towards bedtime, and stop all activities at least one hour before going to bed.
- Write down a list of things to do for the next day so that you are not trying to remember them while in bed. Don't do any further planning; that is for tomorrow. You can try putting a small pad of paper and pencil in your bedside table drawer for any thoughts that you may have in the night.
- Try to avoid any stimulants (coffee, tea, hot chocolate, energy drinks, fizzy drinks, colas, etc.) later than 5.00 p.m., or any deeply emotional interactions (e.g., telephone calls). Try to limit any alcohol intake to reasonable amounts (3 units per night maximum for men, 2 units per night maximum for women). Don't eat cheese, curries, shellfish, or lots of meat late at night.

- Prepare yourself for bed: have a little walk outside around the block, then have a bath or shower, then get into the bedtime routine (teeth, hair, face, pyjamas, etc.), then get into bed and perhaps read a little—but nothing to thrilling or exciting. Don't watch TV in bed.
- Make sure you have enough time for a good sleep—about seven hours. If you do NOT go to sleep within about half-an-hour, get up, relax in a different room, and then try going back to bed again. Make sure that bed is really only for sleeping.
- If you wake up after a little while and cannot get back to sleep easily, do the same: get up, relax somewhere else, and then try again. Have a comfortable alternative in another room, but do not fall asleep there.
- Do *not* take naps in the middle of the day: do *not* take extra sleep to make up for the previous night's deficiencies. You are trying to establish a different routine. Stick to it for at least 3–4 weeks, so as to really give it a chance.
- When you get into to bed and have turned the light out, try just to listen to your breathing. Allow yourself to feel the whole of your body, breathe into all parts of your body, and as you breathe, allow all parts of your body to be connected to your breath.
- Breathe in gently, to a slow count of four or five, making sure your chest expands fairly fully. Breathe out to a slow count of five or six, making sure that your chest empties. Imagine all the stress and tension disappearing as you breathe out. Do this several times.
- If you stay awake for a while, and are thinking about something especially, have a little note pad beside the bed and write down a few words. Then try to let it go. Deal with it in the morning.
- Make sure your bed is properly associated with sleep. For example, don't habitually watch TV, eat, read papers, or talk on the telephone while in bed. This is particularly relevant for students.
- Sexual frustration can sometimes be a problem that affects your sleep. We often associate bed, night-time, and sex, and one part of the equation might be missing. Masturbation can often help to get you to sleep, but try to avoid creating another habit.

- If you really cannot sleep, or if you wake up in the night and cannot get back to sleep, get up. Go downstairs. Have a glass of water or a herbal tea, and read for about 20–30 minutes. Then try again. If this happens regularly, have a blanket or sleeping bag and a pillow easily available in the living room and use the sofa there, rather than disturb other people upstairs in the house with too much coming and going. Try not to get into the habit of sleeping on the sofa.
- Have a regular family planning session one night a week, after a family meal and before the dessert is served. Take a few minutes each to say how the week has been for you. Discuss what will be happening next week and who is doing what, when. Write up appointments, arrangements and travel times, etc., on a piece of paper and post it in the kitchen or on the fridge with a magnet. This is what has been agreed: any changes need to be agreed as well.

These changes should have a beneficial effect. If they don't, try adding a herbal night-time tea, or using a pillow filled with special herbs.

Only when all these remedies have failed, should you consult your doctor. The medications for sleep are often highly addictive, and so it is not a good idea to become reliant on these.

Problems at work

More and more people are experiencing problems at work. Some of this is the employers' fault, as more and more is demanded, overtly or covertly, from the employees. Requirements have grown from good time-keeping, politeness, dress code, lack of absenteeism, diligence, etc. to very high productivity requirements, no personal calls or e-mails at work (yet being expected to accept calls at home or in the evening about work), a lack of job security and short-term contracts, and so forth. There is also much greater awareness about discrimination, health and safety, confidentiality policies and the like that add to the day-to-day stress levels of the employee and manager.

I have mentioned specific problems in the workplace in other sections of this book (e.g., "Parents at work"; "Stress at work"; "Mental health issues at work"). I shall now look briefly at other issues that may arise and be important or significant in the workplace for you.

- Presentation is still important, even on "dress-down Friday" days. This does not only just refer to dress codes; your willingness, calmness, maturity, groundedness, presentation of work, time-keeping, etc., are all equally important. Do you present yourself as the "office clown" (perhaps because of insecurities), or the person who is more interested in other things (including going home) than work? What fundamental attitude do you present with? This is mentioned because, if things are not working out well at work, this is an area where you can quite easily make a difference. In changing how you present yourself, look around: who is generally more accepted, who is not? Does this give you any clues? Ask a friend. Maybe they can help.

- Intimate relationships with other people in the office are generally short-lived, counter-productive, and will probably mean that one person will have to leave when it is over, and always known about at some point in time: generally not a good idea at all. These relationships often start because people are thrown together by work in an otherwise fairly lonely situation. Then our hormones take over! Relationships between a senior person and a more junior person in the office hierarchy are almost inevitably doomed to failure, are probably unethical, and are certainly frowned upon. Don't get involved! Even if it manages to turn into a long-term relationship, do you really want to "take work home"?
- Company policies. Check the company policies, staff manuals, health and safety policy, anti-discrimination policies, etc. These should be readily available.
- Annoying colleagues (or their annoying habits) are a top source of stress in the office, and you cannot get away from them until Friday at 5.00 p.m. Common complaints are: talking on the phone too loudly; constantly whining about work, the wife, a manager, etc.; the "pet" phrase; sitting around gossiping when others are working; and so forth. Try to make sure, too, that you are not one of these annoying people. In a recent office survey, 60% of those polled said these sorts of things affected their work badly, and 40% said it led them to look for another job. So, first, live with it—as much as you can. Then, if it continues, try to find a way to communicate the annoying aspects to your colleague, in private at first. Make sure you praise them for their good points as well. If that does not work, then possibly comment publicly in a team meeting, as other people may be equally annoyed.

- Try not to mix personal things with work things. Personal calls at work are largely frowned upon. Some companies allow personal e-mails to be sent at set times. Some organizations block certain websites. A small partition is not soundproof; do not assume that it is. Just because you cannot see anyone does not mean that they cannot hear every word you say.
- Do NOT take work home! Ever! You are paid to work in the office or workplace and you are not paid to work at home. Do you wish to give your employer some of your free time, unpaid, because he/she is too mean to employ the right number of staff for the job? Working late means you can claim time in lieu. Take it. Don't be the office martyr: no one will thank you, you will only crucify yourself.
- Avoid "office-speak", jargon, acronyms, slang, nick-names, corporate management polysyllabic head-banging nonsense, and swear words. "In the PDQ department, old Trotters and I had to spend all Saturday resurrecting the meta-analysis of last year's Total Quality Initiative, just because Four-Eyes, that a****ole of an MD, wants to suck up to the bigwigs." Ugh!
- Prejudice is absolutely unacceptable. This includes ageism, racism, sexism, religious prejudice, prejudice against disabilities, mental health, and people from some (any) other place. Examine your own prejudices before you condemn others. Would you want your son/daughter to marry one of "them"? How do you come across to others? Going along with other people's opinion can mean that you compromise your own.
- Occasionally you may be the one who is being discriminated against, either by a small clique, or by an individual. The individual will usually be in a superior position to you. Dealing with this sort of discrimination is stressful and difficult. First, you must talk to someone. Someone in Human Resources (HP) or Personnel should be able to help you, or go to your manager or team leader and talk to them. Ask them to sort this out initially without specific reference to the fact that you have complained. Only if this sort of generic approach has not worked can a specific intervention be justified.

Mental health issues at work

There is still a lot of stigma, prejudice, and fear about mental health issues, and these also exist at work, where we often experience a lot of stress and where we also spend a significant amount of our time. When we are under stress, it really helps to admit it, and it also adds to the stress if we cannot say that we are on the point of cracking up: hence all the little "jokey" notices in the office, such as "You don't have to be mad to work here, but it helps!" and "Don't mind me, I'm just having a nervous breakdown!"

In a recent survey, about 70–75% of employees believe that if they admit that they suffer from mental health problems such as stress, depression, and anxiety, they would damage their future career prospects. This is especially true of older employees (45–54 years old). Yet about three in ten of all employees will experience stress, depression, or some other form of mental ill-health every year.

From the management side, in the survey, about 63% of employers thought that their organization's policy on mental health (if they had one) was effective in helping their staff to stay in work. But if employees are not reporting mental health issues for fear of repercussions, employers are less likely to know the extent of the problem and thus be able to provide effective support. The key findings of some research done by the Shaw Trust on these issues were as follows.

- Employers badly underestimate the extent to which employees and fellow managers are suffering from stress, anxiety, depression, and other forms of mental ill health.
- The cost of mental ill health to businesses is as much as £9 billion in salary costs, with a further unknown cost in terms of lost time and productivity.
- Most companies do not have effective policies to deal with employees' mental health and also do not know enough about their legal position. (What are their liabilities? Can they dismiss someone?)
- Most companies do not have effective provisions to identify and manage mental health (particularly stress) in the workplace.

- Workplace attitudes indicate widespread discrimination towards people with any sort of mental health issues, although this may not be conscious or intentional.
- The majority of directors believe industry needs significantly more support to deal with mental health in the workplace.

So what can be done? The best place to start is with the HR department and/or the Health and Safety department in your place of employment. A question to one of these departments should invoke a reply about the company's present policies, and how people in each department can make them more workable and effective. A new poster on the wall is a good start.

If a policy on mental health does not exist in the company or at your place of work, your question should (one hopes) prompt the processes towards creating a new policy, and, in various departmental meetings, you can try to get an agreement about an effective mental health policy or anti-stress policy being put into place.

Such policies should always involve consultation with staff at all levels. This allows for discussion and suggestions without the real necessity for any personal disclosures or discrimination. If there is any resistance to this, a mention that the Health and Safety Executive (HSE) are particularly hot on anti-stress policies (and the lack of them) and that an appropriate risk assessment for stress should therefore probably be made as soon as possible, with appropriate actions to try to prevent stress, might be a good way of starting.

What else can you do?

- You can take the official tea-breaks and the lunch breaks and don't skimp on them. You can work the exact number of hours that you are paid for, and no more. You can stick to your job description. And you can also encourage others—gently—to do the same. Employers often pile on their work demands, but do not necessarily want to pay for the extra hours, and so you end up effectively donating your time to them—free of charge. They (probably unconsciously) rely on your sense of job satisfaction and the power that they have over their employees. Work (employment) is a two-way interactive process that should include clear conditions of work, the promised pay packet, a

relatively safe environment, freedom from bullying and abuse, and as little stress as possible.
- You can try to avoid all emotional confrontations: they usually make things worse (more stressful). Go and cool off, walk around the block (or the corridors with a piece of paper in your hand), talk to a friend or your line manager; try to work out what you really need or don't need, and then say it to the appropriate person in a clear but neutral way (see the section on "Expressing your needs").
- This may sound paradoxical, but if there is any bullying, overt criticism, discrimination, or abuse, then you need to confront this, and not just if it is happening to you, as we all need to confront this. Not speaking up, or not having a quiet word afterwards, saying how you did not like what happened there, is effectively condoning it and allowing it to continue.

The only remaining stressful thing in the workplace not yet mentioned is—managers! Occasionally you get a good one; if you do—go with them when they go. Most people's experience is not very complimentary about how they are managed.

Weight, body image, and eating issues

This is a section with just a few suggestions about a huge set of issues, with a number of quite severe complications. Much has been written about these topics elsewhere and in great depth. First, there is no doubt that most people would probably benefit by losing some weight. Some US statistics state:

- approximately seven million girls and women, and approximately one million boys and men will struggle with eating disorders this year;
- eating disorders have the highest mortality rate of any psychiatric diagnosis;
- anorexia nervosa is the leading cause of death in adolescent girls, with bulimia nervosa a close second;
- 19% of college-aged women in America are (estimated as being) bulimic, although as many as 33% of young women in this age group will experiment with eating disordered behaviours;
- 10% of all persons with eating disorders are male;
- 81% of ten-year-olds (surveyed) are afraid of becoming fat;
- 91% of women recently surveyed on a college campus had attempted to control their weight through dieting;

- 80% of American women (surveyed) are dissatisfied with their appearance, which is indicative of a cultural condition;
- when surveyed, a group of young women were asked: would you rather be maimed in an automobile accident, experience the loss of a good friend, flunk out of school, lose all your hair, or be fat? The overwhelming response was that they would rather have any of the above situations happen to them than be fat.

Obesity in the UK is also high, and getting higher. Body weight is measured by your body–mass index (BMI), a height–weight ratio that should be below 30. There is a simple chart in your doctor's surgery, or available on the Internet. However, irrespective of any objective measures, most women think they are too fat, so losing a little weight should improve your self-image and self-esteem, as well as benefiting your general health. Most men could do with losing some as well, and although they usually will not admit it beforehand, they will feel better about themselves and acknowledge this afterwards.

We are truly experiencing an epidemic of disordered eating and body image in our culture. The question becomes, "Now that we are aware of it, what do we do?" The first step must be education. So here is some fundamental "Do and Don't" information about simple weight loss and dieting.

- Feel that it is a positive thing to do to control your weight, not a punishment.
- You can (and will) control your weight with the right skills and some determination.
- Think about which things were helpful in the past and those that were not.
- Plan to make any lifestyle changes small and sustainable, but continuous.
- Keep a simple "food and mood" diary to help stay conscious of when, what, and why you eat.
- Aim to lose no more than 0.5–1 kilo a week.
- Eat small regular meals, starting with breakfast, and eat regularly throughout the day.
- Include a variety of healthy choices from all the main food groups.

- Eat masses of fruit and vegetables.
- Adopt a flexible approach to eating, rather than all-or-nothing.
- Learn how to cope better with feelings, rather than feeding them.
- Be much more active, more often, in your daily life: deliberately increase the amount of exercise
- Make time for 30–45 minutes moderate activity almost every day.
- Experiment with low-fat products, different cooking skills, skillets, etc.
- Set yourself little goals, giving rewards and treats for achievement: half a kilo lost this week = a massage.
- Tell your friends, encourage them to ask you how you are doing, get some positive support.
- Remind yourself that a healthy diet also helps to reduce your risk of various health problems such as heart disease, certain cancers, diabetes, and lung disorders.
- Note your progress: you will start to feel better after one week, and better still after the second week.
- Drink lots of water: about two litres a day.

There's no single right way to lose weight. But it is important to do it in a healthy and realistic way. This allows you to adapt to this new regime, get the nutrients you need, feel positive about helping your health and well-being, and get on with living your life. It also means you will be developing new skills and attitudes that will help you keep the weight off.

Quick-fix diets are usually designed to be very short-term with a rigid set of rules: it can seem like a form of punishment. While you might lose weight, the diets are often too constraining to sustain for long. They can also be nutritionally inadequate, and might lead to problems such as iron deficiency, poor bone health, or smelly breath. In addition, they can make you lose confidence in your ability to slim successfully: you become reliant on them, rather than on you.

Sustained weight loss—that does *not* involve your weight yo-yoing up and down—is only really achievable by improving your self-esteem, as the main (if not only) route to this sustained weight loss (increased exercise *and* reduced calorific intake) will be perceived as a form of self-punishment *unless* you are doing it for your own decided benefit and from a place of improved self-esteem. Improved self-esteem has to come first, and then you will be much more likely to be successful in achieving your desired weight loss.

The traditional weight-loss programmes (such as Weight Watchers) have some benefits in that you are doing this with a local group, which means increased social contact, with others who have done it already, and your progress is being monitored regularly. Howwever, they also have some disadvantages, such as costing money, creating competition and a dependency, and having a complicated points system.

The essential equation is: calories in *vs* calories out. If these equal each other, your weight remains stable. Otherwise you will inevitably either put on weight, or lose weight. Cutting your food intake (watching your portions for quality as well as quantity) as well as increasing the amount of exercise that you take regularly means that you will be in a win–win situation, and you will inevitably shift this ratio towards a reasonable weight reduction as well as improved dietary intake. You will be fitter, too.

There are 3,500 calories (energy content) in 0.5 kg (1 lb) of body fat. So, to lose 0.5 kg a week (a healthy weight loss), you will need a deficit of 500 calories each day ($7 \times 500 = 3,500$). You can best achieve this by making small changes, essentially eating fewer calories and being more active. For example, swap a chocolate bar for a banana (saving 150 calories) and substitute a small pot of reduced-calorie coleslaw for a standard one (saving 240 calories), or cut out a bag of crisps (280 calories) and add two fifteen-minute brisk walks (burning 150 calories) for a 500–600 calories deficit. Then just keep doing it—every day. Slowly, gently, easily, the weight just drops off.

There are a huge number of factors that lie behind our general weight and body-image: genetics, cultural stereotypes, social and economic class, childhood eating habits, age, current fashion ideals, levels of emotional stress or distress, employment activity, national dietary habits, lifestyle, available medical information, etc. Be as aware as possible about which of these have affected you, to what extent, and how you feel about them. Then decide what you want to do about your weight, body image and eating patterns.

Most of the necessary medical and dietary information is now readily available, either from health centres, low calorie recipes, most women's or home magazines, or on the Internet. There are no simple products, no new medicines, no magic cures, cosmetic surgery techniques, or special treatments that will do it easily for you. You probably need to tackle this one for yourself. Assume you have a moderate food addiction and start from there: it is a little like the 12-Step Programme.

Please also be aware that this is not just your problem: a standard serving of French fries has risen from about 200 calories in 1960 to around a massive 610 calories today: a woman's ideal shape has changed from the flat-chested flappers of the 1920s, to the busty 1950s, to the anorexic waifs of the modern day. Very few people ever look like this: the image is an illusion. It is all very unreal. You need to find out what your ideal shape and size really is, and then "dream" into it.

Eating disorders

Those people who cannot perceive, or accept, their actual weight (excessive overweight or excessive underweight) *and* the fact that this may be very unhealthy for them, may have an eating disorder. The disorder is actually in their self-perception. They really do need to get specialized help, and if you are a member of the family of someone with this disorder please encourage them strongly to get such help, because they almost certainly will not do it for themselves because they have an eating disorder and perceive themselves wrongly. Start by going to their GP with them, or by calling their GP for them. It can be serious.

The other main type of eating disorder is bulimia nervosa, which is where the person "binges" and then purges himself or herself by vomiting, or using laxatives, enemas, diuretics, or other medications, or by over-exercising. This regularly puts their body and digestive system under a massive strain. Again, specialist help is really necessary.

There are a number of specialist websites that can help:

www.b-eat.co.uk
www.eating-disorders.org.uk

www.edr.org.uk
www.eatingdisorderexpert.co.uk

Please contact these or get a referral from your GP to a specialist.

Chronic fatigue syndrome (myalgic encephalomyelitis [ME], or fibromyalgia, or post-viral fatigue syndrome)

Basic principle

A section on this topic is included here as many people suffering from depression either have, or might think they have, chronic fatigue syndrome (CFS). Whether they have got a clear diagnosis of this is somewhat irrelevant: the principles of working with overwhelming tiredness, fatigue, and debilitation are pretty much the same. Don't do too much! The other reason for including a section here is that there is much one can do oneself: in fact, most of the treatment is almost totally self-help.

Symptoms

ME or CFS is now established as a recognized syndrome or illness. It is estimated that at least 300,000 people in the UK suffer from ME/CFS. The overwhelming symptom is long-lasting (chronic) and debilitating fatigue that is medically otherwise unexplained. Other symptoms often associated with this are muscle pains, tender neck or armpit glands, poor sleep, or mood disturbances. There may also be sickness, headaches (of a new type, pattern, or severity), nausea, tingling, shakiness, joint pain (without swelling), sweating, cold extremities (hands and feet), etc. Some people also have an intolerance to certain foods. Frequent sore throats or colds may indicate a run-down immune system. Mental symptoms may include concentration difficulties, memory problems, or the inability to find the right words.

In order to be technically classified as CFS, it needs to have been present for at least six months and the symptoms present for more than 50% of that time. A variety of associated symptoms also usually have to be present, *and* the absence of any other established medical disorders that cause fatigue, such as a major depression, eating disorders, or alcohol or substance abuse.

Causes

The main cause of CFS is not really known. Symptoms often develop after a flu-type virus, or glandular fever, or an Epstein–Barr type of virus infection. The virus is thought to attack the body's immune system, which is essentially why one does not get better quickly. There are (apparently) some similarities to soft-tissue rheumatoid arthritis.

The main suggested common factor, present in most cases, is also a prolonged period of severe overstress, or serious distress (bereavement), before or around the time of the illness. Many sufferers seem to pay a lot of attention to other people, rather than to themselves. Since the children of CFS sufferers can also apparently get CFS, there may be some genetic predisposition, or it might be some sort of a "learnt" syndrome.

Other possible causes of chronic fatigue (physical or psychological) need to be eliminated: doctors will usually test for full blood count, ESR/CRP, LFTs and UandE; thyroid stimulating hormone and thyroid function tests; creatine kinase; blood tests for coeliac disease; urine and blood tests for glucose; and urine test for excess protein. All of these may indicate something else that could be wrong. A doctor will not diagnose CFS without having had these tests. Please do not try to self-diagnose.

What causes the fatigue?

Some CFS sufferers have been found to have much higher levels (increases of 30–50%) of choline than other people in the areas of the brain related to voluntary movement. Choline has a significant role in the synaptic communication of messages to the voluntary muscles and this might explain why CFS sufferers can feel exhausted making simple everyday movements, or why they interpret these as exhausting, since many more messages instructing the muscles to move would need to be made.

If, as the name ME suggests, there has been an infection of the myelin sheath around the motor nerve fibres, then the insulating effect of the myelin sheath could be compromised and it would take many more impulses than usual to make a simple movement. This could feel exhausting. Glial cells are responsible for supporting the main motor messages, and also for restoring the myelin sheath, and so something might be malfunctioning with these. They largely operate using calcium and a phosphate, ATP, so there may be a deficiency there. There also seems to be evidence in some people of reduced red blood cell mass, or reduced magnesium sulphate.

There may be some evidence of damage to the autonomic nervous system; a malfunctioning in the hypothalamus (leaving it switched on and in overdrive), and the immune system is almost certainly affected in many people. What is going wrong with the internal mechanisms might not be so important, unless you are researcher looking for a cure. What is important is the road to recovery.

One set of theories centres around the possibility that you have been ignoring the normal signals coming from your body that you have been overdoing things. These signals may be hormonal, they may be tiredness, there may be a sense that you need a change or a rest. It is like ignoring the temperature warning light on you car instrument panel. At some point the water in the radiator boils, and you have to stop. With CFS/ME, you have to stop, because you have become totally exhausted. However, your body takes a lot longer to "gear up" again: it continues to manufacture the symptoms of exhaustion to make sure that you do not start up again and run it down again immediately. You may need to listen to these symptoms and get the message your body is trying to tell you. You may have to find a way of doing things differently; now, in order to get better, and for the future, in order not to burn out again.

Will I get better?

In some people CFS comes and goes, or gradually gets less severe over time. Sometimes the symptoms just disappear after a significant period of time, especially if there has been a change in lifestyle, attitude, or environment. Reassurance and support is essential. Ignore all criticisms (internal or external) and look at your whole life picture, what (and how much) you have been doing recently, and your (probably unrealistic) expectations of yourself.

Prognosis is reasonably good and most people recover almost completely, becoming well again, but it usually takes time—several months to a couple of (sometimes a few) years. A combination of gentle (graded) exercise therapy and a psychological therapy such as cognitive–behavioural therapy (CBT) currently seems the most effective treatment, especially if conducted with a knowledgeable and empathetic therapist. There are a couple of "new" therapies, "reverse therapy" and "Mickel therapy", which claim to be having good results, but the jury is still out.

Family-focused therapy work and simple psycho-education are also quite effective. For a small percentage of sufferers, their illness is extreme and they become almost bed-ridden: psychological interventions are usually inappropriate or ineffective here.

Are there any drugs I can use?

Some medications can apparently help with some of the symptoms: non-steroidal anti-inflammatory drugs (NSAIDs) for pain relief, sleep-enhancing medication, low dose tricyclic anti-depressants, anti-anxiety medications, etc. Most of these are to relieve the symptoms: there are no drugs yet that address the causes. Avoid any drugs that give you any unpleasant side effects. Discuss these with your doctor, and if your doctor is unsympathetic, find one that is more open to discussion. There is little-to-no evidence of any benefits from herbal medicines, though some vitamin supplements (vitamin B) can probably be useful, and there may be some benefit from nicotinamide adenine dinucleotide (NADH), which assists the body in the normal functioning of a hormone, ATP, which is involved in energy production.

How do I get better?

One of the best ways to get better is by understanding that you have probably/almost certainly been overdoing it in some way, and therefore need to start pacing yourself and using graded exercise before you will even start to get better.

One sufferer, who did get better, says, in a CFS information sharing for sufferers,

> [About] Pacing: I never had to bother before, all I did was step on the gas but, in general, I have found the "50% rule" of great benefit to me. Whatever you feel you can do or would like to do—half it!
>
> [About] Graded exercise: This is now advocated by most medical specialists and has its virtues, providing you take into account several factors:

- Don't try it initially unless you have nothing else to do that day.
- Don't take any notice of what others are doing, we are all different.
- Don't exercise with fit people like those found in gyms.
- Don't expect too much, remember the 50% rule.
- Do keep your activity regular.
- Do build up slowly.
- Do listen to your body.
- Do take into account your energy usage that day, work, reading etc. [Maggs, 2000]

Understanding that your previous way of doing things, the way you had of doing things before that might have, in part, caused the burn-out, is almost certainly *absolutely* and *totally* the wrong way for you to do things from now on. You and your internal systems have become seriously overloaded, or over-stressed, or just burnt-out, and this damage is going to take some considerable time to heal. You will almost certainly need to find a much slower and gentler way of doing things: in first and second gear, if you like. This is the key to successful recovery, and it is the most difficult thing to do, especially for a "high-flyer"— like yourself?

Even though you are seriously fatigued, a little light, regular physical activity is also absolutely essential. Modest regular exercise is very important; don't collapse completely. You will need to rediscover exactly how much to do and especially when to stop. Only increase your levels of activity very gently and gradually. Avoid increasing your overall levels of fatigue, as you certainly will not get better that way. Be gentle, consistent, and increase what you do and can do very, very gradually. Aquatic therapy, light exercise, gentle stretching, some forms of Yoga or Tai Chi, can all be very beneficial.

Doing things much more gently, in a Tai Chi type of way, is also much better than doing things in a Karate style or manner, with sudden bursts of movement and activity. Only do something when you have the energy to do it. Use exercises, like Chi Gung, to build energy. Another useful analogy is considering your body's nervous system as a (now) somewhat faulty electric circuit, so use "constant low voltage" rather than occasional bursts of high voltage that will probably be followed by further burn-out.

Do not do anything that results in exhaustion. Aim for tiredness. Do not try to do too much: split things up into bite-sized pieces. "One thing at a time" is an excellent maxim. Focus or concentrate just on this. This is almost a form of mental discipline, or active meditation, or mindfulness practice. Try to do it well. For example, when you are doing the washing up, just do the washing up; don't start thinking about anything else. Focus totally on just what you are doing in the moment.

If your health has been severely compromised you should try to get professional help and/or some form of supervision. Do not try to do it all by yourself (that's probably your old pattern). You may also need to explain things initially to employers and/or family members and friends, but then they need to co-operate with you (and each other) if they are going to be of any real help to you. They may also need some advice, help, or counselling.

Try to avoid emotional stress or worrying about things overly: that uses up energy. Learn to delegate. Get others to help you. Just concentrate on getting well, rather than on doing what you cannot do, or have not done. Do NOT do things for other people any more:

focus purely on yourself. Cut out things that cause you any level of worry or stress. Get in a cleaner, take a sabbatical, let someone else take over the committee work, use an answering machine for the phone and cut the bell out so it doesn't disturb you, listen to some nice soothing music. Chill out and heal.

Try building in some form of mental relaxation (relaxation tapes, meditation, or similar) as a daily and significant part of your lifestyle. Try focusing on today, possibly tomorrow, but certainly not the far distant future or the past. "Why am I like this now?" or "Will I ever get better?" are not particularly helpful questions: "How do I get through today?" and "What do I need to do to plan for tomorrow?" are much more useful topics for consideration.

Some complementary health therapies, such as massage therapy, acupuncture, cranio-sacral work, therapeutic touch, etc., can be pleasant and might be useful. They are most effective when combined with your own regime of very gentle, regular activity; don't rely on them or use them exclusively. Many of these therapies have not been proved to be effective, and some proposed new treatments or products are unproven and might even be harmful. Any therapy should not aggravate any existing symptoms, or create any new problems. This is very important. Therapies that seem to impose an additional financial burden should also be avoided. If someone says that their treatment works, ask first of all to be put in touch with others who have got better. You should also consult, or at least tell, your doctor about anything else that you are doing or taking.

Avoid caffeine (in all its forms), sugar, and other stimulants, as they will *not* help your body heal. Use something like a timetable to plot when you do things, what your energy levels are hour by hour, and when you get up and go to bed, etc. Once you have drawn up an original, leaving plenty of space to write in, have it printed or photocopied so that you have one sheet per week, fill it in over a period of time, and then compare the weeks to see if there is a particular pattern emerging. Then see if you can gradually change your pattern of activity towards something that works for you, and others, better.

If you find that the day after you have done some particular thing you tend to do much less, then you need to do that thing in a different way: it is still exhausting you. Try taking more time over it, stopping half-way through for a break, doing it with someone, doing half as much and doing the other half another time—or something.

Check to see when your "good" energy levels normally are. Use this time to plan things, make appointments, etc. Most people have a mid-afternoon "low", so don't plan a shopping trip then. If you notice you feel exhausted after meeting a particular person, cut down on their visits. Instead, meet people who give you energy.

See which days of the week you have more energy or less energy. Why is that? Try to build up the "low times" and not to do too much when you do have some energy. This is best done in consultation with someone who can give you objective feedback.

Progress

It takes time to heal, because healing is a process. ME/CFS is not always an illness; sometimes it is more of an attitude. This particular form of healing may also require that you change your whole way of doing things, possibly even how you see the world. This sort of change is difficult. Be more conscious of the way you do things, as well as of how much you do. See your healing as perhaps learning a new set of skills, like a craft or an art: how to do things more gently or gracefully. The more you practise this, the better you get at doing it.

All this sounds like a lot, but take it gently. It is a learning process. It will take time. Achievement is not the only criteria of whether you are leading a full and satisfactory life: whether you are nice to yourself and other people is as important, or more so. You may find that you need to learn how to respond to other people differently, perhaps with greater tolerance, acceptance, and even that four-letter word "love". You will, almost certainly, also need to learn to like, or "love", yourself, instead of pushing yourself. "Good enough" is a concept that many people have difficulty with. Your body has definitely said, "Enough now!" Listen to it: it has a particular, unique wisdom. Don't fight it, or condemn it for being weak or letting you down. Listen to it, instead. It can also tell you how to get better.

Where can I obtain more information?

You should have received some information from your doctor, or your local Health Centre. The easiest other available source is through the Internet. There are a number of websites about CFS or ME: try typing "chronic fatigue" or "fibromyalgia" into a web search engine. Be very careful of any websites that seem to be trying to sell you a particular remedy, or a wonderful new therapy. Do not give out your e-mail address, as you may find your mailbox full of e-mail messages about treatments or products from other sources; some of these messages can also contain computer viruses. You don't need that on top of everything else.

There are also pamphlets put out by Health Boards or specialist CFS groups. Ring up your local Health Information Centre, or ask for these in the local library, or via the Internet. The local groups are particularly useful as you can use them to meet other people with the same (or similar) problems. Such groups can be great, even though it can also be initially quite difficult getting out and meeting new people. Persist with these if you can: otherwise come back later, if you want to. Your local group might not be absolutely right for you: some people need different things at different times. Get from it what you can; maybe even eventually you can help change what doesn't work so well. The best changes happen from within!

Final word

Back to the cured ME/CFS patient:

> How can there be any benefits to having ME/CFS? If you take a philosophical approach, something good always comes out of something bad. ME/CFS is no exception. For me there are a number of things I would never have done like: Learning to cook; Learning to observe more; Having time to think more; Being more effective with my energy levels; Getting closer to some family members than before; Having time to rekindle old relationships; Getting more enjoyment from what I already have; Being more appreciative; and I took my good health for granted before. I am a better person, I think! [Maggs, 2000]

Twelve-step programmes

The original 12-Steps Programme was designed for people with an addiction to alcohol and forms the basis of the Alcoholics Anonymous method of treatment. This programme, way of seeing addiction, or form of treatment has been shown to apply equally successfully to many other forms of serious addiction, such as drug addiction or compulsive gambling. The "12 steps" are really a guide towards living a moral, happy life by trying to conquer the addictions, compulsions, or habitual dysfunctions that hold us back and prevent us from being the person we want to be. Try to see them in this way. They can be used for almost anything.

The twelve steps

1. We admitted we were powerless over —— (our particular addiction), and that our lives had become unmanageable.
2. We came to believe that only with the aid of a Power greater than ourselves could we restore ourselves to sanity.
3. We made a decision to turn our will and lives over to the care of that Power, God, as we understand Him.

4. We made a searching and fearless moral inventory of ourselves.
5. We admitted to that Power, ourselves, and to (at least) one other human being the exact nature and extent of our wrongs.
6. We make ourselves entirely ready to have these defects/negative aspects of our character removed by ourselves and with help from that Power.
7. We humbly asked that Power to help us to clarify and correct all our shortcomings and dysfunctional patterns.
8. We have made a list of all persons we have harmed, affected, or distressed, and we are now willing to make amends to all of them.
9. We will make direct amends to such people, wherever possible, and at their discretion, except when to do so would injure them or others.
10. We have continued to take a personal inventory and, whenever we were wrong, promptly admitted it.
11. We have sought through prayer and meditation to improve our conscious contact with that Power, as we understood Him, praying only for knowledge of His will for us, and for the power within ourselves to carry that will out.
12. Having had a spiritual awakening as a result of these steps, we have tried to carry this message to others, and to practise these principals in all our affairs, and in all aspects of our lives.

Twelve steps in counselling

The remarkably successful "12-Step" programme has some lessons for us in a counselling situation. First, it really does work. About 67% of all people who follow it properly get significant help from it. A high percentage of these people either succeed in stopping their addiction, or gain significant control over it.

The persistent habits that we have been looking at can also be seen as akin to old survival techniques or perceptions about life that we developed in our family of origin, have used fairly religiously ever since, and that are now increasingly inappropriate or dysfunctional. It is these that we need to change, but we have great difficulty in so doing. In that way, they are like addictions, though commonly something considerably less than a full-blown addiction.

These persistent habits can include: low self-esteem; patterns of blame or lack of personal responsibility; persistent self-sabotage; work-a-holism; self-abuse or self-harm; inappropriate anger reactions; heavy drinking or smoking; financial mismanagement; any compulsive or obsessional behaviours; bad eating patterns (eating disorders); persistent flirting, a series of affairs, and/or inappropriate sexualization of other people; persistently staying in an abusive or exploitative situation; and co-dependent relationships.

The first six Steps can usually be applied by anyone, relatively easily, to any of the above situations, without doing any harm, and with the distinct possibility for discovering, or refinding, a degree of self-control or a sense of self-empowerment and self-benefit. They are really outlining the necessary steps towards a radical change of awareness and self-image.

Start going through the Steps and rewriting them out in your own language or terms. Keep the essential point of each step, but rephrase it to fit your present situation. Discuss this with a friend, or with your partner or therapist, saying how these Steps might work for you now. Listen carefully to yourself as you talk about or justify what you have written. Listen carefully also to their advice. They know you quite well and they probably know how this persistent habit has got hold of you, and how you usually avoid dealing with it.

Either try one of these steps at a time (the best way)—or you can try to work on all of the first six Steps. These earlier steps really help one to prepare for the fairly profound, transformative, even spiritual, implications of change. It is difficult to remember any more steps at the beginning, anyway. Step 7, and especially Step 8 onwards, take one into a different phase of the actual work: more one of actual rehabilitation and change.

Please notice that the steps are all written in the past tense, except for Step 9, which is an affirmation of future action. You have not completed the step until you can fully acknowledge, over a period of time, that this step is now true for you. Until such a time, you are working with it, trying to make it happen, struggling with it. This is normal. No one said that any of this would be easy. There is no gain without pain!

Scrupulous honesty and thus heightened self-awareness are the factors that really work in this programme: otherwise you are just fooling yourself. You can try to fool others, but it will not work for long, and then you will have (again) destroyed any trust or goodwill that you might have built up in the interim. Back to Square One! Taking a good, hard (painful) look at yourself is not easy, but it may be the only way that you start to stop.

The other very successful part of the programme is that your compatriots, fellow addicts, sufferers, travelling companions, whatever, those involved in 12-Step programmes, have all been there, done it, and "got the T-shirt", sometimes many times before. They are the only real experts because they have done it already themselves, to themselves. They know all the tricks and self-delusions because they have been there, before you. It is therefore sometimes very useful, if not essential, to try to find, and get into, such a group of like-minded people. Do NOT even think of trying to do this just by yourself: just re-read the early Steps. Self-help here probably will not work, by itself, as Square One will become very, very familiar. But the essential self-awareness, no one else can do for you.

The other useful concept that comes out of the 12-Step program is the perspective that you are a "recovering (whatever-it-is) - oholic" for every single day of the rest of your life. So just take it one day at a time. You haven't succumbed to this addiction today. That is good! You are not cured: the addiction will always be there; the potential to repeat the old pattern will always be there. So do not become complacent. Just remember the addictive component. It is still a part of your life. Live with it—and have a good life—from now onwards!

Trauma and post traumatic stress disorder

Trauma sometimes happens to us. It is a profound psycho-physical experience, even if the traumatic event or events cause the person affected no direct physical harm. As mentioned previously, some people have experienced long-term levels of extreme stress that have actually traumatized them: there does not have to be one single event or incident, or even several. It can happen from a build-up to high levels of ongoing stress over a considerable period of time that creates a situation that is extremely stressful to the point of being traumatic.

We are gradually realizing that trauma, and the effects of trauma, constitute a special case and need specialized handling, mainly because the symptoms do not seem to go away unless this happens, and because it is all to easy to retraumatize an already traumatized person, even in therapy.

The traumatized person often remembers or re-experiences the physical and emotional sensations of the traumatic event, but is usually unable to affect or modulate these experiences in any way. They can feel shocked and helpless and often feel overwhelmed again—simply from the startle effect of the memory or the flashback. Over time, the affects usually decline and lessen, though a particular situation or circumstance (smell, noise, sight) might trigger the memory and the traumatic reaction once more.

Sometimes these memories and their attendant symptoms do not go away gently or easily. In a number of cases (possibly up to 20%), traumatized people can develop a particular condition called post traumatic stress disorder (PTSD), where the effects of the trauma continue to intrude into the person's life, affecting them quite seriously on a day-to-day basis for a fairly long period of time. In people with PTSD, traumatic events are remembered differently from non-traumatic events, where there is a sense of the passing of time since the event. With PTSD, traumatic events or memories are dissociated from the passing of time: the feelings and emotions are all present now, and the person is re-experiencing the trauma in the present time in the form of a flashback.

The symptoms of PTSD are: (1) that sufferers experience these unbidden memories or flashbacks; (2) they quite actively try to avoid any reminders of the trauma; and (3) there is a chronic arousal of their autonomic nervous system (ANS). If these symptoms last for more than a month and are combined with a loss of any regular functioning—such as at work or in social relationships—then a diagnosis of PTSD can be made. The person is not mad. They may feel that they are going crazy, but this is now a recognized condition, albeit only fairly newly recognized as such. People have been traumatized throughout time and history, but previously they were thought to be crazy, or were even shot for cowardice ("shell-shock" was not recognized as a condition during the First World War), or were permanently damaged by the constant repetition of the traumatization.

Effective therapy for trauma and PTSD, and there is effective therapy now, involves helping the person to stay in their body in the present, to understand their somatic and psychological process, to use their internal resources, and to learn to re-experience these physical and emotional sensations without getting retraumatized. This latter point is extremely important, and is the main emphasis for new and effective approaches to treating trauma, epitomized by the work, and in the writings, of, especially, van der Kolk (e.g., van der Kolk, McFarlane, & Weisaeth, 1996), Levine (1997), Rothschild (2000), and Ogden (e.g., Ogden, Minton, & Pain, 2006).

Self-harm

People may find ways of coping with, or simply get used to, difficulties and distress in their lives that are harmful to themselves and also to others. Some people take harmful substances for pleasure: they are not really self-harmers. They may drink too much, overwork, smoke, take drugs, eat unhealthily, use methods to cope that are immoral (like abusing or bullying other people) or criminal in some way and, while these might harm others initially, they are ultimately considerably harmful to themselves as well. These methods are not usually included in the definition of self-harm. However, they are harmful, and you are doing them to yourself, so—if these apply to you—read on and you might learn something. Many people (about 50% men, 25% women), who self-harm have also abused alcohol, or another drug; mixing drugs and alcohol is another form of self-harm, and a very dangerous one.

"Deliberate self-harm" is a term usually used to refer to drug overdoses or attempts at suicide. Other methods of self-harm include cutting and scratching, often the arms, scalding or burning themselves, biting or punching themselves, head or body banging, hair or eyelash pulling, swallowing sharp objects, or inserting objects into various orifices. Most people who self-harm in these lesser ways do not see themselves as suicidal: they are using the pain of the self-harm for a very different reason. Other terms used for this type of behaviour are "self-injury" or "self-abuse".

Self-harm is a way of dealing with very strong and very difficult emotions. For some people, especially those who have been abused in some way, it seems to give the sort of relief to their feelings that crying or getting angry might provide for other people. Some self-harming people are so angry and aggressive that they cannot control these feelings. They feel that they just cannot take it out on the others around them, so they take it out on themselves. It makes a weird sort of sense, but, of course, it has to stop, or be prevented.

People who self-harm are NOT attention-seeking: they are usually not public or overt about their self-harm. Usually, they are more accustomed to, and feel "safe" with, the harm they cause themselves, rather than getting aggressive or angry with those around them. The amount of self-harm that people do to themselves is not usually indicative of the amount of harm caused to them, but of the length of time this behaviour has been happening. Over time, they have to harm themselves more severely to get the same amount of relief. However, this spiral can lead to serious infections, frequent hospitalizations, and even permanent injury— or death. This is not usually intended. The self-harm is a form of addictive behaviour.

The more frequent areas of self-harm are arms, hands, and legs; less commonly the face, abdomen, breasts, or genitals (though this is somewhat more common in people who have been severely sexually abused). Other forms of self-harm include scratching, picking, biting, scraping, and occasionally inserting sharp objects under the skin and into orifices, or burning themselves with cigarettes. Lesser forms of self-harm include pulling out their hair, or eyelashes, scrubbing themselves so hard they break the skin, using caustic substances (to "clean" themselves) or nail-biting. Some people burn or scald themselves, others inflict blows or bangs on themselves, but the most frequent form is cutting.

Women tend to harm themselves in this way much more than men, possibly because of the differences between the experience and the expression of emotions. About 10% of all hospital admissions are as the result of one form of self-harm or another (especially if one includes drug overdose). Men tend to externalize emotions such as anger. Self-harm is often an expression of anger, a reaction to violence, or to an upset-ness that has been turned back on oneself. People may be so inhibited from expressing anger that they internalize it and hurt themselves.

Another cause of self-harm is a build-up of stress. This group regularly self-harm in order to relieve their stress. They have usually found ways to keep their problems hidden, and when the stress levels build up, they self-harm in one of these covert ways. They usually do not harm themselves enough to need treatment, or they have a story prepared, or they will not seek help. Yet, somewhere, they may also be desperate to be discovered. The result may be a permanent disfiguration or a serious infection.

There is a definite distinction between self-harm and attempted suicide, although to the people involved there is often little distinction. They are so miserable that they might want to die, but they cannot bring themselves to kill themselves, yet.

There are many reasons why people might wish to harm themselves. Sometimes it can be a form of asking for help, but many people are ashamed of this behaviour and hide what they do. They can also feel humiliation, low self-esteem, and fear. For others it is a sort of distorted coping mechanism; a way of feeling in control because they are at least doing it to themselves. For some, it is a form of emotional release: they may have difficulty in crying or getting angry when others are around, or they may feel empty or numb inside and this is their way of feeling "real" again, because this pain really hurts. A few people carry "wrong beliefs" about themselves: they believe they are a bad person who has bad thoughts or does bad things and should be punished, so self-harm is then a form of punishment or a "letting out" of these imagined bad parts. Often these "bad" thoughts or actions are relatively normal ones, but they have abnormal associations. They may relate back to a time when the person was abused.

Many (some would say most) people who self-harm have had painful early experiences in childhood, quite often with a history of some kind of abuse, or they may have experienced hurt, rejection, abandonment, or extreme patterns of behaviour or belief in their family of origin. Self-harm does not just happen: it is part of a deeper psychological pattern, set up with a recurring cycle of responses to various triggers that happened in that person's life.

"Days, weeks and months can go by without self-harming, and then the pattern starts again." This is quite a common story. There is a definite pattern here. You are not alone: quite a few people self-harm and then get over it. Speak to someone knowledgeable about this area.

Some of the present-day triggers can be feeling rejected by other people, being blamed for something out of your control, feeling inadequate, abandoned, unhappy, frustrated, desperate, out of control, or angry, or feeling "wrong" or "bad" in some way, and unable to express these feelings more appropriately. These feelings then tap back into the earlier bad feelings and unresolved issues and the pattern of abuse or harm is continued. Most people who self-harm would like to stop hurting themselves or beating themselves up in some way. Try to develop different ways of communication, and of coping.

Getting proper psychotherapeutic help is very important. It is very unlikely that you will be able to cure this pattern by yourself. Initially, it may be hard to speak about these issues: many non-professional people might express shock, or distaste, or will feel unable to help. Counselling and psychotherapy can be very helpful in addressing the deeper underlying issues, the reasons for this type of behaviour, and the possible emotional abuse that started it. You will be listened to properly and taken seriously. It is important to feel accepted, and not judged or condemned, to feel respected, and to feel that someone understands these various feelings and experiences. Once started, it is necessary to feel that there is a relationship of trust that builds with that person and you can then use this as a basis for changing the pattern of self-harm. Talking through the feelings will help you to understand them better. It is also important to overcome some of the negative thinking and belief systems, and to look at other possible behaviours and reactions: (better?) alternatives to self-harm.

Self-harming is not immediate and thoughts usually build up before the self-harming action is actually taken. It is important to try to recognize these thoughts when they first appear, and then try different strategies to get out of the (otherwise seemingly inevitable) cycle. Almost any form of interruption to the usual cycle can be used beneficially. It is best to discuss these strategies with your therapist.

Self-help groups of people with similar experiences of self-harm can also be useful, as an adjunct to counselling or therapy, helping to overcome feelings of isolation, to share experiences, to give mutual support, not to have to explain or justify, and possibly giving acceptance, friendship, and a sense of belonging. Creative experiences like art or drama can also be a very useful way to express such feelings in a non-verbal way. Family and friends can help, but in a limited way, as families can be part of the original problem. However, the acceptance, care, and support that come from people who love you is immeasurable and hugely beneficial. Listen to them and try to take in the concern that they have for you. Try to make sure that you do not alienate yourself from them. You may, however, need to maintain some distance.

Listed below are some self-help techniques for people who self-harm. These can help to reduce the level of injury, and they might help you to reduce the risk of injury, or any further complications. Try them out and see if they work for you.

- First, when you feel as if you want to cut yourself,
  - count down (ten, nine, eight, . . .)
  - breathe in slowly and deeply, then breathe out slowly and long;
  - point out five things in your surrounding environment—one for each sense (sight, hearing, touch, taste, smell)—that help you to bring yourself into the present;
  - breathe slowly—in through the nose and out through the mouth.

- Try to describe any mounting problems or feelings, etc., to those around you in a way that still allows you some choice.
- If you still feel like cutting yourself, try:
  - marking yourself with a red (water-based) felt-tip pen instead of cutting;
  - using a punch-bag or large cushion to vent the anger or frustration;
  - plunging your hands into a bowl of ice cubes (for a few minutes only);
  - using ice (instead of a blade) where you would otherwise cut yourself.

- Make an outline drawing of yourself on A1 (flipchart) paper ahead of time. When you feel like cutting yourself, use a red felt-tip, and mark where you would cut yourself. Try to contact some of the underlying driving feelings that make you want to cut or harm yourself. As you do this, write them out, or talk them out into a small tape recorder.
- Instead of scratching or cutting yourself, imagine scratching or cutting something else in front of you. Make the gestures, make an angry face, growl, grimace, or snarl, and then imagine who you might be getting angry with.

None of these alternatives will be very satisfactory—at first. They will not totally replace the feeling, or the relief, but they have one major advantage—they will not hurt you. As you stop the actual self-harm, you will be changing the dynamic. You will feel better because this time you did not hurt yourself. You will be able to start to rebuild your self-esteem.

Friends and relatives may not know how to help you properly, so some of their demands, suggestions or ideas may be inappropriate for you. It is best to be able to say something like, "Thank you for your concern, and I am dealing with this pattern of behaviour reasonably adequately with my therapist and the situation is improving steadily."

If you have just harmed yourself, you may be expressing a number of strong emotional reactions: panic, anger, fear, hopelessness, or hate comprise just some of these. These reactions will not help you and you need to insulate yourself from them, while not cutting yourself off from the feelings of love and concern behind these expressions. You may well be very sensitive to the feelings of those around you: your "psychic antennae" are possibly able to pick up negative feelings very easily. It is often a lot harder to pick up the more positive feelings. If you feel rejected or abandoned by their anger, don't take it personally: they are reacting to your behaviour, not really to you. They may also be feeling inadequate, a failure, or very anxious about you. Again, some family counselling might be helpful.

Self-harm is a symptom of another underlying problem. One hopes that the symptom can be helped or diminished, but the underlying problem still needs to be addressed. Some form of professional help is usually necessary. Contact your doctor first and see if you can get some help, first through the NHS Counselling Service, then (perhaps) a referral to clinical psychology.

Theories about self-harm vary. It usually starts in childhood, progressing into more obvious forms of self-harm in adolescence. There is, quite frequently but not exclusively, a high correlation between people who self-harm and people who have been sexually abused, or who have grown up in an invalidating environment. In either case, it would have been very difficult to express one's feelings and have them validated. Self-harm is thus a desperate method of self-expression.

Another theory about self-harming, and especially self-cutting, is that it releases the body's natural opiate-type painkillers (endorphins). It is possible that one can become addicted to this heroin-like internal reaction, which is why it gets repeated. Endorphins also make you feel quite relaxed and pleasantly calm, so there is an emotional release from the pain, stress, or agony. Non-addictive drugs used to treat heroine addicts can sometimes be efficacious in extreme cases.

Finally, any type of behaviour can be rewarding. Cutting or self-harm can bring greater attention and thus this can be rewarding. In a specialist treatment unit, there is care taken to avoid reinforcing any such behaviour and finding alternative behaviours (that do not involve self-harm) that can be rewarded.

It is important to try to destigmatize self-harming behaviour. It is then much easier to get help and support and "normalize" this type of behaviour. You may find some negative reactions coming from people who are unfamiliar with this type of behaviour.

Advice to family and friends is: get support for your own feelings from other family members, or your close friends, your family doctor, or a professional counsellor. Do not make any demands on the person who self-harms, except for them to get proper help. Do not set ultimatums, nor try to force that person into different behaviour patters—these strategies will not work because the background problem is not being dealt with. Do not deny, or try to hide, that there is a problem. Accept your own limitations as a family. If you feel rejected by the family member who self-harms, do not take it personally, as it may be nothing to do with you, but the self-harming person might need their own space and distance from you and the rest of the family.

Since many of these feelings come from high levels of stress or agitation, the regular and effective use of relaxation techniques is often very beneficial. Some methods like "progressive relaxation" or the autogenic technique are well established and should be able to help. Other forms of personal relaxation, such as a long hot soak in the tub, walking in the hills or on the beach, listening to your favourite music, can also be very beneficial. Techniques like Tai Chi or Yoga, and therapies like hypnotherapy, reflexology, massage, or acupuncture, can also help you to relax more generally. Since anger is involved, you might like to try Thai kick-boxing, or something similar.

Somehow you are going to have to start learning—yes, start learning—to like yourself. If this behaviour is a "learnt" reaction to high or unbearable levels of anxiety and distress, then you are going to have to relearn how to tolerate and then reduce such levels, and how to develop a behaviour pattern that does not do any harm yourself, one that is much nicer to yourself.

This has to be part of a wider pattern: thinking that you are worthwhile, thinking it was not your fault, realizing there are other ways to feel the pain, and other possible ways to express yourself. It takes time, patience, courage, and (most importantly) the desire, even the determination, to change and do things differently. It is not easy, but it is possible.

One place to contact on the Internet is the National Self-Harm Network (see "Sources of information: self-harm" towards the end of this book). This has a forum for people who self-harm, family, friends, and professionals, and a good list of resources, downloads, and much more. There are also many self-help groups in most major cities, go to "Resources" and scroll down. Try also exploring the Self-Harm Alliance website. This seems to have more sponsored links.

One of the very few specialist units in the NHS for self-harm is London Bethlem Royal Hospital's crisis recovery unit: they may be able to advise you where any self-harm specialist services are nearer to you.

Money worries

Money worries are affecting more and more people. These are usually created by redundancy, sickness, or relationship difficulties: i.e., circumstances outside of your control. Debt levels for individuals (mortgages, credit cards, bank loans, etc.) are at an all time high—more than £1 trillion now! More and more families have to have both parents working in order to get by. More and more people are paying off mortgages later, taking mortgage "holidays", having interest-only mortgages, or even having their houses repossessed. In 2008), we were faced with the "credit crunch" and also substantively increased prices at the supermarket and petrol pump. These have put increasing pressures on the family purse, and what was affordable and within budget is often now not so. We are going to have to "down-size" our spending and our expectations.

The extreme anxiety generated by such financial issues, and when people feel out of control of their finances, is now being called "money sickness syndrome" (MSS). This refers to a group of symptoms of extreme anxiety generated by people feeling that they have lost control of their personal finances, or that they cannot see any way out of a debt situation. This could affect as much as 43% of people (AXA survey); nearly four million people admit that money worries have caused them actually to take time off work; more than ten million people admit that money worries have affected their relationships; and one person in five (20%) says that money worries have affected their sex life. With the availability of all-too-easy credit cards, and average personal debt (excluding mortgages) now exceeding £4,000, MSS could be affecting as much as half the population.

Symptoms of MSS include physical symptoms such as palpitations, shortness of breath, headaches, a tight feeling in the stomach, nausea, sleeplessness, diarrhoea, reduced libido, and a lack of appetite, and emotional symptoms include irritability, mood swings, nervousness, poor concentration, forgetfulness, poor judgement, difficulty in making decisions, depression, and negative thinking. There is a general tendency not to look after oneself properly, for alcohol and other drug consumptions to increase, for "comfort" eating habits to return, and for relationships to be adversely affected. Some people are even ashamed to admit the extent of their debt to their partners or other family members. So! What to do?

First, be totally frank with your partner and/or other close family members. They will find out some time, and the sooner the better. There will almost certainly be a real need to work together on this problem. Many people find they can get short-to-middle-term, low-interest loans from other family members, and then just work their way out of this situation, making regular repayments, and not damaging their credit rating. A word of warning, though: it can be difficult to get "heavy" with a family member who has not repaid a loan on time. Frankness, total honesty, full disclosure, regular communication, and formal family meetings can all be part of such an in-house "rescue package". There are also self-help books, Internet websites, and much good, free advice can be got from the Citizens Advice Bureau (CAB).

Second, develop some tactics to reduce your spending—often the main culprit. These will probably involve surrendering several (or all) of your credit cards, making a budget and keeping to it religiously, selling any unnecessary stuff on e-bay, setting up a support system with a regular check-in process, giving up a (or the) car and using public transport more, cutting out (or down) on a family holiday, or even downsizing on the house. All these tactics need to be discussed in an open, consistent, transparent, and explicit manner.

The next line of approach is possibly to approach a proper debt consultant and look at consolidating all your loans and credit card payments into one reasonable package with regular guaranteed repayments. The CAB, or your bank, are almost certainly the best people to help you out here. Try to transfer of all your high interest loans (credit cards, store cards, loan sharks, etc.) into a much more reasonable single source. Juggling with credit cards and short-term zero interest offers just does not work in the long term. Loan sharks have very high interest rates (exploitative, even) and tend not to be very nice people: avoid them!

The next level of intervention is to persuade some of your creditors to reduce their expectations and lower your repayments. This will affect your credit rating. It is best to get someone professional to negotiate on your behalf. Again, the CAB or your bank will probably advise you best. Debt management is a tricky business and a lot of people are trying to make money out of it. Not everyone has your best interests at heart. The step beyond this is an Individual Voluntary Arrangement (IVA), which is where you come to terms with your creditors.

The final step is not suicide (unfortunately, a choice made by some), but insolvency or bankruptcy: it is rare to have to get to this stage. Again, take professional advice before you take this step.

Don't try to be "clever" and hide money away. Don't hide (or not disclose) any debts; make a clean breast of everything. Don't over-estimate how much you can repay: it is actually better to under-estimate slightly. Don't miss instalments, once you have set up these arrangements. Don't resort to anything criminal.

Ageing issues

Ageing

The most widespread "disorder" today is premature old age. The passage of time doesn't kill you and you don't really die of "old age". The cells in your body have to be constantly replaced, and when your body ceases to be able replace the old cells with new ones, you accumulate an excess of old dead cells and eventually die—usually of complications.

The most recent and seemingly correct theory of ageing is based on damage done by "free radicals". Free radicals are highly unstable chemical "buzz-bombs" that steal electrons from your body's delicate membranes and genetic (DNA) structure in order to balance themselves, causing your genetic code to change slightly and thus your body's ability to repair itself. Free radicals are so chemically reactive that they only exist for a millionth of a second, but there are millions of them around every second. These come from food, water, air, smoking, chemical exposure, even exercise and sleeping cause poor cellular function and waste. Oxidation is another name for this process of cellular damage or decay. It is a lot more serious than you think. Try to avoid these "free radicals".

Many ageing theories have been proposed over the years, the most ancient and incorrect being the idea that blood pressure and cholesterol rise with age, that bone density and strength declines with age, that middle-age is inevitable, and that sexuality disappears. None of these is necessarily true. Studies that indicate these are based on an ageing population ignorant of the fact that one could do something to break these patterns. The average ageing Westerner has had improper nutrition and has generally lived a sedentary (and overweight) life. If that is what you choose to do, then the above ageing signs may be true for you! If it is not, then they are not. There are a number of specific issues that are particular to "ageing" and that affect us, sometimes without us realizing it, as we get older. It seems worth mentioning some of these.

Mobility

The ability to walk freely and easily is mostly taken for granted—until it is threatened or lost. One of the more unfortunate aspects of ageing is such a loss: mobility problems are the most frequent disability, affecting over four million people, 75% of whom are over seventy-five years old. Half the number of people over seventy-five suffers from mobility problems. These can range from discomfort when climbing stairs (that many suffer from) to being totally bedridden (for a few). Causes can be arthritis, strokes, Parkinson's disease, motor neurone disease, tiredness, breathlessness, dizziness ("turns"), faintness, falls and fractures, heart problems, osteoporosis, or spine, hip, knee, and feet problems. Management of this is usually through a combination of adaptations, attitude, specialist advice, physiotherapy, mobility aids, medications, surgery, and alternative forms of mobility. Insurance rates for drivers can increase after the age of sixty; older drivers have slightly slower reaction times and sometimes have difficulty with night vision. UK driving licenses are valid up until the age of seventy, and then a special health declaration is needed. After some illnesses, a temporary cessation from driving is required, or driving is excluded. At sixty, most people can get a free, or reduced, travel pass. Public transport schemes vary considerably: some local authorities run social transport schemes, and there are volunteer groups who can help.

Memory

Just because you're getting older does not mean that you have to accept memory loss as inevitable. Many research studies show that proper nutrition and active stimulation are very important factors in maintaining a sharp and active memory throughout your life. The brain needs nutrient-rich blood to function properly and to create the neurotransmitters that are essential in making sure that your body and mind function and interact well with each other. Besides general nutrition, it is important to combat the damage that free radicals do to your body, and they can do enormous amounts of damage to your memory cells. Green tea is good for you. Eating well will definitely help: vitamin E found in whole grains, nuts, and sunflower seeds is good for prevention of Alzheimer's, oily fish may help to protect against dementia, anti-oxidant rich fruit and vegetables, and leafy green vegetables will all help. For stimulation, try Sudoku, crosswords, quiz games, or learning a new language. These "mental aerobics" can really help: "Use it or lose it" is a maxim that applies to memory as well as other things.

Nutrition and health

It is increasingly important that you should not be carrying any excess body weight, as gradual degenerative changes in your joints and heart mean that these will carry the additional strain. So really try to avoid fats and highly refined carbohydrates (sugar); instead, go for high fibre options, include plenty of fresh vegetables and fruit (mainly for the vitamins), and just watch the size of your portions. Do not overcook food, as this destroys nutrients. Do not try to economize by keeping left-over food, as this can be quite dangerous, especially as elderly people have a lower resistance to infections and the consequences are more severe. Do take plenty of liquids. Keep a stock of frozen, tinned, or dried foods, especially for when the weather is bad. Failure of your normal appetite may mean something is wrong, so consult your GP. Also ensure that you have a back-up heating system.

If you become constipated, it might be the side-effect of a drug. Avoid any purgatives or laxatives, and just increase the fibre in your diet (fruit, vegetables [especially beans], bran, and wholemeal flour), then consult your GP if this doesn't resolve it. Alternatively, diarrhoea, maybe from a mild infection, should clear up quickly with normal hygienic precautions. If it is chronic, increase the fibre in your diet and consult your GP if it doesn't clear up in a couple of days and make especially sure you avoid dehydration by drinking plenty.

Blood pressure and cholesterol

Make sure these are checked regularly (annually) from middle age onwards, but after about the age of sixty, this test should be done every six months or so. The cholesterol test involves taking a simple blood sample. Follow the advice given to you by your GP.

Exercise

While stamina, strength, suppleness, balance, and muscle and bone mass all reduce with ageing, some of the loss may be due to progressive disuse. These effects can be minimized if adequate exercise is taken regularly. Brisk walking, if possible, three or four times a week (as a minimum) really improves general health, stamina, and helps burn off those stress hormones as well. It also boosts one's sense of well-being. Any form of exercise is better than nothing; just be sensible with what you can do and enjoy it!

Living arrangements

Try to avoid any domestic accidents (the most common) by doing a little risk assessment for most normal activities: what could go wrong, and how one can minimize the risk. Look at just what you can do now, rather than what you used to be able to do. Learn to ask for help for those things (like climbing ladders or carrying heavy objects) that are now too much. It is quite common for an elderly person to have to change their home. It is also unfortunate that this is very often very disruptive and unsettling and it is possibly the worst possible time in your life to do it. Elderly people often degenerate physically and mentally quickly after a move. So, try to make any inevitable move happen sooner rather than later. The factors to be considered are usually finance, family ties, proximity and access, the type of accommodation, who to live with, and the sort of support you may need. An active social life can, apparently, reduce the risk of Alzheimer's, etc., by up to about 40%. It is also more mentally stimulating and should even be quite fun!

Finances

Once we have stopped working, our financial situation starts to change rapidly. We become dependent on pensions and savings, and, as inflation cuts into those, we often have less and less available money at times when we might need it more, as our health and mobility can decrease.

There is a huge risk factor in using one's house (often the only major asset) as a form of finance, as there is no knowing what will be needed later, when the funds may become less available, and also, you are potentially depriving other members of your family from their inheritance. Take specialist advice.

Mental health

As we get older our brain shrinks a little and the blood supply to it decreases. A reduced blood supply or a slower heart rate can even precipitate vascular dementia. Neuronal connections (responses) are a little weaker and slower, and plasticity (adaptability) is decreased, both mentally and physically.

However, there are some positive aspects: experience, discrimination, and higher time and energy conservation can mean older professionals perform better than younger ones. The requirements of good psychological health are (as ever):

- an adequate standard of living;
- financial and emotional security;
- reasonable health and diet;

- regular quality social interactions;
- pursuit of personal interests.

For further information, contact Age Concern: www.ace.org.uk, or www.ageconcernscotland.org.uk

Travel

The following list comprises a few pointers about travelling that can affect mental health issues and might be useful.

- First, please get a general "travel and health" leaflet from your GP or travel agent: there are several.
- These leaflets cover the usual preventative measures and precautions to take with regard to food and water, sun protection, protection against insects, infections, local diseases, inoculations, sexually transmitted diseases, and deep vein thrombosis (for long flights). They may include information about accidents and crime, and special advice for the elderly, or pregnant women, or those travelling with children.
- For free health care when travelling in Europe a special European Health Insurance Card (EHIC) is required—this replaces the E111 form. You need to get the application form from a main Post Office, and it takes a couple of weeks to obtain the card.
- Make sure you take all necessary medications and some of the simple remedies you normally use.

- Make sure you know what your travel insurance actually covers, and whether it is up to date.
- Make sure your passport does not expire within about a month (or more) after your anticipated return. Make sure you have all proper visas, and that your flights are correctly booked in the exact name on your passport.
- Make sure your credit cards will allow you to withdraw cash when abroad (you might be over your "cash limit", not your credit limit), or that you have sufficient travellers' cheques and/or foreign currency with you.
- Make sure you have written down somewhere different and safe (not in your wallet) all the telephone contact numbers for credit cards, mobile phone services, family and friends, hotel, travel insurance, etc. Make sure you tell others where this list is.

All this is so you can avoid simple situations or making avoidable mistakes that turn out to be very stressful and might spoil your enjoyment. This is supposed to be a holiday, or a pleasant business trip. Here are a few more suggestions.

- Try to avoid having too many expectations. Read up about the area first, identify things you might like to see and do, but don't get into too much detailed planning. Things will almost certainly be different when you are there.
- Try to avoid doing too much. It is always a bit more difficult doing things in a strange place. Take it easy.
- Don't decide anything dramatic while you are away. By all means think about the home or work situation from this different perspective, plan some changes even—but don't resign from your steady job by text when you are offered (say) a part-share in a bar in Ibiza, or end your long-term relationship on the basis of a holiday fling.
- Take the time and rest and make sure that you get the break that *you* need. That may mean an early night, or not going on an outing, or spending some time by yourself as well as being with others. Just be clear.

- Please don't interfere or involve yourself with other people's lives, especially the people living where you are on holiday. You are the visitor, the transient. You get to go home. This is their home and they have to go on living there. Any interference is usually tragic.

WELL-BEING

Natural health

This section is not really about all the so-called "natural health" remedies that are out there. Some are excellent, some are not so good, and a few are potentially dangerous if you take them without knowing exactly what is in them and how they might affect you. This section is more about what we mean by "natural health".

According to Wikipedia, natural health is an eclectic self-care system of natural therapies concerned with building and restoring health and wellness via prevention and a healthy lifestyle. It is a totally different philosophy to the medical model of "illness". In times gone by (not that they were necessarily any better than today), there was a local, lay presence that relied on knowledge and wisdom and the body's healing capacities. This principle can still be found today in herbal medicine, the midwife, and the alternative medicine practitioner. A person needs to stay healthy, and diet and what we do with our bodies has a large part to play in that.

"We are what we eat" contains some truth. Organic food is better than non-organic; fresh and green, with vegetables (mostly) raw, is better for you than cooked and processed; small, more frequent meals are better than one or two large ones; smaller portions are healthier; a greater variety of foods is more beneficial. You can try getting a juicer, so that you can make smoothies. Cut down on the amount of meat you eat. Make sure you get lots of vitamins A, Bs, and C, folic acid, zinc, magnesium, etc. Drink more water—about 1.5 litres minimum. Breathe, breathe, and breathe. Enough said! Get out into the fresh air and grab whatever sunlight you can. Exercise all your different muscle groups. But you know all this already!

Another definition of natural health is that it is something that has to be worked at and maintained: you do not stay healthy by doing nothing. Sorry about that! But it is true. There is a constant maintenance component that is important: just as you pump up the tyres on your car and put oil into the engine, you need to do something regularly to keep your body healthy.

However, there is another principle, a more social one. John Donne wrote, "No man is an Island", and it is true that we cannot exist, healthily, without other people, without nurturing social contacts, without love and friendship. This is also an essential part of natural health, as is being fully in the world in which we live, and not being adversely affected by our environment.

Natural health is an integrated approach that includes all these social and environmental factors, as well as the internal factors already mentioned. It is something of a philosophy or a way of thought that integrates the person's mind, body, and spirit with their social relationships and environment. When these work together, that is natural health. The process of healing is therefore concerned in working holistically with all these factors. This means that we have to accept full responsibility for our health and look after ourselves.

A new model of health care

My ideas about this came from two main sources. In ancient China (apparently), you paid your doctor only when you were well. It was his job to keep you healthy. When you were ill, you didn't pay him and so he worked hard to get your health (and his income) restored. This means that there is an active principle. When you are well, he should be working to keep you that way, rather than waiting until you fall ill. Modern medicine is not very proactive: little is taught to doctors about actual health. The focus is on illness, diagnosis, and treatment, rather than prevention. So, another insight came in the form of a model of natural health care for the twenty-first century. What do we need to do?

A holistic perspective

This model is an extension or development of the natural health philosophy and the more modern bio-psycho-social model and goes something like this. The position of the person (I won't use the term "patient") is central. Let us put them in the middle and build a system around them that works. All the people (and structures) around them (partners, family, friends, practitioners, teachers, etc.) will have that person's well-being as their main concern and can reflect back to that person all the different aspects of their perception, their knowledge, and their "truth" about that person, their life, and their health. This can be done—and usually would be done—on a fairly regular basis. If the person has a problem, be it a health, financial, social relationship, or work problem, there will then be many different views on that person and their problem. It will be much more of a holistic perspective.

The process of reflection of these views back to this person is a very important part of the perception or "diagnosis", and may even be a large part of the "therapy", but it is done from the perspective that the person involved does not *need* to have a problem or an illness in order to get any help. This is a natural, supportive process that can happen regularly or continually, that is person-centred and proactive, and that happens to everyone: so each one of us also has a similar network around us where they are the central person.

This model also uses the perspective that the person is not ever disempowered so that someone else has to "cure" them. They are responsible for their health and we are responsible for feeding back observations to that person for the betterment of their situation. Maybe it is not a "problem" or an "illness" that is the issue, but a pattern from an old survival technique that is now counter-productive. Their environment has changed, but old, now redundant, habits die hard!

An example: let us consider a man who has been emotionally ignored as a boy, even demeaned sometimes, and is only given warmth and approval for his achievements. He is quite likely to become a workaholic and may well be a perfectionist. These traits are actually socially approved of, and so they can consolidate and become chronic. This is a "survival" technique; it works, and is thus reinforced. People say how much he can do, or how well he does. The cracks may be beginning to show to a few people close to him, but they do not say anything. He is "driven" and they don't want to get in the way.

As a result of this, after many years of these additional stresses of life and work and these inner pressures or tensions, he develops first an inflamed duodenum, and then later—as a result of a number of emotional "pressures"—he develops "malignant hypertension" (high blood pressure). He becomes "ill", because we now have a diagnosis. He is actually quite ill, as it was not properly "diagnosed" early enough, and he is hospitalized for a week with a blood pressure reading of 210/150, is convalescent for three months, and his eye-sight is impaired as the retina breaks up.

So, is he now just prescribed (say) Zantac or Atenolol? Will beta-blockers really help this person? We might possibly consider Autogenic Training if he reacts against the medication. This is the allopathic treatment approach. There are other medications to try as well to keep the blood pressure down.

A more enlightened medical practitioner might recommend Tai Chi, Yoga, or Shiatsu to help reduce the build-up of internal stress, but will these forms of "therapy" work for him? Homoeopathy, massage, acupuncture, flotation tanks, or meditation might also be considered and tried. These are all usually outside of the NHS, and so he would have to pay for them himself. Why not just keep on taking the pills? There are numerous prejudices and disincentives. So, this is not really natural health yet, as we are still essentially trying to "treat" the person's diagnosed high blood pressure. Because he has this "illness", he may be motivated to try this or that "alternative medicine".

If we go one step further, we might even consider psychotherapy, which could help him understand better his neurotic patterns, so that he can begin to try to change them. All of these perspectives involve a process of "treating" the person in some, often quite demeaning, way before we can help to "cure" him. We cannot really avoid this if we put ourselves in the position of "healer" or "therapist", and the person in the role of a "patient" needing "treatment". We have added in a few refinements, but the basic position has not changed.

There are further disadvantages. Any one-on-one position will often have the fundamental positioning of "I don't know what is wrong with me, or what to do" and, opposingly, "I (think I) know what is wrong with you or what you need to do." This is a hierarchy of intelligence, or of perception. It also elevates the position of the "expert" and demeans and disempowers the "I don't know" position. All hierarchies of knowledge, training, and experience usually have a more obvious mal-effect. We all know the dangers of institutionalization of long-term hospital patients: this is one of the extreme examples. But in more ordinary cases, I also think that it is very rare for a one-on-one practitioner to be able avoid this endemic position.

Let us instead consider the (possibly more appropriate) reality of a "many-to-one" situation, since we are not "islands" and other people do exist around us. In this scenario, the person is naturally surrounded by friends, family, colleagues, and so forth. It is relatively rare that a person has only one point of social contact, with only their therapist or doctor. The other people have wisdom and experience "of the person" rather than of the "diagnosis" or "illness". Often these other people in this person's life demean their own perspective, as they don't consider themselves particularly competent or professional. However, in this model, we recognize that they also see aspects of that person that the professional, therapist, doctor, or priest, will never see. These other people see the person's tenderness (or coldness) with their partner, or children, for example. They observe their confidence at work (and lack of it) and how they behave at home in emotional situations. They may be aware of how much the person has "cut off" from other people, at work and at home. So we have a more "holistic" perspective.

By putting the person at the centre of the picture we also see this as their "problem" or "issue", and that they are going to have to do something about it—indeed they are the only person who can. Of course, there can be input from other people, but we are talking about the "whole" of this person's life. That means that they are at the centre of their life and totally responsible for it.

None of these views is complete. They cannot be complete. No one, however skilled or wise, can completely know another person, and thus know what they need (not what is "wrong" with them) and then be able to tell them what they need to do. The person must find this out for him or herself. This is the process of personal development ("Know thyself") and of personal empowerment. With it comes self-regulation, discrimination, and even a degree of wisdom.

So, in this new model, as illustrated in Figure 4, Person P_1 has around them (say) a partner (Pp), friends (Ff), a doctor (MD), a therapist (Psy), a (say) Shiatsu practitioner (Sh) and a somewhat enlightened boss (B). There is also "that which is yet unknown" (a question mark: ?). This gives us a series of views of that person, each view giving (say) approximately a 12% insight on that person—once it has been checked out and affirmed by that person. Ideally they will "collect" or "co-ordinate" these people around themselves.

Let me elaborate a little on this last point. I may think that I can see something of a person. If I share this with them, and if it is done in a way that can be heard, and if the person can receive it relatively clearly, and if it is reasonably correct and confirmed, then we can say that this bit (12%) is part of our consensual reality. It is clear, it

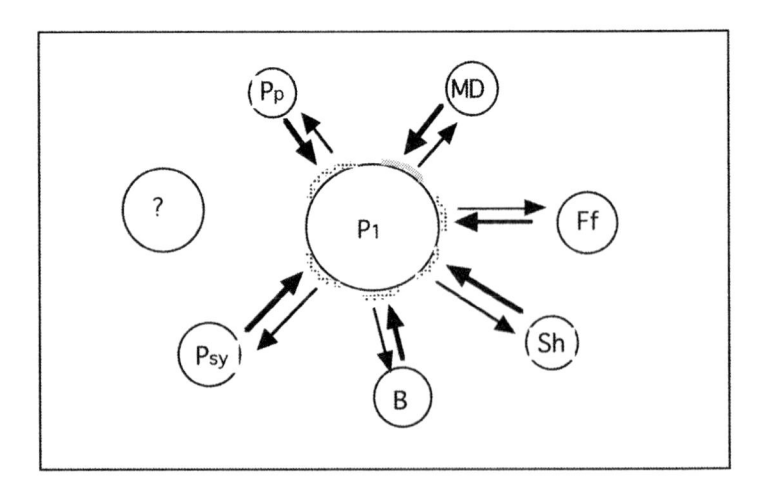

Figure 4. A new model of healthcare.

is open, it is acknowledged, and it is probably accurate and can then be worked with. But this is not the whole story. There are other, totally valid perspectives. At work I am like "this", at home I am like "that", with my friends I am . . . (ask them), with my clients and patients, I (one hopes) am professional and of help to them. Inside, I feel very differently about myself. Ideally, we can bring all these different views together.

In this model, the person thus builds up a more or less accurate picture of a large part of their self from all these different perspectives (no view is totally accurate—and no one view dominates). "Malignant hypertension"—the view from the MD—is just part of the person's process. Unfortunately, this view often predominates.

However there are other perspectives. The "old" workaholic, perfectionist strategy is now obviously counter-productive, as the person has developed hypertension. He needs a new strategy that might or might not be successful. His partner (Pp) has witnessed some of the original parental or familial patterns, either directly or transferentially, and knows (all too well) her partner's ability to cut off emotionally and focus on work, even from home. She would like her partner (P_1) to ease up, chill out, spend more time with the family, relax a little, be less intense, share more of his feelings, and so forth. Will he?

The therapist (Psy) can provide some help, by discussing with the person (P_1) how he originally "adopted" this strategy of cutting off emotionally and pushing himself productively (it *was* a successful strategy—as he survived), and might therefore be able to help him to start to express some of his unexpressed feelings, especially about not being appreciated and recognized for "who" he is, rather than for what he "does". The other therapist (Sh) can support the person's attempts to heal himself, perhaps in ways other than their own therapy, and even to look after himself physically, as well as emotionally. The doctor (MD) can provide a regimen of Zantac or Atenolol (for a while), and also check to see that there is no sign of deeper or more serious problems.

The boss (B) has also realized that this person can push himself too hard, is too much of perfectionist, and is possibly on the way to a really serious break-down or crack-up that will disrupt the work of the company. This person has value and needs to be cared for. He can (maybe) be persuaded to take on less, or do things just a little more gently, perhaps in a "good enough" manner.

Each perspective can help reflect back to the person involved more about himself. This will not only help him to see himself more clearly, both good points and bad points, but often have with it a piece of the possible solution, or at least the tools to help find it.

A new model of treatment

If we take this perspective as the new model of treatment and move towards a more holistic perspective, the person's partner (Pp) can now provide some of the unconditional love and acclaim that he needs, and soften the effects of this "Protestant work ethic" on their relationship, and on their children. The therapist(s) (Psy) and (Sh) can help the person to forgive his parents, and look for more self-esteem within himself, and to learn to care for his self. His doctor (MD) can monitor his blood pressure, encourage more (effective) non-medical treatments, assess how well he is doing, and (possibly) eventually wean him off the hypertensive medication. His boss (B) can put him into a more supervisory role, which takes off the pressure to produce, and possibly uses his perfectionist talents to the best advantage. The friends and family (Ff) can support this person in other ways, perhaps appreciating him, asking him out to dinner, encouraging him to do things with them (instead of work), showing an interest in him as a person, and enjoying his more relaxed persona. We can but dream!

We must not forget that the person himself (P_1) is at the centre of all this. This is his life, and it has got to work better for him. He needs to see all these different aspects, and to work and integrate all these different perspectives. He might have to work on the "triangle" of thoughts, feelings, and actions, going around it in different ways. He might have to correct old, irrational thought patterns and explore some of their locked-in, negative (to the old workaholic pattern) emotions, although these could be possibly supportive to the new nurturing pattern. He has to be the *primum mobile* (prime mover) in his process. It is his empowerment and determination and enthusiasm that will carry him through. And he will heal himself, not just of the diagnosis, but also of the underlying cause of his "illness".

However, there is a further aspect to this model. As can be seen in Figure 4, various parts of the person become more "known" through this group-interactive process. (The shaded areas around the circle, P_1, are an attempt to indicate this.) These shaded areas represent the more "known" and "affirmed" aspects of the person. There are gaps in between, even though a largish area eventually is "known". The arrows represent the interactive process by which these areas become "known". In the diagram, six × about 12% = about 72% "known". The circle with the question mark represents some of the "as yet unknown" aspects. Whether this process of becoming known though the observations of others (as well as by a process of greater self-awareness) happens through a consultative process over time, or through some sort of group interaction process (in medical terms, a case conference), is a matter of choice, as long as there is reasonable communication and clarity, as long as it is self-directed, and as long as there is a fair component of self-awareness.

So far, all that has been determined is essentially the diagnostic stage. Through this interactive process the person involved should have acquired a fair degree (about 72%) of external information about what is happening with him, plus his own increased sense of self-awareness. He should also have had some positive feedback and some proactive help towards resolving of any of his imbalances. He will also (probably) feel a lot more supported by these people around him in his life. This adds to his internal process.

A wider view

Now, these "illnesses" are also part of the person's process of maturation and growth. All major illnesses and traumas can, and perhaps should, be seen in this light. They are opportunities to look at, and even look again at, what is *not* working in our lives: that is transformative. Growth can happen in many weird and wonderful ways.

Pierro Ferruci, a psychosynthesis psychotherapist, studied the lives of 500 famous people and discovered a "peak" experience in every single one of them—many times it was directly connected with a major illness, trauma, or potentially negative life event. These events should, therefore, perhaps not be seen in such a negative light—as an illness, breakdown, or trauma. They can be seen instead as opportunities to rework the old pattern and break through some of the old limiting patterns towards new possibilities and potentials.

So, I want to emphasize the importance of this "unknown" area. A full 28% (in Figure 4) of the person is unknown—perhaps even to them, as it has never been properly affirmed. We really do NOT know what is in this area. Herein lie our horrors and our dreams, our failures or fears, and our potentials. Herein also lie our future creativity, any potential syntheses, the mystery, and the unimagined. For these reasons, it is also very, very scary. We don't like the unknown. We want the quick fix, the pill to take away the illness or the pain, the therapy to "fix" our ailments. We don't like the responsibility, nor do we want it. We prefer having the "expert" telling us what to do and not do. It is a lot safer than having to face the unknown. The fear and "known" pain of demeanour and disempowerment is much less than the fear of the mystery. But it is in this unknown area that we can also possibly grow, mature, find wisdom, serenity, and even enlightenment. We usually have NOT found these in the "known" spaces. So, what is left?

Deep change can only happen in these unknown areas. And the only way to achieve this is to be able to look at our "known" areas more clearly and honestly, and take from these the strengths that we need and the skills that we have developed to explore the "unknown" within ourselves. You find this message over and over again: in poetry, in myths, in modern fiction such as *Star Wars* and the Harry Potter books.

The best thing that the ancient Greeks could think of to write above the oracle at Delphi—the place to which people travelled from all over the then known world to hear the word of God (the god Apollo), more than 2500 years ago—was two words: "Know Thyself".

This is the sort of thing that we mean by greater self-awareness, and certain of these truths have been largely forgotten by the onset of science, medicine, and technology in the past 150 years, yet fundamental truths do not ever change. What we have also lost over the past 150 years (or so) is largely regular, nourishing contact with other people. The nuclear (2 + 2) family in its (semi)-detached living situation, separated from the wider, extended family, does not give one a lot of healthy day-to-day living feedback. Therefore, we often become out of touch with ourselves.

Even if our "illness" or "crisis" is potentially life threatening, like cancer, or AIDS, or criminal charges, many are the true stories of how people find themselves and discover a purpose for their life in their final days or *in extremis*. Perhaps this is just the ultimate rationalization. However, since the one thing that we do know is that we are all going to die (one way or another), maybe it is not such a bad thing after all to be able to get it "right" before we go.

None the less, I would like to return for a moment to the role of the doctor, therapist, or practitioner in this process, because I am one, as well as being the person in the middle of my own process. Please, please never, ever, assume that (I/you/we) know what is "wrong" with (y)our patient. Listen to the person's message, very carefully—and listen to what lies behind the message, the obvious and the stated. You are trying to help them—a whole, complex person with many facets—so try to find out what is right with them, as well as what is wrong with them. What do they do well? Where are their strengths, their pleasures, their achievements? What are their goals and their dreams? Then ask, perhaps, what is preventing them from getting there? What is frustrating them or stopping them? At least then you have got a slightly bigger picture, rather than just focusing on their pathology.

Eva Reich, a paediatrician and the daughter of a controversial psychologist, Wilhelm Reich, was a very strong advocate of home births in America, yet she would never attend one herself. She said that she had the "wrong" outlook as she had been trained (as a paediatrician) in pathology; all the things that can go wrong. That was totally the wrong energy to have at a joyous, natural occasion like the birth of a new life, a new person. We can maybe learn a little from this perspective and do things better in the next century. But we have to admit to our current limitations first.

As therapists, we can also only offer our opinions, our perceptions, our knowledge, and our experience. I repeat the word "offer". The person concerned must feel free to use these insights, or gifts, in whatever way seems appropriate. Otherwise we are imposing our views, our solutions, our perspectives on the person's problems. And this ultimately defeats our aims. The ends do *not* justify the means: we cannot disempower the person before we re-empower them. We have to walk our talk, every single moment of the day.

When these gifts, these insights, these perceptions, are taken in and processed by the person, if we listen very carefully, we will learn whether they are right, or accurate, or appropriate. If we are arrogant enough to assume that we "know" the answer for them, then we will never learn what they really need. We will not hear the "Yes, but . . .", or the silent refusal. This freedom that the person has to interpret and use the ideas that we have is a great gift. It leaves the onus, the work, the development, clearly with the person involved. It frees us, as therapists, from many a burdensome responsibility. We do not have to be "right" all the time. The person can decide, on the basis of an informed consent, rather than being subjected to an objectifying form of treatment.

And, finally, we should also consider offering (again, that word) some tools that the person can use to further their own process. There are plenty of "technologies", perceptions, tools, experiential methodologies, etc., that we have at our fingertips that a particular person might need. We can teach them to fish, rather than just giving them a fish. We can disseminate some of the principles of our craft, instead of hanging on to them and maintaining this sort of mystery for ourselves. We can help educate the person: we can distil, refine, and condense the huge amount of information we have available to what is relevant to that person. We can even try to make ourselves redundant, so that the person is fully empowered to go on and heal what needs healing, explore what needs exploring, and confront what needs confronting—without us, if needs be. And they will. They will have to.

This empowered perspective has the final gracious advantage of freeing us to help others, or to help ourselves. In this new century, the needs of the many can easily overwhelm the few, *unless* we take this route of self-help and empowerment from the start, right the way through any treatment, and on and afterwards as well. We are less likely to burn out this way. We are less likely to hurt others. Our work can become a pleasure rather than a never-ending chore. But it will take a substantively different perspective on twenty-first century health care in order to achieve this.

This is not the age of the central hospital, nor do we need to revert to the barefoot doctor. It is the age of the empowered patient, who is capable of healing themselves, through a social process of interactive feedback and informed consent. This person makes informed decisions for their own welfare.

The path to mental health

Steps to mental health

There are a number of steps towards better health, both mental and physical, or what we might call "well-being". They are simple, but this does not mean that they are easy. You will need to challenge some of the ways in which you are currently *not* staying totally healthy. The definition of health that we are using is that "Good health requires a regular set of active and varied measures in order to maintain, or improve, your general health." This applies mentally as well as physically. The essence of this regular programme can also be described as "taking care of yourself". This means that you need a good routine that is sustainable, and that includes exercise, meditation or relaxation, a good diet, the right clothes to wear, the right home to be in, a good working environment, opportunities for personal growth, some positive thinking, intimacy, and friendship. Mix these, in a flexible fashion (as things change from week to week) with some self-awareness and improved self-esteem (or love) and you have an almost guaranteed winning formula. You determine what it is that you need.

Exercise

As mentioned before, you will need to do some exercise. *Not* using your body is *not* an option: over-using your body verges on abuse. Somewhere in between is a formula that works for you. Find it. If your working day is spent sitting at a computer, your exercise will need to be more varied and regular than if you have been stacking shelves all day, in which case you will need something gentle and flexible. Try to vary what you do from day to day. For example, Yoga one day, swimming another, a work-out in the gym, walking, or whatever on other days. Try to combine it with a creative activity or another leisure pursuit, perhaps gardening, playing tennis with your partner, or football with your children. Now look very carefully at the reasons you give yourself for *not* doing these. How valid are they? Challenge these reasons. What exercise would give you most pleasure? So, go and do it!

Meditation

As also mentioned previously, some form of regular relaxation, mediation, destressing or whatever is also pretty essential. These are usually all quite simple, but to get the full benefit, you *must* do them regularly. It works cumulatively. Try sitting upright, closing your eyes, and breathing in. Imagine taking in the qualities that you need: strength, determination, love, energy, peace of mind, etc. At the top of the breath, hold for a moment so all these qualities can be absorbed. Now breathe out and release all the qualities you do not want: stress, fear, anxiety, depression, selfishness, anger, etc. Then hold again for a moment, before you begin the next cycle. Do this twice a day, every day, for twenty minutes at a time, and see whether it changes your life.

Good food

Good food is essential, but not too much of it! You only need about 1,500–2,000 calories a day, unless you are doing hard manual work. Try to mix the best quality of food (fresh, organic, unprocessed, seasonal, no additives) in an appetizing and varied way, with five portions of fruit and vegetables and a mixture of grains and nuts. This should give you all the vitamins you need. Try to eat foods that give you extra B vitamins, calcium, potassium, magnesium, and vitamin C. Vitamin supplements can help, but it is better to take these in naturally.

Organic food costs a bit more, but it is much better for you. It is healthy (there are no additives or pesticides, and no GM); there are no hidden costs (cleaning up our water supply from pesticides); it benefits animals; it is good for the environment; it benefits children; and it is very tasty. Well worth the extra.

Pay attention to what you eat, and when you prepare it, and cook it, and especially when you eat it: appreciate it, chew it, absorb it. Pay attention to what you crave—which is usually what you are allergic to, or what is not good for you. The cravings usually go away after a few days. Discover instead what it is you need. Pay attention to when you eat, often a heavy meal three times a day is not the best routine, and especially to how much you eat. Watch your portions. Drink plenty of water. Keep alcohol, sugar, and salt to a minimum.

Wash what you buy before you prepare it. Also rinse dishes well so that you are not eating detergent residues. Use biodegradable substances and products wherever possible.

Good hygiene

Cleanse your body well, and care for your skin. It is a major body organ. Use pH-balanced products (soaps, shampoos, shower gels, etc.) where possible, as these do not destroy the slightly acid skin layer which protects against infection. Use a shower brush to help to get rid of old skin. Keep all parts of your skin moist (with pH-balanced lotions) especially in dry weather.

Wash your hair regularly and rinse it well. Use pH-balanced conditioners if you must. Brush your hair lots and it will shine, without extra products. Brush your teeth twice a day; floss your teeth once a day; use mouth washes if you have any gum problems. Get your teeth checked by a good dentist twice yearly. Be careful about washing your hands after going to the toilet, especially before eating or preparing food. Do not smoke.

Rest

The amount of rest and the amount of sleep you need is very personal. Since modern life has speeded up considerably, you will probably need more rest and sleep than you are currently getting. Listen to your body. Don't stay up too late. Take naps, or little 20–30 minute rests, during the day. It really is a lot healthier.

Sit down when you can. Put your feet up when you can. Take a break from routine activity, at least five minutes in every hour. Do a couple of stretches whenever you stand up. Don't rest immediately after a large meal (which you should not have anyway); walk for a while before you rest.

Get into a better sleep pattern. Try to emulate the normal daytime: get up with the sun; go to bed at night. Use daylight bulbs in the house if you don't get enough natural daylight.

Clothing

Many synthetic fabrics (acrylics, polyesters, nylon, etc.) interfere with air getting to your skin, or can cause skin irritations. Try to wear silk, cotton, wool, and undyed fabrics next to your skin where possible: they *are* healthier. Mixtures, such as 50% cotton, etc., are all right. Try different textures to see what you really like.

Some people need to wear certain colours, or different types of clothes. Find out what works for you. Try colours that you don't normally wear occasionally. Again, variation and experimentation are usually quite healthy and fun.

Wear different layers so that you can take something off easily if the home or work environment is hotter, and put it back on when or if it is colder. That way you might also use less heat and will not contribute to global warming so much. That's healthy, too.

Home and work environment

While these can be very different from each other, you will probably spend more than 80% of your time in one or the other.

At work, there are now quite strict health and safety codes about what constitutes a minimum standard for a healthy working environment, but these codes are not always followed. Make sure that you know what these codes of practice are, and therefore what to insist upon. If you are not healthy at work, some one else is responsible. Some people have different individual responses: they react badly to neon light, or are very affected by noise, or smells. Some people have been made very sensitive to certain products or chemicals. Some buildings are just "sick". How healthy is *your* work environment for *you*? Has it changed recently? What works for you at work, and what doesn't? At home, you should have more control over your environment. Is it pleasant? Do you like it? So, do what you can to change it and make it better for you, or move. Try using plants, different colours and fabrics, different lighting, an air ionizer or precipitator. Change things around a little until you feel totally happy with them. What about the mix of space and activity? Would you feel happier with your bedroom downstairs, or your kitchen or living room different? Discuss it with others, get some professional advice, watch some of the TV programmes to get a few new ideas, work out the costs and possible benefits. Then go for it.

Leisure and pleasure

You will not stay healthy unless you have suitable amounts of these. Most people skimp on them, then eventually get run down and get sick, then have to take time off work, etc. It is not a good combination.

Try to rebalance your work, home, and leisure and pleasure activities into a much better mix. Do those things you really like doing, even if it means a bit more effort or expense. At least do them occasionally. Try to do something regularly as well: a night out once a week does not have to break the bank. Combine it with doing a different type of exercise, or going to a special class, or something. It is worth it to be able to have a good time, to laugh more, to glow a bit more, and to start again refreshed.

Try different activities, join different groups, and mix with different people. Challenge those fears, or "scripts" or thought forms that keep you from enjoying yourself more. Someone once said that the secret of happiness is having something to love, something to do, and something to look forward to.

Personal change

This is where we get really serious. You may well have been told, or decided that "something must change". That "something" is actually *you*: surprised? Everyone has things that they need to change, or to work on, or areas where they want to grow. Do *not* get into a rut of disempowerment or apathy. You can change: one step at a time. It is simple, but it is *not* easy, otherwise you would have done it long ago. Now is the time to do it. Don't assume that you will do it tomorrow. This is the day, the time, the moment that you need to decide to change. And you need to keep on deciding, as you may well have some habitual patterns, or even addictions, to break. *Carpe diem*!

The change does not have to be a huge one, yet. Small changes can build on each other. What might you have to do before you change your job, or get to do what you have always wanted? Check it out. Listen to your inner wisdom. Make a plan. Do a little research. Ask others. Check it out again. Then do it.

Your deepest longing may be the one thing that you have always wanted to do in your life. Your best assurance of health is to do what you want to be doing. Start NOW, otherwise you may never start. If you do start, just keep going. The goals may vary as you go, but you are changing and growing.

Included in this is an emphasis on some self-awareness and positive thinking. If you are not self-aware, then you cannot think about yourself. You are living in a fog. If you cannot think about yourself positively, then you cannot conceive that you might change or grow. This self-awareness and positive thinking then leads on naturally to being more proactive. This leads to change, and later to personal growth and development.

Intimacy and friends

We all really need these. We will not be happy and healthy eventually without them. These are also two very difficult areas and by no means easy to resolve or attain. Find out, by asking yourself, what these words "intimacy" and "friends" mean for you. What would you like to do with friends? What sort of friends? What sort of intimacy? Be as precise as you can. Make your own rules: they are what work for you. How much have you been stopping yourself in this area? What is going to have to change? Do you need some help or advice of this?

Is there someone you would like to be friends with, or more intimate with? Have you said anything to them? If it doesn't work, try someone else.

Accident and illness

Before you have need of one, make sure you find a local health care professional that is right for you. Make sure you are registered with a doctor that you like and trust, and who respects your views. If you don't feel good about them, do something about it when you are well.

Please read up on some of the alternative medicine and complementary health disciplines that exist. Most of them work more generally (holistically) than symptom-based allopathic treatments and are concerned with your general all-round health, as well as with any specific symptoms. A combination will probably work best for you. Without knowledge, awareness is limited. Some of these disciplines might be right for you. See which attract you. Try them out gradually.

Keep your doctor informed if you have a specific condition being treated: most doctors are now fairly open about alternative types of treatment. These include such things as homoeopathy, acupuncture, shiatsu, massage, naturopathy, chiropractice, osteopathy, kinesiology, nutritionists, sports medicine, etc., and are mostly reputable. Practitioners have reasonable training, abide by codes of ethics, are members of professional associations, and have appropriate insurance. Ask about these points. Check out some of these remedies out on the Internet, or in the library, if you have not heard of them before.

Self-care

Ultimately we come back to the one person who is totally responsible for your general state of health: *you*! You will need to do all of the above—and more—if you wish to stay in good health. Symptoms are often indications of things going wrong on a deeper level. You can often determine what is going wrong on that level yourself. You will need to "listen in" more and become more aware. Then you can look after yourself better, as you will know what you need. Try the following exercise.

1. Scan your body in any way that you wish, or that works for you. Focus on the area of your body (or mind, or spirit) that you are most concerned about, or most drawn to.

2. Try to give it a form, a colour, a substance, a shape, an intent, or a density. Try to make "contact" with it in some way. If it is a type of pain, what type? When do feel it? How long does it last, etc? If it is a feeling, what exactly? What flavours? What does it make you want to do?
3. What is this area or pain connected with? Has something changed recently? Is there a connection with any recent life event? Has this happened before?
4. Are there any particular feelings connected to this area or pain: fears, anxieties, anger, etc? Are you using a habitual response that does not take these feelings seriously, or causes too much reaction? What other responses may be possible? What if your fears were fewer, or less powerful?
5. Now, place your hands over that area. What does this area of your concern or pain need? How can you help it? What do you need to do? How can you help this to heal?
6. Is there any way that this pain or area of concern could be working *for* you? Is it stopping you doing something, something that you don't want to do? If you consider the question "Why might I have created this?", what would be your answer?
7. By the way, the answer is never that you have done something wrong, or there is something bad about you. This is a wrong answer. The right answer may well be something like: "What I need to do now is . . ."
8. Then go and do that thing. Often it may be something you have avoided doing, or are scared of doing. Pain and fear are likely elements that have prevented you doing what you have identified as needing to do. This is the hard bit. You have to go through these fears and do it anyway. Remember this is "self-care"—or another form of love. You are learning to love yourself and appreciate yourself, and to do things for yourself that you need and can work for you.
9. The points above will not heal you instantly. You will need to keep on doing these things until you know what the connection truly is, and what you need to do about it. Keep on persisting with these points.
10. If there is serious pain, or it gets worse, or if the condition does not go away, then you *must* consult your doctor, *without fail*. This is also an essential part of self-care: knowing when to

consult others. This will not negate anything you have done (as above) or will continue to do for your self.

Personal growth and development

As mentioned at several points throughout the book, we often get into such situations because of, or as a result of, a lack of self-awareness—often imposed through situations of stress, or external difficulties, or an accumulation of life events. The solution, and the path to further personal development, is greater self-awareness. The "search for happiness" that is part of the human condition has also been the goal of most religions and philosophies throughout time. There are several common features in all of these religions and philosophies, which can be condensed into a single Golden Rule: "Treat others as you would like to be treated". This sounds simple—it is, but it is not easy. Many people have thought they knew what this meant. What it implies is that you really need to go inside yourself and have a good, long look at yourself before you can say anything about yourself and how you would like to be treated. Then you have to start, and it can be the start of a lifetime's work, to consider how your actions impinge on others.

Most people treat others with exclusivity; those people are different from us. Even within families and groups there can be some who are treated differently to others, sometimes even with cruelty. One of the major results of personal growth and development is not selfishness, it is a greater kindness (compassion) to others. As we realize how we suffer, through looking inside ourselves, we also realize how we might, can, and sometimes do hurt others. Any disciplined effort to re-educate or better ourselves actually increases or enhances our humanity. It is egoism that creates violence and cruelty, but the way out of this egoism is, paradoxically, not a selfless sacrifice to others, a submergence of the self into the community, it is by an increased process of self-examination, and a focus on what truly works for us. Then we can and do become more of a member of the wider community with something positive to give. We must become more aware of our own actions, then we can become more responsible for them. And it is then, and only then, that we truly become a fuller member of the human race and can live out our true potential, in conjunction with others.

We all desire to be respected. In order to get that, we need to respect, first ourselves, and then respect for others comes. We cannot respect others, and thus be respected ourselves, if we do not respect ourselves first. In order to respect ourselves, we need to know ourselves. In order to know ourselves, we need to look inside ourselves.

This is the major universal insight that led to the formation of most of the main religions in the period of enlightenment that happened in several areas of the world around 500 BCE. It is not an absolute truth. It is a process for becoming a better person.

This section was adapted and expanded from *Hands of Light*, by Barbara Ann Brennan (1987).

The road to change

This is sometimes called "the road less travelled", and it is not an easy road; change is essentially painful. We identify with all our "knobbly" bits, however much they might hurt us, or other people. Some people even believe they cannot change. They might not *want* to—because it is a painful and scary process.

There is a process to change, and we first have to recognize, on quite a deep level, that our present road/lifestyle/way of doing things/habitual pattern (or whatever it is) is often not the best one now. It might have worked up to now, it might even have brought us here or made us who we are (so to speak). But, essentially, it does not work any longer. It is potentially destructive. It hurts other people, as well as ourselves. And that is not an easy pill to swallow. It is an absolutely necessary step to take, but it is also very hard.

We have to start stripping away the illusions that we have about our self: that things are all right, that we can cope, that s/he will come round, that it will be all right the next time, that we can change whenever we want to. These are illusions. They are not true. The time to change them is now. They are illusions that we often use to anaesthetize ourselves, or to convince ourselves that nothing is really wrong, or to plainly deceive ourselves (and others).

However, we also know—somewhere deep inside—that something is wrong, seriously wrong, and we may now be wondering if we actually can ever change. Maybe we cannot; maybe we are stuck with it. Maybe this is who we are? This is a real fear, and one that can cause us to hide all this stuff away again, very quickly. Don't do it. Leave it out on the table. We might even have been told, or we might have told ourselves, that we cannot change, but we also know that we have to change. Otherwise, we will just continue to behave in this way or that, to stay addicted, to give pain and distress to others, and to continue hurting. If we don't allow ourselves to feel this, there is then no motivation to change. We need to realize that we are also hurting deep inside and essentially use that pain as the prime motivator for change. This sounds a bit masochistic, but actually not changing, staying the same, and continuing to hurt is really masochistic.

The next step is to realize that we actually have some "choice points". Things are not quite as black and white or "either or" or "good or bad" as they might seem. It may seem that as soon as we start the old pattern (eating chocolate, drinking too much, getting angry, whatever it is) that we just cannot stop. We are into it absolutely. That is true: we probably are. And this is usually not the whole picture. There is often a little build-up, or some feelings that we do not want to look at, or an inkling that this is about to happen, just a few moments beforehand.

We may have actually been suppressing this awareness—trying to be nice, to be good, not feeling sad, etc., but this is actually our window of opportunity if we know that the old pattern doesn't work for us any more. This is where we can insert a warning signal, an imaginary red light, meter, or dial that will help to tell us we are at the choice point. This is a vital step. Without this choice point sort of awareness, there is little hope of effective change. We will stick in the same groove, continue in the same old pattern, and disappear down the plughole again. We need that red light to warn us, to alert us that we can change—here, now. We usually have about 2–3 seconds that we can use to say, "Uh, oh. I don't want to go that way again!"

This then takes us into the next step: the "I don't know" space. This has been mentioned before, and it is a very important space or place. You don't know, you really don't know, how to do things differently. You do not know what to do if you don't do what you now do not want to do. This is all right. You are taking the first step down the road towards change, and you don't know where it is going to end up. Nor do you know where it is going to take you. You may hope that things can be different from now on.

Try to stay in this "I don't know" space for just a little bit longer. It doesn't have to be too bad a space; it can even be a little bit liberating. If you don't know what to do, do nothing for a while. Just be there, stay there, and see what happens. You also have not gone back down the old road yet. That's different. That's a change. You can now consider doing something—anything that is different.

What needs to happen next is a bit complicated. For change to be really effective, we need to get to the root of the "problem". The "problem" is often the attitude or behaviour that doesn't work, that we want to change; the root of the problem is why we developed this attitude or behaviour in the first place. The chances are that this problem started somewhere back in our childhood, and that it had to do with an unfulfilled need. The chances are that we were not recognized or accepted—in the way that we needed to be—all that time ago. There may also be other reasons.

We may have "learnt" this behaviour and adopted it or copied it from our parents, or significant others. We may have developed this attitude as a survival technique that worked, and so we went on using it. Whatever the original reason, why we keep on doing this particular pattern of behaviour comes from an experience that is usually painful and difficult. We then got used to covering that pain or difficulty with this particular behaviour pattern. It worked and so we kept on using it. We eventually anaesthetized ourselves from the pain and just got stuck with the behaviour. There is nothing wrong with any of this. It worked then. We survived. The problem is that this strategy does not go on working forever.

We are in a different situation now. The old pattern just does not work any longer. However, we just will not change the old behaviour, or those old attitudes, unless we can recontact that original pain and find another way to deal with it. That is the change that needs to be made. It is like getting into an old wound that has not healed and cleaning out all the grungy bits so that the wound can start to heal. It's painful but, unfortunately, necessary.

It is the fear, or the avoidance, of that old pain—of rejection, or abuse, or loss, or degradation, or whatever—that is fuelling that old familiar behaviour pattern, the old avoidance pattern. It is almost impossible to stop this old behaviour and change it unless you contact the old pain and try to find another way of dealing with it, a more suitable way for the present time.

So we have to try to stop—over and over again—and form a new pattern of behaviour, which, one hopes, will be less avoidant. If we have managed to face (some of) the fear or pain, then we will find that, while we now do not want to go down that old road, that old pattern of behaviour, we do not yet know what the new form of behaviour looks like. We are still in the "I don't know" space.

Slowly, we begin to formulate new patterns of behaviour that seem to work a little bit better. Very rarely is there an "Ah-ha!" moment, allowing us to switch immediately into something new and wonderful. That is fairy tale stuff. This is the slow, long, hard, simple slog. We have to learn to do it differently.

An example I often use is that of driving. In the UK, we learn to drive on the left. It works fine (most of the time). However, if we hire a car in Spain or Florida, then—immediately—we need to learn something very different: to drive on the right. There is nothing wrong in driving on the left in the UK. It just doesn't work very well in Spain or the USA. And you need to learn pretty fast. And you have to keep on reminding yourself every time you pull out. It usually takes about 3–4 weeks to really "learn" this new behaviour.

The new behaviour pattern needs to be reinforced. Look for, listen to, even ask for, the appreciations and feedback. You need to learn that this new way of doing things actually works—and better than the old way. You need to fit into the new pattern, adapt to it, adapt it and work with it. Don't be discouraged by the odd setback. This is part of the learning process. Remember the old maxim: "We learn by our mistakes". It is true. So—learn!

Slowly you take on the new pattern. Slowly you adapt. The old pattern is still there. It can be triggered at any moment. And we have to—just have to—stop going down that old road. The new path is the new pattern. Keeping to it, reinforces it. Not keeping to it, doesn't. So, stick to it. Eventually this becomes the way that you are doing things now. This becomes the new way: you have changed! Well done. What's next on the list?

Wider and different perspectives

A wider perspective

Sometimes the crises that happen to us can be seen in retrospect to be the exact and perfect "nudge" that managed to get us out of that stuck position and forced us to change our life. The important words are *in retrospect*, because, at the time of the crisis, there is no way of telling. However, if we accept a fairly matter-of-fact perspective on life, let go of any expectations, and accept just what comes, and then try to work with it, then this can sometimes actually aid our process of change. In such circumstances we are "going with the flow", even if we do not know where that will take us, rather than trying to put the old structures back together again. It is scary, it is traumatic, and sometimes it works out all right—in retrospect.

Sometimes we need to take a wider or a different perspective. Such a perspective might include the possibility that some wounds just do not heal, and that this perspective is actually important. The wounds may heal slightly, but our scars might help to define who we really are, and what has happened to us.

A "family systems" perspective

This type of perspective would say that we are usually playing out some role within our family of origin and that whatever happens to us is seen in a particular light relating to this role. While "normal" roles are father, mother, son, daughter, etc., there are other roles as well. A classic example is someone becoming the "black sheep" of the family. This person carries the unacknowledged problems of the family and they become, or are seen as, "the problem". This means that everyone else is relatively all right—except, of course, that they are not. As soon as the black sheep decides not to be in this role any longer, the family system will tend to try to identify someone else to fit into this role, because this is the way that this family operates. There are many other roles that can be carried by different family members ("clown", "wonder child", "carer", "responsible one", etc. and determining your role, how it affected you, and how to get out of it is quite a skilled task. Some therapeutic help may be necessary if this is your situation. For a good explanation of the family therapy system, go to the relevant page in Wikipedia.

Life-changing situations

People who have been in prison, or in war, had illnesses or accidents, or near-death type of experiences, or who have been in other traumatic or horrific situations, or some extended family crises, describe these events as "life-changing". Their lives have changed, often quite radically. And when they look back, they often talk about those events as having a particular significance. They would not necessarily want to return to being the person they were before that event. But these events have matured them.

Occasionally, when they speak about it, it is almost as if they almost enjoyed the experience, even if it was horrific, as it has had such a positive result. Certainly they could have done without the horror, but to do without the whole experience ... ?

These transformational components are extremely significant to a person, even if they are not necessarily welcomed by the people around them. If, say, a husband, father, brother, son has "changed", often the rest of the family would (initially) prefer the old familiar person, even if they were somewhat dysfunctional. As people nowadays say, "Live with it!"

Changing expectations

If you expect something to happen, or expect a particular outcome, the chances are that you are setting yourself up for a disappointment. Nothing ever happens exactly the way you expect it. Try to get rid of all your expectations. Try to accept things more as they are, or as they seem to be developing. Try to stay "in the moment".

It is absolutely fine to desire a particular possible outcome over another possible outcome, and to try to steer the direction of events more towards the desired outcome than the undesired one. But this is different from having expectations. You are not locked into one particular outcome, or to a particular set of events.

Often you hear the words, in your head, or from someone else, "Oh. I expected this...", or "I didn't expect *that!*" Big mistake! The person may be assuming something about a situation, or another person, that stems more from their desires than from reality. There is then a whole set of issues to get over first. Was the assumption a reasonable one? Did it say this or that in the brochure? Where did that expectation come from? It is better not to have expectations, as far as is possible.

From our children we often hear the words, "It's not fair". When I was feeling a bit rough, I would say to my children, "Whoever said that life was fair?" In childhood we have expectations: "It should be fair." "Things should end happily ever after." Sorry!

Letting go of expectations—any specific ones—is a good way to stop your self from becoming disappointed. A good book on psychotherapy, *The Road Less Travelled* (Scott Peck, 2006) starts off with the words "Life is difficult". It then explains that if you do not anticipate this, then not only do you have the difficulty to deal with, but you also have your own disappointments as well.

Changing goals

Our goals change all the time. When I was about twelve years old, I saw a pay slip on my father's desk. He earned £4,000+ salary in a year. This was a reasonably large amount in the early 1960s. I remember thinking, "I would like to earn £5,000 in a year." In 2006, this would not be enough to pay a family's grocery bill, let alone rent, have a car, or have anything left for holidays, etc. One of the people I worked with was imprisoned for 3–4.5 years because he had been the driver in a car accident that had killed three people. One of the reasons (I think) that he got such a high sentence was because he seemed more concerned that he would now not be able to achieve his goal of making £1 million before he was thirty: there seemed to be a distinct lack of remorse.

So goals can change. In the short term, goals are probably a good idea. They can help achieve a degree of measurement, they maintain a perspective and a direction, they help to get you up in the morning and to relax at night—one hopes—reasonably content with your achievements. Much of this work in psychotherapy, particularly from a Cognitive Behavioural perspective, is trying to identify and help the person achieve reasonable step-by-step goals. In the longer term, it is better, perhaps, not to have too fixed a goal. Being fixated on a goal, or a particular outcome, can mean that you might miss out on other possibilities: you might not see what looks like a side road, but is actually a great opportunity.

We grow up with stories and myths of journeys that have a definite goal: *The Celestial City; The Cracks of Doom; The Wizard of Oz*; etc. The concept of a fixed goal is lodged firmly in our psyche. "If I can get through this—until Saturday, or until retirement, or until . . .— then everything will be all right." But this type of thinking is potentially unhelpful, to the point of being dysfunctional. It means you are not looking after yourself in the moment; you are ignoring the present-day cost in the hope of a future outcome or reward. This is like the addictive gambler, or smoker, "Oh, I'll stop tomorrow." You could try, instead, to focus on how to improve the situation in this moment, right now. Get your direction right, but make your goals very short-term. Going one step at a time along a road, in a reasonably good direction, but without any particular set goal, can help to make the journey quite a pleasant experience. Please think about this point carefully.

Sources of information

There are a number of sources of information, mainly self-help books and websites on the Internet, most of which which give reasonable value and through which you can discover more information about mental health for yourself. Most of the websites have a search function, so specific medical conditions are quite easily found. You can also do a general search of the whole web, but this is likely to bring up a large number of very different sites. Some of these will be commercial sites, trying to sell you something. Please do not pay a lot of attention to these: if it is good for you, your doctor will probably know about it: if it is not, you should not even think of taking or using it. Do not take anything without consulting your doctor. Drugs or treatments purchased over the Internet are *not* guaranteed to be right for you: they can also incur customs duty, and may also be of dubious quality or efficacy.

Self-help reading list

Many of these books can be found in the "popular psychology" sections of large bookshops, libraries, via specialist book websites such as Amazon (www.amazon.co.uk), or the individual publishers' websites. It is worth trying to have a "look" at a copy (by going to a large bookshop, library, or "looking inside" on the website) to see if it is really what you want before ordering it, and there are often readers' coments, synopses, comments, etc., that might help you to decide. To order a book, you will need to note the *name* of the author(s), the *title* of the book, and, ideally, the *publisher*, and/or the *year* published.

In each of the headed sections, the list is by author, alphabetically, rather than by merit. This list is not totally inclusive; there are, of course, many other books, but this is quite a reasonable selection.

Addiction

Horvath, A. (2003). *Sex, Drugs, Gambling & Chocolate: A Workbook for Overcoming Addictions*. Impact.

Marks, D. (2005). *Overcoming Your Smoking Habit: A Self-help Guide Using Cognitive Behavioural Techniques*. Robinson Press.

Anger and irritability

Davies, W. (2000). *Overcoming Anger & Irritability: A Self-Help Guide Using Cognitive Behavioural Techniques*. Robinson.

Dryden, W. (1996). *Overcoming Anger: when Anger Helps & When it Hurts*. Sheldon.

Patracek, L. (2004). *The Anger Workbook for Women: How To Keep Your Anger from Undermining Your Self-esteem, Your Emotional Balance, and Your Relationships*. New Harbinger.

Anxiety

Davis Raskin, V. (1997). *When Words Are Not Enough: The Women's Guide to Treatments for Anxiety and Depression—How to Choose What's Right for You*. Broadway.

Franks, H. (1996). *Hidden Fears Self Help for Anxiety & Phobias*. Headline.

Kennerley, H. (2006). *Overcoming Anxiety Self-help Course: A Self-help Practical Manual Using Cognitive Behavioural Techniques* (plus course in three volumes). Robinson Press.

Leahy, R. (2005). *The Worry Cure: Stop Worrying and Start Living*. Piatkus.

Luciani, J. (2006). *Self-coaching: How To Heal Anxiety & Depression*. Wiley.
Servan-Schreiber, D. (2004). *Healing without Freud or Prozac: Natural Approaches to Curing Stress, Anxiety & Depression without Drugs and without Psychoanalysis*. Rodale.
Sharpe, R. (1997). *Self-help for Your Anxiety: The Proven "Anxiety Antidote" Method*. Souvenir Press.

Assertiveness

Back, K., & Back, K. (2005). *Assertiveness at Work*. McGraw-Hill.
Bishop, S. (2006). *Develop Your Assertivenss*. Kogan Page.
Dickson, A., & Charlesworth, K. (1982). *A Woman in Your Own Right—Assertiveness and You*. Quartet.
Dryden, W., & Constantinou, D. (2004). *Assertiveness Step-by-Step*. Sheldon.
Fensterheim, H., & Baer, J. (1975). *Don't Say YES When You Want to Say NO*. Futura.
Lindenfeld, G. (1996). *Assert Yourself—A Self-help Assertiveness Programme for Men and Women*. Thorson.
Rees, S., & Graham, R. (1991). *Assertion Training: How To Be What You Really Are*. Routledge.

Childhood trauma and sexual abuse

Adamson, L. (2004). *Overcoming Sexual and Childhood Abuse*. Diviniti.
Ainscough, C., & Toon, K. (2000). *Breaking Free: Help for Survivors of Childhood Sexual Abuse*. Ashburn Press.
Bass, E., & David, L. (1993). *Beginning to Heal*. Cedar.
Davies, V., & Andrew, H. (1996). *Betrayal of Trust: Understanding & Overcoming Childhood Sexual Abuse*. Ashburn Press.
Kennerley, H. (2000). *Overcoming Childhood Trauma: A Self-help Guide Using Cognitive Behavioural Techniques*. Robinson Press.
Maltz, W. (1991). *The Sexual Healing Journey*. Harper Perennial.
Saphira, M. (1997). *For Your Child's Sake: Understanding Sexual Abuse (for parents)*. Heineman Reed.

Chronic fatigue syndrome

Burgess, M., & Chalder, T. (2005). *Overcoming Chronic Fatigue: A Self-help Guide Using Cognitive Behavioural Techniques*. Robinson Press.

Campling, F., & Sharpe, M. (2000). *Chronic Fatigue Syndrome (CFS/ME)—The Facts.* Oxford University Press.
Lisman, S., & Dougherty, K. (2007). *Chronic Fatigue for Dummies.* Wiley.
MacIntyre, A. (1998). *M.E.: Chronic Fatigue Syndrome—A Practical Guide.* Thorson.

Depression

Barker, P. (1997). *A Self-help Guide to Managing Depression.* Chapman Hall.
Burns, D. (2000). *The Feeling Good Handbook.* Signet.
Gilbert, P. (2000). *Overcoming Depression: A Self-help Guide Using Cognitive Behavioural Techniques.* Robinson Press.
Greensberger, D., & Padesky, C. (1995). *Mind Over Mood: Change How You Feel by Changing the Way You Think.* Guilford Press.
Martell, C., & Addis, M. (2004). *Overcoming Depression: One Step at a Time.* New Harbinger.
Rowe, D. (2003). *Depression: A Way Out of Your Prison.* Brunner-Routledge.
Williams, C. (2006). *Overcoming Depression: A Five Areas Approach.* Hodder Arnold.
Williams, M., Teasdale, J., Segal, Z., & Kabat-Zinn, J. (2007). *The Mindful Way Through Depression: Freeing Yourself from Chronic Unhappiness: Guided Meditation Practices for the Mindful Way Through Depression.* Guilford Press.

Eating disorders

Cooper, P. J. (2007). *Bulimia Nervosa—A Guide to Recovery.* Robinson Press.
Fairburn, C. (1995). *Overcoming Binge Eating.* Guilford Press.
Freeman, C. (2002). *Overcoming Anorexia: A Self-help Guide Using Cognitive Behavioural Techniques.* Robinson Press.
Hall, L., & Ostroff, M. (2003). *Anorexia Nervosa: A Guide to Recovery.* Gurze.
McCabe, R., McFarlane, T., and Olmsted, (2004). *Overcoming Bulimia Workbook: Your Comprehensive, Step-by-Step Guide to Recovery.* New Harbinger.
Schmidt, U., & Trisure, J. (1993). *Getting Better Bit(e) by Bit(e): A Survival Kit for Sufferers of Bulimia Nervosa and Binge Eating Disorders.* Psychology Press.

Emotional abuse

Elliot-Wright, S. (2997). *Overcoming Emotional Abuse*. Sheldon Press.
Hirigoyen, M.-F., & Marx, H. (2005). *Stalking the Soul: Emotional Abuse and the Erosion of Identity*. Marx.
Ellis, A., & Powers, M. (2000). *The Secret of Overcoming Verbal Abuse: Getting Off the Emotional Roller Coaster and Regaining Control of Your Life*. Wilshire.

Fear

Rowe, D. (1996). *Beyond Fear*. Harper-Collins.

Gambling

Blaszaczynski, A. (1998). *Overcoming compulsdive Gambling: A Self-help Guide Using Cognitive Behavioural Techniques*. Robinson Press.
Milton, S. (29001). *Stop Gambling: A Self-help Manual for Giving Up Gambling*. Pan Australia.
Jantz, G. (2001). *Turning the Tables on Gambling: Hope and Help for Addictive Behaviour*. Shaw.

Guilt and shame

Dryden, W. (1994). *Overcoming Guilt*. Sheldon.
Dryden, W. (1997). *Overcoming Shame*. Sheldon.
Hilliard, D. (2007). *After the Fall: Resurrecting Your Life from Shame, Disgrace, and Guilt*. Destiny Image.
Ruben, D. (1993). *No More Guilt: Ten Steps to a Shame-free Life*. Mills & Sanderson.

General

Burns, D. (2000). *The Feeling Good Handbook*. Plume.
Butler,G., & Hope, T. (1995) *Manage Your Mind: The Mental Fitness Guide*. Oxford University Press.
Dryden, W. (2005). *Ten Steps to Positive Living*. Orient
Neenan, M., & Dryden, W. (2001). *Life-Coaching: A Cognitive Behavioural Approach*. Brunner-Routledge
Rowe, D. (1999). *Dorothy Rowe's Guide to Life*. Harper-Collins.

Young, J., & Klosko, J. (1994). *Reinventing Your Life: The Breakthrough Program To End Negative Behaviour and Feel Great Again.* Plume.

Grief and bereavement

Cerza Kolf, J. (2002). *Standing in the Shadow: Help & Encouragement for Suicide Survivors.* Baker Books.

Matsakis, A. (1999). *Survivor Guilt: A Self-help Guide.* New Harbinger.

McCarthy, S. (1988). *A Death in the Family: Self-help Guide to Coping with Grief.* Self Counsel Press

Morris, S. (2008). *Overcoming Grief: A Self-help Guide Using Cognitive Behavioural Techniques.* Robinson Press.

Health

Lowen A., & Lowen L. (1977). *The Way to Vibrant Health: A Manual of Bioenergetic Exercises.* Harper.

Shealy, N. (1977). *90 Days to Self-Health—Biogenics: How To Control all Types of Stress by Yourself through a Complete Health Program of Autogenics, Diet, Vitamins and Exercise.* The Dial Press.

Marriage and relationships

Beck, A. (1997). *Love is Never Enough.* Penguin.

Duncan, B., & Rock, J. (1991). *Overcoming Relationship Impasses: Ways to Initiate Change When Your Partner Won't Help.* Kluwer/Plenum.

Crowe. M. (2005). *Overcoming Relationship Problems: A Self-Help Guide Using Cognitive Behavioural Techniques.* Robinson Press.

Csoti, M. (2005). *Overcoming Loneliness and Making Friends.* Sheldon Press.

Dryden, W., & Gordon, J. (1991). *How to Untangle your Emotional Knots.* Sheldon Press.

Waines, A. (2005). *Making Relationships Work: How To Love Others and Yourself.* Sheldon Press.

Mindfulness

Naht Hahn, T. (1995). *Peace is Every Step: The Path of Mindfulness in Everyday Life.* Rider.

Kabat-Zinn, J. (2001). *Full Catastrophe Living: How to Cope with Stress, Pain and Illness Using Mindfulness Meditation.* Piatkus.

Negative Behaviour & Thinking

Young, J., & Klosko, J. (1994). *Reinventing Your Life: How to Break Free from Negative Life Patterns.* Penguin Putnam.

Obsessive–compulsive disorder

Baer, L. (2000). *Getting Control: Overcoming Your Obsessions and Compulsions.* Plume.

Clark, D., & Purdon, C. (2005). *Overcoming Obsessive Thoughts: How To Gain Control of Your OCD.* New Harbinger.

Pedrick, C., & Hyman, B. (2005). *The OCD Workbook: Your Guide to Breaking Free from Obsessive–Compulsive Disorder.* New Harbinger.

Roy, C. (2008). *Obsessive Compulsive Disorder: A Survival Guide for Family & Friends.* Hazelden.

Steketee, G. S., & White, K. (1990). *When Once Is Not Enough: Help for Obsessive–Compulsiveness.* New Harbinger.

Tallis, F. (1992). *Understanding Obsessions & Compulsions: A Self-help Manual.* Sheldon Press.

Veale, D., & Willson, R. (2005). *Overcoming Obsessive Compulsive Disorder: A Self-help Guide Using Cognitive Behavioural Techniques.* Robinson Press.

Panic

Silove, D., & Manicavasagar, V. (1997). *Overcoming Panic: A Self-help Guide Using Cognitive Behavioural Techniques* (plus course in three volumes). Robinson Press.

Sheehan, M. (1988) *Fears, Phobias & Panic: Self-help Guide to Agoraphobia.* David Fulton.

Steven, A. (1999). *How to Rush Slowly and Avoid Panic Attacks: A Self-help Therapy Book.* Laid Back Press.

Relaxation

Brewer, S. (2000). *Simply Relax: The Beginner's Guide to Relaxation.* Duncan Baird.

Feldman, C. (2004). *Meditation Plain & Simple.* Element.

Madders, J. (1992). *Stress & Relaxation: Self-help Techniques for Everybody.* Optima.

Self-esteem

Brandon, N. (1997). *How to Raise Your Self-Esteem*. Random House.
Fennell, M. (1999). *Overcoming Low Self-Esteem: A Self-help Guide Using Cognitive Behavioural Techniques* (plus course in three volumes). Robinson Press.
Field, L. (2001). *Creating Self-Esteem*. Vermillion.
Jeffers, S. (2007). *Feel the Fear and Do It Anyway: How to Turn Your Fear and Indecision into Confidence and Action*. Vermillion.
Schiraldi, G. (2003). *The Self-Esteem Workbook*. New Harbinger.

Self-harm

Arnold, L., & Magill, A. (1998). *The Self-Harm Help Book*. Basement Project
Bell, L. (2003). *Managing Intense Emotions & Overcoming Self-Destructive Habits: A Self-help Manual*. Brunner-Routledge
Conterio, L., & Lader, W. (1999). *Bodily Harm: The Breakthrough Healing Program for Self-Injurers*. Little, Brown.

Sexual problems

Ford, V. (2005). *Overcoming Sexual Problems: A Self-help Guide Using Cognitive Behavioural Techniques*. Robinson Press.
Schnarch, D. (2003) *Resurrecting Sex: Solving Sexual Problems and Revolutionizing Your Relationship*. Quill.

Sleep and insomnia

Espie, C. (2006). *Overcoming Insomnia & Sleep Problems: A Self-help Guide Using Cognitive Behavioural Techniques*. Robinson Press.
Burgess, M. et al. (2001). *Self-Help for Nightmares: A Book for Adults with Frequent Recurrent Nightmares*. Blue Stallion.

Social anxiety

Blyth, J., & Glatzer, J. (2005). *Fear is No Longer My Reality: How I Overcame Panic and Social Anxiety Disorder and You Can Too*. McGraw-Hill
Butler, G. (1999) *Overcoming Shyness & Social Anxiety: A Self-help Guide Using Cognitive Behavioural Techniques* (plus course in three volumes). Robinson Press.

Gabor, D. (2000). *How to Start a Conversation & Make Friends*. Sheldon Press.

Henderson, M., & Eunson, K. (1987). *Coping with Shyness & Loneliness*. Penguin.

Trauma and stress

Herbert, C. (2002). *Understanding Your Reactions to Trauma*. Blue Stallion.

Herbert, C., & Wetmore, A. (1999). *Overcoming Traumatic Stress: A Self-help Guide Using Cognitive Behavioural Techniques*. Robinson Press.

Parkinson, F. (2000). *Coping with Post-trauma Stress*. Sheldon.

Richie, R. (1995). *First Aid for Disaster Stress Trauma Victims: A Guide and Self-help Manual for the Lay-person Treating Disaster Stress Trauma Victims*. Richie.

Vermilyea, E. (2000). *Growing Beyond Survival: A Self-help Toolkit for Managing Traumatic Stress*. Sidran Press.

Weight

Gauntlett-Gilbert, J., & Grace, C. (2005). *Overcoming Weight Problems: A Self-help Guide Using Cognitive Behavioural Techniques*. Robinson Press.

US Coast Guard (2004). *Weight Management Self-Help Guide*. Fredonia Books.

McLain, J., McLain, P., & Andreacchio, R. (1998). *Weigh to Go: Self-help Weight Loss Manual*. Aweigh.

Internet websites

About.com: Mental Health: mentalhealth.about.com. A mental health website for consumers and professionals.

Anxiety Disorder Resource Centre: www.anxiety-uk.org. A free resource centre for people with anxiety and anxiety disorders.

Bandolier: www.jr2.ox.ac.uk/bandolier/. A look at the evidence of what works and what doesn't in a bullet-point format, with widely drawn information in a monthly journal. There are a variety of

466 SOURCES OF INFORMATION

studies on different topics, such as diet and prostate cancer risk, electronic pain diaries for children, paracetamol for osteoarthritis, body piercing, etc.

BBC: www.bbc.co.uk/health/. An informative website with short articles on relationships, self-harm, suicide, depression, mental health disorders, men's and women's health, etc.

BBC Mental Health: www.bbc.co.uk/health/mental. A guide to the mental health issues that can affect us all.

Best Treatments: www.besttreatments.co.uk. The site draws its recommendations from "Clinical evidence", the *British Medical Journal's* survey of medical research, so it is a little staid, but very solidly conventional. It covers, to varying degrees, over seventy conditions. It also covers what doctors mean by "risk".

Breathing Space Scotland: www.BreathingSpaceScotland.co.uk. A good resource for information, advice, and sign-posting for various mental health issues and a range of related problems: financial and work issues, bereavement, pain, etc. The organization also provides telephone support for sufferers.

British Autogenic Society: www.autogenic-therapy.org.uk. Information about this particular relaxation technique.

Carer information: www.opsi.gov.uk, or www.thepensionservice.gov.uk.

Children First for Health: www.childrenfirst.nhs.uk. 4,000 pages of content about health information, experiences, games, competitions, and practical information designed for children of different ages: tots (0–3 yrs, with guidance); juniors (3–6), children (7–11), teenagers (12–15) and 16+. It is financed by the charity, Wellchild.

Cochrane Collaboration: www.cochrane.org. This reviews up-to-date information on effective treatments. A little technical perhaps, and you may need a medical dictionary.

Cruse Bereavement Care: www.crusebereavementcare.org.uk helps to support people with all sorts of bereavement and has a national phone line (0870-167-1677).

Department of Health: www.dh.gov.uk/en/PolicyAndGuidance/ HealthAndSocialCareTopics/MentalHealth. Gives recent governmental policy and consultation documents for changes to mental health policies in England and Wales.

Depression Alliance: www.depressionalliance.org. Main website for helping people with depression, with lots of information about symptoms, treatments, support groups, research, publications, campaigns.

Depression Alliance (Scotland): www.dascot.org. Campaigns for better understanding about and support for depression and has a good website with lots of information. DA Scotland also runs self-help groups.

Dipex: www.dipex.org. This is a database of individual patient experiences. It currently contains about 85 hours of audio and video clips on about 14 health topics: including cancer, heart disease, terminal conditions and depression. Individual accounts are supported by further information and links to other sites, including debates and discussion groups.

Doing Well: www.doingwell.org.uk. This website offers extensive advice and information on depression, its treatments, and how it is managed. There are some useful patient's stories and an opportunity to share your own experience. There is a self-assessment function and an emphasis on the management of depression.

Dr Foster: www.drfoster.co.uk. This is an independent organization which collects and analyses information on the availability and quality of health services in the UK so people can make more informed decisions on how to access the right healthcare. You can find thousands of facts on hospitals, doctors, and local NHS and private health services as well as information on complementary therapists and other specialists.

Erowid: www.erowid.org Independent and substantial information site about psychoactive chemicals and plants.

Healthcare Commission: www.healthcarecommission.co.uk. The Healthcare Commission has taken over responsibility for reviewing complaints about the NHS that have not been successfully resolved at a local level.

HealthWatch: www.healthwatch-uk.org. This supports the scientific testing of conventional and complementary or alternative treatments and tries to explain why clinical trials are the best way of assessing a form of treatment. It includes lots of debates about various treatments.

Internet Mental Health: www.mentalhealth.com. The fifty-two most common mental health disorders, medications, news, recovery stories, links, etc.

Joe Panic: www.joepanic.com. A website giving information and advice about stress, panic, and anxiety, with advice on coping skills. Gives information about "good" breathing, some exercises, good links and resource pages.

Living Life to the Full: www.livinglifetothefull.com. Free access to a mental health skills course based on CBT. Includes several teaching sessions.

Mental Health: www.wellontheweb.net; www.shaw.uk.com; www.seemescotland.org; www.scottishrecovery.net; www.smhfa.com; www.nofreudnoprozac.org.

Mental Health Net: www.mentalhelp.net. Offers resources in self-help, psychology and mental health.

Mental Health Foundation: www.mentalhealth.org.uk. The Mental Health Foundation exists to help people survive, recover from, and prevent mental health problems.

MIND: www.mind.org.uk. A national and excellent advocate for people with mental health issues, having a comprehensive site giving information on, and self-help about, depression, mental health, and related issues.

MoodGym: www.moodgym.anu.ed.au. Australian free interactive website designed to help people identify whether they have problems with emotions like anxiety and depression and to develop coping skills.

MoodJuice: www.moodjuice.scot.nhs.uk. This NHS Forth Valley website has a number of downloadable documents containing information on how to cope with anger, anxiety, depression, panic attacks, bereavement, post traumatic stress, sleep problems, etc., with lots of local contacts and further information.

NHS Help Line: www.nhsdirect.nhs.uk. The official website for the NHS 24-hour telephone helpline.

National Debt-line: www.nationaldebtline.co.uk. Help for people in debt: 0808-808-4000.

National Library for Health: www.library.nhs.uk. This site has news stories about health, and gives evidence for many treatments. You can search medical dictionaries.

National Library for Health: www.library.nhs.uk/mentalhealth. Has films, position statements, research reports, hot topics, adult and child and adolescent conditions, and specialist information on schizophrenia, bipolar disorders, and dementia.

National Perceptions Forum: www.voicesforum.org.uk. This used to be called the National Voices Forum. Supported by the Rethink (National Schizophrenia Fellowship) and allows all types of "mad" people to tell their own stories about mental illness, make their own websites, publish their poetry, whatever!

Newcastle, North Tyneside and Northumberland Mental Health NHS: *Self-Help leaflets.* www.nnt.nhs.uk/mh/content.asp?PageName=selfhelp A good set of down-loadable self-help leaflets.

Psychiatry 24/7: www.psychiatry24x7.com

Relate: www.relate.org.uk. Help with any relationship, partnership, or marital probems.

Royal College of Psychiatry: www.rcpsych.ac.uk/mentalhealth information.aspx. Gives readable up-to-date and research-based information about a variety of mental health problems.

QuackWatch: www.quackwatch.org. Tries to be a reputable site that dispels the "quackery" about health and combats health frauds, etc., but seems to be a little bit over-weighted towards conventional medical treatments.

SANE: www.sane.org.uk. A UK national mental health charity giving information on all aspects of mental health.

Self-Harm Alliance: www.selfharmalliance.org

Shaw Trust: www.shaw-trust.org.uk/mentalnealth for problems at work.

Social Phobia/Social Anxiety Association: www.socialphobia.org, or www.social-anxiety.org.uk.

The Samaritans: www.samaritans.org. The Samaritans provide confidential emotional support, on a 24/7 basis, to those experiencing distress or having suicidal feelings.

Weight Watchers: www.weightwatchers.co.uk.

Women's Aid: www.womensaid.org.uk.

REFERENCES

Brennan, B. A. (1987). *Hands of Light*. New York: Bantam New Age.
Bryant, C. (2006). *Benefits of Pilates*. San Diego, CA: ACE.
Ellis, R., & Harper, A. (1998). *A Guide to Rational Living*. Chatsworth, CA: Wilshire Books.
Greenberger, D., & Padesky, C. A. (1995). *Mind Over Mood: Changing the Way You Feel by Changing the Way You Think*. New York: Guilford Press.
Hahn, T. N. (1992). *Peace is Every Step: The Path of Mindfulness in Everyday Life*. New York: Bantam.
Hahn, T. H. (2005). *Being Peace*. Berkeley, CA: Parallax Press.
Holmes, & Rähe, (1967), Holmes–Rähe life changes scale. *Journal of Psychosomatic Research*, 11: 213–218.
Kempis, T. (1427). *The Imitation of Christ*, L. Sherley-Price (Trans.). London: Penguin,
Kübler-Ross, E. (1997). *On Death and Dying*. New Jersey, Prentice Hall
Maggs, P. (2000). My story. Support Me website: www.supportme.co.uk/info.htm
McLuhan, T. C. (1973).*Touch the Earth*. London: Abacus.
Powell, T. (2006). *The Mental Health Handbook*. Bicester: Speechmark.
Rowe, D. (1991). *Breaking the Bonds: Understanding Depression, Finding Freedom*. London: HarperCollins.

Rowe, D. (2003). *Depression: The Way Out of Your Prison* (3rd edn). Hove: Brunner-Routledge.

Scott Peck, M. (2006). *The Road Less Travelled: A New Psychology of Love, Traditional Values and Spiritual Growth*. London: Arrow-New Age.

Servan-Schrieber, D. (2005). *Healing without Freud or Prozac: Natural Approaches to Curing Stress, Anxiety and Depression Without Drugs and Without Psychoanalysis*. London: Rodale International.

World Health Organisation (2007). *Mental health: Strengthening Mental Health Promotion*. Factsheet 220. Geneva: WHO.